Religion in the Age of Reason
A Transatlantic Study of the
Long Eighteenth Century

AMS Studies in the Eighteenth-Century
ISSN 0196-6561
Series ISBN-13: 978-0-404-61470-6

No. 53

Religion in the Age of Reason

A Transatlantic Study of the
Long Eighteenth Century

ISBN-13: 978-0-404-64853-4

Religion in the Age of Reason

A Transatlantic Study of the
Long Eighteenth Century

Edited by
KATHRYN DUNCAN

AMS PRESS, INC.
NEW YORK

Library of Congress Cataloging-in-Publication Data

Religion in the age of reason : a transatlantic study of the long eighteenth century / edited by Kathryn Duncan
    p. cm. — (AMS studies in the eighteenth century ; no. 53)
    Includes bibliographical references and index.
    ISBN 978-0-404-64853-4 (alk. paper)
    1. Church history—18th century. 2. Great Britain—Church history—18th century. 3. United States—Church history—18th century.
    I. Duncan, Kathryn. II. Series.
BR470.R455   2009
270.7—dc22

                      2006045352

All AMS books are printed on acid-free paper that meets the guidelines for performance and durability of the Committee on Production Guidelines for Book Longevity of the Council on Library Resources.

AMS Press, Inc.
Brooklyn Navy Yard, 63 Flushing Ave.-Unit #221
Brooklyn, NY 11205-1073, USA
amspressinc.com

Manufactured in the United States of America

Contents

Acknowledgments

I express my sincere appreciation to all of the contributors to this volume for their hard work and inspiring ideas. I particularly wish to thank Kevin L. Cope, not only for contributing to this book but for being a mentor and friend. I must also thank AMS Press and its president Gabriel Hornstein for believing in this topic and encouraging me throughout my work on it. I feel gratitude as well to Saint Leo University, which has nurtured my career and research interests. I wish to acknowledge Rüdiger Ahrens, editor of *Symbolism: An International Annual of Critical Aesthetics*. Six of the following essays originally appeared in the special section I edited for *Symbolism* in 2004.

On a more personal note, I would like to thank Reverend Gene Zimmerman, who first interested me in eighteenth-century Methodism and who has contributed so much to my intellectual, spiritual, and emotional growth. Two excellent friends and brilliant colleagues, Jacqueline Foertsch and Jennifer Trost, have particularly helped me through the writing and editing process; their support has been invaluable. I thank my parents for fostering my love of learning. And, lastly, but with heartfelt gratitude, I thank my husband, Michael Stasio, and my daughter, Isabella Stasio, for absolutely everything.

Kathryn Duncan

Introduction

When Jacques Derrida died I was called by a reporter who wanted to know what would succeed high theory and the triumvirate of race, gender, and class as the center of intellectual energy in the academy. I answered like a shot: religion.

Stanley Fish, "One University, Under God?"

Protestantism was the foundation that made the invention of Great Britain possible.

Linda Colley, Britons: Forging the Nation 1770–1837

For the majority the Christian religion was real and was a central, perhaps the central, focus in their lives.

W. M. Jacob, Lay People and Religion
in the Early Eighteenth Century

Enlightenment was a product of religious debate and not merely a rebellion against it.

J. G. A. Pocock, Barbarism and Religion

It was an age of enthusiasts against enthusiasm . . .

John Redwood, Reason, Ridicule and Religion[1]

Stanley Fish's call is answered by this volume where the authors examine religion during the long eighteenth century but, importantly, not in a manner that replaces the triumvirate of race, gender, and class. The essays highlight these issues in the context of religion in ways that likely would

---

[1]   Stanley Fish, "One University, Under God?" *The Chronicle of Higher Education*. Jan. 7, 2005. Linda Colley, *Britons: Forging the Nation 1770–1837* (New Haven: Yale University Press, 1992), 54. W. M. Jacob, *Lay People and Religion in the Early Eighteenth Century* (Cambridge: Cambridge University Press, 1996), 11. J. G. A. Pocock, *Barbarism and Religion*, vol. 1, *The Enlightenment of Edward Gibbon, 1737–1764* (Cambridge: Cambridge University Press, 1999), 5. John Redwood, *Reason, Ridicule and Religion: The Age of Enlightenment in England 1660–1750* (Cambridge: Harvard University Press, 1976), 16.

have made sense to those living during the eighteenth century because of the primacy of religion in their lives. Linda Colley, of course, has famously made this point in her breakthrough study *Britons* where she argues that the British defined themselves as a Protestant nation and people against Catholicism. B. W. Young agrees, noting that "anti-Catholicism was a major feature of English identity."[2]

Such anti-Catholicism was inevitable, of course, given the banishment of the French-connected, Catholic-leaning Stuarts and the warring relationship with Catholic France throughout the century. And one may go back farther to Spenser's *The Faerie Queene* to see how virulent hatred for Catholics seemed an essential ingredient in building British identity after the Reformation. This foundational text set the stage with its insistence on the superstitious and duplicitous nature of Catholicism as compared to the reasonable and truthful Church of England. James Gregory writes, "The chief pastoral aim of eighteenth-century clergy was to initiate parishioners into the fundamental message of the Reformation and to educate them out of popery and superstition."[3] The Puritans, with their rejection of the Church of England for seeming still too Catholic, made the division all the more clear during the Interregnum, and the Glorious Revolution cemented things with the rejection of the internal threat to Protantism, James II. W. M. Jacob connects a British nervousness about morality in the period 1690–1745 with the belief that God had intervened to expel the Catholic Stuarts and would punish the British by returning them if they did not follow God's will.[4] And, while, as Jacob notes, the Act of Toleration (1689) undermined the Church of England as a national church, the British still connected church and state. "Religion and politics were not necessarily discrete spheres of activity in the lives of individuals."[5] The Reformation, which inextricably tied church and state together and led to anti-Catholicism, and the Civil War were major ideologically determinant events in the history of England.[6]

And these events reverberated in the average person's life. The eighteenth century, at least at its beginning, was still a communal time with the church as the center of community. "At the parish level, the eighteenth-century Church of England was a people's Church. Lay people managed and maintained the building, determined the frequency of worship, financed the clergy, and, through their good works and generosity, promoted Christian knowledge, relieved the poor and sick, and maintained Christian morality. They were not necessarily saints, but for the great majority of

---

2   B. W. Young, *Religion and Enlightenment in Eighteenth-Century England: Theological Debate from Locke to Burke* (Oxford: Clarendon Press, 1998), 51.

3   James Gregory, "The Church of England," in *A Companion to Eighteenth-Century Britain*, ed. H. T. Dickinson (Malden, MA: Blackwell, 2002), 225–240, 237.

4   Jacob, 124.

5   John Walsh and Stephen Taylor, "Introduction: The Church and Anglicanism in the 'Long' Eighteenth Century," in *The Church of England c. 1689–c. 1833: From Toleration to Tractarianism*, ed. John Walsh, Colin Haydon, and Stephen Taylor (Cambridge: Cambridge University Press), 1–64, 22.

6   Gregory, 228.

people God was very important, and to be right with God was a determining factor in ordering their own lives and the life of their community."[7] For that smaller population not part of the Church of England, the ideologies created by the Reformation and Civil War had material impact on their lives. The Corporation Act of 1661 forbade dissenters from holding public office, the Act of Uniformity of 1662 made the Anglican *Book of Common Prayer* the standard for worship and liturgy, and the Test Acts of 1673 and 1678 required an office holder in a military or civil post to deny transubstantiation and to take Anglican sacrament within three months of receiving the post. The 1689 Toleration Act allowed religious freedom for Protestant Trinitarians who registered their houses of worship, but, even with "toleration," one still had the Test Acts of 1673 and 1678. By 1760, magistrates discouraged prosecution under the acts; in 1778, Parliament allowed Catholics to purchase land and removed the most Draconian aspects of laws against them. In 1791, Catholics were granted freedom of worship, though the sacramental test was not banned until 1828, and Catholic emancipation finally arrived in 1829.[8]

So while scholars have engaged in "a relentlessly secularizing interpretation of the 'Enlightenment,'"[9] one should look later for secularization since, in fact, the eighteenth century was still a highly religious age. This is reflected in print culture, which saw a proliferation of religious material. The Toleration Act of 1689 increased print production to persuade parishioners against Dissenters since no coercion could be used. "More titles were published under the broad category of religious works than under any other category (the vast majority of these written by Church of England clergy), and the sermon was by far and away the most potent means of spreading ideas, not only about issues of belief and theology, but also about politics, society and the economy."[10] While Robert Sullivan claims that "Everywhere theological polemic was a mainstay of early-modern discourse,"[11] a 1713 edition of the *Guardian* asserted, "there is not anywhere, I believe, so much Talk about Religion as among us in England."[12] This "talk" about religion in England extended beyond English borders with the Germans demanding printed material about the Church of England and with writers in the Netherlands accused of plagiarizing English print works on religion.[13] In part, this phenomenon demonstrates another

---

[7]   Jacob, 12, 19. See also Gregory, 238.
[8]   Colin Haydon, "Religious Minorities in England," in *A Companion to Eighteenth-Century Britain*, ed. H. T. Dickinson (Malden, MA: Blackwell, 2002), 241–251, 241.
[9]   Young, 14.
[10] Gregory, 227.
[11] Robert Sullivan, "Rethinking Christianity in Enlightened Europe," *Eighteenth-Century Studies* 34 (2001): 298–309, 306.
[12] Quoted in Jacob, 96.
[13] W. R. Ward, "The Eighteenth-Century Church: A European View," in *The Church of England c. 1689–c. 1833: From Toleration to Tractarianism*, ed. John Walsh, Colin Haydon, and Stephen Taylor (Cambridge: Cambridge University Press), 285–298, 285–287.

instance of anti-Catholicism. Jacob notes that the late seventeenth century showed a new interest in education, even for the poor, as a weapon against dissent and popery with religious material available in cheaper chapbook form. Literacy was a Protestant weapon because it allowed the citizenry to read the Bible for themselves.[14] But beyond looking at this religious material, scholars such as Kevin Seidel remind us that to read the much-studied eighteenth-century novel with relentless secularization is to miss that, for example, "Defoe was writing in a world of letters dominated by a latitudinarian religious sensibility, that is, a print world choked with debate about the proper relationship between morality and religion."[15]

Yet even with the church as center of community and the emphasis on religion in print culture, important, perhaps secularizing, changes did occur during the century. Slowly but dramatically "the old communal world" crept toward "an individualistic and pluralist understanding of religion and society." Migration and the separation of the middle classes from their own apprentices and servants, which led to less of a sense of responsibility to the poor, undermined the church with fewer attempts to regulate morality or at least decreased involvement of the church in doing so. Significantly, at the beginning of the century, only six percent of the population were dissenters with 90 percent Anglicans,[16] but, by 1851, a religious census showed that nearly half of the English were dissenters or Catholics.[17] Peter Harrison argues that the proliferation in print also points to an important paradigm shift connecting religion to the Enlightenment: the scientific objectification of religion as a field of study. In the medieval period, religion meant faith, the "dynamic of the heart," whereas, in the eighteenth century, it came to mean a set of practices or doctrines, moving from a universal notion of religion to the concept of religions. The job of print was to set out articles of belief as the pursuit of knowledge became elevated over the "old way" of faith, love, and duty. This, in turn, led to the notion of comparative religion, being able to investigate and judge other doctrines. "True religion was not genuine piety, but a body of certain knowledge. 'False religion' in this intellectualist conception of things, was equated with ignorance, incredulity, or error."[18] In this way, religion itself became a product of the Enlightenment, something to study as one would study biology, chemistry, or physics.

The key to these doctrinal differences rested in the interlocking perceptions of reason and human nature. Decisions on these two key issues determined attitudes toward salvation by works or faith and the relationship of humans to God. Harrison traces a shift from the medieval period here as well: "Thinkers of the Middle Ages generally maintained that through the exercise of human reason alone man can come to a knowledge

---

14   Jacob, 161–162.
15   Kevin Seidel, "Beyond the Religious and the Secular in the History of the Novel," *New Literary History* 38 (2007): 637–647, 638.
16   Jacob, 17, 224.
17   Haydon, 250.
18   Peter Harrison, *'Religion' and the Religions in the English Enlightenment* (Cambridge: Cambridge University Press, 1990), 26.

of the existence of God in his works, to a knowledge of the human soul with its attributes of freedom and immortality, and can discover Natural Law. This view found its way into traditional Catholic theology. According to the medieval synthesis, two types of knowledge of God, the natural and the revealed, compete each other." Because natural and revealed religion complemented each other within Catholicism, it was inevitable that Protestant England would reject this notion, seeing natural and revealed religion as opposites. For Protestant reformers, humans are so thoroughly marred by sin that the ability to reason is naturally corrupt. A universal knowledge of "God" is possible even among the heathens, but clearly they are all damned since what non-Christian religions know via natural religion/reason is some human construct or even a trick of the devil.[19] One need only think of Milton's connecting the devils newly inhabiting hell to later pagan deities in *Paradise Lost* to see this worked out in literature. This pessimistic view of human nature led to Calvin's doctrine of the elect and Luther's rejection of salvation by works. Such pessimism also entailed a fairly negative view of God, who seemed fully willing to condemn many of his children to eternal damnation since the accident of birth could mean no opportunity to experience revealed—Christian—religion.

Ultimately, this view of human nature and God proved too pessimistic. Isabel Rivers sees this as one of the major shifts in religious thought with a new Anglican emphasis on "the capacity of human reason and free will to co-operate with divine grace in order to achieve the holy and happy life."[20] The Latitudinarians, who arose in the 1650–60s and were the most influential group under William and Mary, rejected the Calvinist and Hobbesian descriptions of human nature. "The latitudinarians held man to have been created and to remain, despite the effects of sin, a rational being endowed with innate knowledge of God, good and evil, and moral duties." As social, self-interested, and rational beings, humans lean naturally toward God and understand that religion leads to happiness.[21] The Cambridge Platonists argued in a similar fashion believing in the *a priori* existence of "irreducible religious truths" in all humans with atheism and impiety arising from a corrupting world. These truths were recoverable via introspection.[22]

Not everyone, of course, shared this optimism about human nature and reason or the easiness of life. Puritans saw the life of faith as active and arduous with John Bunyan giving humans credit for a role in their salvation but making clear that God was the dominant partner in the relationship. Perhaps this bleak view moved beyond the doctrinal as the Test and Corporation Acts "were a daily reminder to Dissenters that they were outsiders in the political establishment." However, the egalitarian instruction at Dissenting academies that embraced a more modern

[19] Ibid., 7, 8.
[20] Isabel Rivers, *Reason, Grace, and Sentiment: A Study of the Language of Religion and Ethics in England, 1660–1780*, vol. 1, *Whichcote to Wesley* (Cambridge: Cambridge University Press, 1991), 1.
[21] Ibid., 59–60.
[22] Harrison, 38.

curriculum taught in English paved the way for a material refutation of Bunyan's gloom as Dissenters made up a disproportionate number of those participating in the boom of an eighteenth-century mercantile economy. "At least a quarter of the late-Stuart London merchants were Dissenters; and Dissenters comprised about thirty-seven percent of the colonial trade, two-thirds of the New England Company, and forty-three percent of the directors of the Bank of England."[23] Calvinists, of course, would read the scene differently, attributing such success to being part of the elect. Key for us is that this dichotomy of natural and revealed religion became crucial in doctrinal disputes with the orthodox arguing for the obvious superiority of revealed religion, deists saying natural religion is sufficient, and latitudinarians and Cambridge Platonists saying something between, that natural religion paved the way for one to believe in revealed.[24]

It is worth reiterating that the distinct differences in opinion over natural and revealed religion rested in attitudes toward reason. And reason itself served as an important component in another binary relationship, that of reason and enthusiasm. The church invoked reason to support the reasonable nature of Christianity versus atheism and Deism and against the enthusiasm of Catholics and Dissenters.[25] Orthodox believers relied on John Locke's arguments in chapter 19 of *An Essay Concerning Human Understanding*. In investigating the sources humans trust in the search for truth, he describes "enthusiasm: which, laying by reason, would set up revelation without it. Whereby in effect it takes away both reason and revelation, and substitutes in the room of them the ungrounded fancies of a man's own brain, and assumes them for a foundation both of opinion and conduct."[26] Enthusiasm, for Locke, means the abdication of reason. In the seventeenth century, Bunyan downplayed reason and even pretended to less education than he had received, perhaps opening the way for Lockean attacks against dissenters as enthusiasts. More importantly, later Englishmen saw the Puritans of the Civil War as engaging in a wild enthusiasm that defied law and order with dire consequences for everyone. Still, even knowing enthusiasm could be wielded as a weapon, later dissenters refused to deify reason. Isaac Watts, the famous moderate dissenting hymnodist, believed "man uses reason to receive, test, and accept revelation" but that reason leads only to knowledge, not action, which requires the passions and affection.[27]

Like Watts, John Wesley, founder of Methodism, shared a similar skepticism about reason as the sole agent of revelation. Young describes his beliefs thus: "Wesley's was an emotional, affective faith, a religion of the heart rather than a systematic theology."[28] Methodism was part of a larger

23   Ana M. Acosta, "Spaces of Dissent and the Public Sphere in Hackney, Stoke Newington, and Newington Green," *Eighteenth-Century Life* 27 (2003): 1–27, 4.
24   Harrison, 24.
25   Gregory, 232.
26   John Locke, *An Essay Concerning Human Understanding* (London: Thomas Tegg, 1841), 516. Google Books: <http://books.google.com/books>.
27   Rivers, 186–188.
28   Young, 151.

international Evangelical revival that began in the 1730s and 40s that was hostile to secularism and characterized by "irregular practices and structures," such as field preaching, and was a rejection of the "largely ethical preaching" of Anglicans. The revival movement expounded a return to "Reformation doctrines of justification and regeneration as expounded in the Thirty-Nine Articles."[29] Wesley's Methodism, therefore, defied eighteenth-century trends in two ways, which partly explains the vituperative response to it. Methodism not only relies on emotion, but it fails the litmus test described by Harrison of being a solid body of knowledge that one can study objectively. Critics, for instance, accused Wesley of being fickle—changing doctrinally and of trying to engage in too many professions—publishing religious but also political and medical tracts, while dispensing medicines to fellow Methodists.[30]

Methodism inhabits a liminal space, sharing some characteristics with dissenters as well as the latitudinarians while still technically a part of the Church of England throughout Wesley's lifetime. Like earlier dissenters, Wesley shared a distrust of human nature believing that humans are born in original sin. For Wesley, "Natural man is evil, and man in his natural unaided state is incapable of knowing God." This leads, of course, to a similar distrust of reason as a saving power. Wesley by no means denies the importance of reason but argues that its powers are limited. Reason cannot control the passions, nor can it "produce faith, because it cannot provide evidence of the invisible world; it cannot produce hope of immortality, nor love of God and our neighbour, nor virtue, nor happiness."[31] Evangelicals, overall, shared "an acceptance of the human facility of reason but not an excessive rationality which might lead to skepticism and unbelief."[32] Yet, ironically, Wesley shares with the latitudinarians an optimism about the Christian life, not seeing it as Bunyan did as a trial, but rather as a happy state, for in spite of his views on original sin, Wesley also preached the doctrine of perfection. While tainted with sin at birth, faith would allow believers to achieve a new birth and ultimately perfection. Rivers describes the necessary steps: "repentance, faith, justification (i.e., the individual's pardon and acceptance of God), assurance (his recognition that he is justified), the new birth (the beginning of sanctification), and sanctification, otherwise holiness or perfection."[33]

The notion of assurance opened Methodists up to great criticism since it was this belief that veered so much on enthusiasm. Wesley's description of his own moment of assurance emphasizes feeling, not reason: "I felt my heart strangely warmed. I felt I did trust in Christ, Christ alone for my salvation; and an assurance was given me that he had taken away my sins,

29 Rivers, 206.
30 Albert M. Lyles, *Methodism Mocked: The Satiric Reaction to Methodism in the Eighteenth Century* (London: Epworth Press, 1960), 118.
31 Rivers, 228, 233.
32 G. M. Ditchfield, "Methodism and the Evangelical Revival," in *The Church of England: A Companion to Eighteenth-Century Britain*, ed. H. T. Dickinson (Malden, MA: Blackwell, 2002), 252–259.
33 Rivers, 234.

even mine, and saved me from the law of sin and death."[34] Later in his career, Wesley would argue that one could be saved without such a visceral knowledge of assurance due to the depression that some of his followers experienced when they did not receive the same kind of clear sign from God. But while Wesley saw himself as hearkening back to the primitive church and as politically conservative in his allegiance to the crown, the charges of enthusiasm continued leading to sanctioned mob attacks against him and his preachers.

Methodism spread best in places where the Church of England was least able to be paternalistic: freehold parishes, industrial villages, mining communities, market towns, ports, and places of migratory population.[35] The movement tapped into the slow deterioration of centralized community as the century progressed moving, for example, to the American colonies where the Calvinist Methodist George Whitefield met Jonathan Edwards and the Wesley brothers lived for a short time in Georgia. "Methodism thus played an important part in a much broader process of religious change in eighteenth-century England, as a centuries-old pattern of enforced ecclesiastical discipline and uniformity on a parish basis slowly gave way to a concept of religion as a voluntary commitment by free individuals in a pluralistic society."[36] As the middle class rose and worked to separate themselves from their servants and apprentices, Wesley, writing in a plain style like Bunyan, appealed to these lower classes employing field preaching and offering a strict moral discipline practiced less often by the Church of England in some parts of the country. Though Wesley did not wish to split with the Church of England but reform it from within, the eventual split from the church was made inevitable by the Deed of Declaration of 1784, making Methodism a continuing body and licensing Methodist chapels as dissenting meeting houses under the Toleration Act and by Wesley's ordination of laymen (twenty-seven total).[37]

Even as the Church of England vilified Methodism for its enthusiasm, some important philosophers critiqued all Christian churches on much the same principles. The second major movement that Rivers traces in eighteenth-century English religious thought is the divorce of ethics from religion and the investigation of human nature—not humankind's interaction with God—as the explanation for human behavior. A number of philosophers and critics of religion did just this, believing "true religion, whatever that may be, was throughout history shuttlecocked by the competing forces of enthusiasm and superstition."[38] In other words, while the Church of England turned its critical eye to Dissenters, Catholics, and Methodists accusing them of enthusiasm and superstition, some eighteenth-century philosophers cast these same aspersions against Christianity itself.

---

[34]   <http://www.flumc.org/bishop_whitaker/salvation.htm>.
[35]   David Hempton, *The Religion of the People: Methodism and Popular Religion c. 1750–1900* (New York: Routledge, 1996), 7.
[36]   Ibid., 158.
[37]   Lyle, 151.
[38]   Young, 300.

Reason again became the lynchpin in arguments against orthodox religion. The Cambridge Platonist Benjamin Whichcote believed, "More than just a property of the functioning mind, reason is both the voice of God in the human soul, and that which enables the soul to distinguish and recognize God's voice in communicating what is good and true."[39] This becomes, much against Whichcote's intentions, the basis of Deism later in the eighteenth century. For the later Deist, Matthew Tindal, reason is all; "the religion of nature for Tindal is the process whereby reason establishes the rules of morality and puts them into practice. Religion and reason are virtually synonymous."[40] Locke, whose works became the foundation for much of these arguments about reason, would have been horrified given his own belief in revealed religion. Locke's pupil, the first Earl of Shaftesbury, disagreed with Locke on key ideas and, along with the later great skeptic David Hume, displaced reason as the seat of morality looking instead to feeling, oddly allying these freethinkers with the great Evangelicals such as Wesley who argued for the necessity of emotion.

Freethinkers, while critiquing religion, also saw its utilitarian value if it led to social harmony; they simply felt that modern Christianity created more problems than it solved. Deists disliked Christianity, seeing it as superstitious and leading to divisiveness.[41] Shaftesbury felt atheism made non-believers hopeless and pessimistic, whereas theism reinforced optimism and natural affection so that religion was healthy psychologically.[42] But Shaftesbury did not feel the theism as practiced by Christianity created these positive results. In fact, the wrong kind of religion—a superstitious mercenary practice where one only does what is right for a reward—damages virtue.[43] Hume, who divorced ethics and religion arguing they are two separate subjects for study, also recognized that religion was psychologically satisfying but felt that Christianity had damaged ethics. He, therefore, wished to investigate moral principles as entirely a human phenomenon with no connection to religion. These ideas inevitably bring us back to views of human nature since placing so much responsibility for morality with humankind itself clearly is predicated upon an optimistic view of human nature. Such claims serve as a counter argument to those made by the mid-century divine William Warburton, who traced moral duty to its first principles: "moral sense (or instinct) and reason in man, subordinated to the will of God."[44]

This thumbnail sketch of religion in Great Britain during the long eighteenth century is not meant to offer a new argument but an overview of some of the main strains of thought and thinkers during the period. The essays in this collection take the reader both deeper and wider. Because of

---

39   Harrison, 31.
40   Isabel Rivers, *Reason, Grace, and Sentiment: A Study of the Language of Religion and Ethics in England, 1660–1780*, vol. 2, *Shaftesbury to Hume* (Cambridge: Cambridge University Press, 2000), 77.
41   Haydon, 247–248.
42   Rivers, 139.
43   Ibid., 135.
44   Ibid., 239, 199.

the centrality of religion during this period, any study of religion looks beyond religion itself into the world of the economy, class, gender, rhetoric, philosophy, and aesthetics. Because, of course, Great Britain included colonies, two essays deal with religion in the American colonies. And, since the roots of the religious controversies originate at least as early as the seventeenth century if not before, our essayists take us back in time as well, allowing us a greater perspective on religion and its representation during the Restoration and Enlightenment.

Anne Barbeau Gardiner's essay, "Division in Communion: Symbols of Transubstantiation in Donne, Milton, and Dryden," investigates a topic easily overlooked in eighteenth-century studies. Given the seeming dismissal of transubstantiation as superstitious Catholic doctrine during the long eighteenth century, Gardiner's careful reading of Donne's, Milton's, and Dryden's treatment of it allows readers to investigate the transformation of transubstantiation during a period of religious upheaval.

In "Fading Fast but Still in Print: The Brink of Visibility and the Form of Religious Experience, Spinoza to Cowper," Kevin L. Cope critiques the modern attempt to separate experience into material and religious components. Cope notes that, while empiricism always sought to see and process experience, even the most famous empiricists such as Locke and Hume move beyond the senses in their writing. By putting English writers, including less-studied English poets, within their broader European context, Cope shows that Romanticism is less revolutionary than part of a larger and longer empirical discourse.

Via an examination of the life of the Benedictine Hugh Paulinus Cressy, Patricia C. Brückmann reevaluates Catholicism and its supposed threat in "The 'Serene Mr. Cressy,' Enlightened and Peaceful Catholicism in the Late Seventeenth Century." Brückmann traces Cressy's social connections as well as reading his work to demonstrate how influential Catholics wished for peace and a unified Christian church not split by schism.

"'Organs of thy Praise': The Function of the Body in Thomas Traherne's Sacramental Phenomenology," Gary Kuchar's contribution, takes readers into the world of an understudied yet important figure of the seventeenth century. Traherne's significance lies in his mystic Neoplatonism and awareness of empirical emphasis on reason. In fact, Kuchar believes Traherne foreshadows the sensibility found in Romantic poets such as Blake and Wordsworth, while also seeing Traherne as a "modern" figure, whose repression was necessary for the success of the Enlightenment enterprise.

Michael Austin's piece, "Bunyan's Book of Ruth: The Typological Structure of Seventeenth-Century Debate on Women in the Church," explores women's roles in worship. Austin provides fresh insight into the debate and one of its major participants, John Bunyan. Austin's reading complicates the view that Bunyan fully engaged in a dismissal of women as valuable spiritual individuals.

Bob Tennant investigates the changes wrought in the church by the Glorious Revolution; he reads key sermons by the important but understudied John Tillotson and offers statistical analysis of sermons in "John Tillotson and the Voice of Anglicanism." Tennant's essay makes clear the centrality of sermons as critical discourse during political upheaval. Tillotson, a Royal Society member, employed a simple style connecting style to ethical, straightforward English Protestantism and hence with substance.

While Edward Taylor, the subject of Harry Clark Maddux's essay, "Effects and Affects: Edward Taylor's Negotiation of Ramist Rhetoric," is often viewed as a conservative, Maddux discusses the emotional affect of several of Taylor's meditations and his indebtedness to Peter Ramus, the Renaissance rhetorician/ logician who appealed to Protestants because of his belief that logic mirrored nature, meaning that individuals could learn logic through experiencing nature for themselves without an intervening authority. In this way, Ramus can be seen as an early empiricist; Taylor's use of Ramism demonstrates, in Maddux's view, that the systematic strain of Ramist theory survived into eighteenth-century colonial Christianity, bringing with it the same kind of reliance on personal experience that is present in Methodism later in the century.

Alexander Pope, of course, has long been seen as an exemplar of the Enlightenment, but Katherine Quinsey's "Dualities of the Divine in Pope's *Essay on Man* and *The Dunciad*" provides new insight into Pope's divided approach to religion and, hence, to tensions present throughout the culture. Through a comparison of the two poems' conceptual and production history, Quinsey shows how these seemingly opposite poems, in fact, share many connections, with much that is suppressed in *Essay* appearing in *The Dunciad*. Our reading of these poems, Quinsey argues, tell us more about Pope on religion than his overt religious statements.

Michael Rotenberg-Schwartz also brings new perspective to Pope's poetry in "'Dishonest Scars': Holiness, Secrecy, and the Problem of Perpetual Peace." Rotenberg-Schwartz examines what it means for a work of literature to be Christian beyond the usual tropes by putting *Windsor Forest* in the context of the Treaty of Utrecht and other poems celebrating peace. Ironically, a "Christian poetics of peace" can be found in texts that strive to but cannot enclose the violence of war, thereby manifesting "holy scars."

Brian Fehler's "Jonathan Edwards on Nature as a Language of God: Symbolic Typology as Rhetorical Presence" takes readers across the Atlantic and moves us beyond Edwards as preacher of "Sinners in the Hands of an Angry God" during the Great Awakening (1735–1742). Edwards is often labeled an anachronistic Puritan, given the heyday of Puritanism had died out before his birth in 1703. Yet Edwards believed firmly in and preached a return to pure Puritan values at his own personal expense. Though his castigation of the youth of the upper class cost him his living, Edwards, as Fehler points out, engaged in more than hellfire rhetoric and, in fact, extended Biblical typology to nature.

Brett C. McInelly's essay "Method or Madness: Methodist Devotion and the Anti-Methodist Response" confronts enthusiasm and the notion of madness as McInelly explores Methodism's relationship with madness. By investigating Wesley's take on reason and madness as well as the vituperative response to Methodism, McInelly offers insight into both

Methodism and Enlightenment anxiety over enthusiasm and the notion that the act of faith requires a kind of relinquishing of control or reason.

Peter Nockles traces the publication history of John Foxe's *Acts and Monuments* to interrogate the assumptions about the use of the book to bolster Protestantism against Catholicism. In "The Changing Legacy and Reception of John Foxe's 'Book of Martyrs' in the 'Long Eighteenth Century': Varieties of Anglican, Protestant and Catholic Response, c. 1760–c. 1830," Nockles argues that Foxe's work was not, in fact, published widely during the century and that dissenters used it to critique the Church of England, generalizing the persecution in the "Book" to the Church of England. As Catholic emancipation became imminent, Foxe's work united Protestants but became a weapon of the Anglican Evangelicals against the Oxford Movement.

B. W. Young has argued that Bishop Warburton influenced his contemporaries far more than Hume did though Warburton has been mostly ignored by modern scholarship. Young's point is well taken; however, new interest in religion by eighteenth-century scholars is encouraging. These essays should do much to promote more such work.

Division in Communion: Symbols of Transubstantiation in Donne, Milton, and Dryden

Anne Barbeau Gardiner

The term *symbol* has long meant a verbal token of membership. In Christian antiquity creeds were called "symbols of the faith," a name they still carry. In the preface to his fourth-century exposition of *symbolum apostolorum* (the Apostles' Creed), Rufinus defined a *symbol* as a password given to an army so that, if someone were asked for his symbol (*interrogatus symbolum*), he would at once reveal if he were friend or foe.[1] St. Augustine among other Church Fathers accepted this definition. In 1538, Luther still spoke of Drey *Symbola* in reference to the Apostles,' Nicene, and Athanasian Creeds, and later the term was applied to articles of faith that divided Lutherans, Calvinists, and Catholics from each other, especially with regard to the sacraments, as in Pareus's 1643 work, *Theologica Symbolica de Sacramentis.*[2]

Donne, Milton, and Dryden each present us with a "symbol" of transubstantiation.[3] Albeit the first two rejected the Catholic doctrine of

---

[1] J. N. D. Kelly, *Early Christian Creeds* (London: Longmans Green, 1952), 54.

[2] Charles Augustus Briggs, *Theological Symbolics* (New York: Charles Scribner's Sons, 1914), 4–9. Johann Adams Mohler used symbol in this way in his *Symbolism: Exposition of Doctrinal Differences Between Catholics and Protestants as Evidenced by Their Symbolical Writings* (1832). And the chief doctrinal handbook for Catholics until the 1950s was Heinrich Denzinger's *Enchiridion Symbolorum*, trans. Roy J. Deferrari (St. Louis: Herder [c. 1957])

[3] The term transubstantiation was used at the Fourth Lateran Council (1215) to explain the modus, the "how" of the real presence in the sacrament. This was in

transubstantiation, they still deliberately used this term and attached a different meaning to it to explain their own idea of communion. Each of the three poets creates an imaginative symbol of faith that shows how he understands Christ's words at the Last Supper, "This is My Body," words over which a controversy had raged since the Reformation. Europe was split apart over what Christ intended by saying that he would feed his followers with his "flesh" and "blood" (Jn 6:53) and by assuring them he would abide with them forever: "I am with you always, even unto the end of the world" (Mt 28:20).

The clergy of the Elizabethan Church of England taught that Christ was really present in the Lord's Supper but only at the moment of communion and only to the soul of the worthy receiver. They condemned as idolatry the Catholic adoration of the sacrament of the altar. As Dryden expressed it:

> A real presence all her sons allow,
> And yet 'tis flat Idolatry to bow,
> Because the god-head's there they know not how.[4]

Nicholas Sander, an Oxford theologian who was papal adviser at the Council of Trent, summed it up neatly when he said that the Church of England taught, "bread only in the hand, and body only in the harte," whereas Catholics believed, "body as well in hand, as in harte."[5] At that time, Puritans were already complaining that kneeling for Anglican communion was idolatry, so spokesmen for the established church such as Richard Hooker defended the posture by explaining that the real presence was a completely interiorized experience. There was no object of adoration. It was in trying to placate the Puritans that Hooker used the term *transubstantiation*, but only to define it as interior change in the receiver after taking communion: "there ensueth a kind of transubstantiation in us, a true change both of soul and body, an alteration from death to life."[6] Like Hooker, Donne used the word *transubstantiation* and defined it to mean an internal alteration happening *after* communion. In his Fourth Prebend Sermon, he wrote: "There is the true Transubstantiation, that when I have

---

response to Berengarius and his followers who, from the eleventh century, claimed that the real presence was only figurative. Among others, St. Thomas Aquinas explained transubstantiation as the modus by which "the whole substance of the bread" is converted to "the whole substance of Christ's body" at consecration (*Summa Theologica* IIIa.75.4). Here substance was distinguished from accident.

4   *The Hind and the Panther*, Part I, 414–416, in *Poems 1685–1692*, ed. Earl Miner and Vinton A. Dearing, in *The Works of John Dryden*, ed. H. T. Swedenberg, Jr. et al. 20 vols. (Berkeley and Los Angeles: University of California Press, 1956–), 3:135.

5   Nicolas Sander, *The Supper of Our Lord* (Lovanii, 1566), 75. Sander is arguing against Nowell's *Apologie*.

6   Richard Hooker, *Ecclesiastical Polity*. 2 vols. (London: Dent and Dutton, 1922), 2:328.

received it worthily, it becomes my very soule; that is, my soule growes up into a better state . . . the more deified soule by that Sacrament."[7]

Both Hooker and Donne used the word *true* to imply they were correcting the Catholic definition of transubstantiation by interiorizing it: Hooker speaking of a *true change*, Donne of a *true transubstantiation*. However, as R. V. Young shows, Donne, because of his Catholic upbringing, was ambivalent even in this sermon. For the rest of his life, he alternated between "hostility and sympathy" for transubstantiation but continued to have a "vexed preoccupation with and longing for the divine presence."[8] As I will show, the poem "Good Friday 1613. Riding Westward," written not long before he was ordained in the Church of England, is a symbol of Donne's belief that a purely spiritual encounter with the real presence, one that leaves the body aside, is enough to transubstantiate one into the image of Christ.

By the late seventeenth-century, few in the Church of England would have used the term *transubstantiation* in a positive way, even by redefining it as Hooker and Donne had. The reason was that the Test Acts of 1673 and 1678 required, as a prerequisite for public employment or a seat in parliament, an oath against transubstantiation. The term had come to mean "gross idolatry." But Anglican Bishop Samuel Parker, representing the high-churchmen, lamented that those who had set up the 1678 Test to exclude Catholics from parliament (and James from the throne) as idolaters were unable to distinguish between real presence and transubstantiation. By the new Test, he said, they introduced into the Church of England that "Zwinglianism" regarding the Lord's Supper that had prevailed in England in the Interregnum, id est, the belief that the real presence was a bare metaphor. Insofar as the new law was about the real presence, Parker said, it was a *"Defiance to all Christendom,"* and insofar as it was about transubstantiation, it required Englishmen to abjure something "unintelligible" to them, because to understand that term one would have to know medieval metaphysics.[9]

An example of what Parker complained about appears in Bishop Burnet's exposition of the 28th Article of the Church of England, on the Lord's Supper. Burnet not only condemns transubstantiation as "gross idolatry" but also urges abandonment of "the phrase real presence," saying that it "were better to be let fall than to be continued, since the use of it, and that idea which does naturally arise from the common acceptation of it, may stick deeper, and feed superstition more, than all those larger explanations that are given to it can be able to cure."

In these "larger explanations" of real presence Burnet includes those of Luther and Calvin, for he asserts that it was only because these Reformers found "the World was possessed of the Phrase of the *real presence*" that

7 Donne's *Prebend Sermons*, ed. Janel M. Mueller (Cambridge: Harvard University Press, 1971), 155.
8 *Doctrine and Devotion in Seventeenth-Century Poetry: Studies in Donne, Herbert, Crashaw, and Vaughan* (Cambridge: D. S. Brewer, 2000), 99.
9 Samuel Parker, Bishop of Oxford, *Reasons for Abrogating the Test Imposed upon all Members of Parliament Anno 1678* (London, 1688), 9–11, 47–49, 69–70.

they kept it in their symbols of faith,[10] retaining it out of policy, not out of principle. In an earlier work where he specifies *what* is received at communion, Burnet says it is Christ's "*dead Body,* which is not now actually in being" but only "conceived of as presented to us," and he adds that what "is present in the Sacrament is Christ *dead.*"[11] Edward Sclater comments that the denial of "Christs real and substantial Presence" in the sixteenth-century led at first to making the consecrated bread and wine "bare signs and figures," and at last, "meer Cyphers."[12]

The English Puritans followed Zwingli on the Eucharist and for this reason objected to kneeling for reception as early as the reign of Edward VI. They insisted that there was a logical contradiction between Christ's ascension and the real presence and that since Christ was confined to the right hand of the Father until doomsday, he could not, even if he wanted to, be present anywhere else. This meant that the substantial real presence of Christ's body to the soul of the worthy receiver, of which Hooker, Andrewes, and Donne wrote, was just as impossible to them as the Catholic real presence in the sacrament of the altar. So they objected vehemently to kneeling for reception. Besides this, Puritans saw no difference between the sacraments of the Old and New Testaments, between the Lord's Supper and the Jewish Passover. They thought a sermon gave the same benefits as communion with less danger of superstition and idolatry, for making Christ present to their faith was the main thing. Little wonder, then, that when Puritans controlled Oxford University from 1648 to 1660, communion was not distributed even once.[13] In Book V of *Paradise Lost,* Milton deliberately uses the word *transubstantiate* to show where he stands in this debate. A passage about transubstantiation in Book V, where he discusses the relation between matter and spirit becomes the basis for his later depiction of Eve's sin in Book IX as her succumbing to a diabolical illusion of transubstantiation.

One of the chief distinctions between Catholics and Protestants was that, for Catholics, the Church was itself a sacrament, a manifestation of real presence insofar as she was believed to be the mystical "Body of Christ."[14] In *The Hind and the Panther,* Dryden creates a symbol of his faith in a Church that embodies the real presence. His design is drawn from the

---

10   Gilbert Burnet, Bishop of Sarum, *An Exposition of the XXXIX Articles of the Church of England* (Oxford University Press, 1845), 384, 357.

11   Gilbert Burnet, *A Discourse Concerning Transubstantiation and Idolatry. Being an Answer to the Bishop of Oxford's Plea Relating to those Two Points* (London: n. p., 1688), 5–6.

12   *Consensus Veterum: or, the Reasons of Edward Sclater Minister of Putney, For his Conversion to the Catholic Faith and Communion* (London: Henry Hills, 1686), 97.

13   Charles Leslie, *The Wolf Stript of His Shepherd's Cloathing . . . By one call'd an High-Churchman,* ([London], 1704), 20. The author cites the *Antiquities of Oxford* and the Archbishop of Dublin's *Discourse Concerning the Inventions of Man* and adds that in Aberdeen communion has not been given in fifteen years, ever since Presbyterianism was established at the Revolution.

14   The Church is called "the sacrament of Christ's action at work in her through the mission of the Holy Spirit." No. 1118 in *Catechism of the Catholic Church* (San Francisco: 1994), 290.

Song of Songs, a biblical book which, at the time, both Protestants and Catholics agreed in interpreting allegorically as the marriage song of Christ and his Bride the Church. The Hind in Dryden's poem represents the Catholic Church as the beloved of the Roe, a figure of Christ. In a memorable confession at the start of this poem, Dryden reveals that, for him, taking communion in the Catholic Church means being incorporated into the public, visible body of Christ.

Donne: The Journey to Interior Transubstantiation

In "Good Friday, 1613. Riding Westward," Donne creates a symbol of his faith. He tells of a private journey that leads to an encounter with the real presence, followed by a substantial interior conversion. The poet begins by picturing the liturgical year as an astronomical cycle: on Good Friday, Christ crucified rises in the east like the sun, but Donne's body is a sphere moving in the opposite direction. He cannot look at the cross with bodily eyes, because his exterior self is not in his control, being driven to "Pleasure or business" by "foreign motions." Even so, his soul turns to worship Christ as he moves bodily away from him: "my soul's form bends toward the east."[15] That his soul should take the posture of adoration toward the east evokes the communion liturgy, since from antiquity to his day, the worship of Christians was directed to the east as to the place of Redemption. Christ was adored by bowing toward an altar with a crucifix situated at the eastern end of the church.

Good Friday has always been the focus of the communion liturgy. Here in an oblique way, Donne hints at the Church of England liturgy where only the soul receives communion. His body faces westward, is subject to natural laws, while his soul alone bends to the east where life is, and it can "see" Christ in an interior I-Thou encounter, so as to be substantially changed to another self. Donne gives a clue to his liturgical groundwork when he says further on: "Though these things, as I ride, be from mine eye, / They are present yet *unto my memory*." His phrase *unto my memory* evokes Christ's words at the Last Supper, "Do this in remembrance of me" (Lk 22:19), a command understood down the ages as the institution of the Lord's Supper.

If his bodily eyes could look to the east, Donne thinks he "should see" something happening in the present moment: "There I should see a sun, by rising set, / And by that setting endless day beget." Then he moves to the past with the verb *did rise*: "But that Christ on this Cross, did rise and fall, / Sin had eternally benighted all." Merging past and present together in this way suggests a liturgy where Christ is both remembered as crucified and adored as divine. The poem can be approached as an Ignatian meditation, but it is a meditation that leads to an intimate encounter with the real presence, a moment of communion.

Donne dares "almost be glad" he is moving bodily in the opposite direction, because the sight would be "of too much weight for me." Since at

---

[15]   *John Donne*, ed. John Carey (New York: Oxford University Press, 1990), 241.

Christ's death the earth quaked (Mt 27:51) and the sun grew dark (Lk 23:45)—"It made his footstool crack, and the sun wink"—he himself might perish if the Crucifixion were visible to his bodily eyes: "What a death were it then to see God die?" Thus he justifies his body's absence from the encounter with Christ in the real presence. Then he ponders how Christ is at once a man and God filling and ruling the universe:

> Could I behold those hands which span the poles,
> And turn all spheres at once, pierced with those holes?
> Could I behold that endless height which is
> Zenith to us, and to'our antipodes,
> Humbled below us?

He zooms in and out from the fixed hands to the vast reaches of the universe to try to conceive how the same person could be nailed to a tree and cause the motion of the spheres. This is not a paradox. He articulates the core belief of Christianity, that Christ is both true man and true God.

Then Donne says that if he turned around, he would "behold" Christ's torn "flesh" and spilt "blood." With the terms *flesh* and *blood* so evocative of the Lord's Supper, the poem comes to its climax. Donne's soul now meets Christ in an I-Thou encounter:

> Though these things, as I ride, be from mine eye,
> They are present yet unto my memory,
> For that looks towards them; and thou look'st towards me,
> O Saviour, as thou hang'st upon the tree

Note that the poet uses the charged word *present* when he says the details of the crucifixion are "present yet unto my memory." In this context, the phrase *present* yet designates the real presence because Donne is immediately aware that Christ is looking straight at him: "Thou look'st towards me, / O Saviour." The three verbs in the above passage—*looks, look'st,* and *hang'st*—are all in the present tense. First Donne "looks" back at Christ in his "memory," and then Christ is suddenly "present" as the intimate "Thou" who looks straight at Donne from the cross. Afterwards, the "eyes" of the two interlock in a timeless I-Thou encounter. This is not the "dead" Christ of Burnet's communion, but a living Christ who can *look* at the receiver. Although the eye-contact is metaphysical, or purely spiritual, it is also intensely personal. This is exactly what the Lord's Supper is in Hooker—the worthy receiver meeting Christ as really and substantially present, but only to his soul, not to his body.

And so, after worshiping interiorly, bending his soul to the east, and looking back to the crucifixion in "memory," Donne reaches a point in his paradigmatic liturgy where his soul encounters the real presence in a profoundly personal way. After this communion, he experiences the start of a substantial conversion, or a transubstantiation. He has been made aware of his "rusts" and "deformity" by the nearness of his "Saviour," and, suddenly overcome with sorrow, he prays to be restored by lashing and burning:

I turn my back to thee, but to receive
Corrections, till thy mercies bid thee leave.
O think me worth thine anger, punish me,
Burn off my rusts, and my deformity,
Restore thine image, so much, by thy grace,
That thou mayst know me, and I'll turn my face.

The encounter with the real presence thus leads to a yearning for complete conversion. Now *conversion* was the word used from antiquity, long before *transubstantiation*, for the change of the bread and wine into the body and blood of Christ. Donne begs for an interior change, to be restored to what he was at baptism, an image of Christ. He wants to regain his true form, though he is now in a state of "deformity." The closeness of Christ makes such a change possible through the application of strong "Corrections" to his "back" or his body.

When Donne pleads with Christ, "Restore thine image . . . / That thou mayst know me," the word *know* alludes to biblical passages like Matthew 7:23, where Christ banishes souls to hell by saying "I never knew you," and Revelation 12:8, where the damned have their names "not written in the book of life." The transubstantiation Donne prays for is a radical change from being *unknown* to Christ to being *known*. When he can be sure that Christ will "know" him, he says "I'll turn my face." Turning or facing God in his body means death, so he is saying he welcomes physical death whenever he can be sure of salvation, the word *face* in "I'll turn my face" evoking the final encounter with the real presence that St. Paul longs for in 1 Corinthians 13:12: "now we see through a glass darkly, but then face to face."

Donne's "Good Friday" is a symbol of his belief in the real presence and in an interior transubstantiation. None of what he writes contradicts what he learned in his Catholic youth, though it reduces it by half. As Nicholas Sander explains: "it is true that we hold Christ by faith, spirit, and understanding in the holy mysteries," but "one truth" does not "stop another," and so, just as a man and his wife must come bodily together to be made one flesh, so the bread which is "turned into Christes flesh" is meant to be "made one with our flesh."[16] Long before Descartes, Sander warned that a great gap was opening between body and soul in Protestantism. But if Hooker and Donne abridged and interiorized the Catholic Eucharist, Milton cast it off altogether. He made belief in a "Food divine" that can nourish "bodie and soul" the basis of Original Sin.

Milton: Transubstantiation and Diabolical Illusion

In his maturity Milton resembled Zwingli in emphasizing the spiritual element in worship as against exterior liturgies. Concerning the Lord's Supper, Zwingli wrote that "To eat the body of Christ spiritually is nothing else than to trust in spirit and heart upon the mercy and goodness of God

---

16   Sander, *Supper 1566*, 81v–82v.

through Christ." Since Zwingli saw nothing in the Lord's Supper that could
not be found more readily in prayer, sermons, and scripture reading, the
rite fell into disuse in those churches that followed his teaching. For
Zwingli, the sacrament could at best inspire "historical faith" by reminding
us "that a certain thing once took place."[17] Likewise, Milton saw nothing
necessary for salvation in the outward rites and ceremonies of Christian
worship. Indeed, these were for him marks of decadence. In Book XII of
Paradise Lost, he showed Church history as a great downward slide from
the Apostles to the Second Coming. The teachers who replaced the Apostles
were already "grievous Wolves" tainting Christ's truth with "superstitions
and traditions," so that the interiorized worship in "Spirit and Truth"
bequeathed by Christ to the Apostles was soon corrupted into "outward
Rites" (12:508–512, 533–534).[18]

In Book V of *Paradise Lost*, Milton pointedly uses the verb
transubstantiate to appropriate the old Catholic term. He uses the word to
describe the way fruits and vegetables are digested by angels and men to
fuel their intelligence. In this way, he suggests, matter is constantly
transmuted into spirit. Now this is the kind of transubstantiation he can
accept. He has Raphael explain that angels, being both corporeal and "pure
Intelligential substances," (note his choice of the word substance here)
require food like Adam, and so "digest, assimilate, /And corporeal to
incorporeal turn"(404–413). Milton names this digestive process, to
transubstantiate:

> And to thir viands fell, nor seemingly
> The Angel, nor in mist, the common gloss
> Of Theologians, but with keen dispatch
> Of real hunger, and concoctive heat
> To transubstantiate; what redounds, transpires
> Through Spirits with ease; nor wonder; if by fire
> Of sooty coal the Empiric Alchemist
> Can turn, or holds it possible to turn
> Metals of drossiest Ore to perfet Gold
> As from the Mine. (434–444)

Whereas Hooker and Donne use the term *transubstantiation* for the
substantial conversion of the communicant into Christ, Milton defines it as
a natural process by which matter is converted to spirit during digestion. He
uses the word *real* for "real hunger," not any presence. Yet, in this scene,
there is a vestige of communion in that angel and man share the same
"viands." In the well-known hymn for the feast of Corpus Christi, St.

17   "The Presence of Christ's Body in the Supper," ch. 4 in *A Short and Clear
     Exposition of the Christian Faith Preached by Huldreich Zwingli, Written by
     Zwingli Himself Shortly before his Death to a Christian King (1531)* in *On
     Providence and other Essays*, ed. William John Henke (Durham: Labyrinth Press,
     1983; first published, 1922), 252–254.
18   John Milton, *Complete Poems and Major Prose*, ed. Merritt Y. Hughes (New York:
     Odyssey Press, 1957), 465–466.

Thomas Aquinas named the sacrament, *panis angelicus*. But in Milton's scene, angel and man share only the viands of earth, not the bread of heaven.

Milton also makes this natural process of transubstantiation the unifying dynamic of creation: everywhere matter is incorporated into higher substances. In Book V, he makes Raphael his spokesman to instruct us about the nature of being. In his heavenly philosophy, the "grosser" creature is always digested into the "purer" (416), as the "drossiest Ore" is turned in the crucible into gold. Matter is purified by being absorbed into spirit, fire, and light. Raphael teaches Adam that matter is first digested into air, and then air feeds heavenly lights: "Earth and the Sea feed Air, the Air those Fires / Ethereal, and as lowest first the Moon" (417–418). Above the moon, air grows purer till the sun receives "alimental recompence / In humid exhalations" (424–425). When Milton teaches that matter moves up by feeding what is more spirit-like, he leaves little room for the Eucharist, where the purer (Christ) comes to nourish the grosser (the communicant).

Milton's idea of transubstantiation as linked to digestion was arguably inspired by St. Gregory Nyssa, a Greek Father whom Milton read, for he quotes him in *An Apology for Smectymnuus* and elsewhere. In his Great Catechism (385 A.D.), St. Gregory explains that just as bread becomes our body during digestion, so the bread eaten by the Word of God while he was on earth "by the indwelling of God the Word was transmuted to the dignity of Godhead." This kind of purification of matter Milton approves of. But then, St. Gregory adds, it is because the bread that Christ digested was converted into his divinity that we now believe that "the bread which is consecrated by the Word of God is changed into the Body of God the Word." If Milton took his idea of transubstantiation from the first part of Gregory's commentary, where bread is digested into a heavenly eater, he makes his heavenly eater an angel, not the Word. In addition, Milton would be sure to reject all the rest of Gregory's comments, such as that Christ "disseminates Himself in every believer through that flesh, whose substance comes from bread and wine, blending Himself with the bodies of believers," so that "by this communion with Deity mankind might at the same time be deified."[19] In Gregory Nyssa, the eater is converted to the substance of the sacrament, but, in Milton, food is converted to the eater's substance.

The reason Milton carefully defines the term *transubstantiate* in Book V is that he intends to depict Eve as falling for a diabolical illusion of transubstantiation in Book IX. Disguised as a Serpent, Satan persuades Eve that a nectar powerful enough to give her divine life has been infused into the Fruit of the forbidden Tree. He implies that by glutting himself on the Fruit, he was transubstantiated from a serpent to an interior "Man," perceiving

---

[19]   Gregory of Nyssa, *The Great Catechism*, ch. XXXVII, trans. William Moore and Henry Austin Wilson, in *Nicene and Post-Nicene Fathers*, ed. Philip Schaff and Henry Wace. 2nd ser. (1893; rprt. Peabody, MA: Hendrickson Publishers, 1995), 5:505–506.

>   Strange alteration in me, to degree
>   Of Reason in my inward Powers, and Speech
>   Wanted not long, though to this shape retain'd. (599–601)

Even though he found himself possessed of speech and reason, the Serpent
kept his outward form, "this shape retain'd." He continued looking like a
Serpent, though his underlying identity was converted to "Man" by this
unexpected "alteration." The Serpent's distinctions recall St. Thomas
Aquinas on the topic of transubstantiation. St. Thomas particularly
distinguished change of *form* from change of *substance*, saying that God
"can work not only formal conversions, so that diverse forms succeed each
other in the same subject; but also the change of all being, so that, to wit,
the whole substance of one thing be changed into the whole substance of
another. And this is done by divine power in this sacrament. . . . Hence this
is not a formal, but a substantial conversion; nor is it a kind of natural
movement: but, with a name of its own, it can be called *transubstantiation.*"[20]

In the temptation speech, the "accidents" or external qualities of the
Serpent remain but now exist without a "substance," since his underlying
identity was transubstantiated to "Man / Internal Man." The passage
parodies St. Thomas but also reaches the Anglican Lord's Supper, since it
deals with the interior transubstantiation or deification of the receiver after
communion which Donne, Hooker, Andrewes, and other high-churchmen
taught.

The Serpent argues that the penalty of death about which God warned
Adam and Eve is only a stage of transubstantiation:

>   That ye should be as Gods, since I as Man,
>   Internal Man, is but proportion meet,
>   I of brute human, yee of human Gods.
>   So ye shall die perhaps, by putting off
>   Human, to put on Gods, death to be wisht,
>   Though threat'n'd, which no worse then this can bring.
>   (710–715)

With the phrases *put off* and *put on*, Milton evokes the Scotists' idea of how
the sacrament was changed from bread to Christ: they taught that the
substance of bread was annihilated and replaced by the substance of
Christ's body, whereas Thomists held that bread was converted without
annihilation. When Donne begs to be lashed, burned, ravished, and
battered by God into a new being, he evokes the Scotist view of destruction
as preceding a new creation.

Milton designs Eve's temptation to suggest that belief in
transubstantiation leads to polytheism and earth-worship. The Serpent
teaches Eve that the Tree, though it seems to be in the plant category, is

---

[20]   *Summa Theologica*, IIIa.75.4, translated by the Fathers of the English Dominican
Province. 5 vols. (1948; rprt. Westminster, MD: Christian Classics,1981),
5:2442–2444.

actually a veiled presence with supernatural powers to infuse divine gifts in the eater. He informs her that there are many gods, not just one, and hints that they reached that level by eating god-making food: "what are Gods that Man may not become / As they, participating God-like food?" (716–717). The Serpent persuades Eve in this way that spirit needs specially-endowed matter to climb to higher wisdom. Gods produce "nothing," while Earth produces a Tree with an "enclosed" power to cause that "whoso eats thereof, forthwith attains / Wisdom." As the Serpent modulates from transubstantiation to polytheism to tree-worship (id est, adoration of the Cross), Milton hints that these are all stages on the road to idolatry.

Eve reflects that the Serpent has indeed become wise: he "knows, and speaks, and reasons, and discerns, / Irrational till then" (765–766). Before she eats, she hails "this Fruit Divine" capable of feeding and healing "Body and Mind":

> Here grows the Cure of all, this Fruit Divine,
> Fair to the Eye, inviting to the Taste,
> Of virtue to make wise: what hinders then
> To reach, and feed at once both Body and Mind? (776–779)

The Eucharist was long believed to be nourishment and remedy for body and mind, as the Serpent claims this Fruit is. While she gorges on the Fruit, Eve is in "expectation high / Of knowledge, nor was God-head from her thought" (790), but she only gets drunk. Even so, she believes transubstantiation has begun and the Tree will soon make her wise. So she invokes it:

> O Sovran, virtuous, precious of all Trees
> In Paradise, of operation blest
> To Sapience. . . . (795–797)

Besides praying to the Tree as a deity, she also pledges to return each morning to sing hymns to it and take communion from its branches,

> . . . henceforth my early care,
> Not without Song, each Morning, and due praise
> Shall tend thee, and the fertile burden ease
> Of thy full branches offer'd free to all;
> Till dieted by thee I grow mature
> In knowledge, as the Gods who all things know. . . . (799–804)

When she says "dieted by thee," Eve shows she has achieved an I-Thou intimacy with the presence in the Tree. Her pledge to offer songs of praise and to communicate each day is entirely Milton's invention. He does this in order to make Eve's sin the type and prefiguration of daily Mass. Moreover, he attacks not just the doctrine of transubstantiation but the ancient mystery of real presence, for he deliberately uses the word *presence* when he shows Eve adoring the Tree:

So saying, from the Tree her step she turn'd,
But first low Reverence done, as to the power
That dwelt within, whose presence had infus'd
Into the plant sciential sap, deriv'd
From Nectar, drink of Gods. (834–838)

She imagines the Fruit is divine because of a presence dwelling in the Tree, a presence she adores with a low bow. In designing this hymn to the Tree, Milton parodied the ancient, well-known hymns of Fortunatus, who hailed Christ's body and blood as the divine Fruit of the Tree of Calvary, made really present on the altar at the sacrifice of the Mass.[21] Thus Milton makes Original Sin into an idolatry that foreshadows Catholic worship. He depicts Eve as succumbing to a diabolical illusion that the divine can be embodied in time and space, on an altar, and in a visible sacrament. As appears in Book XII, Milton himself believes Christ to be absent not only from the visible sacrament but also from the visible Church until the Second Coming.

What underlies Milton's portrayal of Eve's sin is his belief that worship should be spiritual. At the heart of his epic, he inscribes his symbol of faith. Samson-like he tries to shake the twin pillars of the Mass and the Eucharist. Shortly before he died, he created another such symbol in a pamphlet urging the government, on the grounds of idolatry, not to allow Catholics to have freedom of worship, even in the privacy of their own homes.[22]

Dryden: Transubstantiation and the Church as Body of Christ

In *The Hind and the Panther*, Dryden creates a poetic symbol of his faith to counter the attacks against his Church as idolatrous. At the start of his poem, he places a hundred-line passage (Part I, lines 43–149) on the Eucharist, a passage that culminates in an encounter with the real presence. In contrast to the interiorized Presence of Donne's "Good Friday," Dryden experiences Christ as embodied in a visible Church. He begins by comparing the fanatics' hatred of the sacrament during the Reformation to the indifference of those who got rich from pillaging the churches. The fanatic Boar befouled the altars with "fat pollutions" (defecations) in his fury against idolatry, while his fellow-travelling Fox "fed on consecrated spoil," or

---

[21]   In *Vexilla Regis*, Fortunatus calls Christ's body the fruit that hangs from the boughs of the Tree of Calvary. See my essay, "Milton's Parody of Catholic Hymns in Eve's Temptation and Fall," *Studies in Philology* 91 (1994): 216–231.

[22]   In his *Of True Religion* (1673), Milton wrote: "As for tolerating the exercise of their Religion, supposing their State activities not to be dangerous, I answer, that Toleration is either public or private; and the exercise of their Religion, as far as it is Idolatrous, can be tolerated neither way: not publicly, without grievous and unsufferable scandal giv'n to all consciencious Beholders; not privately without great offence to God, declar'd against all kind of Idolatry, though secret." *Complete Prose Works of John Milton*, ed. Don M. Wolfe, Maurice Kelley, et al. 8 vols. (New Haven: Yale University Press, 1953–1982), 8:430.

made his market from the other's iconoclastic zeal. Dryden thinks the Boar and the Fox are closer than they seem. After trampling the real presence, they will both "end" by denying the Incarnation on the same principles. Not only have the Socinians renewed the "blasphemy" of fourth-century Arians, but all the sects (who reject the real presence) are heading in the same direction:

> His impious race their blasphemy renew'd,
> And natures King through natures opticks view'd.
> Revers'd they view'd him lessen'd to their eye,
> Nor in an Infant could a God descry:
> New swarming sects to this obliquely tend,
> Hence they began, and here they all will end. (56–61)

The sects are all traveling this road, he thinks, because they use "natures opticks" or natural reason to look at revealed mysteries. Hence those events are "lessen'd to their eye." Dryden then breaks into prayer and thanks God for a Church that preserves the mysteries:

> What weight of antient witness can prevail
> If private reason hold the publick scale?
> But, gratious God, how well dost thou provide
> For erring judgments an unerring Guide! (62–65)

Dryden sees the Church as a visible, public, historical entity. For him, Christianity is not something only private to the soul. He then addresses Christ directly as "gratious God," distancing himself from the Socinian "blasphemy" he has just condemned. That he is addressing Christ is shown in the rest of his prayer, for he asks to be taught to take "her alone for my Directour" whom "thou hast promis'd never to forsake," alluding to Christ's pledge (Mt 28:20) to remain "always" with his Church until the end of the world. And so, when Dryden exclaims in this same prayer,

> Thy throne is darkness in th'abyss of light,
> A blaze of glory that forbids the sight,
> O teach me to believe Thee thus conceal'd,
> And search no farther than thy self reveal'd . . .

he means that is really present in his Church and in the sacrament. Indeed he uses the very language of the Corpus Christi hymns of St. Thomas Aquinas. Christ is "conceal'd" from the worshiper in the Eucharist, but Dryden asks for the gift of faith to believe him there "reveal'd" in "a blaze of glory." He wants to adore the mystery, not delve into it with natural reason.

With much humility, Dryden admits his "shame" at his former attempts to search the mysteries with private reason. He was impelled by "vain desires" and "Follow'd false lights" which he sometimes created himself: "My pride struck out new sparkles of her own." He wanted to define the doctrines of Christianity by himself, but instead he fell into anguished doubt. His conversion let him see that a more important task for him was to live the Christian life:

> Such was I, such by nature still I am,
> Be thine the glory, and be mine the shame.
> Good life be now my task: my doubts are done,
> (What more could fright my faith, than Three in One?) (76–79)

He hints that the mystery of the Trinity was once a hurdle to his private reason. This would have been years earlier, for the poem *Religio Laici* (1682), written while he was yet a Protestant, contains a moving confession (against a Deist) of his faith in Christ's divinity. The poet's new reliance on the Church lets him exclaim with respect to the mysteries of faith:

> Rest then, my soul, from endless anguish freed;
> Nor sciences thy guide, nor sense thy creed. (146–147).

He confides here that he suffered from "endless anguish" of "soul" before his conversion. His touching admission shows that he was not a skeptic or a rationalist, but a tortured seeker after some security in faith. He hints that a renewed sense of mystery, as seen in *Religio Laici*, made it possible for him to move on, four years later, to the real presence:

> Can I believe eternal God could lye
> Disguis'd in mortal mold and infancy?
> That the great maker of the world could dye?
> And after that, trust my imperfect sense
> Which calls in question his omnipotence?
> Can I my reason to my faith compell,
> And shall my sight, and touch, and taste rebell?
> Superiour faculties are set aside,
> Shall their subservient organs be my guide?
> Then let the moon usurp the rule of day,
> And winking tapers shew the sun his way;
> Form what my senses can themselves perceive
> I need no revelation to believe.
> Can they who say the Host should be descry'd
> By sense, define a body glorify'd? (80–94)

Note his use of the pronoun I, because this long passage defending the Catholic Eucharist will culminate in the use of the pronoun we, once he experiences the real presence. Dryden seems to retrace the steps of his conversion when he says, if I can believe that God could lie "Disguis'd" in the infant of Bethlehem and die on the cross, then I should trust that God's omnipotence can make his glorified body present in the sacrament. Why should I rely on my "imperfect sense" (id est, the *sensuum defectui* of Aquinas's hymn to the Eucharist, *Tantum Ergo*)[23] in this mystery, instead of

---

[23]   St. Thomas's line is, let faith for all defects of sense supply. See my *Ancient Faith and Modern Freedom in John Dryden's The Hind and the Panther* (Washington,

faith? If my natural reason can bow to faith when I confess the mystery of Christ's divinity, or the Trinity, then why should I let my senses rebel against faith when the mystery of the real presence is proposed? My senses should receive light from faith, as the moon from the sun. Alluding to Christ's revelatory words at the Last Supper, "This is My Body," he exclaims: "what my senses can themselves perceive / I need no revelation to believe."

At the very end of the above-cited passage, the poet turns directly to the communion "Host" and shifts to the plural pronoun *they*. He asks whether "they" who make their senses a measure of what the sacrament is can "define" what is possible for Christ's resurrected, glorified body? His word *define* evokes Church councils that have, since antiquity, *defined* the deposit of faith received from the apostles, in opposition to the "novelties" of heretics. The reason Dryden uses the pronoun *they* at the end of the passage is that he is referring to the post-communion rubric inserted in the 1662 *Common-Prayer Book*, a rubric that ends with these words: "And the Natural Body and Bloud of our Saviour Christ are in heaven and not here; it being against the truth of Christs Natural Body, to be at one time in more places than one."[24] Catholic controversialists charged that the new rubric had introduced "Zwinglianism" into the Church of England.[25] Dryden uses the rubric's phrasing in this passage to declare that Christ's *body* can indeed be *in more places* than one:

> For since thus wondrously he pass'd, 'tis plain
> One single place two bodies did contain,
> And sure the same omnipotence as well
> Can make one body in more places dwell. (100–103)

After the Resurrection, he explains, Christ's body was "wondrously" able to penetrate solid objects, as when he "pass'd" through a door to stand in the midst of his disciples (Jn 20:26). If two things (the door and his body) stood in one place, then the same "omnipotence" can cause his body to be multiplied in the sacrament. Dryden is not trying to conquer with reason here, but rather trying to make room for awe and wonder.

Another common attack against the Catholic real presence was that Christ's miracles had appealed to the senses, so the senses should remain the "motive still of credibility." Dryden answers that Christ's miracles were

---

D.C.: Catholic University of America Press, 1998), 101–110 for more on this point.

[24] *The Book of Common Prayer* (London: John Bill and Christopher Barker, 1674). The rubric is in gothic lettering at the end of the unpaginated communion service. Dryden attacks this rubric also in Part II, 31–34, where he echoes its "not here" by saying that "to explain what your forefathers meant, / By real presence in the sacrament," you say, "he's not there at all."

[25] *"Animadversions upon the Alterations of the Rubrick in the Coimmunion-Service in the Common-Prayer-Book of the Church of England,"* the First of Two Discourses Concerning the Adoration of Our B. Saviour in the Eucharist (Oxford: O. Walker, 1687).

intended to "prove the godhead of th'eternal Son," and once this was accomplished, his followers were to believe "Beyond what sense and reason can conceive," taking the mysteries on trust from "heav'ns authority," the Church (113–121). Christ's miracles were the "scaffolding," which comes down when the building "gains a surer stay" (124–125). That is, his miracles were necessary to raise up the Church.

Reaching the climax of this passage, Dryden now compares reliance on the senses in the mystery of the real presence to hugging the shore in a small skiff when "we" could embark in a seaworthy "vessel" and "launch into the deep." This is where he creates a striking symbol of transubstantiation, without using the word: he pictures Christ as the "Pilot" of a great "vessel" waiting for "us" to enter. Once embarked, "we" sail off with a "better guide" to a "better world":

> Why chuse we then like *Bilanders* to creep
> Along the coast, and land in view to keep,
> When safely we may launch into the deep?
> In the same vessel which our Saviour bore
> Himself the Pilot, let us leave the shoar,
> And with a better guide a better world explore.
> Could He his god-head veil with flesh and bloud
> And not veil these again to be our food?
> His grace in both is equal in extent,
> The first affords us life, the second nourishment (128–137)

His use of the pronouns *we* and *us* is of great importance. Dryden experiences the real presence as a public, communal event. The vessel into which "we" enter is at once Christ and the Church. When Dryden speaks of the "same vessel which *our Saviour* bore," his term our Saviour is both subject and object. The "vessel" is at once the body God took at the Incarnation (in 2 Cor 4:7, "vessel" is used for body), and the sacrament and chalice that bore his body at the Last Supper. At the same time, the "vessel" is a ship where Christ is "Pilot," id est, the ark of the Church. Dryden modulates from "vessel" in line 131 to "flesh and bloud" in line 134, to show that it is in receiving communion that "we" enter the body of Christ and his mystical body the Church, of which Noah's ark was a type. St. Paul himself calls the Church the body of Christ where he is the invisible head ("Pilot") and "we" are his members or limbs: "For no man ever yet hated his own flesh; but nourisheth and cherisheth it, even as the Lord the church: for we are members of his body, of his flesh, and of his bones. For this cause shall a man leave his father and mother, and shall be joined unto his wife, and they two shall be one flesh. This is a great mystery: but I speak concerning Christ and the Church."(Eph 5:29–32).

In Dryden's symbol of faith, then, Christ is substantially incorporated with his Church by a mystical marriage, he has become one flesh with her, and so communion means being received into the Church as body of Christ. Dryden laments that by inserting a Zwinglian rubric into the Common Prayer, the Church of England has lost the divine substance in two ways—

in the sacrament and in the church, and he repeats the word *substance* to emphasize this point:

> For *real,* as you now the word expound,
> From solid substance dwindles to a sound.
> Methinks an *Aesop's* fable you repeat,
> You know who took the shadow for the meat:
> Your churches substance thus you change at will,
> And yet retain your former figure still. (2:46–51)

Dryden declares that the real presence is just as necessary for salvation as the Incarnation, "His grace in both is equal in extent," and he explains that God veiled himself in flesh to give immortal life but that life needs to be nourished with the immortal substance in the sacrament. To reject this food on rationalist grounds leads in the end to rejecting the other mysteries: "For who wou'd break with heav'n, and wou'd not break for all?" (1:145). Like Newman after his conversion, Dryden no longer sees a *via media* possible between Catholicism and atheism.

In conclusion, each of these great poets created a symbol of belief regarding the mystery of real presence. In "Good Friday," Donne showed his belief in Christ's Presence to the soul at the moment of communion, as well as in an ensuing "transubstantiation" of the receiver into Christ. In Book IX of *Paradise Lost,* Milton revealed his conviction that a divine food capable of causing transubstantiation in the receiver was a diabolical illusion that led to idolatry. And in *The Hind and the Panther,* Dryden affirmed his belief in the mystery of real presence, in the doctrine of transubstantiation, and in the Church itself as the Body of Christ. Each of these poets had pondered the mystery of the real presence and wrote on this theme some of their most passionate poetry.

Fading Fast but Still in Print: The Brink of Visibility and the Form of Religious Experience, Spinoza to Cowper

Kevin L. Cope

Long before its rise as a prominent mall store, Banana Republic, then primarily a mail-order retailer, offered a style of slacks called "empirical trousers." Advertisements for these pants included snippets from the works of John Locke. What was most revealing about the "empirical trousers" was that they revealed nothing about empiricism. None of the sensible attributes of these pants—whether their color, texture, fragrance, or rustling sound when moved in their shipping box—signified or supported any empiricist propositions. One could not *see* in the zipper anything related to real or nominal essences; one looked in vain at the cuffs for a definition of "ideas." The "empirical trousers" were, it seemed, non-empirical; whatever it was that made them "empirical" could not be discovered empirically.

Whimsical as this example may be, it reveals more than it might seem about long-eighteenth-century empiricism. Empiricism itself was often non-empirical. For every paragraph in the works of John Locke, George Berkeley, or David Hume that reports on empirical evidence, readers find a dozen others dealing with less tangible matters, whether perceiving, abstracting, amalgamating, storing, memorizing, or processing experience. For every "sensible quality" mentioned on empiricist pages, there is an abundance of speculation concerning its rarefaction into "mixed modes" or "general ideas" or "the invisible hand." The discussion of "imagination" that runs through eighteenth-century literature symptomatizes this more-than-empirical tendency within empiricism.

The empiricists are only one strand in the long braid of long-eighteenth-century speculative writing. Their tendency to stand out beyond their statistical place in the history of thought makes a point about how the period "saw" experience. Empiricism was always about seeing, processing, and maximizing whatever experience disclosed, whether that meant, as it did for George Berkeley, linking the perception of a silver disk in the sky to the idea of the distance to the moon or whether it meant, as it did for the Romantic poets, seeing one's own backyard as a parcel within paradise. The eighteenth-century urge to see more than one could see bears a special relevance to the topic of religion and literature. The difficulty that today's readers encounter when trying to reconcile the supernatural with the empirical elements of long-eighteenth-century writing arises from a strait-jacketed definition of "experience." Lady Margaret Cavendish and William Blake both voiced commitments to the empirical, yet both dealt with orders of experience far beyond the range of routine daily life. The rigorous usage of "empirical" and "experience" that twenty-first century readers take for granted seldom came into play during this most experiential of periods. Our contemporary notion of "experience" boils down to what Shakespeare's character Othello calls "ocular proof": straightforward sense evidence gathered during a specific slice of time that contains a specific parcel of information specifically about the physical world. Such an understanding of "experience" results in the division of experience into at least two smaller categories: "experience" in the aforementioned colloquial but highly rigorous sense; and "religious experience," which is understood to be an unusual, extraordinary, minimally verifiable event contrasting with the more ordinary sort of "experience."

This essay attempts to reverse the dichotomizing of long-eighteenth-century "experience" into its material and its religious aspects. Rather than grouping authors from this period into hard-boiled philosophers or eccentric visionaries, this paper will suggest that the most common species of experience in the period is the "simultaneous" or "extended" variety, in which writers perceive a variety of supplemental phenomena—literary form, artistic convention, political implications, and religious significance—as part and parcel of experience itself. This paper will not try to suggest that the "visionary" discourse of the Romantic period characterizes the entire century; on the contrary, it will suggest that the Romantic cult of "vision" has been somewhat overblown, that our modern picture of Romantic writers "renovating" or "revolutionizing" experience results from a misunder-standing of the extensiveness of "experience" earlier in this "long" period. This paper will argue that English writers could be better understood by viewing them within the larger European context, a context that includes the suggestive and yet also empirical speculations of Gottfried Wilhelm Leibniz or Benedict Spinoza. The paper will look at an array of British poets who have received less than their fair share of modern attention precisely because their writings epitomize the broader notion of "experience" that was at play during the "empirical" century.

* Leibniz, Spinoza, and the "Bigness" of Futurity *

There are some authors whom nobody wants to love. Leibniz and Spinoza
lead that unadmired crew. The confident brevity with which these authors
explain entire universes alarms those who value complication or
collaboration. Owing to propaganda from his rival Isaac Newton and owing
to Voltaire's devastating caricature in *Candide*, Leibniz usually looks like
either a sore loser—as someone trying to grab a share of Newton's credit for
inventing the calculus—or as the naive philosopher convinced that ours is
"the best of all possible worlds." Spinoza usually makes his appearance in
cultural history as an ice-cold apologist for a purely "geometrical" account
of ethics and experience (recently, he was spurned by Harold Bloom for
shedding "light without heat").[1] The "best of all possible universes"
formulation is an easy target for satire, but this seemingly glib formulation
is only a shorthand for a core affirmation that the universe *as it is* is as
good as it can be. The "best of all possible worlds" anthem is only the
beginning of a cosmological story line. Leibniz's rendering of the universe is
fundamentally narrative. Mainstream philosophers from Aquinas to
Descartes aim to determine the contents of nature (by postulating the
existence of "substance" or "extension" or "matter" or some other objective
"being"), but Leibniz wants to show that experience has a plan for change
and development as well as an intelligent audience capable of seeing and
appreciating that story.

Leibniz offers a breezy summary of his ontology in his *Monadology*, a
work adapting his technical treatises to the modest capacities of his patron,
Eugene of Savoy. There he explains that the universe is populated by
"monads," indivisible beings internally endowed with a program of planned
changes and improvements. Change occurs not by a monad becoming
something other than it was when the all-foreseeing God created it but by
its sequentially expressing its inbuilt plan for improvement. A monad is
never really "perceived," in a stringently empirical sense, as some one
"thing" or as some set of sensible "qualities" apprehended at some one moment in time. A perception is rather a kind of abbreviation: a shorthand
representation of the series of changes that a monad will eventually
perform. Every being "is big with its future";[2] every monad contains an
anticipation of its future career and so must be seen as a forecast of all that
eventually will be seen in it. Leibniz insures that monads carry plenty of
baggage: his principle of "sufficient reason" affirms that a thing exists only if
there is a power sufficient to produce it and a specific reason to justify its
existence (see *Monadology*, §32). Thus, an elephant, not a mouse, must

1   See Harold Bloom's review of Rebecca Goldstein's *Betraying Spinoza: The
    Renegade Jew Who Gave Us Modernity* (*New York Times Literary Supplement*,
    June 18, 2006). For a historical account of Spinoza stereotypes, see Rosalile
    Colie, "Spinoza and the Early English Deists," *Journal of the History of Ideas* 20
    (1959): 23–46.
2   Gottfried Wilhelm Leibniz, *The Monadology and Other Philosophical Writings*,
    trans. Robert Latta (Oxford: Oxford University Press, 1898 [rprt. 1971]), §22, p.
    231.

produce an elephant; thus, nature may produce elephants only if there is an adequate justifying reason (bamboo needing carrying, peanuts needing eating, trees requiring trampling).

Perceiving an experience requires adducing a working hypothesis about its cause and purpose. Leibniz sets up God as the "final reason of things" (*Monadology*, §38, p. 238), insuring that God will serve as an adequate audience for the familiar Aristotelian and Christian notion that nature is progressing toward perfection. A novel aspect of Leibniz's version of developmentalism is the degree to which he presents the long-term career of a monad as part and parcel of seeing and experiencing. The future progress of a monad is not, as it might be for Aristotle or for any Christian theologian, a matter of speculation about an unseen future; rather, that whole story is "reflected" in the present constitution of a monad. Leibniz inverts the usual procedure for narrative foreshadowing. The image of an object or "monad" is not one partial sign or symbol of a larger developing future. Rather, every object presents a miniature representation of its *whole* future—a very big future that is *part* of the particular monad that we see represented before us.

Leibniz surely qualifies as the most unqualified of thinkers. Monads do not "have" qualities that modify them or that affect their destiny, perception, or reception. They *contain* those qualifying factors. Perceiving the world—experiencing—is both inward and outward: outward, in that the business of a monad is relating to or perceiving of other monads (depending on the degree of consciousness); inward, in that monads *contain* their qualities, modifications, and, in sum, futures. Experiencing the world is hard work: one must look in and through monads in order to make out more than is seemingly visible—to see through to a potential infinity of relationships between one monad and all the others in the universe (in the past and future as well as in the present).[3] Viewers must also maintain the *transparency* of their perceptions. Leibniz presents his universe as a series of luminous, reflective surfaces, as an informative hall of mirrors.

> Now this connexion or adaptation of all created things to each and of each to all, means that each simple substance has relations which express all the others, and, consequently, that it is a perpetual living mirror of the universe.
>
> And as the same town, looked at from various sides, appears quite different and becomes as it were numerous in its aspects; even so, as a result of the infinite number of simple substances, it is as if there were so many different universes, which, nevertheless are nothing but aspects of a

---

[3]   On the ethical, experiential, and narrative characteristics of monads—on monads that contain prospects of future adventures as a form of travel literature—see my "Exit, Intermediary, or Interior: Leibniz, Gay, and Defoe on the Impassability of Moralized Space," in *Proceedings of the XIIth Congress of the International Comparative Literature Association*, ed. Roger Bauer, Douwe Fokkema, Michael de Graat, et al. (Munich: Iudicum, 1990), 62–67.

single universe, according to the special point of view of
each Monad. . . .
I have already noted . . . that souls in general are living
mirrors or images of the universe of created things, but
that minds are also images of the Deity or Author of nature
Himself, capable of knowing the system of the universe.
(*Monadology* §§56–57, 83; pp. 248, 266)

Leibniz is renowned for developing the idea that the universe is a "plenum,"
a rigorously full place in which every possibility is actualized and in which
there are no vacant rungs on the ladder of creation. What is less
appreciated is the degree to which Leibniz builds that sense of fullness out
of a process that might be called "outward-oriented reflection" in which
perceptive minds continually reflect, deflect, and perfect information
streaming in from other monads. Leibniz's universe is a gigantic array of
passively luminous surfaces, of monads constantly detecting other
monads—and likewise detecting both the fullness of those monads'
potential and the majesty of their arrangement in an exquisitely rational,
vigorously developmental universe. His system resolves into a
psychologically enriched narrative in which the most active monads—dare
we say the cleverest persons?—see in any given monad the greatest number
of links in the chain of relations and thereby see the maximum number of
evolving story lines.

      A more religious way to look at Leibniz is to say that he is interested in
two and only two quantities: infinity and unity. His individual monads
contain, if only by "reflection," all that can be known about the infinite
universe. Conversely, the universe and the infinite array of relations spread
through it must be known through individual entities. Leibniz is not the
only philosopher of the period to superimpose the infinite on the solitary.
Early in his *Ethics*, Benedict Spinoza establishes that "every substance is
necessarily infinite."[4] A limited, non-infinite "substance," he opines, would
have to be limited by something; that "something," in turn, would either be
or would derive from a necessary being (otherwise it would not exist)—a
state of affairs requiring that two things would share the identical attribute
of necessary existence (which Spinoza regards as impossible). By
"substance," Spinoza does not mean those objects or other phenomena
comprising day-to-day experience but rather the substratum supporting
those objects, objects that are understood as "modes" of the one necessarily
existing substance. Spinoza's commitment to the simultaneous unity and
diversity of substance leads to a mentality like Leibniz's: to confidence that
particular experiences reconcile empirical immediacy with the suggestion of
a huge matrix of supplemental information. Nothing can be conceived,
Spinoza argues, without conceiving it to be in God. This argument might
seem tautological—God *being* being—were it not that Spinoza uses it to

---

4   Benedict de Spinoza, *The Ethics*, in *Benedict de Spinoza: On the Improvement of
     the Understanding, The Ethics, Correspondence*, ed. and trans. R. H. M. Elwes
     (New York: Dover Publications, 1955), proposition VIII, 48.

create complexity within a monist universe: to affirm that the one substance is truly infinite and not composed of finite parts and to attribute the apparent differences among phenomena to a multiplicity of "modes" (see *Ethics*, proposition XV ff., 55ff.). Individual things, including thinking minds, emerge as *modes* of being that reflect the panoply of relations among all the other monads in the universe. To emphasize that individual "modes" depend on the one substance—that is, on God—Spinoza adduces what Leibniz would later call the "principle of sufficient reason." He argues that there must be some adequate external cause to account for both the existence and the exact number of beings (see proposition VIII, 50). It is not enough to say that twenty apples exist simply because there happens to be one substance with twenty modifications; one must also explain why that one substance was modified in such a way that precisely *twenty* apples appear in the cart. Being and perceiving require the constant eliciting of explanations concerning details (one might, for example, ask why the one substance was modified so as to create twenty green apples or twenty Washington State apples or twenty pie apples). There is no experience in Spinoza's system that is truly simple and that does not require the transfer of additional information. Intelligent beings are always attending to the reasons underlying the qualification of objects and to the reasons for their apparent complexity as sentient beings. Spinoza adduces a pair of propositions: that "in God there is necessarily an idea, which expresses the essence of this or that human body under the form of eternity" and that "the human mind cannot be absolutely destroyed with the body, but there remains of it something which is eternal" (*Ethics*, propositions XXII–XXIII, 259). From these propositions, we might conclude that for each of us there is an ideal human body that persists in the mind of God even while the physical body deteriorates (so as to allow the mind to find its post-mortem way to a suitable haven): an admittedly strange notion that amounts to a secular philosophical account of the Resurrection and that points up the supplemental philosophical meaning of even the degenerate physical body. Everything that Spinoza "sees," whether it be the physical body or the rings of Saturn or the Pegasus on the old Mobil Oil trademark, is always stretching to be and to convey more than it is. A mode of being, the individual human body always seems to stretch toward its metaphysical counterpart in the mind of God. Spinoza, like his many contemporaries who wrote treatises on disciplining the mind—Descartes, Pascal, Locke—veers away from his stated commitment to strictly "geometric" methods of proof. He emphasizes *habituation* to the philosophical lifestyle, showing how to train the mind to see more than the sluggish senses are initially able to disclose. It is odd to think of such cool celestial lights as Leibniz and Spinoza as lively storytellers, yet that is precisely the role in which their philosophical stances position them as they push to see through and beyond "clear and distinct" experiences.

* Repairing as Well as Restoring: The Quick Path to God *

If one were to look for a new suburb in the sprawling "long" eighteenth century, an attractive subdivision could be made of that awkward period of challenged sovereignty running from the elevation of Archbishop Laud to the premature conclusion of the reign of James II. During this underappreciated period, poets who were neither "metaphysical" versifiers in the manner of Donne and Herbert nor public wits in the manner of Pope and Gay developed a refined verse for a declining regime, directing the nascent energies of early neoclassicism not into the kind of spectacular public culture that would arise during the early eighteenth century but into seemingly harmless entertainments that concealed the threatening Republicanism incipient in the Roman ideal. Unpopular in our own time owing to its unabashed elitism and acerbic wit, this highly cultivated verse participates in the project to enhance "experience" that animated the thought of Leibniz and Spinoza. Poets such as Edmund Waller, whose adventurous temperament combined with his political ineptness to ruin repeatedly a repeatedly resuscitating career, or Abraham Cowley, possibly the most popular poet of his day but now exiled from politically correct literary canons, were not religious in any conventional sense. They did, however, develop a religiously alert poetry that would play a part in producing that strange mixture of sallying rhetoric and skeptical philosophizing found in the poems of Dryden or Rochester.

Edmund Waller should be regarded as less a *Restoration* than a *repair* poet.[5] His claim to fame rests on a smattering of poems concerning renovating, upgrading, or restoring. Waller's most famous poem, *Instructions to a Painter*, in which he gives continually revised orders to an artist, is built on the celebration of repair. One can only imagine Waller's painter daubing, covering over, and re-daubing for hours, until his canvas cracks under the weight of paint. Waller's short panegyric, "Upon His Majesty's Repairing of St. Paul's," makes for a fine introduction to the art of rehabilitating art.

Discussion of "metaphysical" poetry usually addresses the physical properties of extravagant metaphysical imagery. Donne's flea is applauded as an unlikely but ingenious embodiment of the idea of love. The first generation of "metaphysical" verse explores a timeless realm in which "conceits" are examined for their logic (or witty lack thereof) or are appreciated for their apparently easy realization of physical or conceptual impossibilities. For a writer like Waller, "metaphysical" moments, in which contradictions flash-freeze into staged moments of baroque imbalance, are rendered even more complex by introducing *time* as a supplemental factor. Donne might ask readers to evaluate how this or that flea at this or that

---

[5]   Waller might also be called a "dilapidation" or "entropy" poet in that he frequently stresses decay, even questioning commonplaces about the immortality of verse by pointing up the susceptibility of poetry to linguistic change and other varieties of erosion. See Richard Hillyer, "Better Read than Dead: Waller's 'Of English Verse,'" *Restoration: Studies in English Literary Culture, 1660–1700* 14 (1990): 33–34. Will Pritchard takes note of the "repair" motif in the St. Paul's panegyric and suggests that "restoration," whether in the form of home repair or of the reestablishment of monarchy, is one of Waller's favorite themes. See "The Invention of Edmund Waller," *Restoration: Studies in English Literary Culture, 1660–1700* 22 (1998):9.

moment explicates the concept or experience of love, but Waller keeps the ball rolling and the flea flying, wondering whether an aging bug is as suitable as is a hatchling for such a task.[6] One could easily imagine Waller speculating on the amorous potential of senescent fleas in entomological assisted living facilities. The topics and images in Waller's poems appear to be both more and less than they might seem. They develop through a series of time-specific phases and degenerate with age.

The "repair" topic suits Waller because it links decline with improvement. The theme fixes attention on time and its consequences. It insists that things and experiences are more than they seem, that they have a life cycle—a beginning, an acme, a decline, and a rejuvenation. Things and experiences are more than they seem specifically because they are less, because they decline and require restoration.

In 1633, King Charles I tried to "repair" St. Paul's by adding a neoclassical façade to its west entrance, an event that Waller celebrated in a panegyrical poem. Waller sets up the poem with a time-spanning analogy that links St. Paul's Cathedral in London with St. Paul's shipwreck in Malta some sixteen centuries earlier:

> That shipwreck'd vessel which th' Apostle bore,
> Scarce suffer'd more upon Melita's shore,
> Than did his temple in the sea of time,
> Our nation's glory, and our nation's crime.[7]

From the outset, the principal object within the poem is washed and eroded in "the sea of time." Readers are never allowed to see the cathedral in an extratemporal frame. They must reach back to the time of the apostles, seeing the church as part of a huge conceit that stretches far back in time. A side-by-side comparison of Paul's rocky Maltese altar to the great church along the Thames never materializes owing to the suggestion that the sea of time is somehow confluent with the Mediterranean and by the accompanying suggestion that that sea of time surrounds both churches. This running together of images in the flood of time also occurs at the level of syntax. The awkward word order of the opening line leaves readers momentarily wondering whether the vessel bore the apostle or the apostle bore with the rickety vessel. If the "vessel" is "shipwreck'd," it could not "bear" the apostle while in that ruined state. Waller presents a shipwreck but seems to describe it in a time prior to Paul's calamity. A few lines

---

6   Waller's taste for extravagant poetic techniques has drawn its share of criticism. Waller's excesses, however, serve aesthetic as well as moral and para-religious purposes. They highlight his self-conscious quest to become an *exemplary* poet with respect to both diction and thought. See Warren L. Chernaik, *The Poetry of Limitation: A Study of Edmund Waller* (New Haven: Yale University Press, 1968), 209–210.

7   Edmund Waller, "Upon His Majesty's Repairing of St. Paul's," in *The Poetical Works of Edmund Waller and Sir John Denham*, ed. Charles Cowden Clark (Edinburgh: William P. Nimmo, 1869), 9, lines 1–4. Subsequent citation from this volume is intratextual, by line number.

further down the poem, time is again juggled. King Charles, "like Amphion, makes those quarries leap / Into fair figures from a confused heap" (11–12). This classical analogy allows Waller to pass over several steps in the construction process, to move directly from raw stones to finished building while only implying the intervening steps. Waller complicates cause-effect and past-future relations by comparing ancient architects to "antique minstrels" for whom "cities were lutes," who played upon building materials and who built towns in the same way that musicians make music by strumming a lyre.[8] A more conventional comparison might suggest that King Charles resembles ancient musicians insofar as he plays upon building contractors in the same way that ancient minstrels once plucked strings. Waller reverses and complicates the comparison by suggesting that these ancient artists were *a priori* imitations of Charles: "Those antique minstrels, sure, were Charles-like kings" (15–16). The expectation that readers are seeing one present thing (Charles at work on the cathedral) that resembles some bygone item (the projects of antique minstrels) gives way to the more exciting thought that one might be seeing much more than one is actually seeing.

A remarkable aspect of Waller's technique is that it remains *optional*. One may read his poem and do no more than visualize workers repairing or updating a building. Waller operates in the world of *possibility*, suggesting ways in which his images and ideas *might* mean more than *might* seem. This technique differs from that of the first generation of "metaphysical" poets, whose difficult conceits *require* readers to explicate and often lead into extended versified explanations. Waller's technique also differs from the meaning-saturated approach of post-romantic symbolists, who require readers to process aggressively complicated images. Waller simply opens up options. He defines categories into which a passing image *could* fit. One of his common techniques is to split an experience into two or more aspects (or consequences or interpretations), allowing readers to see the event and then decide whether to proceed further in its interpretation. Looking at Charles's restoration project, for example, "Two distant virtues in one act we find, / The modesty and greatness of his mind" (29–30): the action appears but then can be parsed into its apparently contrary components. With regard to the financing of this project, we learn that "The King built all, but Charles the western end" (54). The entirety of the rehabilitation was a royal project, but we are allowed to note, if we decide to inquire, that another aspect of Charles, his private person, financed part of the work. The cathedral itself evidences bipolar moods: "So proud a fabric to devotion

---

8   Paul J. Korshin calls attention to this passage as an example of Waller's use of typology not in the usual way—to credential the present by referencing similar, laudable events in the past—but to play up ambiguity by invoking a classical figure, the minstrel Amphion, who used the power of music to build fortresses rather than temples. For Korshin, Waller's verse shows that the passage from the "metaphysical" to the neoclassical mode in poetry was complex, deliberate, and evolutionary rather than sharp or decisive. See "The Evolution of Neoclassic Poetics: Cleveland, Denham, and Waller as Poetic Theorists," *Eighteenth-Century Studies* 2 (1968): 102, 128.

given, / At once it threatens and obliges Heaven!" (55–56). The church appears as an emblem of devotion, but then, in an afterthought, is subdivided into at least two moods—moods that many readers may overlook and that never hinder a basic understanding of the poem.

It is not only in sacred buildings that Waller discovers possible supplemental meanings. Charles II's renovation of St. James Park extends and refines the techniques that Waller developed in his celebration of St. Paul's. The poem opens with a complicated morph in which the present, developing garden blends in with the Edenic garden of the deep past:

> Of the first Paradise there's nothing found;
> Plants set by Heaven are vanish'd, and the ground;
> Yet the description lasts; who knows the fate
> Of lines that shall this paradise relate?[9]

The technique is familiar, but the application is enhanced: a deep-historical prototype of the developing garden rushes into the present, in the first line, where it links up to the modern garden, also denominated "paradise" (4), only to be vacated and left, like St. Paul's shipwrecked vessel, in the ambiguous world of things that no longer exist. Waller anticipates the eventual wreck of his own poetical lines; he presents a ruined future as part of the full temporal extension of St. James Park. A vast block of time and a very wide range of phenomena are linked to Waller's tense rendering of the present garden; readers choose whether to view the present park or to see through to its past and future phases.

Waller also enhances experience by maintaining a diffuse focus on the penumbra of objects. He keeps readers aware of the *surroundings* of those things that he describes. Shadows play an especially important role as oracular foreshadowing supplements plain old shade. Waller describes the ranks of trees planted in the St. James marsh as "future shade" that will extend their penumbra as their royal planter's future reputation grows, eventually casting future shadows over future palaces (13–20). A "feather'd cloud" (30) creates an even less substantial shadow in the air, something that remains invisible to those visitors that it cools but something that nevertheless casts a supplementary philanthropic veil over Charles's landscape installation. By the eightieth line of the poem, shade itself has become an actor on the stage of the future. "Oraculous shade" outlines a venue in which King Charles may plan the future of nations. The accurate description of shade makes at least dark reference to all those things, events, and phenomena that occur when it is cast. Shade, the absence of light and energy, is a natural companion for other phenomena that reside on the cool and dark side. So the ice storage pits in St. James Park:

> Yonder, the harvest of cold months laid up,
> Gives a fresh coolness to the royal cup;
> There ice, like crystal firm, and never lost,

---

9   "On St James Park," lines 1–4, in Clarke, *Poetical Works*, 74.

Tempers hot July with December's frost;
Winter's dark prison, whence he cannot fly,
Though the warm spring, his enemy, draws nigh. (49–54)

Waller finds a park facility that not only endures through time but that seems to store and dispense time, that delivers December in July. St. James Park provides many such "storage" devices by which unusually capacious, extended, or complex experiences can be stored, managed, or displayed. "Strange! That extremes should thus preserve the snow, / High on the Alps, or in deep caves below" (55–56). Waller presents St. James Park as part of an elaborate time machine with a vertical extension: as a system for maintaining the winter months outside their normal time by means of managed altitude (i.e., high-altitude snow in low recesses). Properly viewed, landscapes can store seemingly incompatible experiences, as in Waller's trans-seasonal view of bathers and ice-skaters winking in and out of the St. James pond (24). Later in the poem (101–104), Waller reflects on Mt. Etna, where providence allows snow fields and subterranean fires to reside within inches of one another, thereby showing off the full range of time and nature in a compact space. Westminster Abbey appears in one sweeping view as a time-extended system for producing and dismantling monarchs: "It gives them crowns, and does their ashes keep" (93). Everywhere we look, we see complex storage devices. The park brings together Biblical records, still life painting, high cuisine, and landscape architecture:

All that can, living, feed the greedy eye,
Or dead, the palate, here you may descry;
The choicest things that furnish'd Noah's ark,
Or Peter's sheet, inhabiting this park;
All with a border of rich fruit-trees crown'd,
Whose loaded branches hide the lofty mound,
Such various ways the spacious alleys lead,
My doubtful Muse knows not what path to tread. (41–48)

It is not enough for Waller simply to present a variety of things. Rather—in a reversal of the usual order, in which nature precedes art—he offers a carousel of media and of genres through which to view one landscape. We see St. James Park as an architectural achievement, as a menu, as an extension of a still-life painting, as a continuation of the story of Noah, and as an extreme pedestrian experience. Changes in perspective abound. We get a submarine view of the park barges (31–32); we see Charles seeing himself going about his renovating toils (105–110). Waller wryly offers us a picture of no less than Charles II at the central, monadic viewpoint of the universe, seeing one small thing after another through an amazing succession of perspectives and relations.

The kind of royal grandeur that Waller would like to see in everyday experience is implicitly religious, whether in its continual references to biblical archetypes or in its zest for whatever is greatest. By emphasizing repaired rather than achieved grandeur, Waller opens the possibility that grandeur may increase or improve through time.[10] He asks readers to see accomplishments not only in space but also in time—as more than what strikes the eye at any given moment. Abraham Cowley, certainly among the most popular writers of the seventeenth century, provides another example of a repair-oriented poet who is eager to enlarge on experience. Cowley's "On the Queens Repairing Somerset House" makes for a good example of the extensiveness of the techniques used by Waller. Cowley venerates a grand house through a heroic evacuation that recovers this monumental pile from the brink of non-existence while suggesting a broad range of future possibilities:

> When God (the Cause to Me and Men unknown)
> Forsook the Royal Houses, and his own,
> And both abandon'd to the Common Foe;
> How near to ruine did my Glories go?[11]

Cowley opens the poem by gashing at the foundations of experience.[12] God withdraws from the scene, leaving the physical as well as the political royal house to wither away. Somerset House speaks for itself (rather like Waller's chatty Pauline shipwreck), reporting its disappearance: "And Me, when nought for Robbery was left, / They starv'd to death, the gaping Walls were cleft, / The Pillars sunk, the Roofs above me wept [...] Nothing was seen which could content the Eye" (11–15). It is only a few more lines before the renovated house explains that it is not what it once seemed: that the evanescence of the old house allows the queen to convert it into a glorious new structure.

> It does not fill her Bounty to restore
> Me as I was (nor was I small) before.

---

[10]   A few critics have accused Waller of gilding the wilted lily of Charles's reign, cautioning that Waller's fantastic predictions and lavish panegyrics contrast with real-life conditions in the seventeenth century. Piqued in part by Waller's not altogether altruistic political career, these overly literal if attentively historical critics forget about the temporal, futuristic element in Waller's *forecasts* of glory (and ruin). For an example of an uncomplimentary historicist interpretation of Waller's panegyrics, see Jack G. Gilbert, *Edmund Waller* (Boston: Twayne Publishers, 1979), 91–95.

[11]   Abraham Cowley, "On the Queens Repairing Somerset-House," in *The Works of Mr Abraham Cowley*, 8th ed. (London: 1684), sigs. Hhh1v–Hhh2v [cited from *Early English Books Online [EEBO]*, lines 1–4].

[12]   Cowley's frequently voiced commitment to Baconianism, empiricism, virtuosity, and science seems to contrast with his habit of emptying his scenes and writing high-flying odes. The resolution of this apparent contradiction resides in Cowley's embrace of "temerity" as an aesthetic value: his *use* of experience to produce startling, unstable, and highly extenuated viewpoints. "Temerity" can thus be reconciled with the Baconian program to extract the maximal *use* from evidence and to draw out utopian schemes from pedestrian evidence. On "temerity," see David Trotter, *The Poetry of Abraham Cowley* (London: Macmillan, 1979), 112.

> She imitates the kindness to her shown;
> She does, like Heaven (which the dejected Throne
> At once restores, fixes and higher rears)
> Strengthen, Enlarge, Exalt what she Repairs. (19–24)

Cowley is not so much describing an object as the myriad processes that transform it into something else: into something bigger and better. Rather than following Donne or Herbert by forcefully combining inconsistent ideas or images, Cowley's softened conceits show different phases of a building that is on the way to becoming more than itself. To appreciate Somerset House, readers must imagine it as it once was, running through the Civil War and its disassembly, viewing the renovation of the ruin, and then projecting a glorious future for the repaired monument.

Cowley amplifies experience by running in rapid succession through ever-new perspectives on the objects that he describes. By continually repositioning himself, he pays less attention to Somerset House *per se* and more to unusual vantage points—to perspectives that highlight potential enhancements and transformations.[13] Cowley, for example, creates a complicated viewpoint that shows both sides of Somerset House within one short paragraph. That side of the house that is most easily seen and that is most engaged with the physical world—the streetside façade—is mentioned only in passing while the riverside elevation gets a beautiful, philosophical elaboration:

> My other Fair and more Majestick Face
> (Who can the Fair to more advantage place?)
> For ever gazes on it self below,
> In the best Mirror that the World can show. (43–46)

The street side of the house is solid, physical, and familiar. The river side ripples in reflected abstraction along the great river of British commerce, waving with images of the great world and of British imperial power. Cowley's philosophically bifurcating perspective shows how the house, lodged between town and court, sits between "Wealth on the Left, and Pow'r on the Right" (54)—how it rests on the thin line dividing monarchical prerogative from capitalist expansion. Somerset House itself reminds readers of another viewpoint, that of the ships that guard it from the Thames anchorage (61). The poem concludes with the House trying to see itself from an English pastoral viewpoint and trying to reconcile the "Active" and "Quiet" "Mind" implied in its double urban and rural perspectives.

---

13   Achsah Guibbory argues not only that Cowley accepted the Baconian idea of progress but that his enthusiasm for that ideal correlates with the gradual transition from the Renaissance taste for imitation to a more modern commitment to originality. By generating new perspectives on objects, Cowley moves toward the *original*, both in the older sense of "the original object described" and in the emerging sense of "creative" originality. See Guibbory, "Imitation and Originality: Cowley and Bacon's Vision of Progress," *SEL: Studies in English Literature, 1500–1900* 29 (1989): 112–113.

Thames waters bearing the reflective imprint of Somerset House drain out to sea charged with inspecting every building, port, or scene by which they might flow by way of confirming that no site is nobler than the Thames-side panorama (93–102). Somerset House is thus evacuated. Its image is dissolved within the world's waves while its grandeur is aqueously distributed throughout the world and while the appreciation of Somerset House swells into a global project.[14] Cowley's poem is an exercise in secular panegyric, yet it acquires transcendent characteristics, even while undergoing what passes as empirical description.[15] The poem continues Waller's quest to see experience in more dimensions than experience discloses.

* Intermezzo: When Empiricists Elaborate *

The poetry of George Berkeley makes for an intermezzo in our study of the expansion of "experience." Berkeley lived long after Waller, Cowley, and the Stuart court culture, but he shares with these poets an interest in "apparent impossibilities": in poetic representations that exceed the semantic or physical limits of normal experience. Most of Berkeley's writings deal either with impossibilities or with entities on the brink of visibility. An accomplished mathematician, Berkeley, for example, penned numerous treatises challenging the fundamental assumptions of the calculus. For Berkeley, the notion of an "infinitesimal," an infinitely thin quantity that could be used to calculate the length of a curving line or the area under a curve, literally made no sense. Infinitesimals could not be visualized and therefore could not be reconciled with Berkeley's central tenet, "to be is to be perceived." Infinitesimals could not appear on the field of vision or anywhere else, for sensible things always have some size. Berkeley argued that the knowable world must be comprised of perceptions, a requirement that, in turn, leads to an interest in very small, perception-challenging phenomena. Although Berkeley had little patience with metaphysical wit or cavalier banter, he prizes liminal experiences that extend the range of possibility. Berkeley takes a "ground up" approach to poetic language; he pushes experience to enhance itself by exposing its minima, maxima, and varia.

---

[14]   The Somerset house is by no means an exception to Cowley's usual poetic practice. He follows a similar procedure in his "Ode. Sitting and Drinking in the Chair, Made out of the Relics of Sir Francis Drake's Ship," where, with a curious mixture of comedy and enthusiasm, he emblematizes Drake's worldwide voyages with this fragmentary chair and then sends both that chair and the great explorer's reputation sailing out into the world on a mixed sea of salty waves and inebrious wine. See James G. Taaffe, *Abraham Cowley* (New York: Twayne Publishers, 1972), 99–100.

[15]   Although Cowley presents himself as the celebrant of empiricism, his poems routinely move toward a universalist, context-free viewpoint. For a further discussion of Cowley's tendency to fuse with physical with the metaphysical or to "decontextualize" knowledge, see Frank Boyle, "Old Poetry and New Science: Swift, Cowley, and Modernity," *1650-1850: Ideas, Æsthetics, and Inquiries in the Early Modern Era* 4 (1998): 253.

Berkeley's poem "On the Prospect of Planting Arts and Learning in America" is a study in the art of pitching up of experience until it opens more possibilities than it could possibly reveal at any one glance. Waller and Cowley rely on frequent changes of perspective to multiply the ways in which an object can be seen—to suggest, for example, that a pleasure boat, when seen from the surface and then seen from below, may amount to more than one *experience* of a boat. Berkeley goes further, writing poetry from so remote a transoceanic perspective that it precludes viewing what he describes. Berkeley opens his poem by transporting his muse to the new world:

> The Muse, disgusted at an Age and Clime,
> Barren of every glorious Theme,
> By distant Lands now waits a better Time,
> Producing Subjects worthy fame.[16]

Writings these lines some years before his visit to America, Berkeley removes his muse to a distant place while he remains in her Britannic headquarters. Berkeley's muse is also displaced into future time. She awaits the moment when she can celebrate adequately worthy topics. The poem seems to happen before it happens; in a fine example of an "apparent impossibility," Berkeley seems to write a poem before it can be written, in a place thousands of miles from the prospect he portrays. Berkeley presents his vision as if looking at it on a stage from a distant mezzanine. In the "happy Climes" of distant America, "Scenes ensue" from "the genial Sun" and the "virgin Earth" (5–6). The action of Berkeley's utopian drama (and future poetry) takes place somewhere in a band between the solar and the mundane boundaries, like long and narrow cinemascope projections from Hollywood's golden age. Berkeley's third stanza continues piling on conditions that must be met before his demanding muse can inspire proper poetry. Among these requirements we find expectations that nature shall guide, virtue rule, and scholastic folly give way to "Sense," even in this most unempirical of empiricist pardises. Presumably those genres that thrive on mistakes—satire, farce, burlesque—would be excluded from Berkeley's Mecca for noble verse.

Berkeley asserts that all the foregoing shall occur in some specific place, that his song belongs not to the golden world of pastoral but to anticipated experience. The fourth stanza opens with the emphatic proclamation that "There shall be sung" (10) odes appropriate to the predicted golden age, driving home the importance of specific location. A series of double goals—spreading empire and art, cultivating the good and the great, educating the head and ennobling the heart—suggests a continuing branching and expanding of Berkeley's visionary undertaking. In the last stanza, anticipated experience overcomes European inertia as

---

[16] George Berkeley, "Verses by the Author on the Prospect of Planting Arts and Learning in America," in *The Works of George Berkeley, Bishop of Cloyne*, ed. A. A. Luce and T. E. Jessop (London: Nelson, 1933), 7:373–374, lines 1–4. Subsequently cited intratextually, by line number.

British civilization sweeps westward. "Westward the Course of Empire takes its Way; / The first four Acts already past, / A fifth shall close the Drama with the Day" (21–23). Britain itself is sucked into the western vista. As experience seems to fly westward, readers almost feel themselves in motion as the American prospect picks up the supplemental attractive power of moral magnetism. Presenting America as the fifth act in the tragedy of European degeneracy, Berkeley demands a high degree of coherence between art and nature. He speaks as if history is literally a drama; he anticipates a genial apocalypse in which the imagined American future draws out and enhances the best that Europe once had to offer. "Time's noblest Offspring is the last" (24).

Berkeley designated *Siris*, his apology for the powers of tar water, as a "chain of reflections," a metaphor that also fits his "America" poem. Berkeley conjures up a remote vision of an American future and then credits that vision with something more than conventional sensibility: with a magnetic power that reconfigures present experience, that draws observers into observations, one step, one link in the chain of reflections, at a time. It is as if Berkeley were viewing experience aboard a movie camera trolley, making motion toward imagined experience into a part of current experience. Berkeley's poem "On Tar" postulates a progression "from lowest earth" through "air, fire, æther to the highest skies."[17] Motion and progress are added to point-of-view, time, and space as factors in what constitutes "experience": as means of enhancing and extending experience, its meanings, and its implications. It would be challenging to find an experience that Berkeley did not regard as leading to something else. The religious function of poetry becomes easy and pleasant as the suggestion of progress toward a goal mixes with the material of vision.

* Viewing the Invisible Sea: Falconer's Cruise into Eternity *

"Progress" like that in Berkeley's American poem seems to imply a destination. Stranded in Rhode Island while planning to found a college in Bermuda, Berkeley soon discovered that travel to any destination could follow many routes and could take longer than expected. Berkeley's futuristic view of the new world requires an uplifted glance, a look out and above the horizon to distant points in distant futures. Berkeley unveils a visionary panorama that contains little in the way of particular detail, scenery, or even content yet that, owing to its elevated angle of vision, gives the impression of a vast impression.

The sea is an ideal medium for those who want to look beyond the brink of visibility to see more than one can see. Vast and level, the sea allows for roaming, elevated, probing perspectives. It abounds in suggestions and occasionally tosses up extraordinary phenomena, but its flat topography and undifferentiated vistas seldom block the line of vision. Among those who looked to the sea to perfect the art of looking was William Falconer. Until the success of his poem *The Shipwreck*, Falconer belonged

---

17   George Berkeley, "On Tar," in Luce and Jessop, *Works*, 5:225.

to the lower echelon of sailors. A literary prodigy who quickly became a favorite among genteel readers, Falconer converted his own experience on a wrecked vessel into a three-canto epic mixing the tragic loss of promising youth with a (nearly) accurate description of seafaring as well as with a kind of intellectual travelogue. However sensational or sentimental Falconer may be, his verse goes further than almost any other when it comes to the visual filling of vacancy—to seeing more than is to be seen and to appending literary form to topics that resist or subvert it. *The Shipwreck* is a modest manual for the kind of enhanced "seeing" advocated by Leibniz and Spinoza; set aboard rickety ships in the hostile vacancy of stormy oceans, the poem rides the wave of repair, renovation, and long-distance anticipatory vision that emerges from Waller, Cowley, and Berkeley.

A humble mariner somewhat overawed by neoclassical verse, Falconer never hesitates to deploy introductions, invocations, and the entire armada of poetic devices. The sheer number of devices used allows him to explore the outer limits of an otherwise very conventional verse. Falconer's "Introduction," for example, opens with an invocation to the muse of memory, an invocation that tackles the problem of a setting for his poem that is, in the last analysis, an undifferentiated sheet of water. "Say on what seas, for thou alone canst tell, / What dire mishap a fated ship befell":[18] it is not so much that Falconer is unable to recall which venue on the aqueous plenum provided the setting for his shipwreck but rather that most watery venues look alike. Calling attention to the unrelenting similarity that characterizes the open ocean proves more interesting than does jotting down some particular navigational fix on the salty plane. Despite the salience of the storm in his poem, Falconer repeatedly highlights the still, stable, and undifferentiated nature of marine environments. Languishing in the southern hemisphere, "Four days becalm'd the vessel here remains" (I:90), sitting on a vast and level desert of flat water; even when in motion, the ship moves in an undifferentiated way, as "Along the glassy plain the vessel glides" (I:706). The recurrent image of a "glassy plain" or "pathless tide" (I:47) emphasizes Falconer's apparent plan to extrapolate a high-seas drama from this baldest and cleanest of stages, to build a story, a seascape, and a poetic idea on a platform that is almost not there: that, if touched, literally dissolves and that, if viewed, tends to level itself out of view. Falconer is fond of using what might be called the "youth afloat" trope, in which a promising youth floats about the Mediterranean, drifting with the tide and indulging in reveries. Palemon, the tragic hero of the tale, floats along the main while his beloved "Anna's image swims before his sight" (I:301), with neither dreamer nor dream in any clearly defined venue but rather on the sea of dreams. Despite the harsh physical realities that it represents, *The Shipwreck* never tells readers where the story might be occurring. The sailors are on an inbound course from Egypt, but how far they have progressed remains unclear (I:1 ff.); the protagonists wander into

---

18   William Falconer, *The Shipwreck*, ed. John Mitford (Boston: Little, Brown, 1863), "Introduction," lines 109–110. Subsequently cited intratextually, by canto and line.

hidden alcoves with a fairy ambiance (I:365–366); now and then Falconer draws back into a remote perspective so as to compare his characters' experiences to events in classical epic (see, for example, II:394–411 and III:1–58); characters even gather atop heaving masts, waving to-and-fro somewhere out on the bounding main (III:596–597).

These indeterminate "settings" juxtapose a plentitude of information— what could be draw more commentary than either a sea voyage or a sea disaster?—against a paucity of information or detail. Falconer asks readers to do more than a little bit of work in passing from a "glassy plain" that could lie anywhere between Pago Pago and Rejkavik to the highly descriptive, highly tangible world on deck (and the diffuse stage on which that stage, in turn, floats). Falconer's poem functions as a training program in which readers learn to see an abundance of detail in a field of routine or repetitive information. So with time: Falconer opens each of his cantos with a note indicating that the cantos take place over specific but somewhat dispersed intervals ranging from four and one-half days to seven hours— intervals rather longer than the two hours of action-packed Elizabethan drama. The intervals decrease as the poem progresses, and Falconer's readers learn to pick out and see the interesting junctures in the field of time. The poem as a whole deals with the protracted nature of sea travel— with the fact that it takes a long time to get anywhere and even longer to get into position for a once-in-a-lifetime event such as a shipwreck—by introducing time-consuming set-pieces such as laments and soliloquies that elide the drifting of open time. Falconer is more "empirical" than hard-edged naval novelists like Daniel Defoe or Tobias Smollett, who present adventure after adventure and utterly distort the usually tedious experience of shipboard life. Falconer at least attempts to give something of the flavor of the long dull hours, training his audience to look out for an excess of information in routine events.

One technique that Falconer uses to get more than can be seen out of sense experience is the incorporation of time and motion into experience. Poets prior to the era of Albert Einstein generally regard time as something separate from experience, something that wears out the pleasures of the moment. Falconer's verse evidences a high degree of spatio-temporal elasticity. Sailors who are stationery in Venice, awaiting departure for Britain, are shown as if they are already running through their journey and already anticipating debarkation in Britain:

> From gay Venice [the sailors] soon expect to steer
> For Britain's coast, and dread no perils near.
> Inflamed by hope, their throbbing hearts elate
> Ideal pleasures antedate,
> Before whose vivid intellectual ray
> Distress recedes, and danger melts away.
> Already British coasts appear to rise,
> The chalky cliffs salute their longing eyes. (I:31–37)

Falconer may give too much philosophical credit to his sailors—few peg-legged gobs have much to say about "intellectual rays"—but, in his rendering of the sailors' longing, he presents a psychological seascape in which time and motion are equally present with the experiences represented. The psychological "antedating" of pleasures, the anticipated voyage, and the long-distance apprehension of Britain's shoreline coincide in a picture that is less an individual picture than a broad slice of time and space. There are almost no "still" experiences in Falconer's poem. His is a world in which every experience is stretched, extended, and enriched across time and space. Time, space, and the psychological states pertaining thereto are factors in every perception. One of Falconer's favorite techniques is to couple an emotionally charged "glance" with the commencing or concluding of a long voyage (see I:601–608 and I:629–630). In such melodramatic moments, the entire shipwreck story seems to stretch out within the elastic moment of the glimpse. Falconer often uses multiple negations to turn simple events into extended dramas. "With cruel haste the shades of night withdrew," he remarks of the moment when Palemon must leave his inamorata for his ill fate; night, the negation of day, withdraws, in reversal of entering, to allow for a departure. What is barely a perception—the disappearing of darkness—spreads out into a vignette. This technique is stretched still further when Falconer presents a variety of semi-invisible phenomena:

> The watchful ruler of the helm no more
> With fix'd attention on the adjacent shore,
> But by the oracle of truth below,
> The wondrous magnet, guides the wayward prow.
> The powerful sails, with steady breezes swell'd,
> Swift and more swift the yielding bark impell'd:
> Across her stem the parting waters run,
> As clouds, by tempests wafted, pass the sun. (II:103–110)

Falconer conducts a symphony of invisibility: invisible magnetic powers guide the needle that guides the ship; felt but unseen breezes push the ship; waters seem to run past the bow, even though, in fact, the bow runs through the waters; clouds, from our limited perspective, seem to "pass" the sun. One could argue that these images are the stock and trade of nautical poetry, but Falconer was an experienced mariner who was proud of his mastery of maritime science. By concentrating attention on non-visible phenomena, he summons a surplus of information from a minimum of experience. Characters in Falconer's poems need do almost nothing in order to communicate a great deal. The high point of the crisis—when the imperiled ship is allowed to run before the tempest—is a kind of passive travelogue in which the disembodied voice of the poet offers a cultural and geographical account of the countries that the ship passes as it slams along toward its doom (III:145–377). Strange as it may seem, Falconer spends over 200 lines near the climax of his poem pointing out sites of cultural, historical, political, and scientific interest while his foundering ship thrashes along hazardous coastlines. The moment of crisis opens up into a leisurely review of world geography—into a less physical sort of time and space where one can view both the sublime story of the shipwreck and the more deliberate story of cultural evolution all at once. As Falconer says, "the

sad Muses with prophetic eye / At once the future and the past explore,"
putting a genuine emphasis on the *at once*.

"At once" is a good phrase to use in describing Falconer's poetic
technique. Aboard ship and at sea, a good deal happens "at once," suggesting
that Falconer's art is about choosing highlights. Falconer's highlighting is of a
very special kind: it draws attention to what might be called "barely attached
imagery," to properties that barely cling to an object and that tend to lead the
poet and his viewers off in some tangential direction. Falconer, for example,
develops a description of the motion of a ship:

> Along the glassy plain the vessel glides,
> While azure radiance trembles on her sides;
> The lunar rays in long reflection gleam,
> With silver deluging the fluid stream. (I:706–709).

The water through which the vessel progresses barely grazes the ship while
"azure radiance" barely clings to it (or to the vessel or perhaps to some
infinitesimal space between ship and water) and while lunar rays acutely skid
across the sea. It is easy to visualize the scene but hard to determine in which
object or experience these phenomena inhere. Although his poem is about
turbulence and shipwrecks, Falconer abounds in descriptions of calm
sunrises or sunsets, when conditions are optimal for rarefied effects such as
sparkling, glittering, reflecting, diffracting, glowing, and even perfuming (see,
for example, I:639–654). The storm itself arrives in a superficial way as its
wind "with foaming sweep / Upturns the whitening surface of the deep"
(II:147–148), telling a story about wind and wave through an impression of
volatile spray: spray that rises from the water and descends from the air, that
detaches itself from the experiences Falconer reports.

This use of detached imagery is interesting enough as a poetic
technique, but Falconer also uses the procedure as a tool of (modest)
philosophical analysis. Falconer's characters have a way of looking along
and through experience in the hope of catching some barely visible
philosophical impression. Battered by the fatal storm, the ship's master
surveys the raging seascape and wonders whether "Perhaps this storm is
sent with healing breath / From neighbouring shores to scourge disease
and death" and then concludes, like some latter-day Pope or Leibniz, that
"whatever is, is just" (II:870–873). The ship's master does not simply view
the scene and then offer some remote reason for its devastation. He
considers the storm as it is and perceives in it some very extenuated
attribute—its cleansing power—that arises directly from the perception but
that leads the mind in more philosophical directions. Often Falconer
renders experience as if it were turning itself into something more
philosophically suggestive. For example, he presents the process of
cognition as part and parcel—and distraction—of any event. "E'en now my
ear with quick vibration feels / The explosion burst in strong rebounding
peals" (III:446–447): the physical event of a thunderstorm is associated with
its physiological consequences and with the psychological process of
cognition and memory; the event is turned into a perception and the
perception into a memory that merits commentary. The poem culminates in

a philosophical speculation on the elusive ways of divine justice, yet that searching question resolves not into an answer, but into a vignette: into an artful, indeed sculptural setting of survivors and their rescuers—"In mournful silence on a rock reclined"—that suggests that there may be sound philosophical answers out there somewhere, that lets speculating readers move from the images before off toward some philosophical gleam. Given his aptitude with neoclassical formulae, Falconer could easily have come up with a few closing lines of condolence. Instead, he leaves the poem in the midst of unfinished processes and images, allowing the philosophical implications of those phenomena to "detach," or nearly so: to hover just above the surface of his otherwise stock representations.

The suggestion of the imminent detachment of the most meaningful aspects of experience from those experiences in which they originate accounts in part for the confusing changes in tone and attitude that erupt throughout Falconer's poem. As mentioned above, Falconer is fond of inserting sunrise or sunset scenes in his poems, but what is most remarkable about those scenes is that they have a way of arising in the midst of emergency actions. In his second canto, for example, Falconer inserts a calm sunset scene in the middle of his account of a raging storm (see II:274–283). Such a decision—to insert ten lines of decorative art into a tempest—would be bewildering had not Falconer trained readers to expect almost any meaning can arise, erupt, and detach itself from almost any experience. A moment in a beautiful sunset with sun rays shimmering on the glassy sea can suggest the sublime rapidity with which the sea can likewise shimmer and shake into a (philosophically perplexing) enemy to mariners. Falconer offers up mixed-media passages in which watercolor-like renderings of sunsets intermingle with textbook descriptions of the "hard" sciences such as navigation, with all its highly technical instruments (see I:736–753). The proximity of these two descriptions suggests an interdependency: misty conditions at sea call for good navigational skill while navigational expertise is all too likely to lead mariners into dangerous waters. The two sets of images shimmer into one another.

Falconer's poem might be described as both philosophically and aesthetically "jittery." Contemporary science has talked about the "jitteriness" of space—about its tendency to warp, twist, and bring material in and out of existence, even when otherwise unperturbed. There are certainly no grounds for declaring Falconer a "quantum mechanical poet," but this anachronistic analogy helps us to understand aspects of his verse that puzzle modern readers. There is never a dull or even calm moment in Falconer's verse. He offers many a scene in which literally nothing is happening and yet the atmosphere remains jittery, as if the world were on the brink of calamity:

> Deep midnight now involves the livid skies,
> When eastern breezes, yet enervate, rise:
> The waning moon behind a watery shroud
> Pale glimmer'd o'er the long protracted cloud;
> A mighty halo round her silver throne,

With parting meteors cross'd, portentous shone:
This in the troubled sky full oft prevails,
Oft deem'd a signal of tempestuous gales. (I:671–678)

Day is done, yet the moon pierces the livid (in the archaic sense of "bluish black") skies; breezes are only incipient; thin, languid clouds conduct light. Yet anticipation seems to sit on every atom. With respect to plot development, the very few turning points in Falconer's one-way journey to destruction always draw attention to a sudden leap from calm to agitated conditions. The voyage begins while Palemon and the other heroes are asleep, in the midst of prophetic dreams, "upstarting from his couch" in startled reaction to the "unmoor" cry (I:693–695); even the anchor is yanked into the scene from repose in the abysmal calm ("Up-torn reluctant from its oozy cave / The ponderous anchor rises o'er the wave") (I:702–703). For Falconer, the field of poetic description—everything in the world that poetry describes—is energized, unstable, and "jittery": on the brink of becoming or leading to or meaning something else, to something new, big, threatening, or sublime. Falconer completes the project of those *restoration* poets like Waller and Cowley who specialized in conversations about renovated houses and gardens. True, his sea wrecks rather than rebuilds oceangoing habitations. Nevertheless, it subtends a world where everything, even the foundering of a ship, seems to yield improvements, in which nothing can be perceived without the accompanying perception of a better version or useful application of it. Like Leibniz and Spinoza, Falconer sees the world as a network of improving relations—of perceptions that harmonize with other, better perceptions—even while he preserves the sense of empirical engagement. Like Berkeley, he accomplishes this through a poetry centered on an empirical "sense" of motion, change, and—with luck—destination.

* Coda: Cowper *

Shipwrecks, like park or palace renovations, usually happen to someone else. Few people find themselves cast away on a desert isle or at the center of London's urban redevelopment. The poets and philosophers examined in this paper have, in their various ways, seen, if not God, at least something promising in otherwise grim experience. None, however, have presented *themselves* as the locus of such divine epiphenomena. The habit of looking to the *brink of visibility* reaches its outer limits in the case of William Cowper, who had the simultaneously tragic and comic habit of seeing more in or pertaining to himself than experience supported. Cowper's psychiatric hijinx—his belief that he was the murderer mentioned in a tabloid report, his conviction that he was the man whom the Bible had charged with the unforgivable sin, his abortive if melodramatic suicide attempts—are the stuff of literary legend. Cowper's strange habit of *over*cognition, of knowing more about what he experienced than apparently could be known, remains misunderstood. It fits neatly within and brings to a climax the Leibnizian habit of seeing more than can be seen.

In his short poem "The Castaway," Cowper incorporates the "wreck-age" motif that was adopted by many writers who were interested in making more of their environment than could presently be seen. The scene that Cowper presents is a famous shipwreck, reported in Anson's *Voyages*, in which a crew member slipped overboard during a nighttime storm, perishing when all rescue efforts failed. "Of friends, of hope, of all bereft, / His floating home for ever left,"[19] the castaway is psychiatrically indistinguishable from the unstable Cowper. Although the theme and story of this poem might seem excruciatingly simple, Cowper manipulates viewpoint to assure that readers see more than can be seen. The poem is delivered by a disembodied omniscient narrator writing in the past tense, but it seems like a first-person account when Cowper zooms in on the castaway's miseries, making an obvious a parallel between the castaway and Cowper. Cowper offers a narrative report about a first-person account delivered by someone who has already drowned—certainly one of the most complex viewpoints that literature has produced.

Cowper's poem is a virtual if miniaturized tour through the ideas and techniques of Spinoza, Leibniz, Waller, Cowley, Berkeley, and Falconer. Cowper's second stanza offers a one-way, partial itinerary in the manner of Falconer. A ship departs from port to sail not to a particular destination but into eternity. What might be called the "vehicle-in-unlimited-indeterminate-motion trope" forces what might otherwise pass as a sublime seascape to take on unexpected religious significance, to emerge as an old-style metaphorical "journey" that has been confined within the minimally allegorical language of the empiricist and the neoclassical traditions. Like Falconer, Cowper asks relentless tempest winds to bracket philosophical questions as well as to render them picturesque, if only to delay receipt of an unwelcome answer. The winds rush through the poetic canvas that Cowper paints, but whence they come and whither they go remain outside the frame. The implied question of God's role in natural evil, whether storms or plain old mortality, disappears behind the drama of the castaway's struggle. We see a scene and get the impression that it is about both natural and religious topics, but the degree that those topics intrude on the scene is carefully controlled lest the skeptical philosophical analysis interfere with fragile religious suggestiveness. Readers know very well that the poem invokes religious ideas, but they also know equally well that those ideas resist articulation in this context. A twenty-first century audience might be tempted to say that the poem has a religious "feeling," but it would be more accurate to say that it makes a religious impression, that it uses shockingly violent scenes in order to make a minimal religious statement, to give the impression of motion toward a religious goal and yet to lock the discussion into what is palpable or visualizable, going to go to the brink of visibility but no further.

Curiously, then, the religious aspects of Cowper's poem support its apparent skepticism, desperation, and nigh-on irreligiousness. As long as the world remains cruel and unjust, sublime scenes may be painted and

---

19   William Cowper, *The Castaway*, "Representative Poetry Online [University of Toronto]," <http://rpo.library.utoronto.ca/poem/560.html>. Subsequently cited intratextually, by line number.

repair efforts undertaken. In Waller and Cowley, the repair and restoration process proved more provocative than the finished facility; so in Cowper, the bustle of a rescue operation makes for an interesting scene because it seems to serve a useful purpose, because it seems to pertain to someone passing into the eternal goal of life, and because the patina of religion makes the rescue efforts seem heroic.

> Some succour yet they could afford;
>   And, such as storms allow,
> The cask, the coop, the floated cord,
>   Delay'd not to bestow.
> But he (they knew) nor ship, nor shore,
> Whate'er they gave, should visit more. (25–30)

Cowper's inventory of rescue devices keeps pushing our attention back into the scene. Readers, Cowper, and the seamen know very well that the case is desperate, yet Cowper's focus on rescue equipment seems to keep the process going, holding viewers in his frame and yet also reminding them that the drama may end in eternity. Readers are forced to think about the "big," religion-related issues in the poem in and through an array of objects—to see in marine paraphernalia more than a "cask" or "coop" or "floated cord" seem to reveal.

Despite the brevity of his poem, Cowper introduces details that emphasize the limits of brevity. Drawing on sea lore and a rudimentary knowledge of hypothermia, he tells us, for example, that "He long survives, who lives an hour / In ocean, self-upheld" (37–38), thus concentrating both the castaway's physical and his own spiritual drama within sixty minutes and some sixty lines even while playing up the immensity of the ocean and the grand scope of the implied philosophical problem. Unusual attention is also paid to the sonic aspects of this calamity: to the vain cries of the lost seaman and their fading volume aboard ship and to the failure of the divine voice to still the waters (41–48, 61). The concluding couplet of the poem—"But I beneath a rougher sea, / And whelm'd in deeper gulfs than he"—draws all the way back to Cowper, who has declined to "descant" on the fate of the castaway (56) but who begins speculating on his own comparatively worse fate in the gulf of melancholy. Cowper presents himself as a quasi-religious image of despair and potential recovery. Despite being "whelm'd" in the troughs of depression and despite having "perish'd" (64), he is apparently still going strong. He seemingly speaks from out from the eternal world, taking advantage of an induced confusion as to whether he has "perish'd" physically or psychologically to give the impression that he addresses us from some very remote, marginally supernatural place. The spiritual equivalent of the idealized restored houses and renovated parks found in Waller's and Cowper's verse as well as a practitioner of the indefinite motion characterizing the poems of Berkeley and Falconer, Cowper fulfils, in an unexpected way, the Leibnizian and Spinozan appreciation of beings that are defined as relations to everything else—including by relations to God, misery, and everything else that shimmers on the brink of invisibility.

The "Serene Mr. Cressy": Enlightened and Peaceful Catholicism in the Late Seventeenth Century

Patricia C. Brückmann

The last thirty years have slowly brought the history of early modern and modern English Catholicism into the mainstream and considerably revised old-fashioned views of Catholics as either members of a sect, eventually content to accept their place as such, or as those persuaded that they might take back monastic lands and cathedrals and reestablish themselves, possibly with some violence, as the rightful, true, and old religion. As Anthony Milton makes clear, (contrary to some writers, mostly commenting on literary figures), not all popish recusants[1] spent their lives in priest holes

---

I would like to dedicate this essay to the memory of the Very Rev. Dom Daniel Rees, Monastic Librarian of Downside Abbey until his death in January, 2007. I owe a great debt to Dom Daniel and to the Community for monastic hospitality and assistance during the years in which I have worked on Cressy. Were Cressy alive today, he would be a monk of St. Gregory's, i.e., of Downside.

[1]   The term *recusant*, from the Latin *recussare*, means "to refuse." Recusants refused to attend religious services of the reformed church. They were not, among other matters, allowed to hold public office. It should be noted that Protestants also could be described as recusants, as in the title of J. C. H. Avelings's *The Handle and the Axe: The Catholic Recusants in England from Reformation to Emancipation* (London: Blond and Briggs, 1976).

or fending off Protestant attack.[2] We should also not be surprised to find that there were those in every church who deplored schism, whose ideal was church unity, even when those who hoped for it did not necessarily want to be wholly inclusive. My principal subject here, although there were other Catholics who shared his goal,[3] is Hugh Paulinus Cressy, whose intellectual history and work vividly illustrate Catholic concern for peace. The name he chose when he became a Benedictine after his conversion in Rome in 1646 suggests his central concern: Serenus, or peaceful.[4]

    Cressy (1605–1674), son of a judge of the King's Bench in Ireland, went from Thorpe Salvin in his native Yorkshire to Oxford in 1619, first to Magdalen Hall, then to Merton College.[5] As a Fellow from 1627, he held a variety of college offices before leaving in 1638 on the recommendation of Archbishop Laud to serve in Ireland as chaplain to Thomas Wentworth, Earl of Strafford. Made prebend of Windsor in 1625, he was given two further preferments in Ireland before returning to England. His attachment to Oxford and to Merton was lifelong and so, of course, were his connections with the University and his college. His last letter, written three weeks before his death, went to Oxford to the Benedictine John Mallet from the Sheldon estate in Warwickshire.[6] He complains about Dr. John Fell's misrepresentations of the numbers of Catholics in the army during the Civil War. This complaint is the last of the comments he made to stress the loyalty of Catholics to the Crown, an issue he insists upon in all his work. In the continuation of his *Church History of Brittany*, still in manuscript at the Bibliothèque Municipale de Douai, he praises Merton elaborately. The Merton College Library has a copy of *The Church History*, of a set of

---

2   See Anthony Milton, *Catholic and Reformed: The Roman and Protestant Churches in English Protestant Thought, 1600–1640* (Cambridge: Cambridge University Press, 1995). See also Milton, "A Qualified Intolerance: The Limits and Ambiguities of Early Stuart Anti-Catholicism," in *Catholicism and Anti-Catholicism in Early Modern Texts*, ed. Arthur F. Marotti (New York: St. Martin's Press, 1999), 85–115. For a comment on the use of priest holes or hides in the later eighteenth century, see Michael Hodgetts, *Secret Hiding Places* (Oscott Series 3; Dublin: Veritas, 1989), ch. 12.

3   See the entries for Christopher Davenport (A. Camber), James Maurus Corker (G. Scott), and John Vincent Canes (P. Brückmann) in the new *Dictionary of National Biography* (hereafter "the new *DNB*," or simply "the *DNB*" for the earlier edition).

4   John Brückmann argued (in private conversation) that Cressy's abbot or novice-master would choose his name. At the time of his conversion, Cressy was a man of mature years, and, as a highly educated former Anglican dean with important English connections, a considerable addition to the community. He would, I think, be given his choice.

5   For a biographical sketch of Cressy, a list of his works, and my sources for the sketch, see my article in the new *DNB*.

6   Much work remains to be done on the Catholic Sheldons, not least on the iconography they worked into their tapestries and their carpets. Georgina Stonor proposed (June 23, 2004, Conference on Recusant Archives, Downside Abbey, Somerset) very plausibly that the red markings on a huge Sheldon carpet marked the places of Catholic houses.

controversial queries about reasons for being a Catholic, and a volume of
Bishop George Morley's works with a letter from Cressy.

At Merton, he would have met William Berkeley, future governor of the
state of Virginia. In the 1640s, he tutored Berkeley's brother Charles, later
Earl of Falmouth. Charles was, in the title of Cyril Hartmann's study of him,
The King's Friend.[7] For all his foolishness,[8] Berkeley, who later helped to
support his former tutor, had considerable influence at court.[9] Cressy may
also have met Henrietta Maria during her stay in Oxford. He would dedicate
The Church History of Brittany (1668) to the Queen Mother, perhaps because
she funded his later journey from Paris to Douai. Stephen Goffe was at
Merton in the early 1620s, so Cressy must have met him too. Goffe (Gough)
(1605–1681) was an ardent royalist, chaplain to Laud, ultimately a Catholic
convert and an Oratorian. Goffe's French connections were useful to Cressy
in Paris in the 1650s after he arrived there from Rome. As an Oratorian, Goffe
could keep his personal wealth; he helped to support Catholic exiles, an
enterprise made easier by his place as Henrietta Maria's chaplain.

Berkeley, Goffe, and Henrietta Maria were significant later for Cressy:
two other Oxford influences are more important in his formation and in his
Church History of Brittany, the text that will be my main concern later. The
first is his membership in the Tew Circle, the group that met at Lucius
Cary's Burford House in Great Tew, about fifteen miles outside Oxford. The
Lord Falkland's circle included George Morley, John Hales, John Earle,
Henry Hammond, William Chillingworth, Thomas Barlow, and Edward
Hyde, future Earl of Clarendon and author of the great *History of the
Rebellion*. In a late controversial work, where Hyde differs sharply from
Cressy, he says that he has known him "for near fifty years."[10] Brian
Wormald and Hugh Trevor-Roper have written of Tew, whose spirit is best
caught by J. C. Hayward's unpublished Cambridge doctoral thesis.[11]
Formed by their reading of writers like Grotius, Erasmus, Cassander, and
Castellion, the men of Tew preached a gospel of peace, whose virtues were
vividly illustrated by their reading of history and especially of war. When
Falkland threw himself into danger and death at the battle of Newbury in

---

7   Cyril Hartman, *The King's Friend: A Life of Charles Berkeley, Viscount
    Fitzhardinge, Earl of Falmouth (1630–1665)* (London: Heinemann, 1951). For a
    brief view of Berkeley's connections, see Ronald Hutton's article in the new *DNB*.
8   See Sir John Denham's view (1667) in "Directions to a Painter," 183–184: "His
    shatter'd Head the fearless Duke disdains, / And gave the last first proof that he
    had Brains."
9   See Hartmann, 105, for a quotation of a letter from Cressy to Berkeley: he has
    received advice of "the continuance of your great liberality to Mee, though
    absent."
10 Edward Hyde, *Animadversions* (London, 1673), 8.
11 B. H. G. Wormald, *Clarendon: Politics, Historiography and Religion, 1640–1660*
    (Chicago: University of Chicago Press, 1964), Hugh Trevor-Roper, *Catholics,
    Anglicans, and Puritans: Seventeenth-Century Essays* (Chicago: University of
    Chicago Press, 1988), J. C. Hayward, "The 'mores' of Great Tew: Literary,
    Philosophical and Political Allusion in Falkland's Circle" (PhD diss., Cambridge
    University, 1982). See also Hayward's "New Directions in Studies of the Falkland
    Circle," *Seventeenth Century* 2 (1987): 19–48.

1643, his circle lost its centre, and its members largely dispersed. That the others kept up with Cressy's later career can be illustrated from Oxford libraries associated with them. There are copies of his work, for example at Hammond's Christ Church. Thomas Barlow, later Bodley's Librarian and Provost of Queen's, gave his marked-up copies of two of the three editions of Cressy's *Exomologesis* to Bodley, the differences carefully indicated in the text and in the margin. The Queen's Library has a copy of the controversy with Morley and a large number of unpublished papers whose marginalia show that Barlow read Cressy with care. Merton, his own college, has a large number of his works. All four colleges that hold some of his work also hold *The Church History*.

Cressy's own decisions after his time at Tew were formed in part by Falkland's formidable convert mother, Elizabeth Cary, whose chaplain was Dom Cuthbert Fursdon, a pupil of Augustine Baker, Benedictine, lawyer, historian, and mystic. Four of Lady Falkland's daughters became Benedictines in France and had Baker as their spiritual director. She had less success with two of her sons. The nuns were important to Cressy later in Paris partly because of their court connections, lively even from the cloister.[12] He dedicated his *Arbor Virtutem* (1649) to Maria Cary and served briefly as chaplain to the nuns. *Arbor Virtutuem*, as the title suggests, is a version of an old genre—the tree of virtues, meant to suggest the inevitability of certain choices. It is still in manuscript at the Australian National Library, which now houses the Clifford family's extensive collection of books, manuscripts, and pamphlets. The Benedictine Abbey of St. Mary's, at Colwich in Staffordshire, has a splendid collection of books and papers critical for study of Cressy; these were brought back to England when the exiled English nuns were ejected during the French Revolution. His preface to his edition of Baker's treatises, *Sancta Sophia* (1657) shows his early knowledge of "Baker's way."[13] I don't think that these two influences—the reasonable and pacific atmosphere of Tew and the beginnings of a considerable interest in mystics and mystical theology—are opposed. The tendency of mystical prayer is towards unity.

Reconciled in Rome in 1646, he wrote the *Exomologesis; or, A Faithful Narrative of the Occasion and Motives of the Conversion into Catholique Unity of Hugh Paulin de Cressy, Lately Dean of Laghlin &c. in Ireland and Prebend of Windsore in England* in 1647.[14] Because I want to emphasize Cressy's

---

[12] See my unpublished essay on the ways in which necessarily new architecture enhanced the ability of nuns to move more freely than they had in more traditional structures, "Material Culture and Cultural Production in a Seventeenth-Century Convent," Aphra Behn Society Conference, Fall 1998, Daytona Beach, Florida.

[13] For "Baker's Way," see Michael Woodward, *The Mysterious Man: Essays on Augustine Baker with Eighteen Illustrations* (Salzburg, Austria: Three Peaks Press, 2001) and James Gaffney, *Augustine Baker's Inner Light: A Study in English Recusant Spirituality* (Scranton: University of Scranton Press, 1989).

[14] For an account of this genre of conversion narrative, see Susan Rose, "'Il était possible aussi que cette conversion fût sincère': Turenne's Conversion in Context," *French Historical Studies* 18 (1994): 632–666. Members of the Tew

connections with Catholic families who would be an important part of the audience for his *Church History*, let me note that the Pontifical Institute in Toronto has a copy of the *Exomologesis*, part of the Bergendahl Collection curated by Joseph Pope, with the signatures of Thomas Howard (d. 1657) and Fr. Michael Gascoigne (1644–1718). The Howards and the Gascoignes were very important Catholic families.

Cressy became a Benedictine (the usual pension was waived) in 1649, an event recorded in his neat hand in the Profession Book in the monastic library of Downside Abbey, Somerset, for he was a monk of St. Gregory's. He was given, like Leander Normington, five years seniority in the habit five years after his profession. As a novice exercise in 1648, he wrote *A Treatise on the Passion*, still in manuscript in the library of Ampleforth Abbey.[15] Henry Holden, of whose Gallicanism the late Antony Allison has written,[16] was an important influence on Cressy in Paris. These strains come together: the desire of Tew for a peaceable kingdom, one founded on allegiance to bishops and to councils, not to the "court of Rome." Cressy makes this distinction, notably in his later correspondence with Sir Thomas Clifford, a strong supporter of toleration and of an ecclesiastical government whose structure helped to reflect it. Councils and synods are important to Cressy in the *Exomologesis*, and these are later emphasized in *The Church History*.

Objections to some "liberal" construction of the Church of England in the first edition of his apology occasioned a second in 1653. I have outlined these changes in an essay on the two editions.[17] He modifies praise of the Church of England, toning down the sections on Hooker and his own friendship with Chillingworth of Tew. Chillingworth's *Religion of Protestants* (1638) is the principal text with which Cressy differs. He considerably expands the section on mystical theology and the list of writers in that tradition. As the Rt. Rev. Dom Placid Spearritt O.S.B. has shown in an important article, Baker and Cressy were responsible for preserving the mediaeval English mystics.[18] Cressy condensed Baker's disparate treatises into the single large volume called *Sancta Sophia*. This appeared in 1657, four years after the second edition of the *Exomologesis* with the expanded section on mystical theology. Without *Sancta Sophia*, Baker would not have

---

Circle surely would have known Erasmus's 1536 treatise on confession called "exomologesis."

[15] Dom Placid Spearritt transcribed and partly annotated the *Treatise* long ago. He and I have prepared an introduction. As a sample of its kind and as the only wholly "original" text Cressy wrote, it should be published. I put original in quotation marks because his editing of other documents and his reconstruction of *History* make them original in a different way.

[16] Antony Allison, "An English Gallican: Henry Holden (1596/7–1662) part 1 (to 1648)," *Recusant History* 22 (1995): 319–349.

[17] Patricia Brückmann, "'Paradice It Selfe': Hugh Cressy and Church Unity," *1650–1850: Ideas, Æsthetics, and Inquiries in the Early Modern Era* 1 (1994): 83–107.

[18] "The Survival of Mediaeval Spirituality among the Exiled Black Monks," *American Benedictine Review* 25 (1974): 287–316.

been available to those outside the tradition of Benedictine monachism[19] although Cressy's tidy editing changes Baker's characteristic digressive style.[20]

In 1659, Cressy issued a "third edition" of the *Exomologesis*. I know of only two copies, one in the Library of Congress in Washington, D.C., the other at Worcester College, Oxford. I want to stop over it because it helps to describe what Cressy did to texts and the reasons for his alterations. This may serve as a cue for his *Church History*.

When I collated the third edition with the first and second, I was puzzled. I was about to give a paper on the implications of the changes from first to second. I could see nothing different in the text of the third edition. Then I looked again at the title page, which is, of course, part of the text. Everything counts. There were two brief but important additions: one called attention to the appendix on John Pearson on infallibility; the other highlighted Holden's answers to Cressy's queries on his conversion. The reader is warned by an addition not to miss the important matter at the end. Marking out what is important is always central to Cressy's presentation of texts. In his edition of Julian in 1670, for example, we get not only the text but also glosses on hard words. His edition of Baker as history (although John Clark is gradually providing the original) comes from the same principle. Baker's highly digressive style is part of "Baker's way." In contrast to Jesuit spiritual advisors who counselled the structure of the *Spiritual Exercises*, Baker's direction allowed a measure of freedom; this method (or absence of it) made him suspect.[21] In his preface to *Arbor Virtutem*, Cressy says that he always studies with pen in hand, sorting out meaning, in preparation for handing it on.

Cressy left France for the mission in 1661, a year after the Restoration, formed by his experience at Tew and with Fursdon further shaped by Holden, by his conversion and profession as a Benedictine, and as chaplain to nuns formed by Baker's teaching. While he eventually served as one of Catherine of Braganza's domestic chaplains, his principal commitment, made firmer by his time in France, was to Henrietta Maria. Rapidly enlisted as a Catholic controversialist, he was never so fierce as those who wrote against him nor so fierce as the standard controversial rhetoric of the period. I have listed all his titles in the entry in the new *Oxford Dictionary of National Biography*. His work responded to attacks on what was perceived as his support of the alleged fanaticism of the mystics, especially Julian and Birgitta of Sweden, and of images and infallibility. After the *Exomologeses* of 1647, 1653, and 1659, he wrote no major work for nearly ten years. His edition of Julian of Norwich (the first) is 1670, two years after *The Church History*.

---

[19]   The Rev. John Clark has been making Baker available in modern editions published by the University of Salzburg in an enterprise managed by James Hogg.

[20]   See my review of *Fr. Augustine Baker, secretum*, ed. John Clark and Justin McCann, O.S.B., *Mystics Quarterly* 25 (1999): 114–115.

[21]   Cressy's editorial changes for *Sancta Sophia* were not made to turn it into a version of the *Exercises* but to make the text as a whole available.

No one knows exactly when he met Sir Thomas Clifford, Baron Clifford of Chudleigh, first of that creation, nor is anyone sure when Clifford himself began first to think about conversion. It is usually argued (safely) that he made his change in 1672 or 1673 (the year of his death) and had then to resign as Lord Treasurer. Clifford (of the Cabal) was on the side of toleration, peaceful and charitable accommodation. Toleration was one of the principal issues of the decade after the Restoration. We also do not know when Cressy first visited Ugbrooke Park, the Clifford estate in South Devon, one of the two houses thought to be the place where, twenty years later, Dryden wrote *The Hind and the Panther*, his own apology for conversion. There is a knoll on the estate known as Dryden's Seat. His conversion was assisted, as T. A. Birrell has shown, by James Maurus Corker, O.S.B.[22] Corker was also one of those who wanted an end to ecclesiastical war.[23] We do know that Cressy bought books for Clifford, because there is a list among the Clifford papers: I read these at Ugbrooke; they are now in the British Library. The list, with titles, authors, and prices, is dated in Cressy's hand as August 17, 1669. The items are perhaps predictable, as additions to the library of a person interested in religion, possibly in conversion: the fathers of the Church, lives of the saints.[24] Hartmannn is more tentative, but I think that the list argues for a close connection between Clifford and Cressy before 1669, with the Benedictine as both spiritual advisor and counselor about matters of state concerning religion, especially toleration. Among the Clifford papers there is, for example, a review of what might be done to achieve church reunion, notably by accommodating Catholic practice. The purpose was ecclesiastical peace. Cressy feared that the Jesuits might try to prevent this design.

The only item Hartmann omits from Cressy's list is the Jesuit Michael Alford's enormous *Annales Ecclesiastici et Civiles Britannorum Saxonum, et Anglorum . . . . Authore R.P. Michaele Alfordo Alias Griffith, Anglo Societatis Iesu theologo*.[25] This work, published in 1656, four years after Alford's death in France, is four volumes folio so just over two thousand pages. Clifford also had a copy of Cressy's *Church History*, published in Rouen in 1668, the year before Cressy bought Alford's *Annales* for Clifford.

---

22 T. A. Birrell, "James Maurus Corker and Dryden's Conversion," *English Studies* 54 (1973): 461–469; "Books and Buyers in Seventeenth-Century English Auction Sales," in *Under the Hammer: Book Auctions since the Seventeenth Century*, ed. Robin Myers, Michael Harris, and Giles Mandelbrote (London: British Library, 2001), 51–64; and D. Geoffrey Scott's biographical notice in the new *DNB*. See also see Anna Battigelli's forthcoming study of the context of Dryden's conversion.

23 James Maurus Corker, O.S.B., *Roman Catholick Principles in Reference to God and the King*, 1680. This brief work, which argues that there is no conflict of allegiance, continued to appear in many editions. Corker was abbot at one point of his career at the Benedictine Abbey at Lambspringe in northern Germany, near Hanover.

24 Cyril Hartmann, *Clifford of the Cabal: A Life of Thomas, First Lord Clifford of Chudleigh Lord High Treasurer of England (1630–1673)* (London: Heinemann, 1937), 189.

25 Alford is sometimes known as Griffith.

How do I know that Clifford had a copy, either before or after he acquired the Alford? In 1963, the Cliffords, who had an Australian connection, sold their enormous library of seventy-five manuscripts, ten thousand books and fifteen hundred pamphlets, many of the last two categories rare, to the National Library of Australia. In addition to Alford's *Annales* and three copies of Cressy's *Church History*, the Clifford Library also had the *Exomologesis* of 1653, and the *Reflexions upon the Oathes of Supremacy and Allegiance*. This last item is bound with John Vincent Canes' *The Reclaimed Papist*, 1655, and his *Roman Catholick Doctrines No Novelties*, 1663,[26] *A Non Est Inventus . . . . to Mr. Edward Bagshaw* 1662, and three other short works printed after 1671. The Clifford library had many volumes of Grotius and Erasmus. Canes would have been attractive to a supporter of toleration. I have given an account of him in the new *Oxford Dictionary of National Biography*.

As Philip Caraman, S.J. has argued, Alford saw himself as the "English Baronius."[27] Caesar Baronius's twelve folio *Annales Ecclesiastici*, begun in the year of the Armada and finished in 1607, was a response to the *Magdeburg Centuries* (1559–1574), the first history of Protestantism,[28] a work Baronius styled *opus pestilentissimum*. History, *ipso facto*, offers recognition, legitimation. The cardinal saw the danger of a positive account. Alford's history would make clear the Catholic history of England as a response to those who attacked her for innovations that destroyed, they argued, the Scriptural basis.

Who was Michael Alford, apart from being a Jesuit with a grand scheme? His own history is part of the history he wrote and part of what I would argue was Cressy's deliberate and Benedictine response. As Fr. Caraman tells us (there is, of course, a longer account in Foley[29] and a shorter *DNB* entry by J. T. Rhodes), Alford came from a recusant family in London. He was sent by John Gerard to St. Omer when he was 11. At 17, he went to the seminary at Valladolid to Douai in 1606 and to the Jesuit novitiate in 1607. After ordination, he acted in Naples as chaplain to exiled English gentry (1615–1620). Having ministered to English Catholics in Rome for the next five years, he assisted Gerard as Master of Novices in Flanders. Only in 1628 did he return to the English mission in Leicestershire, having spent nearly thirty years out of England, with whose affairs he was obviously not in immediate touch, however sophisticated

---

26   See my biographical notice of Canes in the new *DNB*. Canes, a Franciscan, belonged to the more liberal group, along with Christopher Davenport and Maurus Corker. Given the binding of these texts together, their relationship is here perceived as such.

27   Philip Caraman, S.J., "The English Baronius," *The Month* 15 (1982): 30–34. See Cressy, *Exomologesis*, 625–626, on how he has had more profit from reading Charles Borromeo than from "those famous *Cardinalles, Baronius, Ballarmin*, and *Perron*."

28   See Gregory B. Lyon, "Baudouin, Flacius, and the Plan for the Magdeburg Centuries," *Journal of the History of Ideas* 2 (2003): 253–272.

29   Henry Foley, *Records of the English Province of the Society of Jesus* (Manresa Society, 1875), 299–308.

Jesuit communication. At his return, he began to collect materials for the *Annales* and was simultaneously in charge of other missionaries in Leicestershire, Derbyshire, Rutland, and north Nottinghamshire. He also founded a school. No one knows how he managed to collect material and to write. Caraman speculates about his access to the Cotton collection, to Augustine Baker's papers, but nothing is certain. By the time he returned to St. Omer in 1652 meaning to carry on his historical work, he had probably finished at least three of the four folios (there is a cumulative index at the end of the third), but he died of a fever in the year of his return.

The *Annales* were not published until 1663, in Liège, eleven years after Alford's death. In the preface, he says that he wished to render the British and English church the same service that Baronius rendered to the Church Universal. The volumes were published, of course, by permission of his superiors. One of those who lent permission in 1655 was Edward Knott, a leading Jesuit controversialist.[30] Knott died in 1656, leaving the books to be published, presumably by the Society, seven years later. Let me emphasize once again the centrality of the issue of toleration in the 1660s. For some, toleration was a goal to be sought. For others, it was (nearly) anathema.

It is important to look at the volumes physically. Text and ancillary matter are in Latin. Modern cataloguers describe the books as provided with an index and some images. There are in fact several indexes. The first three volumes have an index that covers these; the fourth (which brings the narrative past the Conquest with which volume III ends to 1189) has its own. The third has several others as guides to readers. This is generally true of early indexes. Books of this period were, in fact, by modern standards, over-provided with tables, hence Jonathan Swift's satire on indexes in *A Tale of a Tub* (1690) and Pope's later barb in *The Dunciad* (1728): "Index learning turns no student pale, / but holds the eel of Science by the tail." Steven Zwicker, a student of humanist and post humanist habits of reading, says, "By the end of the seventeenth century . . . printed index and epitome have begun to short circuit manuscript annotation, and the printed commonplace book itself has appeared as a strong alternative to the manuscript compilation."[31]

In addition to the conventional alphabetical table, Alford provides a chronological table of a hundred and fifty-three pages, twenty-six of the saints in England, two indexes of English apostles of thirteen and four pages respectively. There is a particularly striking table of forty-four pages using the double column format of the book to play off the good against the wicked. The running title of this "index" is (in Latin) "Thou art Peter and upon this rock I shall build my church and the gates of Hell shall not prevail against it" (Mt 16:118). Under the first part of the phrase, a column lists positive events and people, under the latter, negatives and villains. This index is especially important. It comes after chronology, after saints and

---

30   See Peter Holmes's entry in the new *DNB*.
31   Steven Zwicker, "The Constitution of Oeinion and the Pacification of Reading," in
     Reading, Society and Politics in Early Modern England, ed. Kevin Sharpe and
     Steven Zwicker (Cambridge: Cambridge University Press, 2003), 298.

apostles—to emphasize, in one of the most discussed passages in Matthew, the importance of Peter as the foundation of the church and, presumably, of the history whose end it marks. Peter will have the power to bind and to release; this power will reflect what has been bound and loosed in heaven. The heading, in other words, emphasizes the primacy of Peter and articulates in its own way the Jesuit fourth vow of allegiance to the pope.

The first page of the volume gives us a complicated image that sums the emphases of the book and mark it as a Jesuit document.[32] (See figure 1.) We are not surprised to find a major emphasis on Marian devotion. At the top, the Father and the Son crown the Virgin, who looks down on a cross over which the title of the book is draped. Papal figures wearing the early modern (fourteenth century) triple tiara are to the left: Eleutherius (174–189) is associated in the Liber Pontificalis with the British King Lucius, first, as the pope to whom the king wrote expressing his wish to be a Christian. Gregory the Great (ca. 540–604) is next; we know his zeal for the conversion of England and his strengthening of the primacy of Peter. The third is Alexander II (1061–1073), who gave a consecrated banner to William of Normandy (part of the image to the right) for his invasion of England and elevated Lanfranc, his former teacher, to the see of Canterbury. None of these popes, given their regnant dates, would have worn the triple tiara.[33] St. Augustine is in back with a mitre. There are Roman figures below. Lucius, the first Christian, is at the foot of the Cross holding a map with the donation of England. Sts. Fugatus and Damianus, both associated with Glastonbury, and Helena, mother of Constantine, paragon of charity and finder of the true cross, frame the cross, so that the Christianity of England is put even farther back than the mission sent by Gregory. Apart from a few identifications of some of the figures, no words apart from these distract the viewer from the image. The figure at the left corner, vested for mass, is St. Ignatius.

The title page itself gives the author (with his alias of Michael Griffith) and his membership in the Society. On the next page is a biblical epigraph suitable for a historian, and one with a context Alford would have known. It is Jeremiah VI: "Stand on the ways, and look to the ways that are past and walk in those ways and you will find refreshment for your soul" (6:39). The people of Israel, having displeased Yahweh, are now threatened by foes from the north, the traditional place from which the wicked arrive. Chaucer's Summoner fails to see the implication of the green clad yeoman, who tells him that his home is "fer in the north contree." The people of Israel (like the Summoner, because everyone gets a second chance) stand at a crossroad. Alford's book will, like his opening image, sort out the right choice. As for

[32] The use of images to make a point is, of course, a Jesuit habit. For instances of this use, see François Marc Gagnon, La Conversion par L'Image: Un Aspect de la Mission des Jesuites (Montreal: Bellarmin, 1975) and Anne Dillon, The Construction of Martyrdom in the English Catholic Community, 1535–1603 (Burlington, VT: Ashgate, 2002), ch. 3.
[33] See Bernard Sirch, Der Ursprung der bischölichen Mitra und päpstlichen Tiara (Frankfurt: Verlag, 1975).

Baronius, Alford's model, history is moral. The indexes emphasize this point and cater, as well, to those with limited Latin.

According to the article on Cressy in the old *Dictionary of National Biography*, Alford's *Annales*, with material from Dugdale, and Augustine Baker's papers at Jesus, Oxford were the sources Cressy used for his *Church History of Brittany*. For Thompson Cooper, author of the early article in the *DNB*, and those who have followed him, without, I think, examining the books closely, Cressy's *Church History of Brittany* is no more than a raid on earlier work, especially on Alford.[34] I would argue rather that Cressy's book makes clear its debt to Alford and that in reducing the *Annales* to half its length, translating the whole and making other critical changes, he alters the book in major ways, most critically, in what the book is meant to do. He did so, if not at the suggestion of his superiors, then with their full support.

In 1669, Benedictine convents and provinces were taxed to support Cressy's *Church History*.[35] Not all libraries now have copies of Alford, but *The Church History* is easy to come by. As I have noted, the Cliffords had three. My own university has two, one in the Fisher Rare Books Library, the other at the Pontifical Institute of Mediaeval Studies, part of the Bergendahl Collection curated by Joseph Pope. St. Michael's College, to which the Institute is related, has a copy of Alford; Emmanuel College, part of Victoria College, Toronto, has another. There are fourteen copies of *The Church History* in libraries in Great Britain, one each at Leeds, London, the Wellcome Library, Bristol, the National Library of Wales, and the National Library of Scotland, with two in Exeter (one in the Cathedral Library, one in the University Library, the latter from the Syon Abbey Collection), and four in each of Oxford and Cambridge. On the continent in France, there is one in the Bibliothèque Nationale, one at Troyes, and one at Toulouse. The Vatican has one and so does Munich. There are also copies in major American libraries, like Harvard, Yale and Texas. The Downside Library has one copy; the northern Benedictine house, Ampleforth Abbey, has two. A systematic search of private collections in English Catholic houses would reveal more and testify to the book network among this group.[36]

I would first like to make some comparisons between The *Church History* and the *Annales*, chiefly to try to document the effect each might have on a reader. There is more detail in my paper on Cressy and the unity of the Church.[37] Alford's opening page is gone. Now in English, the book is also only 1002 pages, half the size of Alford. The title is as instructive: *The*

---

[34]   See Thompson Cooper's entry in the *DNB*, ed. Leslie Stephen and Sidney Lee (London: Oxford University Press, since 1917), 5:75–76.

[35]   Athanasius Allanson, *A History of the English Benedictine Congregation*. 14 vols. MS, Ampleforth Abbey, with copies at Downside Abbey (1843–1858): 468–469. Available on microfiche, V. Rev. Placid Spearritt and D. Bernard Green (Oxford, 1978).

[36]   I would be glad to hear of others. Email address: bruckman@trinity.toronto.edu.

[37]   I presented this paper to the meeting of the Catholic Record Society, Oxford, 1981 and revised it for publication in the *English Benedictine History Symposium* in the following year.

Church History of Brittany from the beginning of Christianity to the Norman Conquest under Roman Governors, British Kings. The English-Saxon Heptarchy. The English-Saxon (and Danish) Monarch. Containing I. The Lives of All Our Saints Assigned to the Proper Ages wherein They Lives. II. The Erections of Episcopall See's, and Succession of Bishops. III. The Celebration of Synods, Nationall, Provinciall and Diocesan. IV. The Foundations of Monasteries, Nunneries and Churches. V. And a Sufficient Account of the Successions of our Kings, and of the Civill Affaires of this Kingdom. From All Which Is Evidently Demonstrated: That the Present Roman-Catholick Religion Hath from the Beginning, without Interruption or Change Been Professed in This Our Island, &c / By R. F. S. Cressy of the Holy Order of S. Benedict.

Cressy uses the quotation from Jeremiah but adds the next verse: "but they answered, we will not walk." This antiphonal structure comes from Jeremiah. The audience is asked to listen, but they will not listen and so forth. Despite this admission of the unlikelihood of the audience for conversion into primitive and godly ways to be represented in *The Church History*, the opening is positive, no reading of church history in images supporting, say, the Court of Rome. Alford's negative impact on refusers has already been considerably muted. The audience (think of Cressy's connections with gentry families) has been vastly increased by translation and, in Cressy's characteristic orderliness, helped to see the pattern of the book and its purpose—to demonstrate continuity. As Dom Daniel Rees has noted in his article in the new *DNB*, Augustine Baker understood that the aggregation of two younger monks to Sigebert Buckley, last of the English congregation, demonstrated the continuity of the monastic tradition in a very literal way. Baker was not only a mystic; he was also a lawyer. The commendatory poem for *The Church History* may not be great verse, but the person who describes "this reviving *Book* . . . this *Eternall Monument* . . . restorer of the unity lost by sects and schisms," is Edward Thimelby, a poet from the Tixall circle.[38] There should be further works on Catholic networks, from books to poems to carpets.

But in what does this continuity consist? It is very clear (not only from the column and a half in the index, very different from the amount of space Alford gives) that the major work of unity, continuity, and peace has been achieved by the monks. Immediately after Alford's section on the death of Joseph of Arimathea (Alford, 76), Cressy adds: "We may likelie prudently judge that it was the speciall design of the *Divine Providence* to make choice of these particular *Saints* to be not only Preachers of his word, but examples also of a *Monasticall Conversation*, in an *Island* so commodious for it. Excepting S. Mark in the deserts of Egypt, we doe not find an other of the *Primitive disciples* which seem'd to had such a design. There wanted not, indeed from the beginning, many who relinquish'd their worldly employments . . . that without any impediments they might wholly give themselves to God, and being freed from all distinctions practise the exercises of Divine Contemplation" (31). The text, as the title page suggests,

---

38   For the Tixall circle of poets, see Arthur Clifford, *Tixall Poetry* (Edinburgh: J Ballantyne, 1835).

favors the orderly succession of bishops and celebrates national, provincial, and diocesan synods, images of order Cressy earlier described and defended in his *Exomologesis*, even in the edition in which he makes the changes I have described.

One of the items I like best are the Alford and Cressy items in the indexes on Oxford. Cressy, in a three-line index note, emphasizes the age of his university. Alford gives a column to Oxford, first emphasizing, for half a column, its age and distinction, then half a column on the sadly reformed present state of the university. Cressy on Cambridge is worth a look. The index entry reads: "*Cambridge*: its pretence of *Antiquity* to K. *Lucius* his dayers [sic] IV." The entry is nearly jocular: "Our famous University of *Cambridge* . . . will not take it ill, if an *alumnus* of her sister suspend his assent to her pretention of being founded . . . by *King Lucius*" (67). Observations like this underline Cressy's construction of the index as a document very likely to be read, even as Alford provides indexes for his audience—of a very different kind.

What would have prompted the Benedictines perhaps to commission and certainly to support Cressy's *History*, and why would he order Alford for Thomas Clifford the year after he published his own? I think that the answers to these questions lie in toleration—a critical issue, as I have remarked, in the middle 1660s, made more so by the revival of anti-Catholic sentiment after the Great Fire and, with Cressy's desire, shared by Clifford, to attempt measures that would unify the churches of England and of Rome. As John Miller reminds us, the measures for toleration were not to apply to the Jesuits.[39] Alford, as I have suggested, spent nearly thirty formative and informative years out of England; his formation was the formation of a Jesuit. The clarity of his indexes, notably the one that demonstrates the dichotomy of those on the rock and those swallowed by the gates of hell, is the clarity appropriate to a soldier of Christ who had ministered to refugees and exiles from the reformed church and taken the Jesuit fourth vow of allegiance to the pope. Cressy's preface recognizes Alford's enormous effort and approves his dedication to his patron saint, the war-like archangel, goes on, without noting the changes, to alter the format and the content, in other words, to produce a different book.

The effect of the *Annales*, from the opening images to the indexes at the end was confrontational. This would have surprised neither Cressy nor his Benedictine superiors. When he was preparing *The Church History*, he was, at the same time, discussing proposals for unity. Clifford quotes the *Exomologesis* in his (unedited) Commonplace Book, four times, once under the heading "Unio." As Cyril Hartmann says in *Clifford of the Cabal*, Cressy distrusted the Jesuits "believing that their fervent zeal for their faith was apt to carry them too far in delicate situations."[40] As Cressy says, in the

[39]   John Miller, *Popery and Politics in England 1660–1688* (Cambridge: Cambridge University Press, 1973), 98.
[40]   Cyril Hartmann, *Clifford of the Cabal: A Life of Thomas, First Lord of Clifford of Chudleigh Lord High Treasurer of England (1630–1673)* (London: Heinemann, 1937) 193.

manuscript in the Clifford papers marked Q. Q. Q., "Wee and our forefathers have seen one Active Party among us, who to ingratitiate themselves
with the Court of Rome, have without the consent or knowledge of any
others of the Clergy, and by misinforming the Pope, obtained severeall Bulls
very burdensom and pernicious to the common peace and safety. Which
Bulls, contrary to all order in Catholick countryes, they have presumed to
publish and enforce upon Catholicks in generall."[41] He adds that Catholic
clerics in England have "hitherto too generally . . . been zealously addicted
to the Spaniards, and by their example exalted in Books the Power and
Juridiction of the Roman Court: By means whereof the French, both State
and Clergy, have looked on us with suspicious eyes, insomuch as the
Conversion of England to the Catholic Faith has been esteemed by them
dangerous to their Nation. Whereas if Ecclesiasticall affairs among us were
ordred according to the Modell of the French, it would be a powerfull mean
to procure their assistance: which is of infinitely greater advantage, both as
to Religion and generall Amity, then that of any other Nation can be." While
Cressy's friendship with Clifford, who was pro-French, might seem to
explain this comment, his earlier work, and the *History* itself give a pacific
view that is counter, in his judgment, to the Jesuit position.

I have emphasized the chronology of Alford deliberately so as to
contrast his history to Cressy's. Cressy began as an Anglican divine of
Oxford and Great Tew and all the values that group suggested. He
remained, so far as we can tell, in touch with its members throughout his
life. He was, as his chosen name in religion suggests, a man of peace,
attracted to the Benedictines because of their peaceful commitment. As he
prepared his *History*, directed and supported by his superiors, he was not
simply huddling together his own text from his major source. He was
making what was important in that source available to his recusant
audience and giving direction about how they should respond, not with
insistence on what he calls more than one time "the Court of Rome" but
with charity. These are the old ways in which they ought to walk. The
History, as I have said, is not a rare work. It was meant to have a wide
audience, including those whose Latin could not have coped with Alford. I
have cited some names of prominent Catholic families in Cressy's own
history. Thimelby (and through Thimelby, Aston and Constable and others
associated with Tixall), Howard and Gascoigne, Clifford and Sheldon. He
wrote his last letter from the Sheldon house, died at the Caryll estate in
West Grinstead in 1674, and was given financial support by the Carylls.[42]

Why would he direct Clifford to add Alford to his library with lives of
the saints and Bede and others change this? If I am right about his reading
of Alford, he was not recommending the *Annales*, certainly not in 1669.
When I realized that Hartmann had inadvertently omitted the list, I thought
that Cressy, in making his list, was simply recommending the reading of

---

41   Clifford MSS in Cressy's hand.
42   Timothy J. McCann. "West Grinstead: A Centre of Catholicism in Sussex, 1670–
      1814," *Sussex Archaeological Collections* 124 (1986): 193–212. See 196: Cressy is
      to have £12 per year, one third of the interest on 600 for life.

history to Clifford. Writing history is a Benedictine habit. Given what I have said of the *Annales* and *The Church History*, that now seems quite wrong. The history he recommended was the *History* he wrote, a volume reflecting his characteristic taste for orderly presentation and his defense of the monastic way as well as of peace and unity. The *Annales* represented a quite different position but a position about which Clifford had to know. The other Ugbrooke manuscripts, also initiatives for peace and unity, support this view. History is a powerful tool. Bede saw that as clearly as he saw everything. He declares (because he was honest) that he has assigned the reigns of two bad kings to two good ones, presumably lest they get the fame of remembrance. Cressy alters the size, language, emphases, and, most critically, the spirit of Alford. His *Church History of Brittany* is a Benedictine history. Pax is his theme throughout his work and the work of those whose orientation was like his own. Anthony Milton is right to stress the way in which common life asked for neighborly feeling and support; a religious order founded in community promotes this ideal.

With considerable irony, Stillingfleet played on Cressy's chosen name in religion, implying that the "Serene Mr. Cressy" was simply another agent of the Court of Rome, its images and foggy mystics and, as a controversialist, hardly serene at all.[43] As we know, Dryden speaks in nearly similar tones about "Fr. Cres" in the context of quarrel and potential regicide.[44] But Mr. Cressy, in all his writing, would, like his monastic brothers, frequently hear and read in *The Rule of St. Benedict*, including chapter 4 on the instruments of God's works. Among these, near the end, we hear, from Matthew 4:44, the injunction to pray for one's enemies and in the next, from Ephesians 6, the admonition to reconcile before the end of the day.[45] Cressy underlines peace and the scandal of disunity. He lived in community, bound by obedience and, in addition, by a vow of stability, surely not always easy. He was not alone. There were others, like Corker and Canes and Davenport, the last two Franciscans. Their continued concern for and work for unity and for the peace that enables it was enlightenment of a critical kind.

43 Edward Stillingfleet, general preface to *An Answer to Several Late Treatises* (London, 1673), n.p.
44 See the preface to "Religio Laici," in *The Poems of John Dryden*, ed. James Kinsley. 4 vols. (Oxford: Clarendon Press, 1958), 1:307.
45 Translations will vary, but none alter the sense of forgiveness and peace.

Figure 1. First page of Michael Alford's *Annales*.

"Organs of Thy Praise": The Function and Rhetoric of the Body in Thomas Traherne

Gary Kuchar

> Meaning is invisible, but the invisible is not the contradictory of the visible: the visible itself has an invisible inner framework (membrure), and the invisible is the secret counterpart of the visible, it appears only within it—one cannot see it there and every effort to see it there makes it disappear.
>
> Maurice Merleau-Ponty, *The Visible and the Invisible*

In the final chapter of *The Body Emblazoned: Dissection and the Human Body in Renaissance Culture*, Jonathan Sawday situates the work of Thomas Traherne against the "technological regimes" of the Royal Science, focusing particularly on how Traherne's representation of the body both reflects and resists changes in linguistic perception taking place during the Restoration. The rise of empirical disciplines that occurred in the last third of seventeenth century—disciplines grounded in the philosophies of Bacon, Hobbes, and Descartes—rested, Sawday contends, on a "reform of the very language of science."[1] Among other things, these reforms undid the metaphorical matrices of analogical

---

[1]   Jonathan Sawday, *The Body Emblazoned: Dissection and the Human Body in Renaissance Culture* (London: Routledge, 1995), 231. For an account of Traherne's rebuttal of Hobbes's *Leviathan*, see Stanley Stewart, *The Expanded Voice: The Art of Thomas Traherne* (San Marino: Huntington Library, 1970), ch. 3.

correspondence that had long provided the conceptual bedrock for representing the body in favor of an empirically focused, metonymically based language of dissection and mechanization. Reacting against the objectification of the body in isolation from the thinking soul and troubled by the desacramentalizing implications of such decontextualization, Traherne, according to Sawday, asked how "would it be possible to create a new language of the body which, whilst it acknowledged the discoveries within the microcosm, could retain the dimensions of sacred anatomy?[2] [. . .] To simply deny the force of Cartesian analysis was hopeless. But to reinvent the body as its own peculiar, reserved space, was an altogether different possibility."[3]

Part of Traherne's answer was to appropriate the taxonomic methodology of the Royal Science for sacramental ends. Traherne's catalogs were "to become a stylistic device in their own right, an attempt at suggesting endless complexity which the discourses of reason would never succeed in refining into a system."[4]

While my essay is occasioned by Sawday's argument that the very unreadability of Traherne's cataloging technique—its opaqueness to modern interpretation—is a function of the historical triumph of mechanism, I think it is misleading, if not simply inaccurate, to suggest that Traherne sought a "reserved space" for the body. On the contrary, Traherne positions the body within the field of being-in-the-world, making it not an object unto itself, but a medium of experience as such. Situating Traherne's work against "the culture of anatomy" and ignoring some very important prose passages, Sawday overlooks the phenomenological dimensions of Traherne's articulation of the body and the relationship this experiential account of embodiment has to Traherne's sacramental vision of the self's relationship with the world. Although Sawday provides a compelling analysis of how Traherne resists the systematizing aims of the Royal Science, he does not reflect on how Traherne's reaction to the desacramentalizing implications of scientific anatomy anticipates the phenomenological thesis that scientific explanation is a second-order expression. We need to take closer account, that is, at how Traherne resists the way that empirical explanation detaches the knowing consciousness from the object known without acknowledging the epistemological incoherence of such a rupture nor its debilitating existential implications. This philosophical concern with modes of knowing is of particular importance in regards to Traherne's fashioning of the ideal or felicitous self as an embodied being. For Traherne, felicity is achieved when "the soul of a man actuates his Body," when the body is revealed not only in its sacramental character,

---

[2] By sacred anatomy, Sawday refers to a mode of corporeal analysis that looked to the body in order to perceive the divine design of the cosmos. See ch. 5, "Sacred Anatomy and the Order of Representation," 140.
[3] Sawday, *Body*, 258.
[4] Ibid., 262.

but as the medium of encountering and communing with others and with the world.[5]

By describing Traherne's articulation of the body in phenomenological terms, I am developing a line of thinking that begins with A. Leigh Deneef's reading of Traherne vis-à-vis Heidegger. While Deneef offers a compelling argument that Traherne thinks of being-in-the-world in terms that anticipate Heideggerian phenomenology, he does not address the importance of the body to Traherne's philosophy. In an effort to illuminate the function of the body in Traherne's vision of the *felicitous* self, I not only situate his work within and against the taxonomic practices of Baconian science, but I also place it alongside Maurice Merleau-Ponty's phenomenological account of embodied being. As we shall see, Traherne conceives of the body not simply as an object open to analysis (as Sawday has shown, Traherne insists that the body ultimately resists the aims of anatomical analysis) but as a "living hymn," an expressive articulation of desire for God. As such, Traherne's account of embodiment offers a sacramental counterpart to Merleau-Ponty's view that the body has the ontological status of a work of art: "A novel, poem, picture, or musical work are individuals, that is, beings in which the expression is indistinguishable from the thing expressed, their meaning accessible only through direct contact, being radiated with no change of their temporal or spatial situation. It is in this sense that our body is comparable to a work of art."[6]

In this account, the body is not an object but "is our general medium for having a world."[7] Similarly, Traherne views the body as a site of ethical obligation, metaphysical speculation, and as the occasion for communion with the world as distinct from, but accessible to, consciousness. Thus what Traherne and Merleau-Ponty fundamentally share is the conviction that, if one isolates the body as an objective entity, one fundamentally misconceives what (or more precisely how) the body is.[8] Moreover, Merleau-Ponty's account of the chiasmic structure of intersubjectivity, along with his focus on the role of the body vis-à-vis

---

5   *Commentaries of Heaven*, ms. fol. 30r2, British Lib., London; cited in Cynthia Elizabeth Saenz, "Thomas Traherne's View of Language in Restoration England" (PhD diss., University of Oxford, 1997), 40.

6   Maurice Merleau-Ponty, *Phenomenology of Perception*, trans. C. Smith (London: Routledge, 1962), 151.

7   Merleau-Ponty, *Phenomenology*, 1962, 146. For a discussion of Merleau-Ponty's conception of embodiment in relation to saintliness see Edith Wyschogrod's *Saints and Postmodernism: Revisioning Moral Philosophy* (Chicago: University of Chicago Press, 1990), 14–19.

8   Merleau-Ponty makes this point in the preface to *Phenomenology of Perception*: "I am not the outcome or the meeting-point of numerous causal agencies which determine my bodily or psychological make-up. I cannot conceive myself as nothing but a bit of the world, a mere object of biological, psychological or sociological investigation" (viii). This essay is an attempt to demonstrate that Traherne not only shares this view but that he thought through some of its phenomenological, ethical, and metaphysical implications.

self-other relations, provides a view that illuminates Traherne's thinking more effectively than Deneef's Lacanian conception of intersubjectivity as a function of one's alienation within signification—a view that is quite at odds with Traherne's sacramentalism. Thus while I build on Deneef's Heideggerian reading of Traherne, I offer an alternative to his Lacanian view of Traherne's concept of "intermutuality." What is ultimately at stake in Traherne's account of embodiment and the view of "intermutuality" that follows from it is nothing less than the most intimate dimensions of sacramental experience and knowledge at a point in time when the metaphysical framework grounding such sacramentality had begun to shift towards a dualist, and in this respect wholly non-sacramental, view of the body/mind relation.[9]

In his early prose work, *Select Meditations*, Traherne outlines the continuous relation he believes exists between the body and the soul. He summarizes his conception of this relationship when he suggests that the "little actions of our confined being"—the actions, that is, of our body—are coextensive with the internalized presence of Being that "prepossesses our soul": "External affaires, as Animated and flowing from the Soul within, have an Imputed Greatness by the Inward Sphere" and "all the works of joy and Glory are Radically *there*, And thence doth all the Beauty and valu flow which is on the Inside of every operation."[10] In this economy of being, the body's exteriorized actions are imagined as having a sacramental continuity with the indwelling soul's outward moving presence: "Thoughts are the springs of all our actions here / On earth, tho they themselves do not appear."[11] For Traherne, Being can only be approached through the actions of being-in-the-world, through, in other words, the body as medium of experience. Inside and outside, soul and body, become continuous, interwoven as it were, as each reveals the other in an ever renewing process of mutual disclosure. It is precisely this intertwining relation between the inside and the outside, between the visible and the invisible, that Traherne captures when says: "You never enjoy the world aright, till the sea itself floweth in your veins, till you are clothed with the heavens, and crowned with the stars."[12] Poetic imagery is at the service of serious philosophical speculation. This passage evokes the sense that at the highest levels of perception, body and world, thinking and being, thing and thought, become inter-mutually coordinated with one another. As Traherne puts it in "My Spirit," the fully realized mind "acts not from a centre to / Its object as

---

9   For an account of desacramentalization from the perspective of the history of
        ideas see Michel Foucault, *The Order of Things* (New York: Vintage Books,
        1970). For an analysis of desacramentalization within the context of English
        religious practice see Keith Thomas, *Religion and the Decline of Magic* (New
        York: Penguin, 1971).
10   Thomas Traherne, *Select Meditations*, ed. Julia J. Smith (Manchester: Fyfield,
        1997), 45, my emphasis.
11   Thomas Traherne, *Centuries, Poems and Thanksgivings*, ed. H. M. Margoliouth. 2
        vols. (Oxford: Clarendon Press, 1958), 175, lines 7–8.
12   Ibid., 15.

remote, / But present is, when it doth view, / Being with the being it doth note."[13]

By understanding the body as a medium of experience rather than an object of scrutiny, Traherne grants the body an integral role in the constitution of an ideal subject who coordinates being and knowing— uniting past, present, and future into itself through a complex series of "intermutual" relations with other beings. He summarizes his conception of this ideal subject in *Christian Ethics* when he writes: "JANUS with his two Faces, looking backward and forward, seems to be a fit Emblem of the Soul, which is able to look on all Objects in the Eternity past, and in all Objects before, in Eternity to come. Faith and Hope are the two faces of this Soul. By its Faith it beholdeth Things that are past, and by its Hope regardeth Things that are to come."[14]

This vision of the soul beholding past and future in a simultaneous present[15] does not entail an effacement of the body, as one might expect given Traherne's Neoplatonism, but rather it coincides with a sacred, rather than anatomical vision of the body. This body is figured not only as something in excess of representation, but it operates as one of the central means by which the self realizes a view of itself as "a seeming Intervall between Time and Eternity, the Golden link or Tie of the World, yea the Hymenaeus Marrying the Creator and his Creatures together."[16] Operating as a copula within the sacramental grammar of his work, the Trahernian body functions mystically, filling up, as it were, the loss inflicted through the desacramentalization of the "corpus mysticum."[17] Facing both the demystification of Eucharistic theology and the increasing pressures of Cartesian dualism, Traherne focuses attention on the human body as the source or ground that, along with the soul, links oneself to God and to the world. It is for this reason that he is interested not only in the body's interiorized depths, which had long been associated with Christian faith,[18] but he is also focused on the body's

---

13   Ibid., 50, lines 18–21
14   Thomas Traherne, *Christian Ethics*, ed. Carol L. Marks and George Robert Guffey (Ithaca: Cornell University Press, 1968), 117.
15   For an account of how Traherne's conception of time "reconciles" the scholastic view of eternity as a perfect simultaneity (Nunc-stans) and the Hobbesian view of eternity as endless duration see Richard Jordan's *The Temple of Eternity: Thomas Traherne's Philosophy of Time* (Port Washington: Kennikat Press, 1972).
16   Traherne, *Centuries*, 208–209.
17   We might recall here Michel de Certeau's account of the rise of mysticism (*la mystique*—translated as "mystics") as a discourse in the seventeenth century: "Sixteenth- and seventeenth-century mystics proliferated about a loss. It is the historical figure of that loss, making readable an absence that has multiplied the productions of desire. At the threshold of modernity, an end and a beginning are thus marked—a departure." Michel de should the Certeau remain? Certeau, *The Mystic Fable*, trans. Michael B. Smith (Chicago: University of Chicago Press, 1986), 13.
18   Christianity, as David Hillman suggests, "has always positioned the body's inner realm as the ultimate site of faith" (85). Similarly, Elaine Scarry points

outward parts, its "naked" surfaces. As such, Traherne's representation of the body participates in the pursuit that Michel de Certeau claims characterized seventeenth-century mystics in general. The early modern mystic quest, according to de Certeau, is an obsessive quest after the body. The goal of seventeenth-century mysticism, "was to produce a mystic body, [. . .] an alien body against which the institution of medicine would eventually win out in imposing a scientific body."[19]

Writing both within and against the de-contextualization of nature that made this scientific body analyzable, Traherne's texts present a complex version of the Pauline principle that faith precedes and is the condition of knowledge. As the Epistle to the Hebrews puts it, "Faith is the substance of things hoped for, the evidence of things not seen" (11:1). Even more strongly, the author of Hebrews suggests that "through faith we understand that the worlds were framed by the word of God" (11:3).[20] Having been influenced by the emergence of Baconian induction and other rationalist and empiricist practices, Traherne's work moves, sometimes uneasily, between St. Paul's uncompromising view of the precedence of faith and the Royal Society's emphasis on the necessary role that experience and experimentation play in consolidating knowledge of the world.[21] Ultimately though, the knowledge of the body that Traherne is concerned with in such texts as "Thanksgivings for the Body" is knowledge mediated by and originating from faith, for as he argues in the *Centuries*: "He that Knows the Secrets of Nature with A Magnus or the Motions of the Heavens with Galilao or of whatever else with the greatest Artist; He is nothing. if he Knows them meerly for Talk or idle Speculation, or Transeunt and External Use. But He that Knows them for Value, and Knows them His own: shall Profit infinitely."[22]

---

out that in both the Old and New Testaments "the interior of the body carries the force of confirmation [of belief] (137, cited in Hillman, 85). See David Hillman, "Visceral Knowledge," in *The Body in Parts: Fantasies of Corporeality in Early Modern Europe*, ed. David Hillman and Carla Mazzio (New York: Routledge, 1997), 81–105. Elaine Scarry, *The Body in Pain: The Making and Unmaking of the World* (Oxford: Oxford University Press, 1985), 137.

19   de Certeau, *The Mystic Fable*, 85.

20   *King James Holy Bible* (Nashville: Thomas Nelson, 1992), 709.

21   For an examination of Traherne's Dobell sequence in terms of Baconian induction see James J. Balkaier, "Thomas Traherne's Dobell Series and the Baconian Model of Experience," *English Studies* 3 (1989): 233–247. Balkaier contends that "Traherne has adapted the scientific model of the mutually beneficial relationship of Experience and Understanding to give his marvelous cognitions and intimations a comparable objectivity of expression" (247). While I concur that Traherne's work possesses an emphasis on the relationship between experience and understanding, it is misleading to assert that he aims at an "objectivity of expression." On the contrary, his experiential tendencies are in the service of his sacramental epistemology. They move, that is, towards a convergence of the subjective and objective, self and world: "You never enjoy the world aright, till you see all things in it so perfectly yours, that you cannot desire them any other way" (*Centuries*, 19).

22   Traherne, *Centuries*, 134.

Like the Jesus of *Paradise Regained*, who refuses to invest in mundane things so long as such an investment is motivated by pragmatic ends rather than by an apprehension of creation as an extension of God's will, Traherne emphasizes a sacramental relation between knower and known—one where the perceiver adapts him or herself to the object in its permanent, ontological dimension rather than in its transient or ontic aspects. Yet Traherne's critique here is not aimed at those who seek knowledge for worldly profit, but at those who seek it for its own sake, as something distinct from one's relation with God. Traherne is ultimately concerned, that is, with articulating an enigmatic mode of knowing in which the subject is involved with and in the object known: "Knowledge is that which does illuminate the Soul, enkindle Love, excite our Care, inspire the mind with Joy, inform the Will, enlarge the Heart, regulate the Passions, unite all the Powers of the Soul to their Objects."[23] Consequently, knowledge is only in the service of wisdom, which is to say in the service of Being, when it possesses an existential, rather than simply pragmatic, dimension: "Wisdom is not a meer Speculation of Excellent Things, but a Practical Habit, by Vertue of which we actually atchieve and compleat our Happiness."[24] Knowledge is only real for Traherne when it improves our comportment towards ourselves, when it affects, that is, the structure of our relation to the world: "Thoughts are the things / That us affect."[25] This existentially committed mode of apprehension is made possible, indeed is exemplified by, the sacramental relationship between the body and the soul.[26] The beginning of wisdom for Traherne, in other words, lies in the way one understands and experiences oneself as an embodied being. Traherne addresses this issue in *Select Meditations* when he outlines the various risks made possible by unbodied or existentially ungrounded thought. The following passage, for instance, appears designed, both philosophically and stylistically, to counter the Cartesian *cogito ergo sum*, arguing, as it does, that the (resurrected and mundane) body cannot, unlike thoughts, be removed from the orbit of God's Being: "To Liv in his kingdom is not by Body to be removed thither, but there to Abide in mind and Spirit. for there my Body Always is. where my Thoughts are, there am I. since therefore my Body is Always in Gods Kingdom, and cannot chuse while it is here upon Earth: it is by my thoughts alone that I can goe out of it, into I Know not what coasts of Emptiness and vanity [. . .] Heaven and earth is full of the Majesty of his Glory which to awake to the understanding, is all within."[27]

Rather than viewing the body as a discrete entity standing apart from the operations of the soul, as anatomists like William Harvey do,

---

23 Traherne, *Christian Ethics*, 39.
24 Ibid., 65.
25 Traherne, *Centuries*, 175, lines 7–8, 21–22.
26 For an account of Traherne's own political commitments see N. Matar, "Prophetic Traherne: 'A Thanksgiving and Prayer for the Nation,'" *JEGP* 82 (1982): 16–29.
27 Traherne, *Select*, 50, original punctuation and capitalization.

Traherne sees the body as ethically, if not epistemologically, de-limiting the soul's proper sphere of motion. While the idea that the body resurrects with the soul into "God's Kingdom" is an orthodox one, Traherne's emphasis is placed on the existential dimensions made possible by this ideal body-soul relation rather than on the theological issue of whether or not the body ascends with the soul. More specifically, the accent is laid on the act of *dwelling* with, abiding in, being present to the body whose loss would constitute a dissolution of self. It is the *experience* of this sacramental relation that interests Traherne, its phenomenological character rather than its purely theological status. The being of Being is thus presented here as the coincidence of body and thought: "there my Body Always is. Where my Thoughts are, there am I." In this view of things, the body is not, as Merleau-Ponty puts it, "an object for an 'I think,'" it is a grouping of lived-through meanings"—a series of potential actions and relations that participate in the disclosure of Being.[28]

While Traherne, unlike Merleau-Ponty, does not see thought as epistemologically confined by the body ("The eye's confin'd, the body's pent / [. . .] In narrow room: limbs are of small extent / But thoughts are always free"[29]), he does suggest that the body ethically and existentially focuses the proper sphere of thought. For instance, in his poem "Apostasie" from his incomplete encyclopedia *Commentaries of Heaven*, Traherne situates the soul's ability to remain "in love" with God through an investment in and on the body.[30] More specifically, and perhaps more strangely to modern sensibilities, the poem situates the soul's strength in the body as "all eye." In this view of corporeality, the body appears as an analogical reflection not of the harmonious orchestration of the cosmos but of the soul's faculties of perception. In other words, the Paracelsian body of analogical correspondence has now shifted from a set of metaphysical alignments to a series of epistemological and devotional operations. This analogical structure is thus internalized as a means for expressing the continuity between body and soul. In this poem one finds and sustains a relationship with God through an investment upon the body's various organs, orifices, and surfaces:

> The Ey is there the Mouth: it is the Ear
> The nostril and the Tongue the very Sphere

---

[28] Merleau-Ponty, *Phenomenology*, 153.

[29] Traherne, *Centuries*, 1958, 169, lines 61–63.

[30] The entire aim of the commentaries is to show "ALL THINGS [. . .] to be Objects of Happiness" (3). By taking objects of knowledge as the means of sacramental enjoyment, Traherne attributes to the encyclopedia form a religious value it is not normally thought to possess. He thus conceives of how and why one collects knowledge in a way that has not yet been theorized in Traherne studies. Indeed, the *Commentaries* pose a range of generic problems that Traherne scholars have yet to address. Thomas Traherne, *Commentaries of Heaven: The Poems*, ed. D. D. C. Chambers (Salzburg: Institut für Anglistik und Amerikanistik, Universität Salzburg, 1989).

Of strength and Power. All the faculties
Are in the Ey, all there are full of Eys.
O give me but a Strong and perfect Sense.
Of all thy Beauty Lov and Excellence
And all my Faculties being turned to Eys
I never will in Heart Tongue Hand apostasize.[31]

The threat of withdrawing from God due to a lack of faith is countered here
by a deepened investment in the body whose organs reveal God's presence
in time. Indeed, just as the body's tendency towards sin makes apostasy a
risk, so its divine origins make a renewal of faith a constant possibility.
More precisely, Traherne's account of how God's "living presence" is
inscribed upon the body enacts the Augustinian thesis that "Thou [God]
wert more inward to me, than my most inward part."[32] This intense, even
uncanny, mode of intimacy is figured in Traherne's poem, as it is in George
Wither's 1635 emblem book, with a heart that is at once an eye. In this
configuration, the internalized other, the divine mind, is the thing that it
sees. As Plotinus puts it, the divine seer "will be that which he sees, if
indeed it is possible any longer to distinguish seer and seen, and not
boldly to affirm that the two are one."[33] In Traherne's hands, this divine
mode of contemplation is given form through an unusually exaggerated
violation of the borders between distinct parts of the body. In this poem,
each part of the body emanates the same internalized presence, thereby
drawing God closer to him than his own self.

This vision of the body-as-eye discloses the extent to which
Traherne's thought operates according to an economy of sight that is
derived from a reflexive theory of optics in which, as A. Leigh Deneef
explains: "beams from the Sun pass vainly through the air unless and
until they meet an object. As the Sun's light illuminates that object—lets
it be seen and thus known for what it is—so the object itself illuminates
the light that shines upon it—lets it be seen for what it is [. . .] The Sun
is thus imagined as a metaphoric Eye."[34]

As an Eye, the body, like the Sun, allows one to perceive and be
perceived, to love and to be loved, to abide with and among other beings.
The body, like the world, speaks to the self in such a way as to disclose
the self to itself. Traherne thus imagines the body as a process of
perception as much as an object to be perceived. It is a mirror in which
one sees oneself as an image of God. Given the specular nature of this

---

31 Traherne, *Commentaries*, 66, lines 15–22.
32 St. Augustine, *The Confessions*, trans. Edward B. Pusey (New York: Collier, 1961), 44.
33 Plotinus, *The Essential Plotinus*, trans. Elmer O'Brien, S.J. (New York: New American Library, 1964), 141. For a fuller discussion of Traherne in relation to Plotinus and the mystical tradition more broadly see A. L. Clements, *The Mystical Poetry of Thomas Traherne* (Cambridge: Harvard University Press, 1969).
34 A. Leigh Deneef, *Traherne in Dialogue: Heidegger, Lacan, Derrida* (Durham: Duke University Press, 1988), 27.

epistemological economy "not to *be*, and not to *appear*, are the same thing."[35] Traherne exaggerates the porous, open nature of the sacramental body thereby shifting its analogical character from a synchronic vision of the cosmos to an epistemologically oriented view of the body's role in spiritual reflection. Despite his disavowal of "curling metaphors" in "The Author to the Critical Peruser," this vision of the body as all eye hyperbolizes its sacramental, which is to say its fundamentally metaphorical character, making embodiment an aid, rather than an obstacle, to spiritual love. Moreover it implies an analogy between the faculties of the mind and the structure of the body, a position he also articulates in *Christian Ethics*: "Powers are in the Soul, just as Limbs and Members in the Body."[36]

The body that Traherne imagines through his work is neither the classical body of idealized form, although it partakes of it, nor is it the fluid, anatomized, grotesque body that circulated through Jacobean culture, although it is mediated by this conception of the body and certainly shares its porous nature. It is, rather, a view of the body as "living hymn," an animate, incarnate, expression of God's will and love towards humans. In this sacramental context, the body functions as a kind of gerund, an action that has taken on a substantive form. For instance, in his hexameral work, *Meditations on the Six Days of Creation*, Traherne lists various parts of the body not as objects but as mediums of praise. The following passage is not only a celebration of the body as a form, it is also an exposition of how the very act of celebration itself is determined by the body. What is disclosed here, in other words, is that the body's being *is* praise:

> I Praise thee, O God, that thou hast so compassed me in on every side, as with Gates and Bars, make my Heart, and all that is within me, to resound thy Praises. My Bones, like the Beams and Posts of a House, uphold the Structure; in my Ribs like Laths make up my Walls, which are varnish'd over with a curious Skin, and united together [. . .] Cause my Flesh and my Heart to cry unto thee, the living God, and all that is within me to say, God be magnified. Make even my Bones and Sinews, my Senses and Members, cry aloud with singing.[37]

Moving from an image of the body as a prison cell to a temple, this passage tethers together various organs and structures until they emerge as elements within a polyphonic chorus—until they disclose themselves as acts of praise rather than a static structure. This vision of the body as both temple and hymn, singer and song, medium and message, constitutes an imaginative extension of the Anglican practice of public

35   Traherne, *Christian Ethics*, 37.
36   Ibid., 26.
37   Thomas Traherne, *Meditations on the Six Days of the Creation* (Los Angeles: William Andrews Clark Memorial Library, 1966), 77.

worship which, after the Restoration, included genuflection.[38] It not only makes worship a bodily activity, however, it also renders the body the basic medium of praise. This vision of the body as hymn comes as the climax to a sacred anatomy in which the hands, feet, eyes, and other parts of the body are celebrated for both their form and their function. A similar panegyric unfolds in "Thanksgivings for the Body" where Traherne celebrates the body's role in opening or more precisely "framing" the world as a series of relational sites in which one becomes the acts that one engages in, projecting oneself into the world and the future that appears through it: The volubility and liberty

> Of my hands and members.
> Fitted by thee for all operations; [. . .]
> For all the mysteries, engines, instruments,
> wherewith the world is filled, which we are *able to*
> *frame and use* to Thy glory.
> For all the trades, variety of operations, cities, temples,
> streets, bridges, mariner's compass, admirable picture,
> sculpture, writing, printing, songs and music; wherewith
> the world is beautified and adorned.
> Much more for the regent Life,
> And power of perception,
> Which rules within.
> That secret depth of fathomless consideration
> That receives the information
> Of all our senses [. . .]
> The involved mysteries
> Of our common sense;
> The inaccessible secret
> Of perceptive fancy;
> The repository and treasury
> Of things that are past;
> The presentation of things to come;
> Thy name be glorified
> For evermore.[39]

This catalog explicitly thematizes the work such sacred taxonomies perform. That is to say, it explains how the body "frames" the mysteries of the world in such a way as to disclose, unveil (alethia), or make appear the "glory" with which Traherne seeks to dwell. Such dwelling or abiding with, for Traherne, consists of an ongoing act of praise between the self, body, world, and Being. This intertwining relationship between the body, world and Being, a relation that is enacted in the accumulation of the taxonomy, aims to speak to the "fathomless depth of consideration" and

---

38 For a recent account of the politics and poetics of public worship see Ramie Targoff's *Common Prayer: The Language of Public Devotion in Early Modern England* (Chicago: University of Chicago Press, 2001).
39 Traherne, *Centuries*, 217–218, lines 112–114, 121–132, 135–143; my italics.

"perceptive fancy"—that primordial and impalpable source of sensations that is the meeting point of mind and world. Traherne's catalogs do not expose or anatomize each individual part of the body or world, but rather each part works to reveal the sacramental mode in which "intermutual" relations are lived. The taxonomy gives form to something which cannot be represented as such. In this sense, Traherne pursues something very much like Merleau-Ponty when the philosopher suggests that what he wants to do "is restore the world as a meaning of Being absolutely different from the 'represented,' that is, as the vertical Being which none of our 'representations' exhaust and which all 'reach,' the wild Being."[40] The inexhaustible accumulation of Traherne's taxonomies "reach," in Merleau-Ponty's sense, in excess of representation. Thus, unlike the proto-scientific catalogs of Baconian science which situate an object spatially, making it a static, concrete and most importantly a de-contextualized object, Traherne's catalogs emphasize the verbal as well as the substantive aspects of the body, thereby resituating the body's relationship to Being as an ongoing, ever-renewing process. The body is not an object so much as it is a thing, an entity, a living act of praise.

The difference between Traherne's cataloging technique and that of Baconian science can be further clarified by considering how Baconian taxonomy presumes the decontextualization of nature, the separation of distinct units from a total order. We see such de-contextualization, as M. M. Slaughter observes, "in the enumerative lists being compiled, in the collections of instances and specimens that underlie, for example, the Baconian methods of induction as well as the collections plant, animal and mineral specimens that abound."[41] Taxonomy as a science of order, Slaughter observes, proceeds in two ways. First of all, it analyzes wholes into units: constituents, parts, elements, variables, etc. The aim or outcome, depending on the success of the analysis, is the establishment of relations of identity and difference between things. Secondly, taxonomy brings things together in groups and arranges the groups in a hierarchal system. Wholes are decomposed in order that they can be recomposed or reconstituted in a system that expresses the totality of their relations.[42]

Traherne's lists, on the other hand, shift the focus away from the relationship between parts and wholes, from what the objects "mean," to what the relationship between beholder and beheld might consist of in sacramental terms. As Carl Selkin argues, Traherne's catalogs ask that one "become like the organ of God as described by Nicholas of Cusa, who contrasts man's limited vision with God's unlimited sight by comparing them as readers; the first reads a page linearly, each word in succession,

---

[40]   Maurice Merleau-Ponty, *The Visible and the Invisible, Followed by Working Notes*, ed. Claude Lefort, trans. Alphonso Lingis (Evanston: Northwestern University Press, 1968), 253.

[41]   M. M. Slaughter, *Universal Languages and Scientific Taxonomy in the Seventeenth Century* (Cambridge: Cambridge University Press, 1982), 42.

[42]   Ibid., 9.

but God sees the entire page at once."[43] Traherne's focus is thus on the ethos of the perceiver rather than on the objective nature of the perceived. It implies a projection of consciousness into the world but one that is ethically and existentially organized by the body and, to this extent, quite distinct from the form of disembodied vision that the Renaissance Neoplatonist Nicholas of Cusa imagined.[44]

Traherne's mode of perceiving implies an ethical as well as an epistemological relation between knower and known. For instance, further on in his hexameral work, Traherne offers up a list that lays out the obligations between oneself and other beings. These obligations are again situated in relation to and as a function of the body:

> Men being Angels by their Souls, have Bodies besides, that they may be united as the Angels are, and in another manner make use of the World, and serve each other, and glorify God. And indeed infinite are the ways wherein our Bodies become useful to us; all Obligations, Relations, Education, Pleasure, History, Trades and Service, Devotion Learning, Language, Bounty, Laws, Counsels, Temples, Altars, Universities and Colleges, Churches, Festivals, Governments, Magnificence, Liberality, &c. uniting us infinite ways together; all which Benefits arise from our Bodies: God being so marvellous in the creating of them, that he hath super-added something to his Image.[45]

The obligation or responsibility between oneself and other beings is presented here along the axis of the body as an ethical site, a sacramental space in which beings encounter each other. Moreover, this sacramental space is situated as a supplement of God, an excess that unites creation with its Creator: "he hath super-added something to his Image." The body is an excess that makes "intermutuality" possible—a divine gift that allows man and God to draw closer together. This notion of the body as something "super-added" to Being suggests that the condition of possibility for the Body is a negation of Being as spirit. In other words, when Traherne speaks of the body as something "super-added" to God's image, he is addressing the conditions of possibility for the dehiscence of Being, its differentiation into or through beings and bodies. As such, Traherne is extremely close to Jacob Boehme's idea that

---

43 Carl Selkin, "The Language of Vision: Traherne's Cataloguing Style," *ELR* 6 (1976): 92–104.

44 Merleau-Ponty calls this projection, an "intentional arc": "The life of consciousness—cognitive life, the life of desire or perceptual life—is subtended by an 'intentional arc' which projects round about us our, past, our future, our human setting, our physical, ideological and moral situation. It is this intentional arc which brings about the unity of the senses, of intelligence, of sensibility and motility" (*Phenomenology*, 136).

45 Traherne, *Meditations*, 74.

"a spirit is raw without a body, for there is no understanding without a body, and also the spirit does not last in itself without a body."[46]

The paradox of such lists is that they do not so much accumulate greater and greater modes of meaning, but rather they each display this dehiscence of Being, its differentiation into things. As Deneef puts it, Traherne's rhetoric of accumulation says the same thing over and over again and that thing is the "unsaid surplus of language itself."[47] What is important here though is the way that surplus gets articulated as correlative with the human body, an image that is "super-added" to Being. Traherne enacts how the body is the source of the "unsaid surplus" of the being of language in "The Person" where he lays a series of identities against one another as a strategy for allowing the body to emerge in its aseity, in its ontological essence. The act of emblazoning is given an apophatic twist in "The Person," as the accumulation of "reds" does not cover but unveils the body's essence. Situating the blazon form within an apophatic context, Traherne, in effect, subverts the rhetoric of mastery and domination that, as Nancy Vickers and others have demonstrated, characterizes the blazon as a rhetorical form:[48]

> Ye sacred limbs,
> A richer blazon I will lay
> On you, than first I found:
> That like celestial kings,
> Ye might with ornaments of joy
> Be always crown'd.
> A deep vermillion on a red,
> On that a scarlet I will lay,
> With gold I'll crown your head,
> Which robes of glory and delight
> I'll make you bright.
> Mistake me not, I do not mean to bring
> New robes, but to display the thing:
> Nor paint, nor clothe, nor crown, nor add a ray,
> But glorify by taking all away.[49]

---

[46]   Cited in David Walsh, *The Mysticism of Innerworldly Fulfillment: A Study of Jacob Boehme* (Gainesville: University of Florida Press, 1983), 59. Boehme's work was beginning to circulate in England during Traherne's lifetime. See Nigel Smith, *Perfection Proclaimed: Language and Literature in English Radical Religion, 1640–1660* (New York: Oxford/Clarendon Press, 1989).

[47]   Deneef, *Traherne*, 65.

[48]   See, for instance, Nancy Vickers "'The blazon of sweet beauty's best': Shakespeare's Lucrece," in *Shakespeare and the Question of Theory*, ed. Patricia Parker and Geoffrey Hartman (New York: Methuen, 1985), 54–74. For an account of Traherne's indebtedness to the *via negativa* see Rosalie Colie's *Paradoxia Epidemica: The Renaissance Tradition of Paradox* (Princeton: Princeton University Press, 1966), 145–168.

[49]   Traherne, *Centuries*, 74, lines 1–16.

As Deneef has argued, such passages disclose the fact that "it cannot be emphasized too much that Traherne is especially committed to hearing what conceals itself as unsaid in language."[50] What needs to be emphasized here though is that Traherne's mode of listening for the unsaid, for the sacramental disclosing of Being, is often achieved through a mode of estranging what is ostensibly most familiar, namely the body. For Traherne, the emblazoned body reveals not an object, but an inaccessible "glory": "Survey the skin, cut up the flesh, the veins / Unfold: the glory there remains."[51] Elsewhere he celebrates the ineffable quality of humans as "A sphere of sense, And a mine of riches, / Which when bodies are dissected fly away."[52] Despite the explicit aims of anatomization, dissection reveals, according to Traherne, what Merleau-Ponty sees as the end of phenomenological inquiry: "It is the things themselves, from the depths of their silence, that [philosophy] wishes to bring to expression."[53] And although this invisible "glory" speaks to consciousness (it is there as Merleau-Ponty would say), any attempt to bring it directly into language "makes it disappear."

In the final stanza of "The Person," Traherne poses the challenge of seeing the "truth" of the body—seeing it as the source of one's "sacred treasures." Here again, it is the comportment towards the body as the basis for sacramental perception that is at stake, a comportment that seeks to make the body an "organ of praise":

> Let verity
> Be thy delight: let me esteem
> True wealth far more than toys: [. . .]
> My tongue, my eyes,
> My cheeks, my lips, my ears, my hands, my feet, Their
> harmony is far more sweet;
> Their beauty true. And these in all my ways
> Shall themes become, and organs of Thy praise.[54]

Such passages enact a transformation of the body, a radical shift from experiencing the body as an object in isolation from the world, seeing it "alone" as he says in the second stanza, to experiencing it as the site of a divine presencing. In this sense, the body is, from its very beginning, written on and by God and the poet's task is to listen for the voice behind that writing and to repeat back to God in praise the "verity" of his own image. For this voice is concealed not only, as Sawday suggests, in the body's depths, but also on its surface, on its most "naked" outward part: "The naked things / Are most sublime, [. . .] Men's hands than angels' wings / Are truer wealth even here below."[55]

---

50   Deneef, *Traherne*, 65.
51   Traherne, *Centuries*, 76, lines 28–29.
52   Ibid., 216, lines 85–90.
53   Merleau-Ponty, *Visible*, 4.
54   Traherne, *Centuries*, 75, lines 49–51, 61–64.
55   Ibid., 76, lines 17–21.

As "The Person" makes clear, Traherne's focus on the "naked" body
as the site upon which one can renew one's perception of the mystery of
Being leads him to adopt a unique rhetorical strategy that consists of an
apparently tautological juxtaposition of identities. Traherne explains the
strategy in "The Author to the Critical Peruser" when he describes his
poetic technique as a "baser Heraldry," a form of the plain style that runs
counter to the principles of the *ut pictura poesis* tradition:

> No curling metaphors that gild the Sence,
> Nor Pictures here, nor painted Eloquence;
> No florid Streams of Superficial Gems,
> But real Crowns and Thrones and Diadems!
> That Gold on Gold should hiding shiningly
> May we be reckon'd baser Heraldy.[56]

What exactly is Traherne after here when he suggests that his version of
the sermon simplex involves situating "Gold on Gold" so as to reveal
what in "hiding shining" lies? Certainly, Deneef's Heideggerian account of
how Traherne seeks the "thingness" of the thing is relevant here.
Traherne thinks things in a particularly Heideggerian fashion: things are
and appear, things gather and summon, things set forth and set up the
specific regions of man's relatedness. This fact requires some critical
adjustment, for what in most other seventeenth-century contexts we
would applaud as the detailed imagery of concrete things is, in Traherne,
merely the surface substance, the ontic matter concealing the thing's
true phenomenological and ontological being.[57]

Yet we can be more precise than this by referring to the work of
Merleau-Ponty. By situating identities against one another, Traherne
evokes, as Merleau-Ponty does in his later work, the invisible conditions
of visibility, the way that Being is disclosed as a "shining forth"
(*rayonnement*) within and against an unperceived ground.[58] The "shining
forth" or "advent" of an object's essence, for Merleau-Ponty, is situated in
an indeterminate field that extends before and beyond the object. As our
epigraph suggests, "the visible has an invisible inner framework."[59] In
other words, perception relies on an unseen setting against which an
object appears. The ontological and phenomenological essence of a thing
"appears" or "shines forth" through the dynamic interplay between the
object itself, the "inner framework" of the background against which it is
set and the perceiver. Juxtaposing a thing against itself (Gold on Gold)
Traherne draws attention to this relational structure of apprehension. By
doing so, he estranges the object, unhinging it, as it were, from its
everydayness in order to open up a space for hieratic perception. This
estranging of the object discloses the background or dispositional field

---

56   Ibid., 2, lines 11–16.
57   Deneef, *Traherne*, 74.
58   Gary B. Madison, *The Phenomenology of Merleau-Ponty* (Athens: Ohio
      University Press, 1981), 228.
59   Merleau-Ponty, *Visible*, 1968, 215.

out of which the thing appears, thereby revealing, as he puts it in "Thoughts III" "the only Beauty that doth Shine":[60]

> Here Ornament on Ornament may still
> Be laid; Beauty on Beauty, Skill on Skill,
> Strength Still on Strength, and Life it self on Life.
> Tis Queen of all things, and its Makers Wife.
> The Best of Thoughts is yet a thing unkown,
> But when tis Perfect it is like his Own:
> Intelligible, Endless, yet a Sphere
> Substantial too: In which all Things appear.[61]

As the title of the poem suggests, this situating of identities against one another discloses the structure of thought itself. Such activity, as he puts it, "beautifie[s] even all his Dwelling place."[62]

Indeed, the most precious thought possible is, as Traherne would have it, yet "unthought"—for such a thought would disclose "pure Being." In other words, by drawing attention to the structure of perception—the need, that is, for a framework in which to perceive the being of Being—Traherne aims to think the unthought, thereby disclosing the endless or inexhaustible nature of the "perfect thought." In such passages, Traherne approaches Merleau-Ponty's view that the "transcendence of the thing compels us to say that it is plentitude only being inexhaustible, that is, by not being all actual under the look—but it promises this total actuality, since it is there."[63] Likewise, Traherne's juxtaposition of identities is an attempt to speak to the being-there of the object. This active mode of thought can reveal "the only Being that doth live. / Tis Capable of all Perfection here, / Of all his Love and Joy and Glory there. / It is the only Beauty that doth shine."[64] Addressing this process of the "shining forth" of being, Traherne aims, as we have suggested, at evoking a mode of perception that "acts not from a centre to / Its object as remote, / But present is, when it doth view, / Being with the being it doth note."[65] Merleau-Ponty addresses a similar mode of apprehension when he speaks of an "inspiration and expiration of Being, action and passion so slightly discernible that it becomes impossible to distinguish between what sees and what is seen."[66] In such cases, perception is not of an "object" as such, but of the perceiving agent's own relation with the "thing" that transforms the perceiving I. It is the interrelated field of perception that Traherne and Merleau-Ponty evoke, not the object in

---

[60] Traherne, *Centuries*, 176, line 57.
[61] Ibid., 176–177, lines 63–70.
[62] Ibid., 176, line 32.
[63] Merleau-Ponty, *Visible*, 191.
[64] Traherne, *Centuries*, 176, lines 54–57.
[65] Ibid., 50, lines 18–21.
[66] Maurice Merleau-Ponty, *The Primacy of Perception and Other Essays on Phenomenological Psychology, the Philosophy of Art, History and Politics* (Evanston: Northwestern University Press, 1964), 167.

radical isolation from the perceiver's existence. In an ideal act of perception, knower and known form what Traherne calls an "intermutual joy," a participating of beings with and through one another in a way that discloses the Being that grounds such a relation. This is intersubjectivity not as a form of self-alienation, as it is in Lacan's account of the specular relations between self and Other, but the realization of the self through genuine communication with the Other. While Traherne constantly enacts this process of intermutuality, he explicitly describes it in "Ease" when he imagines that "all may happy be, each one most blest, / Both in himself and others; all most high, / While all by each, and each by all possess'd, / Are intermutual joys, beneath the sky."[67] The chiasmic structure of this form of intermutuality ("While all by each, and each by all possess'd") more than approximates Merleau-Ponty's notion of intersubjectivity as a chiasm: "the chiasm is not only a me other exchange (the messages he receives reach me, the messages I receive reach him), it is also an exchange between me and the world, between the phenomenal body and the 'objective' body, between the perceiving and the perceived: what begins as a thing ends as a consciousness of the thing."[68] We return here to Traherne's "unthought thing," where phenomenon and essence meet. Moreover, we cross paths with the intertwining structure of perceiver and perceived that we have suggested characterizes Traherne's phenomenology, a chiasmus that is exemplified by and grounded in the continuity between body and soul.

---

[67] Traherne, *Centuries*, 66, lines 25–29.
[68] Merleau-Ponty, *Visible*, 1968, 215. Helen A. Fielding's defense of Merleau-Ponty's notion of intersubjectivity against Lacan's critique is relevant here. According to Fielding, "Lacan would assert that we can never know what the other is thinking; such thoughts would always be our own projections, and sight lends itself to these misconceptions. For Merleau-Ponty, however, vision helps to confirm for us that we live in the same world" (191). Not only sight, but the sentient nature of our being enables, for Merleau-Ponty, a relation with the other that Lacan precludes: "Because as corporeal beings our bodies are both sensed and sentient, visible and invisible, our perceptions arise from the midst of our relations and not from the periphery as is suggested by the image of Lacan's voyeur. Merleau-Ponty thus adds another dimension to our understanding of intersubjectivity and that is the dimension of our intercorporeal relations" (Fielding, 191). As the following argument suggests, Traherne not only shares Merleau-Ponty's sense of the chiasmic structure of intersubjectivity, but he also places the body at the axis of the self's relation with others. Helen A. Fielding, "Envisioning the Other: Lacan and Merleau-Ponty on Intersubjectivity," in *Merleau-Ponty, Interiority and Exteriority, Psychic Life and the World*, ed. Dorothea Olkowski and James Morley (New York: State University of New York Press, 1999), 185–200. Lacan is primarily concerned with the notion of the disembodied gaze, the way the subject perceives itself as gazed upon in all directions, that Merleau-Ponty's account of embodied vision occasions. This leads Lacan away from Merleau-Ponty's view of the chiasmic nature of self-other relation. For Lacan's account of the gaze of the Other see *The Four Fundamental Concepts of Psychoanalysis*, ed. Jacques-Alain Miller, trans. Alan Sheridan (New York: Penguin, 1994), 67–105.

Traherne imagines the origins of this mind/body relation in "The Salutation." The estranging of "things" through tautological juxtaposition (placing for instance "a deep vermillion on a red") recreates the sense of strangeness that he associates with the earliest moments of his consciousness:

> A stranger here
> Strange things doth meet, strange glories see;
> Strange treasures lodg'd in this fair world appear;
> Strange all, and new to me.
> But that they mine should be, who nothing was,
> That strangest is of all, yet brought to pass.[69]

For Traherne, the first act of consciousness consists of a greeting and then a celebration of the body, a gathering together of its various joints into a single unified thing, a gestalt: "These little limbs, / These eyes and hands which here I find, / These rosy cheeks wherewith my life begins, / Where have ye been?"[70] This movement from bodily fragments to corporeal integrity informs the unifying structure of consciousness itself as the mind moves outward gathering first itself, then the world and finally the cosmos as a whole:

> I that so long
> Was nothing from eternity,
> Did little think such joys as ear or tongue,
> To celebrate or see:
> Such sounds to hear, such hands to feel, such feet,
> Beneath the skies, on such a ground to meet [. . .]
>
> From dust I rise,
> And out of nothing now awake,
> These brighter regions which salute mine eyes,
> A gift from God I take.
> The earth, the seas, the light, the day, the skies,
> The sun and stars are mine; if those I prize.[71]

In Traherne's account, the awareness of being-in-the-world emerges through an appropriation of the body as an emergent unity: "When silent I, / So many thousand thousand years, Beneath the dust did in a chaos lie, / How could I smiles or tears, Or lips or hands or eyes or ears perceive? / Welcome, ye treasures which I now receive."[72] He returns to this scene in "The Preparative": "My body being dead, my limbs unkown: / before I skill'd to prize / Those living stars mine eyes, / Before my tongue or cheeks were to me shown, / Before I knew my hands were

---

69   Traherne, *Centuries*, 6, lines 37–42.
70   Ibid., 4, lines 1–3.
71   Ibid., 4–6, lines 13–18, 25–30.
72   Ibid., 4, lines 7–12.

mine, / Or that my sinews did my members join."[73] Unlike Milton's
Adam, who, upon his creation, gazes first at the upturned sky and then
himself "Limb by Limb surveyed"[74] Traherne "receives" his body in order
to ground his sense of self. This process of "receiving" is both passive and
active. While it entails an appropriation of the body, this appropriation is
conditioned by the body's disclosing itself to him: "before my tongue or
cheeks were to me shown." The origins of the Trahernian I are thus more
similar to Freud's narrative than Milton's.[75] Like Freud's, Traherne's I
appears something like an internal screen onto which the illuminated
and projected image of the body's outer surface are directed. It is the site
for the gathering together and unification of otherwise disparate and
scattered sensations provided by the various sense organs, in all their
difference spaces and registers.[76]

In both Freud and Traherne, the self emerges through a narcissistic
investment onto the surface of the body. The self in this developmental
narrative is not simply an effect of the body, but is a projection or outline
of bodily forms. Thus when Traherne estranges the body, he is
estranging the very origins of the self, remaking identity in its most
primordial dimension while reconstructing the conditions of thought
itself.

In "Thanksgiving for the Body" Traherne seeks to recreate the sense
of holy strangeness that he describes in "The Salutation" through a set of
elaborate rhetorical strategies that again address how the body calls for a
certain kind of ethical disposition. More precisely, Traherne's elaborate
taxonomies in this poem intertwine self and world, body and soul, visible
and invisible as a means for evoking the interrelatedness of
consciousness and world. In this respect, the text enacts Traherne's anti-
Cartesian principle, "for there my Body Always is. Where my Thoughts
are, there am I." Traherne here approaches Jacob Boehme's idea that
spirit requires bodily form in order to reveal itself fully to itself: "there
must be a contraction [of spirit into body] and a closing in from which

73   Ibid., 20, lines 1–6.
74   John Milton, *Complete Poems and Major Prose*, ed. Merritt Y. Hughes (New
     York: Macmillan, 1957), 369, line 267.
75   Freud, as Merleau-Ponty suggests, is part of the philosophical tradition that
     runs from Hegel to Heidegger. Moreover, Merleau-Ponty's interest in Gestalt
     psychology is mediated by Freudian psychoanalysis. For a recent account of
     the relationship between Freud and Merleau-Ponty see Richard Boothby's
     Freud as Philosopher: Metapsychology after Lacan (New York and London:
     Routledge, 2001), 54–61.
76   Elizabeth Grosz, *Volatile Bodies: Toward a Corporeal Feminism* (Bloomington:
     Indiana University Press, 1994), 37. See also Freud's "The Ego and the Id":
     "The ego is first and foremost a bodily ego; it is not merely a surface entity,
     but is itself the projection of a surface. [. . .] The ego is ultimately derived
     from bodily sensations, chiefly from those springing from the surface of the
     body" ("Ego and Id," 364). Sigmund Freud, "The Ego and the Id," in *On
     Metapsychology: The Theory of Psychoanalysis*, trans. James Strachey
     (Penguin: New York, 1984), 350–404.

the revelation may shine."[77] The body's central place in Traherne's account of the revelation of Being is established in the longest and perhaps most important catalog in the poem:

> Even for our earthly bodies, hast Thou created all things.
> Visible.
> All things { Material.
> Sensible.
> Animals,
> Vegetables,
> Minerals,
> Bodies Celestial,
> Bodies terrestrial,
> The four elements,
> Volatile spirits,
> Trees, herbs, and flowers,
> The influences of Heaven,
> Clouds, vapours, wind,
> Dew, rain, hail, and snow,
> Light and darkness, night and day,
> The seasons of the year.
> Springs, rivers, fountains, oceans,
> Gold, silver, and precious stones.
> Corn, wine, and oil,
> The sun, moon, and stars,
> Cities, nations, kingdoms.
> And the bodies of men, the greatest treasures of all,
> For each other.[78]

Traherne's taxonomy does not constitute a dissection of creation but functions as a kind of moving image of it. This is not the Great Chain of Being laid out in taxonomic form, but rather it is a symbol of an embodied and highly permeable cosmos that is at once an image of an embodied being: microcosm and macrocosm thus do not disappear entirely but shift from a metaphysical to an epistemological register. More precisely, Traherne's focus on the embodied nature of creation is encapsulated here in the way the catalog begins with an emphasis on the "visible" and ends with a celebration of the "bodies of men." Beginning and ending with the "visible" Traherne enacts the process by which "the invisible" "shines forth" from within the visible world. The taxonomy thus functions as an expanding metaphor, rather than as a set of discrete units separated from the unity of the whole—enacting the motion and interrelations between parts.

The rhetorical efficacy of the catalog form is most discernible in the way that it encourages not only a God-like perception of everything at

---

[77]   Cited in Walsh, *Mysticism*, 58.
[78]   Traherne, *Centuries*, 220–221, lines 240–263.

once, but more importantly it suggests that there is always more, always an abundance that representation fails to account for but which can nonetheless be felt like the invisible insistence that Traherne speaks of at the beginning of the *Centuries of Meditations* when he asks: "There are invisible ways of conveyance, by which some great thing doth touch our souls, and by which we tend to it. Do you not feel yourself drawn with the expectation and desire of some great thing?"[79] The taxonomic structure is designed to inspire desire for God rather than satiate it. Stanley Stewart speaks to this aspect of Traherne's mode of representation in his discussion of *Christian Ethics* when he argues that Traherne's rhetorical and argumentative structure, particularly as it pertains to his principle of inclusion, is an affront to logical boundaries: "He exceeds the limits [of his own argument] precisely because they are 'limited and bounded.'"[80] Writing two years before the publication of Stanley Fish's *Self-Consuming Artifacts*, Stewart articulates something very much like Fish's idea that seventeenth-century texts violate their own rhetorical structure as a means for undermining the limitations that temporality places on representation.[81] With Traherne however, it is not textual self-consumption that is at issue, but something less epistemologically skeptical and more phenomenologically suggestive. For while Stewart argues that "Traherne piles up words and phrases, taking pains to proliferate synonyms as if the mere weight of the word itself—the word intensified and isolated by the junctures produced in series and periodic sentences—were enough to summon forth the sense of the universe in small part,"[82] we are also left with the sense that words can evoke or inspire the expectation for "some Great thing," can open a space or clearing for an encounter with Being without representing it as such. In this sense, the meaning of Traherne's catalogs is found in their effect, in their capacity to lead a reader both backwards and forwards to the Thing which inspired them: "I have found, that things unknown have a secret influence on the soul: and like the centre of the earth unseen, violently attract it."[83]

The expansive, supplementing movement of a catalog is an index of the very subjectivity that Traherne is at pains to articulate, a subjectivity whose desire for God is as inexhaustible as God himself: "Till I what lies / In time's beginning find: / Must I till then forever burn?"[84] For Traherne, the issue is not about resolving this impossible desire, but realizing that it is itself the means by which one has access to the divine. For Traherne the effort is to constantly renew one's sense of wonder before Being: "So will he have us be a perpetual Conflux and Activity of thought to maintain all Things and in our selves to uphold our

79   Ibid., 3.
80   Stewart, *Expanded*, 1970, 68.
81   Stanley Fish, *Self-Consuming Artifacts: The Experience of Seventeenth Century Literature* (Pittsburgh: Duquesne University Press, 1972).
82   Stewart, *Expanded*, 71.
83   Traherne, *Centuries*, 2.
84   Traherne, *Centuries*, 145, lines 8–10.

Treasures: for they are no longer ours then they are within us."[85] The union of thought and being does not result in a cessation of desire "for some great thing," but in an apprehension that the desire itself is a function of being an (embodied) image of God. If phenomenology is an attempt to constantly renew the questioning of being, and if this questioning is, in part, a function of how "the use a man is to make of his body is transcendent in relation to that body as a mere biological entity,"[86] then Traherne's religious thought marks one of the first moments in this ongoing critique of Cartesian dualism.

---

[85]   Traherne, *Select*, 1997, 51.
[86]   Merleau-Ponty, *Phenomenology*, 1962, 189.

Bunyan's Book of Ruth: The Typological Structure of the Seventeenth-Century Debate on Women in the Church

Michael Austin

> Intreat me not to leave thee, or return:
> For where thou goest, I'll go, where thou sojourn,
> I'll sojourn also. And what people's thine,
> And who thy God, the same shall both be mine.
> Where thou shalt die, there will I die likewise,
> And I'll be buried where thy body lies.
> The Lord do so to me, and more, if I
> Do leave thee, or forsake thee till I die.
>
> Scriptural Poems, "Ruth," attributed to John Bunyan

Feminist interpretations of the second part of John Bunyan's *Pilgrim's Progress*—one of the most sustained treatments of a woman's spiritual journey to come out of the seventeenth century—generally flow between two critical orthodoxies. The first and most common of these holds that, while Bunyan necessarily places Christiana's story within the seventeenth century's definition of women as the weaker vessel, the work itself presents a gentler, more feminine Bunyan who has taken pains to ensure that, in Kathleen Swaim's words, "the overall narration occurs within an atmosphere of family, general charity, specific mercies, and social bonding."[1] The

---

[1] Kathleen Swaim, *Pilgrim's Progress, Puritan Progress* (Urbana: University of Illinois Press, 1993), 161.

second standard interpretation of the work has been recently advanced by
N. H. Keeble, who claims that the second part of *Pilgrim's Progress* initially
promises "what we would recognize as feminist sympathies," but that the
subsequent portrayal of Christiana and Mercy as weak and spiritually
immature does not live up to this promise. "Bunyan . . . welcomes women
on pilgrimage," Keeble concludes, "but he welcomes them not as fellow
wayfarers . . . but as persons in need of especially solicitous ministerial care
and guidance."[2] Margaret Olofson Thickstun presents an even stronger
version of this argument, claiming that "Bunyan's firm belief in the social
and spiritual inferiority of women requires that he restrict the heroic activity
available to Christiana until her story can no longer sustain his attention."[3]

My primary argument in this article will be that both the custodial and
the communitarian rhetoric of *The Pilgrim's Progress, Part II* form what was,
for Bunyan, part of a coherent position on the status of women in the
Church. I will further argue that this position cannot be reduced either to
the critical orthodoxies that now dominate discussions of the work, or, for
that matter, to any of the standard positions about women's spirituality
that were common among Bunyan's contemporaries. *The Pilgrim's Progress,
Part II* should be considered, not merely as a sequel to its more famous
predecessor, but as Bunyan's major entry in a much larger rhetorical
project: the seventeenth-century debate between mainstream religions and
radical dissenters, principally Quakers, about proper ecclesiastical roles for
women—a debate that Bunyan officially entered a year before publishing his
famous sequel with a densely worded—and little read—theological tract
entitled "A Case of Conscience Resolved."

The occasion for "A Case of Conscience Resolved" was a request by
some of the female members of Bunyan's Bedford congregation— apparently
led by a man known only as "Mr. K."—to be allowed to hold separate
woman's meetings.[4] This close proximity between the two of Bunyan's sixty
or so published writings that most directly deal with women and women's
issues has always suggested a connection, as has Bunyan's closing promise
in the tract that "there are some other things, concerning Women, touching
which, when I have an Opportunity, I may also give my judgment."[5] That at

2   N. H. Keeble, "'Here is Her Glory, even to be under Him': The Feminine in the
     Thought and Work of John Bunyan," in *Bunyan and His England, 1628–1688*,
     ed. Anne Laurence, W. R. Owens, and Stuart Sim (London: Hambledon Press,
     1990), 147.
3   Margaret Olofson Thickstun, *Fictions of the Feminine: Puritan Doctrine and the
     Representation of Women* (Ithaca: Cornell University Press, 1988), 88.
4   The most likely identity of "Mr. K." is the London Baptist preacher, William
     Kiffin, in response to whom Bunyan had written the pamphlet *Differences in
     Judgment About Water Baptism, No Bar to Communion* (1673). Bunyan was
     apparently criticized for using Kiffin's name in *Differences in Judgement About
     Water Baptism* and so, in another pamphlet, *Peaceable Principles and True*
     (1674), he referred to him simply as "Mr. K." See T. L. Underwood's introduction
     to *The Miscellaneous Works of John Bunyan*, 4:xxx-xxxiii; xliii.
5   John Bunyan, "A Case of Conscience Resolved," in *The Miscellaneous Works of
     John Bunyan*, general ed. Roger Sharrock (Oxford: Clarendon Press, 1976–1989),
     vol. 4.

least some of these other things concerning women are contained in Part II of *The Pilgrim's Progress* has never been much in doubt. Swaim, noting the close correspondence between the dates of the two works, acknowledges that "it is difficult not to read in the allegory an encoded version of the controversy that arose in the Bedford Meeting when church women . . . sought to justify their practice of separate women's prayer meetings."[6]

Bunyan's primary objection to women's meetings is that they are unscriptural. Mr. K., he insists, has "stretched and strained the Holy Word out of place . . . to shore up his found conceits." "In all the Scripture," he insists, he "find[s] not that the Women of the Churches of Christ, did use to separate themselves from their Bretheren, and as so separate, performe Worship together among themselves or in that their Congregation." But Bunyan does not stop at a simple argument for the lack of scriptural precedent for women's meetings. He presents women as weak and frail creatures who cannot, of their own accord, "orderly manage that Worship to God" because they "are not builded to manage such Worship." For the author of *Grace Abounding to the Chief of Sinners*, the possibility of a massive theological misstep is always very real, and the act of leading people in worship is fraught with peril. "If the weightiness of this Worship be, as indeed it is, so great, that the Strongest, and best able to perform it, do usually come off with . . . repentance for their shortness," he asks pointedly, "What will they do who are much weaker?"[7]

Like the proper interpretation of *The Pilgrim's Progress, Part II* itself, the nature of its relationship to "A Case of Conscience Resolved" is not a matter of consensus. Christopher Hill sees *The Pilgrim's Progress, Part II* as an attempt by Bunyan to "make some amends" to the women of his congregation for his harsh treatment of them in the pamphlet.[8] Swaim, too, sees the famous sequel as a mitigation of the harsh rhetoric that Bunyan occasionally uses towards women in "A Case of Conscience Resolved" and as a fulfillment of his promise to "remedy women's despair and redefine their position in the church."[9] Others, though, see the existence of the earlier tract as proof that the feminist tendencies of *The Pilgrim's Progress, Part II* have been greatly exaggerated. Thickstun, for example, invokes Bunyan's rhetoric in "A Case of Conscience Resolved" to support her argument that "Bunyan insists throughout *The Pilgrim's Progress* on the dangers for women of social and spiritual independence."[10]

Like *The Pilgrim's Progress, Part II*, "A Case of Conscience Resolved" is part of a much larger debate that Bunyan and other dissenting Protestants were conducting over the role of women in the Church. To a great extent, this was a debate over the proper biblical symbols to attach to the female worshipper. Bunyan wrote during precisely that period of English history in which, as Paul Korshin tells us, Protestants took the symbolic discourse of

6   Swaim, *Pilgrim*, 227–228.
7   Bunyan, *Case of Conscience*, 300, 301, 306, 307.
8   Ibid., 300.
9   Swaim, *Pilgrim*, 229.
10 Thickstun, *Fictions*, 95.

typology, which had previously been used as a way of interpreting the New Testament in light of the Old and began "regarding their own history as an antitype of Old Testament history or typological events."[11] The standard and all but ubiquitous typological understanding of women in seventeenth-century worship was constrained by two biblical texts. The first was Paul's injunction in the first Letter to the Corinthians: "Let your women keep silent in the churches: for it is not permitted unto them to speak; but they are commanded to be under obedience, as also saith the law. And if they will learn anything let them ask their husbands at home: for it is a shame for women to speak in the Church."[12] The second crucial text, which almost always accompanied the first, constituted what was perceived to be the typological rationale for Paul's injunction: the narrative of Eve's subordinate creation from Adam's rib in Genesis 2:22. "This passage," Charlotte Otten writes, "was regarded as definitive: the male was created first and hence was superior to the female; the female was created second, out of the body of the male, and hence was inferior to the male. The ancillary but silent position of the female was supported first by the Pauline prohibition and second and perhaps more fundamentally, by the inferior metaphysical position of the female."[13]

Owing perhaps equally to the Book of Genesis and *Paradise Lost*, the figure of Eve was doubtlessly the most common type for women in the mid-to-late seventeenth century, and would remain so for much longer. The Eve type fits very nicely into most seventeenth-century conceptions of women's roles: wife, mother, helpmate, seductress, and spiritual inferior. Not only was Eve created first, she was tempted first and, for most contemporaries, including Milton, bore primary responsibility for the Fall. If given spiritual responsibility, all women would prove as weak and incompetent as Eve. This Eve type comes into play significantly in Bunyan's "A Case of Conscience Resolved," but it is even more important to his posthumously published *Exposition of the First Ten Chapters of Genesis*, in which he writes,

> I reckon a great fault in the woman [Eve], an usurpation, to undertake so mighty an adversary, when she was not the principal that was concerned therein; nay, when her husband who was more able than she, was at hand, to whom also the law was given as chief. But for this act, I think it is, that they are now commanded silence, and also commanded to learn of their husbands (1 Cor xiv. :34, 35. 1 Tim ii. 9-15.) A command that is necessary enough for that simple and weak sex: Though they see it was by them that sin came into the world, yet how hardly are some of them to this day dissuaded from attempting unwarrantably

11   Paul J. Korshin, *Typology in England, 1650–1820.* (Princeton: Princeton University Press, 1982), 31.
12   1 Cor. 14:34–45.
13   Charlotte F. Otten. *English Women's Voices, 1540–1700.* (Miami: Florida International University Press, 1992), 353–354.

to meddle with potent enemies, about the great and
weighty matters that concern eternity.[14]

This harsh assessment of Eve's crime and its implications for all women
was fairly standard faire across the spectrum of seventeenth-century
thought. However, in the unique, upside-down world created by the English
revolution, another major female type flashed briefly across the English
stage—just long enough for Bunyan to be aware of its presence. Beginning
in the 1640s, women who were described as "prophetess" began preaching,
exhorting, and publishing their revelations throughout the nation. In the
years that followed, between 1640 and 1670, works that could be described
as "prophetic discourse" would account for more publications by women
than any other category of text.[15] Phyllis Mack writes that the seventeenth
century's development—however marginal—of the social category of
prophetess gave women of that century "virtually the only taste of public
authority they would ever know." And with increased authority came an
increased visibility that scholars are just now beginning to appreciate. Some
women, Mack continues, "used that authority to write and publish their
own works, to organize separate women's meetings, or to challenge the
greater authority of the male leaders."[16]

During the Civil War and Interregnum, the religious phenomenon of
the female prophet spread across the entire spectrum of Protestant dissent;
from 1640 to 1660, women played significant roles in a collection of sects
and denominations that included Baptists, Ranters, Familists, Fifth
Monarchists, Brownists, and a great number of unaffiliated independent
congregations.[17] With the Restoration of the monarchy, however, most of
these groups either ran out of steam or were persecuted out of existence. By
1680, George Fox's Quakers were the only one of the radical fringe groups
that had managed to evolve the theological and ideological moderation
necessary to survive the return of the established order. Many of the women
who first experienced a religious voice in radical dissenting sects during the
Civil War turned to the Quakers after the Restoration as one of the only
remaining religious sites where such a voice was not only allowed, but
encouraged on the grounds that spiritual authority derived from a non-
gendered "inner light." As a result, Quaker prophetesses "could criticize

---

[14] John Bunyan, "An Exposition on the First Ten Chapters of Genesis, and Part of
the Eleventh," in *The Complete Works of John Bunyan*, ed. Henry Stebbing (New
York: Johnson Reprint, 1970), 3:382.
[15] Patricia Crawford, "Women's Published Writings 1600–1700," in *Women in
English Society, 1500–1800*, ed. Mary Prior (London: Methuen, 1985), 223.
[16] Phyllis Mack, *Visionary Women* (Berkeley: University of California Press, 1992), 5.
[17] For general overviews of the genre of women's prophecy in the seventeenth
century, see Dorothy P. Ludlow's "Shaking Patriarchy's Foundations: Sectarian
Women in England, 1641–1700"; Thomas Keith's "Women and the Civil War
Sects"; and Phyllis Mack's "Women as Prophets during the English Civil War,"
Feminist Studies 8 (1982): 19–45. For a chart of specific known prophetesses and
their religious affiliation, see Mack's *Visionary Women*, 413–414.

men's views because the equality of Spirit in women and men gave equal validity to their interpretations of God's will."[18]

For the Quakers, the typological defense of women's prophecy rested on the undeniable existence of three women in the Old Testament who were referred to as "prophetesses": Huldah, Miriam, and, most important of all, Deborah, the female prophet and military leader who wielded significant political and ecclesiastical power during the reign of the Judges.[19] Taken as a single narrative entity, the prophetess narratives of the Old Testament proved to be a powerful rhetorical tool for Quaker controversialists. The first Quaker publication to invoke one of these prophetess narratives in support of women's right to speak is Richard Farnworth's 1654 tract, *A Woman Forbidden to Speak in the Church*. In this pamphlet, Farnworth focuses primarily on the story of Deborah and argues that her calling as a prophetess, and her position as a judge in Israel, proves conclusively that there was no absolute prohibition in the Bible against a woman acting in the name of God or exercising either ecclesiastical or civil power. God alone is authorized to speak in Church, he argues, and the narrative of Deborah shows a woman who "had the manifestation of the Spirit of God ruling in her, by which she, or the Lord in her, did administer justice to the Israelites, which were the Church and People of God."[20]

A year later, in 1655, a Quaker woman named Anne Audland published a tract entitled *The Saint's Testimony* in which she expanded this argument to include all five of the prophetess narratives in the Old Testament:

> So was there women guided by the Spirit of the Lord, that were the Lord's Prophetesses, as wel as there were men that were his Prophets; and the Lord spoke his word by his own Spirit, in and through the one as wel as the other: *Miriam, Arons* Sister, was a Prophetess, and spake forth the praise of God, in that dispensation and administration. . . . And Deborah a Prophetess by the Spirit of the Lord which taught her to prophecie, she therewith judged Israel, and were a Minister of Justice amongst the Lord's people in her dayes, and in that

---

[18] Elaine Hobby, *Virtue of Necessity: English Women's Writing 1646–1688* (London: Virago Press, 1988), 36–37.

[19] The term "prophetess" actually occurs six times in the King James Version of the Old Testament: once to describe Miriam (Ex 15:20), once to describe Deborah (Jgs 4:4), twice in reference to Huldah (2 Kgs 22:14; 2 Chr 34:22), once to refer to Nodiah (Neh 6:14), and once in relation to the otherwise-unnamed wife of Isaiah (Is 8:3). The term also occurs twice in the New Testament: In a positive reference to a faithful woman named Anna who testified of the infant Jesus (Lk 2:36) and in a mocking condemnation of the Old Testament figure of Jezebel, "which calleth herself a prophetess, to teach and seduce my servants to commit fornication, and to eat things sacrificed to idols" (Rv 2:20).

[20] Richard Farnsworth, *A Woman Forbidden to Speak in the Church, The Grounds Examined, the Mystery Opened, the Truth Cleared, and the Ignorance both of Priests and People Discovered* (London, 1654), 3.

dispensation, insomuch that the Children of Israel came up to her for judgement, and did not dispute the counsell of the Lords spirit in a woman preacher, or a *Judge* in *Israel*, and a *Prophetess* of the Lord. . . . And in the days of *Josiah*, King in *Israel*, there was one *Huldah* a *Prophetess*, that lived in *Jerusalem*, a *woman Preacher*, or one, who by the Spirit of the Lord, declared and spoke to the people the word of the Lord, and to her the Priest and people went to enquire and hear the word of the Lord, according also to the King's command. . . . Besides, several other *Prophetesses* as well as *Prophets*, there was in the time of old among the Lords people, as the *Prophetess* in *Isajah's* time, and in *Nehemiah's* time.[21]

This tract by Audland set the tone for nearly all subsequent Quaker defenses of a woman's right to speak. George Fox opens *Concerning Sons and Daughters* with the statement, "*Miriam* was a Prophetess the sister of *Aron*, and *Moses* a Magistrate, and *Aron* the Priest did not judge this Prophetess nor other Women for they came forth praysing God together." He continues his introductory paragraph by noting that "*Helkiah* the Priest and others, went unto *Huldah* the prophetess . . . and she dwelt in Hierusalem in the house of Doctrine, and they communed with her." And like Audland, he makes a brief allusion to the prophetess in Isaiah 8 before moving on to the all-important narrative of Deborah and using it to draw a conclusion for his contemporaries:

Deborah a Prophetess the wife of Lapidoth judged Israel, and she dwelt under a Palm-tree, and the Children of Israel came up to her for Judgement and she prophesied . . . from the Lord, here again you may see a woman Prophetess and Teacher, to whom all Israel was to give Eare. . . . Therfore ye Children of darkness, limit not the holy one, despise not Prophecying nor the Prophetesses, who professes yourselves to be Christians.[22]

Never a fan of the Quakers, Bunyan uses "A Case of Conscience Resolved" as much to reject their claims to female prophecy as he does to answer the immediate question facing his congregation.[23] Bunyan

[21] Anne Audland, *The Saint's Testimony Finishing through Sufferings* (London, 1655), 15–16.
[22] George Fox, *Concerning the Sons and Daughters, and Prophetesses Speaking and Prophecying, in the Law and in the Gospel* (London, 1661), 1–2.
[23] Bunyan feuded with the Quakers for most of his public life. His first two published works were part of a debate with the Quaker writer William Burroughs, and negative references to Quakers appear in many of his published works, including, most famously, the character of Ignorance in the first part of *The Pilgrim's Progress*. For overviews of the relationship between Bunyan and the Quakers see Christopher Hill's "Quakers and Ranters," in *A Tinker and Poor Man: John Bunyan and His Church, 1628–1688* (New York: W. W. Norton), 75–84,

addresses the typological argument of the biblical prophetess head on, stating simply that "*Miriam* was a *Prophetess*, and I suppose that none of our Women will pretend to be such" (310). However, Bunyan knew very well that there were women in England—specifically Quaker women—who did "pretend" to be prophetesses cut from the same cloth as Miriam, and he almost certainly understood the need to confront their interpretation of biblical narrative with one of his own. And though Bunyan does still acknowledge that some extraordinary women were granted the title of prophetess, and were allowed to speak in public (but not in church), he constructs his version of the biblical narrative around the supposed inferiority of these prophetesses to their male counterparts. In Bunyan's narrative, then, their stories become a support for, rather than a challenge to, his prohibition of women speaking in church:

> In what I have said about Womens Meetings; I have not at all concerned myself about those Women, that have been Extraordinary ones, such as Miriam, Deborah, Huldah, Anna, or the rest. . . . for they might Teach, Prophecy, and had power to call the People together to do so.
> Though this I must say concerning them, they ought to (and did, notwithstanding so high a calling, still) bear about with them the badge of their inferiority to them that were Prophets indeed. And hence 'tis said, under pain of being guilty of disorder, that if they prayed in the Church, or Prophesied there, with their head uncovered, then they dishonoured their Head.[24]

As this argument continues, the prophetess becomes the test case for a woman's ecclesiastical authority. Bunyan briefly relates the narrative of Exodus 12, when Miriam spoke against Moses and was punished by God with leprosy. He insists that this story proves that even those women called "prophetesses" were not empowered to speak against men, or even to speak about spiritual things when men were present. To conclude the argument, Bunyan invokes the narrative of Miriam's punishment, which the Quakers had presented as proof of a woman's right to speak, as a warning to women who might want to defy male authority and organize their own meetings: "remember what God did to *Miriam* and be afraid."[25]

Though "A Case of Conscience Resolved" rejects any typological association between contemporary women and biblical prophetesses, it also rejects the harshest implications of the typological associations between women and Eve. In his *Epistle Dedicatory*, Bunyan carefully parses his words to avoid equating spiritual weakness with essential inferiority. He tells the women that they "stand fixed forever by Faith upon the same foundation with us" and that "the Lord doth put no difference betwixt Male

---

and Richard Hardin's "Bunyan, Ignorance, and the Quakers," *Studies in Philology* 69 (1972): 493–508.
[24] Bunyan, *Case of Conscience*, 326.
[25] Ibid., 329.

and Female, as to the communications of his saving graces."[26] In *The Pilgrim's Progress, Part II*, there is no association whatsoever between Christiana and Mercy—the two principal heroines of the work—and the biblical figure of Eve. In fact, Eve's name appears only twice in the entire text, in an innocuous passage in which Christiana is shown a museum of biblical relics, including Eve's apple and Jacob's ladder. This fact alone would be remarkable in any biblical allegory involving women written in the seventeenth or any other century.

Bunyan does, though, invoke two other biblical women throughout the narrative: Ruth and Naomi. The association is made explicit in the House of the Interpreter, who refers to Mercy as "Ruth":

> Thy setting out is good, for thou hast given credit to the truth. Thou art a Ruth, who did for the love that she bore to Naomi, and to the Lord her God, leave her father and mother, and the land of her nativity to come out and go with a people that she knew not heretofore. The Lord recompense thy work, and a full reward be given thee of the Lord God of Israel, under whose wings thou art come to trust.[27]

The Book of Ruth, however, is more than just one more biblical allusion in a work made up of little else. It is the overall typological underpinning of the entire work, just as the Book of Exodus, with its story of a chosen people fleeing spiritual slavery and wandering through the wilderness en route to the Promised Land is the typological underpinning of Part I. In many ways, Christiana herself follows in Ruth's footsteps: she marries one of the Chosen People, her husband dies, and, years later, she, too, sets out to become one of the elect and is graciously received and supported by those who knew her husband. In other particulars, Mercy is the Ruth antitype and Christiana's journey follows that of Naomi: like Naomi, Christiana assumes responsibility for a daughter figure (who literally becomes a daughter-in-law like Ruth during the course of the narrative); like Naomi, she journeys away from an idolatrous city with her family in tow, finds ways to support that family, and arranges a marriage that ensures her family's continued position among the elect.

For my purposes, though, the most important similarities are those that Christiana shares with both Ruth and Naomi: both biblical women must, for their own salvation, arrange to be protected by a man, Boaz, who becomes Ruth's husband and who allows Naomi to reconstitute the lineage that gives her legitimacy. However, neither Ruth nor Naomi can survive through passive submission to this authority; rather, they must actively and diligently seek it. In this, the heroines of *The Pilgrim's Progress, Part II* represent Ruth negatively as well as positively. Though Mercy and Christiana are given a great deal of agency on their journey, the narrative

26   Ibid., 295.
27   John Bunyan, *The Pilgrim's Progress*, ed. Roger Sharrock (New York: Penguin, 1987), 267.

makes it clear that they are expected to use that agency to recognize their spiritual weakness as women and actively seek a male authority to submit to. On two occasions, Christiana comes very close to losing her salvation, not because she is overcome by obstacles on the path, but because she fails to anticipate her weakness and request protection. The first occurs soon after she and Mercy cross to the other side of the gate. As they are traveling on the path, two men referred to as the "ill-favoured ones" approach and threaten rape. When they are rescued by the Reliever, who comes from the House of the Interpreter, he does not comfort or console them for the ordeal they have just gone through; rather, he chastises them for failing to ask for a guardian when they first crossed through the gate: "I marvelled much when you was entertained at the Gate above, being ye knew that ye were but weak women, that you petitioned not the Lord there for a conductor. Then might you have avoided these troubles, and dangers, for he would have granted you one."[28] Christiana initially protests that she had no way of knowing about the danger so close to the manor and that, if the Lord of the House knew that there was peril, he could have sent a guardian without a specific request. The Reliever answers, however, that it was necessary for the women to "bewai[l] that oversight . . . in not asking for one" so that they would not make the same mistake again. Like Ruth and Naomi, Mercy and Christiana must recognize their weaknesses and work actively and diligently to secure a male interlocutor.

An almost identical scene occurs a few pages later, as if to demonstrate that Christiana and Mercy failed to learn their lesson the first time. As Christiana's party leaves the House of the Interpreter, their assigned guardian, Mr. Great-heart, conducts them to the House Beautiful and fights all of their battles along the way. Once they arrive at the house, Great-heart announces his intention to leave them alone, not because the Lord wants them to fight their battles alone, but because Christiana fails once again to anticipate their need and request his continued presence. When the women and children beg Great-heart to stay with them, he answers, "I am at my Lord's commandment. If he shall allot me to be your guide quite through, I will willingly wait upon you; but here you failed at first: for when he bid me come this far with you, then you should have begged me of him to have gone quite through with you, and he would have granted your request. However, at present I must withdraw."[29]

When Great-heart leaves, the pilgrims begin to lose their way: Mercy falls briefly under the spell of the rakish Mr. Brisk, Christiana's oldest son Matthew eats a poisoned fruit and almost dies, and the journey comes to a complete standstill in the House Beautiful for the next week. However, when Christiana (at the bidding of her young son Joseph) petitions for the return of Mr. Great-heart, all is set aright. We can have little doubt that Matthew correctly admonishes his mother to "fear nothing, as long as Mr. Great-heart is to go with us, and to be our conductor."[30] From this point on, the

28   Bunyan, *Pilgrim*, 255.
29   Ibid., 282.
30   Ibid., 298.

party's ultimate salvation—which had been in extreme peril only moments before—is assured, and the remainder of the narrative need only work out this certain conclusion.

In both of these passages, and in the whole of *The Pilgrim's Progress, Part II*, Christiana's principal sin is the belief that she can negotiate the path to the Celestial City alone—a belief that directly parallels desire of the women in Bunyan's congregation to meet in separate meetings. However, her failing is not one of pride. She does not set out with the intention of making the journey herself, and she is only too glad for the services that the Reliever and Great-heart render. Her failing, rather, is that she does not anticipate this need in advance and seek spiritual assistance in time. She does not follow Ruth in the carefully planned submission that is at the heart of that work and that, for Bunyan, constitutes the religious duty of the weaker vessel. The active submission of women, whom Bunyan perceives as inherently incapable of managing spiritual affairs, benefits the entire community, as he argues in "A Case of Conscience Resolved": "when Women keep their places, and men Manage their worshipping of God as they should, we shall have better days for the Church of God, in the World."[31]

Though Bunyan makes it clear that women must actively submit to spiritually stronger men, he does not suggest that this is a uniquely female requirement. Indeed, of the sixteen pilgrims that Great-heart leads to the Celestial City, ten of them are men, all of whom are under the same obligation as Christiana and Mercy to recognize their weakness and seek the protection of those spiritually stronger than they. Even the names of these male pilgrims—such as "Feeblemind," "Ready-to-Halt," and "Despondency"—demonstrate their spiritual weakness and need of the same kind of protection that Great-heart affords to Christiana and Mercy, and throughout the narrative, the two women demonstrate substantially more spiritual strength than most of the men.

For Bunyan, as for most Protestants of his day, spiritual weakness was not a uniquely female trait but an essential element of the human condition. Nobody, as Bunyan asserts in tract after tract, is capable of attaining salvation by overcoming his/her spiritual weaknesses. Salvation comes only through election, grace, and a limited atonement granted to those who, through absolutely no merit of their own, have been predestined to receive it. All of the pilgrims in the narrative community—men and women alike—represent the elect who have been predestined for salvation. The primary purpose of the community, which is Bunyan's allegory for the Church, is to give them peace, comfort, and spiritual guidance along the way. The fact that Bunyan portrays women as constantly in need of peace, comfort, and spiritual guidance does not, therefore, justify Thickstun's conclusion that "Bunyan's belief in the spiritual inferiority of women makes it impossible for him to assign positive allegorical significance to a female character."[32] The submission of the spiritually weak, be they male or

---

[31]   Bunyan, *Case of Conscience*, 329.
[32]   Thickstun, *Fictions*, 90.

female, to Great-heart and Valiant allows for the formation of the spiritually nurturing religious community that stands at the heart of the allegory in *Pilgrim's Progress, Part II.*

As Christiana and her community negotiate the path to the Celestial City, Bunyan includes as positive a passage on the spiritual importance of women as can be found anywhere in Restoration literature. This passage, which comes near the end of the journey, is in a speech in which the innkeeper Gaius specifically removes the "reproach" that was popularly believed to have come to women through Eve's disobedience:

> I will now speak on the behalf of women, to take away their reproach. For as death and the curse came into the world by a woman, so also did life and health. . . . I will say again, that when the Saviour was come, women rejoiced in him before either man or angel. 'Twas a Woman that washed his Feet with Tears, and a Woman that anointed his Body to the Burial. They were Women that wept when he was going to the Cross; And women that followed him from the Cross, and that sat by his Sepulcher when he was buried. They were Women that was first with him at his Resurrection morn, and Women that brought Tidings first to his disciples that he was risen from the dead. Women therefore are highly favoured and show by these things that they are sharers with us in the grace of life.[33]

Ironically, Bunyan's use of biblical narrative in this passage corresponds very closely to a passage in Margaret Fell's arguments in *A Woman's Speaking Justified* (1667), perhaps the most important Quaker tract in defense of women participating in ecclesiastical affairs. In the pages that Fell devotes to the strong women of the Bible, she includes the following statements about women in Christ's life:

> Thus we see that Jesus owned the Love and Grace that appeared in Women, and did not despise it, and by what is recorded in the Scriptures, he received much love, kindness, compassion, and tender dealing towards him from Women . . . both in his life time and also after they had exercised cruelty upon him. . . .
>
> For when he met the women after he was risen, he said unto them, All Hail, and they came and hold them by the Feet, and worshipped him. . . .
>
> Mark this, you that despise and oppose the Message of the Lord God, that he sends by women, what had become of the Redemption of the whole Body of Mankind, if

---

[33]   Bunyan, *Pilgrim*, 327–328.

they had not believed the message that the Lord Jesus sent
by these women, and concerning his Resurrection.[34]

Though Bunyan and Fell could not have disagreed more about the
propriety of women's meetings or women speaking in Church, the close
correspondences between their arguments on the spiritual worth of women
deserve careful attention. Both of them invoke the same biblical
descriptions of the women who tended to the literal body of Christ as
precedents for understanding the role of women in the metaphorical Body of
Christ. Both see women as nurturers and protectors of this body, and both
credit women with bringing to the male authorities the "tidings . . . that he
was risen from the dead." For Fell, guiding metaphor here is clear: that
women have the right to preach the gospel (which is, after all, simply the
"good news" of Christ's resurrection). Bunyan is not able to come to this
same conclusion, though his own typology leads him most of the way there.
He does, however, state quite clearly that the actions of these women "take
away the reproach" that God gave to Eve—thus neutralizing one of key
proofs of woman's inferiority that some of his contemporaries relied on.

The allegorical role that Bunyan assigns to women in *The Pilgrim's
Progress, Part I* is the role of follower. About this fact there can be little
doubt. The women can never be the leaders of the community and must
always submit to the protection of male authority figures for their own
safety and spiritual progress. However, Christiana and Mercy are not
passive followers. In every step of the journey, Christiana and Mercy, like
Ruth and Naomi, have both the right and the responsibility to make certain
choices in regards to their own spiritual growth. In *Pilgrim's Progress, Part I*,
Christiana elects to stay behind when her husband begins his journey. In
the beginning of Part II, she decides, with no outside influence at all, that
she must begin her own pilgrimage. When she announces her intentions to
the other women in the town—in what may well be a burlesque of a Quaker
women's meeting—the character Timorous attempts to dissuade her on the
grounds that the journey would be too hard for a woman:

> You have heard, I am sure, what your husband did meet
> with, even in a manner at the first step, that he took on his
> way, as our neighbor Obstinate yet can testify; for he went
> along with him, yea and Pliable too, until they, like wise
> men, were afraid to go any further. We have also heard,
> over and above, how he met with the lions, Apollyon, the
> Shadow of Death, and many other things. . . . For if he,
> though a man, was so hard put to it, what canst though
> being but a poor woman do?[35]

Bunyan's narrative plainly rejects this anti-feminist rhetoric when
Christiana rebuffs Timorous by exclaiming, "I have now a price put into

---

[34]   Margaret Askew Fell, *Women's Speaking Justified, Proved, and Allowed by the
       Scriptures* (London, 1667), 6–7.
[35]   Bunyan, *Pilgrim*, 240.

mine hand to get gain, and I should be a fool of the greatest size, if I should have no heart to strike in with the opportunity."[36]

When Bunyan exclaims in "A Case of Conscience Resolved" that, if he believed that women should lead worship services, he "should be a Ranter or a Quaker,"[37] he is correctly assessing the extreme minority of such a position. Despite Bunyan's unequivocal resolution that his congregation should not allow separate women's meetings, however, his overall approach to the question of women's spiritual roles is much more difficult to define, and this ambiguity carries over into *The Pilgrim's Progress, Part I*. The overall position on women in the Church that emerges from these two works is conflicted, but not incoherent. Bunyan clearly intends to convey to female worshippers that they need to submit to male authority. But he does not advocate passive or even uncritical submission, nor does he suggest that the submission required of women is, in the end, remarkably different than the submission required of men. The careful consideration that Bunyan gave to these issues shows, if nothing else, that he considered them extremely important. And here again, the Book of Ruth constitutes a precedent. Ruth and Naomi are unquestionably important, as the central figures of an important biblical narrative, as symbols of devotion and spiritual maturity, and as the progenitors of King David, and, consequently, of Jesus Christ. Here are two women who simply can't be written off as insignificant in any way, but their narrative is problematic. The Book of Ruth foregrounds female agency and female submission at the same time, qualities for which it has been alternately applauded and excoriated by generations of feminist scholars. These very paradoxes make Ruth a perfect symbol for the contradictory views of women that Bunyan presents in "A Case of Conscience Resolved" and *The Pilgrim's Progress, Part II* and a perfect typological counterweight to both the Eve-type and the prophetess-type so integral to the rhetorical milieu in which Bunyan lived and wrote.

---

[36]   Ibid., 241.
[37]   Bunyan, *Case of Conscience*, 305.

John Tillotson and the Voice of Anglicanism

Bob Tennant

—I—

It is very rare that an Archbishop of Canterbury emerges from outside the existing bench of bishops: Thomas Cranmer, the first archbishop of the reformed Church, Matthew Parker, who resumed the reformers' work after Mary I's reign, and John Tillotson, promoted over the heads of several credible candidates to consolidate the 1688 Revolution, were all appointed at crucial moments of national history.[1] In itself, this makes Tillotson a quite exceptional figure, but despite his key historical role and his fame as the leading preacher in a period of great preachers,[2] some modern scholars have found him an intractably problematic figure, calling him, among other things, naïve, foolish, apolitical, gullible, and maladroit and even questioning his moral integrity. When scholars become adjectival, it may be that there is an underlying frustration at the recalcitrance of material in

---

[1] The only other case is Tillotson's predecessor, William Sancroft, who refused the see of Chester specifically because he wanted at that time to continue supervising Wren's rebuilding of St. Paul's.

[2] For Tillotson's biography, see *Oxford Dictionary of National Biography* (Oxford: Oxford University Press, 2004). Robert Beddard, "The Unexpected Whig Revolution of 1688," in *The Revolutions of 1688,* ed. Robert Beddard (Oxford: Oxford University Press, 1991) gives a Whig perspective on Tillotson's role at the crisis. The absence of surviving primary materials, however, makes it difficult for historians to document his diplomatic role in 1688–89 and thus gives weight to the contemporary case for his subsequent promotion to the archbishopric.

relation to theories; with Tillotson, this is mostly traceable to the question of his intellectual relationship with Hobbes.[3] Yet in the paradigm shift that the Glorious Revolution constituted for the Church of England, Tillotson made the central contribution, one that lies perhaps just on the usual limits of intellectual history but which profoundly affected English thought in the eighteenth century and beyond: a new way of constructing doctrinal discourse. The Church of England changed fundamentally after 1688 in its cultural nature, and, despite routine statements by modern scholars, the assumption is highly dubious that an "Anglican orthodoxy" existed that would have recognized itself in that term. Rather, the leading group of senior clergy edged towards concepts based on an interpretation of Hobbes's voluntarist and contractual account of politics, acknowledging the realities of the process of change and the validity of revolution.[4] Because each local arrangement (if based on the Protestant reformed faith, of course) was seen as valid, this led not only to the localization of politics—a theoretical restatement of nationalism and patriotism—but also the toleration of any diversity that did not undermine contractual priorities. This approach is reminiscent of concepts developed recently by John Gray to handle valid intellectual uncertainty: "agonistic liberalism" ("grounded, not in rational choice, but in the limits of rational choice") and "value pluralism" ("an irreducible variety of ultimate values").[5] If reason and argument, however they might arise from natural law, established only local settlements, they became detached from more universally consistent concepts like "truth." We can see why Tillotson was able to combine loyalty to the rather *ad hoc* 1689 Settlement, a closely-reasoned outline structure for his preaching, and a latitudinarian breadth of intellectual tolerance.[6] I will take this context for

---

3   A brief flurry of activity in the mid-1980s failed to create a consensus: for example, John Spurr, "'Latitudinarianism' and the Restoration Church," *Historical Review* 31 (1988): 61–82; John Marshall, who emphasizes the likeness of Hobbes's and Tillotson's thinking, "The Ecclesiology of the Latitude-Men 1660–1689," *Journal of Ecclesiastical History* 36 (1985): 407–427; Mark Goldie, "The Political Thought of the Anglican Revolution," in *The Revolutions of 1688*, ed. Robert Beddard (Oxford: Oxford University Press, 1991), 102–136, who postulates an Anglican third way between Hobbes and Locke. One great value of William Gibson, *The Church of England 1688–1832: Unity and Accord* (London: Routledge, 2001), ch. 2, is that it draws attention to the fluidity of affiliations and ideologies at this time.
4   See, for example, Thomas Hobbes, *Human Nature and De Corpore Politico*, ed. J. C. A. Gaskin (Oxford: Oxford University Press, 1994), xxviiff, esp. xxxii. For Tillotson, language was subject to natural laws. See n. 34 below and associated main text.
5   For example, John Gray, *Enlightenment's Wake* (London: Routledge, 1995), 68 and *passim*, but especially ch. 6, where Gray outlines the case for Hobbes (as against Locke) as a political philosopher of relevance.
6   Clinching an early nineteenth-century controversy with an evangelical bishop Richard Warner, surveying great Anglican divines, characterizes Tillotson excellently as "the sensible, the perspicuous, the argumentative." *A Letter to the Hon. and Right Rev. Henry Ryder* (London: Longman, Hurst, Rees, Orme and Brown, 1818), 16.

granted, setting four texts in the highly stressed context of revolutionary change.

The sermons to be considered are *The Parable of the Ten Virgins*, preached on 2 September 1688 in Tunbridge Wells before Princess Anne of Denmark (the future Queen Anne); *A Thanksgiving Sermon for Our Deliverance by the Prince of Orange*, preached on 31 January 1689 in Lincoln's Inn Chapel, London before the Lincoln's Inn Society of lawyers; *Of Forgiveness of Injuries, and against Revenge*, preached on 8 March 1689 in Whitehall before the Queen; and *The Care of Our Souls the One Thing Needful*, preached on 14 April 1689 at Hampton Court before the King and Queen. I will refer to them, respectively, as *Ten Virgins, Thanksgiving, Forgiveness*, and *Care of Our Souls*. They were evidently conceived as a sequence and, although initially published singly, were printed in sequence in Tillotson's authorized *Works*.[7]

While I will approach the texts in a critically holistic way, there will be a degree of reliance on a cautious use of statistics. This is for two reasons. One is that Anglican sermons are still a relatively unmapped but populous literary genre—over 20,000 were published in the long eighteenth century—so that at least some misconceptions can be corrected partially by number-disciplined methods, helping us in the absence of the "feel" that generations of scholars and critics have given us for secular genres. The other is that performance texts, which is what sermons are, depend heavily for their success on factors such as length, complexity, and pace, all things that can be measured using very simple arithmetical tools, although their interpretation, like all acts of criticism, is fundamentally a metaphorical process.

—II—

Tillotson's career witnessed a largely unacknowledged but profound change in the public role of the published single sermon in England.[8] It would be

---

7   John Tillotson, *The Works . . . Containing Fifty Four Sermons and Discourses, on Several Occasions, together with the Rule of Faith, Being All That Were Published by His Grace Himself . . .* (London: B. Aylmer et al., 1696), sermons XXXI–XXXIV, 369ff. The texts have been checked against the first publications as single sermons; there are no textual differences significant for present purposes.

8   The statistical information that follows is mostly sourced, directly or indirectly, from the late J. Gordon Spaulding's *Pulpit Publications, 1660–1782*. 6 vols. (New York: Norman Ross, 1996). I would like to record my gratitude to Professor Spaulding for the gift of an early trial copy. In the present essay, "single sermon" includes those very few topical sermons that were published in pairs or small collections. Spaulding's listings of sermons are virtually comprehensive—at least 99 percent of Anglican sermons are included, and the lists he generates are considerably larger than those obtainable from the Stationers' Company Register, which leads even recent, ground-breaking, historians like Tony Claydon to underestimate the share of the total publishing market they enjoyed. See Claydon's excellent overview, "The Sermon, the 'Public Sphere' and the Political Culture of Late Seventeenth-Century England," in *The English Sermon Revised*, ed. Lori Anne Ferrell and Peter McCullough (Manchester: Manchester University Press, 2000). My thanks are also due to James Currall for commenting on the analysis of the data presented in this essay. Any mistakes are mine alone.

expected that such a great public event as the Glorious Revolution would see the publication of a flood of celebratory sermons, so it surprises that only four Thanksgiving sermons appeared, three of them by the senior latitudinarians, Simon Patrick, Gilbert Burnet, and Tillotson himself. Since there were issues of fundamental political and religious importance to settle, the question why the published single sermon was so inactive during this crisis merits detailed consideration.

The Restoration saw an initial rush of published single sermons (156 in 1660, 112 in 1661), as the King's return was celebrated, followed by 80 in 1662 and 78 in 1663, when large numbers were published by ejected ministers saying farewell to their congregations. Thereafter, in 1664–1674, an average of only 35 single sermons was published each year, until 1675 saw a 50 percent expansion of output, to an annual base of about 57 in the remaining years before the 1688 Revolution.

In the 10 years between 1677–1686, this base of 57 single sermons is greatly exceeded in four "high" years, which average 102 sermons. These four years witnessed specific pulpit initiatives (1682–1683) in discussing forms of worship during the "comprehension" debates, mostly from the dissenting side (it might be called the "left"), and (1683–1685) events surrounding the Whig plot and the Monmouth rebellion, mostly by Tory clergy (the "right"): sermons were serving as a sub-genre of pamphlet literature, sometimes displacing, but rarely being displaced by, non-sermon and secular material.[9] This suggests that publishers saw a market for controversial material that was assigned a relatively inflexible proportion of the print industry's productive capacity, while an assignment of production to the ecclesiastical "centre" was not an option: it was weaker in attracting sales than the extremes. There is, moreover, a remarkable lack of increase in the gross numbers of single sermons during the Exclusion Crisis of 1679. While, by precedent, there was productive capacity available for additional sermon production, it just did not happen; there was merely somewhat of a squeeze on sermons treating less topical subjects. The Exclusion Crisis was clearly seen as primarily a political rather than religious issue, the publication of secular material taking priority.

Figures 1 and 2 present some data about the numbers and subjects of contemporary sermon publications in the years 1677–1686, the crisis years 1687–1688, and 1689–1698.

The firm base in 1677–1686 of published single sermons crumbled in the crisis years 1687–1688, which saw by far the lowest numbers issued in the period between 1675 and 1800. Since the base was reestablished

---

9   The increases in single sermon production in the four years 1682–1685 correspond roughly to the number of items dedicated to these issues. One hundred seventy-nine more sermons were published than the underlying annual norm of fifty-seven would predict. One hundred sixty-two (twenty-eight concerning forms of worship and one hundred thirty-four the rebellions and associated affirmations of loyalty) dealt with immediate political crises and ecclesiological controversy. Since these one hundred sixty-two are identified only from abbreviated title-page details, it is likely that the actual figure was somewhat higher.

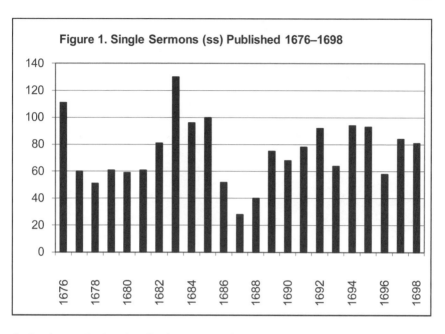

Figure 1. Single Sermons (ss) Published 1676–1698

(indeed, at a higher level) after 1688, these exceptionally low years do not indicate an instability of the market but the single sermon's relatively low status as a means of intervention in public events, the virtually complete absence of sermons defending James II being a sharp expression of the lack of practical commitment to rallying support for him in the parishes, incorporated bodies, and other public associations. This reticence of the genre even affected the publication of sermon collections so that at least 200 fewer sermons were published in the crisis years than might have been expected.[10] While the post-Revolution period (1689–1698) had a slightly lower aggregate number of single sermon publications, divergence from the average was much smaller, and there were no exceptionally high years: the base rose from about 56 annually to about 79, an increase of over 40 percent. The single sermon had become a discrete marketing genre and was more resistant to displacement by ephemeral and secular material. This sense of a changed definition of market role is confirmed by the consistency of output despite the periodically wide variations in the treatment of three key subjects (see figure 2): the role of the Church in the political process, the continuing process of self-definition in contra-distinction to the Roman Church, and the relationship of the liturgy to the strategy of comprehension (in the earlier period) and toleration (in the later).[11]

---

[10]   Reckoning a collection, conservatively, as a single volume containing fifteen sermons.

[11]   These figures are generated only from title page details so that levels of the general climate of opinion are understated.

Figure 2. Sermon Publications, 1677–1698			
	1677–1686	1687–1688	1689–1698
Sermon collections	38	1	36
annual average	3.8	0.5	3.6
Single sermons	751	68	787
annual average	75.1	34.0	78.7

Key subjects of single sermons
(expressed as gross numbers and as % of total ss publications)

Anti-Roman Catholic[12]	48 (6.4%)	0	19 (2.4%)
Political occasions and church unity	70 (9.3%)[13]	0	54 (6.9%)
Liturgy, prayer book and forms of worship	72 (9.7%)	2 (2.9%)	35 (4.4%)

The precrisis period had, predictably, a much higher incidence of sermons establishing anti-Roman Catholic positions and defining the liturgy in the context of the policy of comprehension, while, even if the enormously high level of anxiety around the succession to Charles II is discounted (see note 13), the post-crisis period put much more emphasis on civic and public occasions: public affairs were being normalized as subject matter for the pulpit. Although immediately after the 1660 Restoration preachers like Robert South produced quantities of sermons that were political in the party sense, there was not, after the Revolution, any significant replication of this until the Sacheverell controversy of 1709. The low "anti-Roman Catholic" figure for the post-Revolution period is all the more remarkable in that it includes all those giving thanks for "the deliverance of this kingdom from popery and arbitrary power."[14] The process of exploring the identity of the Church of England shifted from sectarian apologetics to doctrinal exposition, and this process was led by Tillotson.

The complexity of the politico-religious situation may be gauged from a comparison of figures 1 and 2 with figure 3:

12 Most sermons in this category (at least twenty-two in the early period, fifteen in the later) were preached on 5 November, the public set-piece occasion for restating the case against the Roman Church.
13 Another sixty-five (about the rebellion, the death of Charles II and the accession of James II) were published in 1684 (twenty-eight) and 1685 (thirty-seven) but have not been tabulated as they constitute a unique, coordinated intervention by Tory churchmen, who were thereafter politically marginal. If these are included, the proportion of published single sermons dealing with church unity and politics rises to a historically high 18.0 percent.
14 Gilbert Burnet, *A Sermon Preached before the House of Commons, on the 31st January 1688* [i.e., 1688–89] . . . (London: John Starkey and Richard Chiswell, 1689), title page.

Figure 3. Sermon Collections and Single Sermons (ss) Published in Two Eighteenth-Century Crisis Decades
(Bottom row = averages for the eight "non-crisis" years of each decade)

Year	Collections	ss	"Crisis" ss	Year	Collections	ss	"Crisis" ss
1711	5	114		1741	11	66	
1712	4	139		1742	14	81	
1713	8	143		1743	11	66	
1714	5	141		1744	6	63	
1715	6	201	74	1745	5	145	85
1716	7	199	61	1746	4	162	90
1717	8	130		1747	9	69	
1718	5	72		1748	16	66	
1719	7	74		1749	10	87	
1720	14	89		1750	11	92	
av	7	113			11	74	

Here the columns labeled "'crisis' ss" refer to "single sermons relating directly to the crisis, as judged by title-page information" and correspond with the sermons listed under "key subjects" for 1677–1698 in figure 2. Figure 3 shows that the number of sermons directly relevant to the crises roughly corresponds to the increase in the publication of single sermons. In the decade 1711–1720, the crisis years produce 77 percent more single sermons than the average for the decade's non-crisis years; in the decade 1741–1750, this increase is 149 percent. In these eighteenth-century decades, the sermon genre is sufficiently firmly established as a marketing entity to expand its share of the print sector's productive capacity at a time of national domestic crisis, replacing secular material. The Church had assumed a leading role in setting the national agenda so that, indeed, during the Whig Hegemony, the published sermon is a prime vehicle of political and intellectual innovation.

In the precrisis period of 1684–1685, a brief efflorescence of loyalist Tory sermons had merely confirmed that public support could not be rallied for James. While the Revolution might have been "glorious" in its bloodless method and its establishment of Protestant Christianity in the centre of England's polity, the collapse of sermon publications in the crisis period also shows that while there was undoubtedly a strong anti-Roman Catholic consensus, there was no agreement in the country over a positive project. The Revolution was a top-down Whig initiative, which, to survive, had to establish its credentials after the event. This helps us see the significance of Tillotson's series of four sermons: they were the first attempt at creating a consensus—in the event, the authoritative one. We will therefore expect to find in them elements of hesitancy and improvisation.

—III—

Tillotson's association with Royal Society circles was a powerful factor in his thinking and compositional style. He collaborated closely with John Wilkins, especially with the latter's *Essay towards a Real Character and a Philosophical Language* (1668) and *Of the Principles and Duties of Natural Religion* (1678), for which he wrote the preface, while Wilkins's *Ecclesiastes* (1669) formulates much of the rhetorical and exegetical method found in Tillotson's sermons.[15] More broadly, Tillotson is associated with Wilkins's project of creating a clear and plain style of discourse.[16] Richard Kroll has characterized Wilkins's method in attacking his epistemological and linguistic interests as "probabilistic, comparative, and historical,"[17] and these categories are evident in the tripartite exegetical method that Tillotson developed. Tillotson was also a member of a circle discussing comprehension that originated "in the chamber of that great Trimmer and Latitudinarian Dr Hezekiah Burton in Essex House, beyond Temple Bar, being then the habitation of Sir Orlando Bridgeman."[18] As well as reminding us of the intimacy of a country of only five million people, this reinforces the ideational framework described by Kroll. In Tillotson's mid-career sermon, *The Protestant Religion Vindicated from the Charge of Singularity and Novelty* (Joshua 25.15, preached before Charles II, 2 April 1680), he remarked, that, having instructed the Israelites in the true faith, Joshua had left them to "their own election" of their religion, saying that "it [is] the nature of man to stick more stedfastly to that which is not violently imposed, but is our free and deliberate choice."[19] It is in this context that the Wilkins/Tillotson method achieves its full relevance. In his stylistic textbook, *Ecclesiastes*, Wilkins had written that ". . . some men are fain to *divert* their Hearers with little tricks about Words or Phrases, or to *amuse* them by pretending to discover some deep mystery in every Metaphor or Allegory of Scripture . . . The great End of Preaching [is] either to *inform* or *perswade*."[20] Reasonable persuasiveness is

15   Jon Parkin, *Science, Religion and Politics in Restoration England* (Woodbridge: Boydell Press, 1999), 34.
16   For example, *Oxford Dictionary of National Biography*, article "Tillotson, John" and Richard W. F. Kroll, *The Material World* (Baltimore: John Hopkins University Press, 1991), ch. 6.
17   Kroll, 188.
18   Anthony Wood, *Athenae Oxoniensis*, ed. P. Bliss (Oxford: Oxford University Press, 1813–1820), iv.512–513, cited in Parkin, 28. Tillotson wrote a preface to Burton's posthumous *Discourses*.
19   J. Tillotson, *Works (ed. cit.)*, 309–310. Citing this sermon, Parkin (33, n. 47) remarks that Tillotson was a vocal opponent of toleration (as against comprehension). In fact, this sermon is anti-Roman Catholic, something separate from the toleration debate (see also Isabel Rivers, *Reason, Grace, and Sentiment* [Cambridge: Cambridge University Press, 1991], 1:84), and in it Tillotson is careful not to overemphasize the right and duty of the monarch to determine what is the true faith for his subjects: he says (310ff, esp. 311) that a subject has a right, however circumscribed, to dissent.
20   John Wilkins, *Ecclesiastes: or, a Discourse Concerning the Gift of Preaching, as It Falls under the Rules of Art* (sixth impression, London: S. Gellibrand, 1675), Preface, not paginated.

indeed the core of Tillotson's strategy, as is seen in the outline structures of his sermons and his developments of the catechism,[21] and Wilkins's concept of language and its component words as objects created in and projected from the vocal organs is peculiarly appropriate to a public oratory that so obviously studies and measures its effect on the congregation.[22] What is unusual and innovative in Tillotson is the dynamic relationship between sermons' language and their situational context.

As Addison recognized (*Spectator* 106), Tillotson's sermons are "like the composition of a poet in the mouth of a graceful orator." Like Dryden, he pared his style beyond anything achieved by his contemporaries and colleagues. Pepys's description of Stillingfleet's preaching as "the most plain, honest, good, grave sermon, in the most unconcerned and easy yet substantial manner" is yet more relevant to Tillotson.[23] Of the three published sermons preached by latitudinarians during the Revolution crisis, Gilbert Burnet's before the Prince of Orange on 23 December 1688 is densely metaphorical: the Roman Church's "hostile force [is] . . . a crown of thorns [which] . . . had blazed and crackled a little, but was soon spent . . . [the Church of England experiencing] a torrent of success, . . . a chain of Providence . . . a strong and prosperous Gale [which] . . . brought us near our Port."[24] The figures, metaphors of martyrology and English mercantilism (a perceived betrayal of which to the French by James II had helped trigger the revolutionary process[25]), sum up a stage in Burnet's narrative of the Church's triumph. Burnet's 31 January thanksgiving sermon is just as dense in metaphorical figures ("bank . . . waters . . . breaches . . .")[26] and he neatly locates Protestantism between the "extreams" with his formula, "Atheism denies God, and Idolatry degrades him," although his Erastianism is not in the last analysis shared by Tillotson.[27]

Simon Patrick's thanksgiving sermon is similar in density of argument and metaphor. Starting from a statement of the relationship between the "superintending" God and the "curious frame of the World," it builds on a distinction between the psychological "Foundation of that Admiration, Reverence, and Awful Regard which we pay to the Divine Majesty [when

---

21 For developments of the catechism by Tillotson, Patrick, and Burnet, see Gibson, 122.

22 Kroll, 187–191, discusses this in relation to Wilkins's *Essay towards a Real Character* (London: Samuel Gellibrand, 1668) and in particular Wilkins's chapter "Writing Being the Picture or Image of Speech."

23 Samuel Pepys, *Diary*, ed. Robert Latham and William Matthews (London: Bell & Hyman, 1972), 6:87 (1665).

24 Gilbert Burnet, *A Sermon Preached in the Chappel of St. James's* (London: Richard Chiswell, 1689), 8–11.

25 Charles Jenkinson, ed., *A Collection of All the Treaties of Peace, Alliance and Commerce between Great Britain and Other Powers* (London: J. Debrett, 1785), 1:261ff.

26 Burnet, *A Sermon Preached before the House of Commons*, 14.

27 See Burnet's comments on the role of Parliament, page 3 and 32ff. G Mischler, "English Political Sermons 1714–1742: A Case Study in the Theory of the 'Divine Right of Governors' and the Ideology of Order," *British Journal for Eighteenth Century Studies* 24 (2001): 33–61, has documented the survival of divine right theories.

contemplating the creation . . . and] that Devotion of Mind which we express in Humble and Hearty Prayers of Thanksgivings to [God]."[28] The "thankful Temper of Spirit" required on a day of official thanksgiving is grounded in obedience, without which thanksgiving is mere "complements" and flattery, and William becomes virtually God's sole agent, Patrick establishing that the proper response is to "let our Thankfulness . . . be great, in some proportion to his wondrous Works," marrying the voluntary and the emotional into a political-cum-natural philosophical vision, a version of divine right mediated by the voluntary and quasi-contractual subordination of subject to king.[29]

Tillotson is much more committed to colloquialisms than any of his colleagues—"they could not on the sudden recollect themselves," he remarks of the *Ten Virgins*[30]—but it is in his use of metaphor that the creation of a distinctively Anglican rhetoric and strategy may be seen. In 1680, he had written, "Laws are a good security to religion; but the example of governors is a living law, which secretly overrules the minds of men, and bends them to a compliance with it . . . The lives and actions of princes have usually a greater sway upon the minds of the people than their laws."[31] Hence it was Charles's and James's intemperate natures that Tillotson saw as oppressing and alienating their subjects. This psychological approach generates a language of emotional protest. Thus in a lengthy passage condemning the Roman doctrine of supererogation, metaphor follows metaphor: individuals' supererogatory good works are described in the meretricious language of the counting house:

> and from that time forwards may put the *Surplusage* of their *good Works* as a *Debt* upon God, to be laid up in the *Publick Treasury* of the *Church*, as so many *Bills of Credit*, which the *Pope* by his *Pardons* and *Indulgences* may dispense, and place to whose account he pleases: and out of this *Bank*, which is kept at *Rome*, those who never took care to have any Righteousness of their own, may be

---

28   Simon Patrick, *A Sermon Preached at St. Paul's Covent Garden . . . January XXXI. 1688 for the Great Deliverance of this Kingdom by the Means of his Highness the Prince of Orange from Popery and Arbitrary Power*, (London: R. Bentley, 1689), 1. The phrases following are quoted from pages 6, 13, and 28.
29   This adaptation of Hobbes by the Latitudinarians is discussed at some length by Parkin, ch. 1. It is worth comparing Burnet's sermon with his pamphlet, *An Enquiry into the Measures of Submission and the Supream Authority*, in *Collection of Eighteen Papers* (London: John Starkey and Richard Chiswell, 1689), 123–128, *e.g.*, the Hobbesian principle, "[If the King] goes to subvert the whole Foundation of the Government, he subverts that by which he himself has his Power, and by consequence he annuls his own Power, and then he ceases to be *King*, having endeavoured to destroy that upon which his own Authority is founded" (127f). Burnet's *Review of the Reflections on the Prince of Orange's Declaration* (in *Collection of Eighteen Papers*) is remarkably similar to the resolution passed by the States authorizing William's incursion (see Charles Jenkinson, 1:263–265).
30   *Ten Virgins*, 375.
31   *The Protestant Religion Vindicated from the Charge of Singularity and Novelty*, *Works*, 250.

supplied at reasonable rates. . . . [When] we are called *to meet the Bridegroom*, we shall not be put to those miserable and sharking shifts which the *foolish Virgins* were driven to, of *begging*, or *borrowing*, or *buying Oyl* .[32]

It is almost always the case that overtly metaphorical and alliterative language is used by Tillotson to signal the presence of Roman Catholicism. Thus: "[Yet] how soon was this bright and glorious Morning overcast, by the restless and black Designs of that sure and inveterate Enemy of ours, the Church of *Rome*;" "[A] sowre humour had been fermenting in the Body of the Nation;" "[the Jesuits'] *Kingdom of Darkness*;" "If we consider the cheapness and easiness of this Deliverance . . . Had it come upon harder terms, and had we waded to it though a *Red Sea* of Blood, we would have valued it more . . . [We undervalue it] because it came to us so easily, and hath cost us so very cheap."[33] The metaphors seep into "our" own actions, vividly illustrating the dangers of cultural and doctrinal contamination.[34] Although Tillotson's rhetoric is less overtly patriotic or triumphalist than Burnet's, he does consistently associate what he identifies as the unreasonable, irrational, and anti-social nature of Roman Catholicism with particular streams of metaphors and, contrariwise, the ethically good and English Protestantism with plainness of style and serenity of mind: "So that this is a *Day* every way worthy to be solemnly set apart and joyfully celebrated by this *Church* and *Nation*, throughout all Generations; as the fittest of all other to comprehend, and to put us in mind to commemorate all the great Deliverances which God hath wrought for Us, from *Popery*, and its inseparable Companion, *Arbitrary Power*. And we may *then* say with the *Holy Psalmist, This is the Lord's doing, it is marvellous in our eyes. This is the Day which the Lord hath made, we will rejoice and be glad in it.*"[35]

There remains, however, a substratum of unacknowledged metaphor, continually jutting through the sermon's superficially plain language, projecting a specification for the ideal English Christian. This may generally be called natural and constitutional: "the Thraldom and *Bondage* . . . of *Soul*;"[36] "We may . . . be forced to huddle up an imperfect, and I fear an insignificant *Repentance*."[37] Note, in this passage from *The Care of Our Souls*, the repetition of "business" interweaved with metaphors of animal activity: "Let us then shake off this sloth and security, and resolve to make that the great business of Time, which is our great concernment to all Eternity: and when we are immers'd in

---

32   *Ten Virgins*, 377, 379.
33   *Thanksgiving*, 389, 390, 392.
34   Of especial interest here is Adrian Hastings's studies of English nationalism, for example, *The Construction of Nationhood* (Cambridge: Cambridge University Press, 1997), chs. 1 and 2.
35   *Thanksgiving*, 392f.
36   Ibid., 391.
37   *Ten Virgins*, 379. *OED*: "Huddle, v. (8)": "Formerly, in the University of Cambridge, To go through in a hurried and slovenly way certain formal exercises in lieu of those regularly required for a degree." Tillotson was educated at Cambridge.

the cares and business of this Life, and *troubled about many things*, let this thought often come into our minds, That there is *one thing needful*, and which therefore deserves above all other things to be regarded by us."[38] The sequence, "business of time [. .] all eternity . . . cares and business of life . . . one thing needful," is shapely and balanced, moving from time to eternity and back again, the return being secured within scripture ("one thing is needful," Luke 10:42, Jesus in the house of Martha, a favorite episode for seventeenth-century Puritans and eighteenth-century evangelicals). The structure of the metaphor too is noteworthy: "the great business of time" is muted by the literally mundane: "business of this life." *Forgiveness* quotes Seneca ("The sun riseth even upon the most vile and profligate persons, and the seas are open to pirates"), whose introduction is itself highly significant in terms of ethical and stylistic positioning,[39] but this web of metaphors of constitutional and national perfectionism resolves itself ultimately into the exegetical: "*Be ye therefore perfect, as your Father which is in Heaven is perfect*; which St. *Luke* renders, *Be ye therefore merciful, as your Father which is in Heaven is merciful*. So that in that very thing [*i.e.*, forgiveness], which we think to be so hard and difficult, you see that we have Perfection it self for our Pattern."[40]

Such examples could be multiplied. This strategy of metaphors and such patterns is all-pervasive and anchors the physical and human nature of preacher and congregation in the activities of a structured society conceived within a scientific world view.[41] Tillotson's apparent Erastianism is really part of his modest acceptance of the spiritual validity of mundane human affairs. In the *Application of Forgiveness* he risks an empirical claim: "I cannot for my life but think *that* to be the best Religion which makes the best Men, and from the nature of its Principles is apt to make them so; most kind, and merciful, and charitable; and most free from Malice, and Revenge, and Cruelty."[42]

Eschewing the contemporary habit of vituperation, Tillotson makes humor a key component of his rhetoric. When he writes ironically of the Roman Church's withholding the Bible from the people that "[it believes that] the generality of Mankind are mad and have need to be kept in the dark,"[43] he refers to standard contemporary therapeutic practice. When he writes of "Spirits . . . [and] unnatural fermentation and tumult," he introduces a metaphor from chemistry.[44] Such examples proliferate but are combined with a more social wit. Preaching before the new King and Queen, he says, "You that are young [Tillotson was 59, William 38, Mary 26], be pleas'd to consider that

---

38   *Care of Our Souls*, 416.
39   George Williamson, *The Senecan Amble* (London: Faber & Faber, 1951) remains essential.
40   *Forgiveness*, 401. Adrian Hastings, *Church and State: The English Experience* (Exeter: University of Exeter Press, 1991), ch. 2, especially 20f, argues persuasively the context of English Erastianism.
41   Harvey Hill, "'The Law of Nature Revived:' Christianity and Natural Religion in the Sermons of John Tillotson," *Anglican and Episcopal History* 70 (2001): 169–189, gives a useful analysis of Tillotson's theology in this regard.
42   *Forgiveness*, 405f.
43   *Care of Our Souls*, 411.
44   *Forgiveness*, 397.

this is the best opportunity of our Lives, for the minding and doing of this work . . . those that are old, if there be any that are willing to own themselves so."[45] The playfulness of such passages is grounded in a firm sense of community and communion. Thus *Care of Our Souls* begins with a throw-away line astonishing in an archbishop-designate: "[The] care of . . . our Souls is the *one thing necessary* . . . and . . . [I] shall endeavour to perswade you and my self [*sic*] to mind this."[46] Lightness of touch is always available to Tillotson: his style is adaptable to circumstances to a degree unprecedented in the English pulpit and perhaps the more difficult to appreciate in that its lightness continues to be a resource in Anglican preaching.

—IV—

Tillotson's use of metaphor is rather schematic, and his great innovation is the local adaptability of his structures and syntax to emotion, values, and situation. He wrote and delivered his sermons in numbered outline form, a tacit claim to logic, proportion, and consistency that survives in the published texts. The normal proportions of Tillotson's sermons, a model widely imitated in the eighteenth century, are, very roughly, 7 percent initial exordium, 65 percent exegesis (often tripartite in structure), 25 percent application, and 3 percent final peroration (usually in the form of a doxology). Remarkably, only one of the present four (the last in the series) approximates to the model. I will consider briefly each of the four sermons in turn, these observations being based on the data presented in the Appendix.

The first in the series, *Ten Virgins*, was a component of the "Princess's Plot,"[47] which, Edward Gregg writes, "crystallized during the two months which [Anne] and Prince George spent at Tunbridge Wells before their return to London in mid-September 1688 . . . [during which she] was sought out by leading Protestant political and religious figures, including Sir John Trevor, the speaker in the last Parliament, and Dr John Tillotson . . . who recorded that 'I left the good Princess very well, and I think much better than ever I saw her.'"[48] It was Tillotson's task to gain Anne's support of Mary's claim to the throne should it become vacant and accept the promise of the succession, given that Mary was judged medically unlikely to produce an heir. By implication, his sermon's theme was that Anne should imitate the wise virgins and play a waiting game.

The structure of *Ten Virgins* is far removed from the Tillotson norm: it has a uniquely long Exordium (18 percent of the total length), a long Exegesis, and only a rudimentary Application, which gives little guidance to its principal auditor, Princess Anne. Its structure expresses the improvisatory nature of the

---

45   *Care of Our Souls*, 417.
46   Ibid., 410.
47   For a historical narrative from the Whig viewpoint see Beddard, "The Unexpected Whig Revolution of 1688," 11–101, which emphasizes the determination of the Whigs and William in forcing through the change of monarch.
48   Edward Gregg, *Queen Anne* (London: Routledge and Kegan Paul, 1980), 59f. Tillotson was not actually nominated Dean of St. Paul's until later in the year.

thought process: the exegetical part is much-divided into a linear sequence of irregular sections whose lengths are determined by their content rather than by a sense of proportion. It is the most variable of the four sermons in the distribution of adjectives and verbs among its parts. Syntactically, it has the longest sentences and by far the widest variation in the complexity of its sentences (the "total words/simple sentence" measure). Very few verbs are in simple sentences, and it has the fewest verbs: this means that there are long phrasal structures. These indicators point to a slow and involved syntax in the Exegesis: it is not making sharp and clear doctrinal points but feeling its way, hesitatingly, through its subject. The sermon is improvisatory in its style and effect.

> And the true Reason why men are so very apt to deceive themselves in this matter, and are so hardly brought to those things wherein Religion mainly consists, I mean the fruits of the Spirit and the practice of real Goodness; I say, the true reason of this is, because they are extremely desirous to reconcile, if it were possible, the hopes of eternal happiness in another World with a liberty to live as they list in this present World: They are loth to be at the trouble and drudgery of mortifying their lusts, and governing their passions, and bridling their tongues, and practising all those duties which are comprehended in those *two great Commandments* of the *Love of God* and of our *Neighbour*."[49]

Like its subjects, and like its chief auditor, the sermon is literally waiting for something to happen—at least part of which will lie between preacher and princess in private conversation. It is a document about the experience of possessing oneself patiently in uncertainties, of coming to conviction through prolonged meditation, not through doctrinal authority: Tillotson speaks of Christ's "*charitable Decorum*" and of those who "enjoy the *Gospel*,"[50] an aesthetic approach to Gray's agonistic liberalism. Faith is defined through a sanctified engagement with the cultural milieu of each particular human society and is expressed in complex, "inclusive," first person plural, discourse, embracing a plurality of Protestant perspectives on redemption and on ethical values.[51]

Turning now to the *Thanksgiving* sermon, towards the end of 1688, Tillotson had been instrumental in persuading Anne to accept William as King[52] and had been recruited by Burnet into the group of Whig propagandists

---

49   *Ten Virgins*, 373.
50   *Ten Virgins*, 371.
51   See Appendix for the characteristics of *Ten Virgins'* Exegesis 1 where this passage is located.
52   Gregg, 70. The anonymous *Life and Reign of Her Late Excellent Majesty Queen Anne* (London, 1738), allegedly based on first-hand testimony, claims that Princess Anne "went away from Whitehall the 25th of Nov. the Day before his Majesty [James II] returned to London. 'Tis said his Majesty being acquainted

around William.[53] He preached an unpublished sermon before William on 6 January, the special General Convention declared the throne vacant on 28 January and a national day of thanksgiving was called for 31 January. As with *Ten Virgins, Thanksgiving's* approach is indirect: seeking to mobilize his accustomed audience of lawyers (he had been elected preacher to the Lincoln's Inn Society as long ago as November 1663), he emphasizes the sin of ingratitude in both people and King James, rather than setting out the political justification for the Revolution.[54] This was in accordance with his method of identifying the strategy of the Roman Church to encourage atheism and terrorism.[55] He mentions the 5 November 1688 landing date explicitly to turn inside out the Church's constitutional commitment to that date as a merely defensive celebration of the Gunpowder Plot's failure.[56]

Thanksgiving has a relatively perfunctory Exegesis. It is remarkable for the extreme contrast between the main exegetical section (Ex2 in the Appendix) and the Application. The exegetical section is formed of short sentences, with many simple sentences, low in adjectives and high in verbs. The low (1.91) ratio of verbs to sentences will be noted: the syntactical flow is unusually unimpeded by subordinate clauses. The Application is exceptionally long, with few verbs and, in relation to its Exegesis, longer and more complex sentences (see the "verbs/sentence" measure). Compared with the rest of the series the syntax is simple and direct, with few verbs and a low count of total words per sentence. All this indicates a text driven by a fast and emphatic rhetorical pace.

> [The revolution] was brought about in a very *extraordinary* manner, and by very *strange* means: Whether we consider the *greatness* and *difficulty* of the enterprise; or the closeness and *secrecy* of the Design, which must of necessity be communicated at least to the *Chief* of those who were to assist and engage in it: Especially the *Estates* of the *United Provinces*, who were then in so much danger themselves, and wanted more than their own Forces for their own Defence and Security: a kindness never to be forgotten by the *English* nation. And besides all this, the

---

with her going away, the Tears fell down his Cheeks, and he cry'd out, God help me, my own Children have forsaken me" (19).

53   Tony Claydon, *William III and the Godly Revolution* (Cambridge: Cambridge University Press, 1996), 65.

54   It is unlikely that his obliqueness was for fear of prosecution for treason or seditious libel: Tillotson had rebuffed the politically secure Charles II's attempts to change his emphasis on anti-Roman preaching, while James II commanded too little public support to make prosecution viable as it had been during the Exclusion Crisis. See John Feather, *A History of British Publishing* (London: Routledge, 1988, rprt. 1991), 53.

55   See *ODNB*, art. "John Tillotson" and Burnet's *History of My Own Time*. 2 vols. (Oxford: Clarendon Press, 1897), 1:411, for the basis of Tillotson's beliefs about the Roman Church in forensic evidence and the Recorder of London's judgment.

56   *Thanksgiving*, 392. Tillotson's point was developed in a more constitutional way by Burnet in his *Sermon Preached before the House of Lords November 5th 1689* (London: Richard Chiswell, 1689).

difficulties and disappointments which happen'd, after the
Design was open and manifest, from the uncertainties of
Wind and *Weather*, and many other *Accidents* impossible
to be foreseen and prevented. And yet in Conclusion a
strange concurrence of all things, on all sides, to bring the
thing which the Providence of God intended to a happy
issue and effect."[57]

Note the repetition of "strange," hinting at the miraculous, and the damping
down of the rhetoric as the sentences wind through phrases and clauses,
ending in the subtly tautologous "happy issue and effect." The Protestant
leaders are contrasted with the Jesuits, "those formal politicians by book
and rule."[58] Protestant politics are, by implication, "natural," in the
progressive sense used by Hobbes.[59] Tillotson, with psychological acumen,
left his lawyers to work out for themselves their personal and professional
commitment to the Revolution's legality but allowed them no doubt of its
spiritual and ethical legitimacy. Parliament (with Burnet's sermon) could
afford to indulge its triumphalism, but the lawyers might yet be needed to
keep the politicians' heads on their shoulders—the legal justification for the
Revolution was still incomplete.[60]

William and Mary were declared monarchs on 12 February. Then on 8
March, the day before the United Provinces declared war on France, Tillotson
preached *Forgiveness* before Queen Mary at Whitehall, conveying a message of
national unity and toleration. *Forgiveness* offers both likeness and contrast to
Thanksgiving. Again there is a very long Application, emphasizing the sermon's
strongly functional role. Its core—the Exegesis and Application—is sparse in
adjectives and verbs; its sentences are consistently short and the pattern and
level of distribution of simple sentences is like *Thanksgiving's*; its Application,
as usual, is syntactically more elaborate, although, in comparison with the
flanking pair's, still rather simple. One would expect, *Forgiveness*, preached to
the new King and Queen securely on their thrones, while functionally focused,
to be rhetorically more shapely and syntactically less extreme than its predecessors with a lower emotional temperature. Overall, there is a rapidity and
simplicity of syntax in these two sermons of crisis, which contrasts sharply with

---

57   *Thanksgiving*, 391f. Note the hint, to England's leading lawyers, that the wording
     of the United Provinces' resolution, which permitted William's intervention, had
     originated in England.
58   *Thanksgiving*, 392.
59   Richard Peters put it succinctly: "The law of nature . . . was a godsend to those
     who feared absolutism, as a set of principles binding on kings as well as on their
     subjects." *Hobbes* (Harmondsworth: Penguin, 1956), 167.
60   Perhaps because so many clergy were also Justices of the Peace, there are great
     similarities not only in political alignment but also in style between sermons and
     charges to the Grand Jury throughout the period. See Georges Lamoine (ed.),
     Charges to the Grand Jury 1689–1803 (London: Royal Historical Society, 1992), 5
     for the constancy of charges to Whig principles and, as an unusually elaborate
     example, Sir Richard Cock's charge of 30 April 1717 to the Gloucestershire
     Grand Jury (81–88). A comparative analysis of charges and assize sermons
     would be enlightening.

the flanking pair. This is matched by the pressure to express values. Passages of some length without adjectives occur; then, the demands of values to find expression become irresistible, and adjectives come with a rush, although, typically, such episodes die away in a complex of subordinate phrasal structures, often with alliteration ("provoke and procure") supplying a full stop.[61]

> *The Enemy*, as our *Saviour* calls the *Devil*, will sow these *Tares in the night*, and when we least discern it will scatter the Seeds of Discord and Enmity among men; and will take an advantage either from the Envy, or the Malice, or the Mistakes of Men, to make them Enemies to one another. Which would make one wonder to see what care and pains some men will take, to provoke Mankind against them; how they will lay about them, and snatch at opportunities to make themselves Enemies, as if they were afraid to let the happy occasion slip by them: But all this care and fear surely is needless; *we* may safely trust an ill-natur'd world, that *we* shall have enemies enough, without our doing things on our part to provoke and procure them.[62]

Notice also how the flow of syntax stumbles, allowing the speaking voice to emphasize the argument's emotionalism and improvisation, a frequent and characteristic resource when context and strategic aims come into tactical conflict. As in the other sermons, these key values, psychological and "natural" in the Hobbesian sense, are set out in the syntactically relatively spacious and "inclusive" sections, with carefully selected adjectives pointing up the relationship between spirit, emotion, and degenerate world: Tillotson is conveying the suggestion that the limits of political choice are narrow, but within them there may flourish a wide diversity of religious life and freedom.

The last of the series, *Care of Our Souls*, was preached on 14 April, a fortnight before William and Mary concluded a treaty with the United Provinces (29 April) that provided for the supply of a battle fleet and which was followed by the declaration of war on 7 May. This sermon was delivered at Hampton Court Palace before the King and Queen. It reached beyond the military crisis and sought to set the spiritual agenda for the Church of England into the next century: by this time Tillotson was already William and Mary's choice as Sancroft's eventual successor as Archbishop of Canterbury.

Stylistically, this sermon is his home base: the end of the crisis is in sight and the spiritual project underway. It recalls *Ten Virgins* only in the length of its sentences. Its balance and shapeliness approximate the classic Tillotson model; there are more adjectives—by hypothesis a key indicator of the expression of values—and the complexity of its spacious syntax varies little between sections: it is rhetorically slow, elaborate and even-tempered. It has

---

61 For visual representation of this, there are several computer programs available that map texts graphically, although at present the necessary preparation of texts is laborious.
62 *Forgiveness*, 403f. Adjectives underlined.

the longest sentences (the words/sentence measure) and the most words per simple sentence, these two indicators pointing to the fact that there are some very long complex sentences, especially in the Application, again with Tillotson's characteristic use of chains of phrasal structures. Having previously established forgiveness as psychologically and spiritually central to his religion, and, by implication to his politics, Tillotson offers here an elegant meditation on Christ in the house of Martha—the "one thing needful"—in which the listeners would inevitably recognize William in Martha, pious but burdened with business, and Queen Mary in Mary, a characteristically gentle pun reminding that the queen's principal assigned role was in Church relations.

The above analysis is reinforced by another noteworthy feature: the development of the rhetorical direction through the series. Sermons are highly directional performance texts: typically, "I" (the preacher) addresses "you" (the congregation) about "Him" (God) and "them" (a group acting as comparator for the congregation—such as "evil men" or "martyrs"), drawing "us" together into a Church with a reaffirmed and reapplied doctrine. For this reason, I call the first person plural "inclusive," as its occurrence in this series becomes increasingly proportional to the subject of "our" relationship with God. The rhetorical strategy may reliably be gauged from the varying proportions of the persons. So, in this series, *Ten Virgins* is relatively unfocussed, starting with emphasis on "them" (not the Virgins but humankind in general) and only drawing preacher and auditors together in the final sections, most notably, of course, the Application. *Thanksgiving*, by contrast, is heavily "inclusive," as are the remainder of the series, but there is no distinct polar structure. This emerges in *Forgiveness*, the most "Godly" of the series (the relative prominence of the third person singular, which refers mostly to God as the source of forgiveness), while *Care of Our Souls*, less "Godly" than *Forgiveness*, is, while still distinctly "inclusive" in the key Application section, less so than its predecessors and generally less dynamic in its use of persons. It is notable that persons, as defined in this essay, comprise an extraordinarily high 9.21 percent of the total words of the two sermons of the immediate crisis—*Thanksgiving* and *Forgiveness*—an increase of 18 percent over the incidence in the two sermons flanking them (7.79 percent).[63] While it is not possible here to provide statistical comparators, as a rough guide, the thanksgiving sermon of Gilbert Burnet, Tillotson's close associate, achieves 6.5 percent. Burnet's use of the first person plural stands at 2.1 percent, Tillotson's at 4.3 percent—a dramatic difference and wholly due to Tillotson's rhetorical strategy.

Thus, although the rhetoric appears improvised, the syntax regulates the distance of subject and context. The sermons guide the practice of a Christian life, but as the voice of the preacher appears to lose control of the material, the listeners are impelled to seek the source of stress—in the context of current events. The listener's act of engaged criticism is an intrinsically

---

[63]   These figures have been calculated from the raw data, whose presentation is precluded by considerations of space. Work in progress suggests that these are extraordinarily high rates, subsequently approached, but not equaled, only by some evangelical and thanksgiving sermons.

metaphorical activity, and it is his strategy of drawing his listeners and readers into this activity that makes Tillotson so effective.

—V—

Shortly after *Care of Our Souls* was given, William's draft for his first King's Speech to Parliament included the claim that, "L'Eglise Anglicane étoit le principal Apuy de la Religion Protestant." This was translated as "The Church of England is one of the greatest Supports of the Protestant Religion." The phrase "Church of England" was then objected to by Sir Thomas Clarges MP "for fear it should be understood to make the *Dissenters* a part of the *Bulwark*, and therefore he would have had, as by *Law establish'd* added to it."[64] Clarges's amendment shows his appreciation that an entity was emerging comprising both a Church and a State: an Anglican communion defining itself as an increasingly dominant nationalistic part of a Church of England still largely confined to the home territories.[65] Tillotson, by redefining the relationship between doctrine, context, and speaking voice, made a claim about the special, culturally persuasive nature of English Protestantism. His criticism of the Roman Church over supererogation, as we have noticed, was less for bad theology than for the spiritual and psychological usuriousness that flows from it. His conversational rhetoric, with its subtle changes of pace and texture, identified such things as offensive to the "way" of English Protestant Christianity, one from which some Protestant sects wished legitimately, however regrettably, to separate themselves. The nationalism implicit in this became problematic only when the Church engaged in missions to non-English peoples; meanwhile he projected (what, a century later, the anti-slavery bishop Bielby Porteus was to elaborate[66]) a doctrine of multiculturalism, a liberalism grounded in what may be called value pluralism and defined dynamically by psychological and cultural borders.

---

[64]   John Oldmixon, *The History of England During the Reigns of King William and Queen Mary* (London, 1735), 29.

[65]   The transformation of this proto-Anglicanism into the authentic version is mapped in the present writer's chapter on missionary sermons in *A New History of the Nineteenth-Century Sermon*, ed. Robert Ellison (Brill, forthcoming).

[66]   See Bob Tennant, "Sentiment, Abolition, and Empire: A Study of Beilby Porteus's Anti-Slavery Sermon," in *Discourses of Slavery and Abolition*, ed. B. Carey, M. Ellis, and S. Salih (London: Palgrave, 2004), 161, 171.

Appendix.
Some Verbal and Syntactical Features of the Four Sermons

	Words	Comparative lengths (Appl=100)	Adj %	Verbs %	Words/sentence	Total words/ simple sentence	Verbs in simple sentences %	Verbs/sentence
Ten Virgins								
Exord	1439	227	6.74	11.33	20.27	42.32	21	2.30
Ex1	829	131	7.24	8.69	37.68	138.17	8	3.27
Ex2	1027	162	10.03	7.40	57.06	256.75	5	4.22
Ex3	328	52	8.54	10.37	21.87	65.60	15	2.27
Ex4	1613	254	6.26	11.10	26.02	64.52	14	2.89
Ex5	595	94	8.07	10.25	31.32	99.17	10	3.21
Ex6	1069	169	6.64	8.51	42.76	213.80	5	3.64
Appl	634	100	6.31	8.20	48.77	317.00	4	4.00
Per	260	41	6.92	7.31	32.50	260.00	5	2.38
Totals	7794	1229	7.26	9.58	30.81	88.57	12	2.95
Thanksgiving								
Exord	533	13	7.50	9.01	21.32	48.45	23	1.92
Ex1	594	15	7.91	11.11	21.21	54.00	17	2.36
Ex2	2235	56	6.31	10.96	17.46	32.39	28	1.91
Appl	4007	100	7.14	8.36	29.04	66.78	18	2.43
Per	295	7	6.10	8.81	49.17	∞	0	4.33
Totals	7664	191	6.94	9.39	23.58	50.75	21	2.22

"Exord" = Exordium
"Ex" = Exegetical section
"Appl" = Application
"Per" = Peroration

Appendix, cont.
Some Verbal and Syntactical Features of the Four Sermons

	Words	Comparative lengths (Appl=100)	Adj	Verbs	Words/sentence	Total words/ simple sentence	Verbs in simple sentences	Verbs/sentence
			%	%			%	
Forgiveness of Injuries								
Exord	590	20	6.95	10.17	28.10	118.00	8	2.86
Ex1	452	15	8.85	9.96	15.59	22.60	44	1.55
Ex2	899	30	7.12	10.68	23.05	64.21	15	2.46
Ex3	700	23	7.86	8.71	25.93	77.78	15	2.26
Ex4	1992	66	6.58	9.54	23.44	55.33	19	2.24
Appl	3021	100	7.12	9.63	26.97	70.26	15	2.60
Per	245	8	5.71	12.24	17.50	27.22	30	2.14
Totals	7899	261	7.09	9.79	24.16	58.08	18	2.36
Care of Our Souls								
Exord	516	30	5.81	9.69	20.64	46.91	22	2.00
Ex1	3153	182	7.87	9.42	32.17	126.12	8	3.03
Ex2	707	41	7.07	9.90	25.25	117.83	9	2.50
Appl	1729	100	7.81	9.77	34.58	133.00	8	3.38
Per	217	13	5.07	12.44	13.56	21.70	37	1.69
Totals	6322	366	7.50	9.70	29.13	97.26	11	2.82

Appendix, cont.
Incidence of Grammatical Persons

	1st sing %	1st pl %	2nd (all) %	3rd sing %	3rd pl %
Ten Virgins					
Exord	0.97	1.46	0.63	0.49	3.68
Ex1	0.84	1.69	0.00	1.45	2.05
Ex2	0.39	0.78	0.00	1.27	5.06
Ex3	0.30	1.52	0.30	2.44	5.79
Ex4	0.62	1.43	0.56	2.29	3.41
Ex5	0.34	0.84	0.50	0.67	4.20
Ex6	0.19	5.80	0.19	1.96	0.47
Appl	0.32	4.42	0.16	1.74	0.47
Per	1.54	3.46	3.08	1.54	0.38
Totals	0.59	2.25	0.42	1.50	2.95
Thanksgiving					
Exord	0.94	4.32	0.38	2.81	2.44
Ex1	0.51	6.73	0.67	0.84	1.35
Ex2	1.21	1.88	1.70	2.33	2.55
Appl	0.50	4.79	0.27	0.85	1.50
Per	0.34	8.14	0.34	2.03	0.00
Totals	0.73	4.19	0.73	1.46	1.80

Appendix, cont. Incidence of Grammatical Persons	1st sing %	1st pl %	2nd (all) %	3rd sing %	3rd pl %
Forgiveness of Injuries					
Exord	1.36	5.76	1.69	0.51	2.03
Ex1	0.22	2.65	0.00	1.55	0.88
Ex2	0.22	5.12	0.00	3.00	1.11
Ex3	0.14	2.43	0.00	2.43	0.14
Ex4	0.20	4.82	0.75	3.16	1.61
Appl	0.56	4.70	0.96	1.56	2.05
Per	0.41	2.45	4.49	3.27	2.04
Totals	0.43	4.47	0.82	2.18	1.60
Care of our Souls					
Exord	1.16	2.91	0.39	1.74	0.19
Ex1	0.79	2.60	0.41	2.22	1.74
Ex2	0.28	4.67	0.00	1.27	2.12
Appl	0.52	5.26	0.23	0.58	0.98
Per	0.46	8.76	0.92	3.23	0.92
Totals	0.68	3.78	0.35	1.66	1.42

Note: In identifying sentences, punctuation and paragraphing are ignored entirely. "Sentence" means "any string of words ended by a semantic discontinuity (including syntactically anomalous cases)" so that sentences appear shorter than with other analytical models; "simple sentence" includes co-ordinate main clauses. "Adjective" excludes possessives (which count as "persons"), and "person" includes all grammatical parts of each word-family: thus first person singular comprises all occurrences of "I, me, mine, my, myself." For the syntactical analysis, the definitions built into the Linkparser program have been used, although modified to take account of the anomalous structures mentioned. Wordsmith version 4 was used to compile the lexical data. In the third person singular, "she" (virtually non-existent) and "it" (usually a merely syntactical device) are left out of account.

Effects and Affects: Edward Taylor's Negotiation of Ramist Rhetoric

Harry Clark Maddux

Both the poetry and the recorded life of Edward Taylor (1642–1729) have provided students of early American culture with rich research material ever since Thomas Johnson discovered manuscripts of Taylor's *Preparatory Meditations* in 1937. Since then, too, there has been a remarkable (if general) consensus about the aims and effects of Taylor's work. In this regard, the proposition that Taylor depended in his writing upon Ignatian methods of meditation, made by Norman Grabo in the first book-length study of Taylor,[1] is not all that different from recent complementary assertions of Ivy Schweitzer and Jeffrey Hammond that the *Meditations* exemplify a failed cultural quest for an ineffable personal identification, premised upon the covenant of God's grace.[2] Each of these critics agrees fundamentally that in his life, as in his verse, Taylor epitomizes the paradox of Puritan devotion: an intensely experienced disjunction between the opposing forces of ritual meditative practice and Calvinist dogmas of God's sovereignty. In the words of Ivy Schweitzer, Taylor specifically attempted to answer the question of how he might "speak divine praise uncontaminated by fallen, selfish desire . . . by strategic and doctrinally sanctioned representations of the sinning and saintly speaking subject" as a passive female, waiting to be ravished by a male deity.[3]

---

[1] Norman S. Grabo, *Edward Taylor* (Boston: Twayne Press, 1988), 34–36.
[2] Ivy Schweitzer, *The Work of Self-Representation: Lyric Poetry in Colonial New England* (Chapel Hill: University of North Carolina Press, 1991), 22; Jeffrey A. Hammond, *Sinful Self, Saintly Self: The Puritan Experience of Poetry* (Athens: University of Georgia Press, 1993), 20.
[3] Schweitzer, *Self-Representation*, 79.

The combined investigations into Taylor have without doubt improved our understanding of the emergence of Christian belief in America.[4] Such examinations have not, however, usually observed how the *Meditations* are a very precise mirror of orthodox intellectual development in Massachusetts. From this perspective, what distinguishes Taylor's poetry is not so much his representation of himself as female, as is his rigorous application of scholastic logical procedure to matters of the affective will. The singular fact of his writing is not its reliance upon moments of expressive failure, as much as it is its celebration of them.

Moments like those in the *Meditations* operate in essence as formal confirmations of Taylor's belief that the structures of Ramist dialectic (or logic) inhered in all of nature, as well as reflecting the two main lines of modification to Peter Ramus's original reform of teaching, first published in 1543 as *Dialecticae Partitiones*. Almost from the instant of his death during the St. Bartholomew's Day massacre, Ramus's ideas had undergone alteration. In particular, German proto-encyclopedists such as Bartholomew Keckermann and Johannes Piscator developed Ramus's disjunctive method into cataloguing procedures of various kinds, which aimed at comprehensive treatment of a subject.[5] The most famous, albeit parodic, example of this tendency in English letters is Robert Burton's *Anatomy of Melancholy*. At around the same time as these first changes to Ramus's scheme were occurring in Germany, elsewhere in that country followers of Philip Melanchthon, who had developed his own reform of learning, were grafting Ramus's schematic techniques onto Melanchthon's more traditional Aristotelian principles.[6] The result was a manner of intellection that was able to value—even esteem—rationality, without wholly submitting individual experience to it. In effect, Ramism retained its cultural primacy in matters of expression, though not always in expected experience. Later Puritans more obviously than their predecessors, in part because of events such as the Antinomian crisis and local and distant political upheavals since 1630, were less willing than their forebears to claim that Ramist methods had a virtue in themselves, but as late as 1718 they still found in such approaches a satisfying description of the world as they encountered it. It is even possible to say that stalwarts of Puritan orthodoxy, such as Edward Taylor, had by the late seventeenth century been able to domesticate the charismatic, ecstatic strain of Protestantism represented in colonial history by Anne Hutchinson and (more circumspectly) John Cotton.[7]

4   Crucial works treating Taylor include not only those of Norman Taylor, Ivy Schweitzer, and Jeffrey Hammond, but those of Ursula Brumm, Barbara Lewalski, Karl Keller, William J. Scheick, and Thomas and Viriginia Davis as well.
5   Walter J. Ong, *Ramus, Method, and the Decay of Dialogue: From the Art of Discourse to the Art of Reason* (1957) (Cambridge: Harvard University Press, 1983), 300.
6   Ibid., 299.
7   Janice Knight, *Orthodoxies in Massachusetts: Rereading American Puritanism* (Cambridge: Harvard University Press, 1994), 22.

I want to propose that Taylor's work deserves to be considered in this context of intellectual adaptation, contention, and negotiation. Two of the *Meditations* from the two ends of his professional life offer convincing evidence that he at least participated in this process of cultural construction, by drawing from both Systematic and "Mixt" or Philippo-Ramist sources for his poetry. Meditation 1.8, in brief, emblematizes the cognitive procedures of Systematic Ramism; Meditation 2.146, one of Taylor's last verses, is a neat instance of specific Philippo-Ramist techniques as advocated (among others) by the English sermonist John Flavel (1630–1691).

The *Meditations*, regular devotional exercises written by Taylor to be used before those occasions when he administered the Lord's Supper to his congregation at Westfield, thus suggest that Taylor operated within the discursive mainstream of his culture rather than at its edges as is more commonly thought. Moreover, recognizing that Taylor was fully engaged with and not marginalized by his peers encourages us to rethink certain of our conclusions about the disintegration of Puritan culture: if Taylor's language is less reactionary than it has often been made to seem, then the controversies in which he was engaged might have occurred along different axes than those that are frequently mapped. The distinctions between evangelical revivalism and filiopietistic rationalism might be far less distinct than we have easily made them to be. What cannot be ignored facilely, without occluding our understanding of American culture, is that Taylor employed the same discourse in his poetry, to the same purpose, as the most fervent evangelist did in any representative New English sermon of the Great Awakening.

It is probably no surprise to anyone familiar with Louis Martz's thesis in *The Poetry of Meditation* that the opening stanza of Taylor's Meditation 1.8, on John 6:51, sensately composes the matter of meditation.[8] Taylor characteristically approaches his subject obliquely and through a fracture of his own understanding:

> I kening through Astronomy Divine
> The Worlds bright Battlement, wherein I spy
> A Golden Path my Pensill cannot line,
> From that bright Throne unto my Thresholdly.
> And while my puzzled thoughts about it pore
> I finde the Bread of Life in't at my doore. (1–6)[9]

As Michael Wigglesworth had in *The Day of Doom*, and as Taylor himself had in the "Prologue" to his own *Preparatory Meditations*, the poet here sees, but cannot say, divine teleology. What is curious in this instance is that the ritual complaint begins in a rare moment of spiritual satisfaction for Taylor

8 Louis L. Martz, *The Poetry of Meditation: A Study in Religious Literature of the Seventeenth Century* (New Haven: Yale University Press, 1954), 27.
9 Unless otherwise noted, all references to Taylor's poetry are from *The Poems of Edward Taylor*, ed. Donald E. Stanford (Chapel Hill: University of North Carolina Press, 1989). Parenthetical references within the text are to line numbers in the respective poems.

and ends with a rapid (but unproblematic) refiguration of the meditative object. So Taylor begins by reporting how he caught a brief glimpse of "Astronomy Divine" (1). He is, of course, unable to follow with his finger the star chart of God from "that bright Throne unto my Threshold" (4), and yet, while he puzzles over the imperfection of his own understanding, he discovers in that gracious glance "the Bread of Life in't at my doore" (6).

The images are conventional enough. Understanding as a line of rationality (3), from sovereign to subject (4) is a central trope of, among other texts, *Leviathan*. In Meditation 1.8, however, there is a new sweep to Taylor's figures. The old spatial illustration stretches into astral navigation, and it is there that Taylor reveals his growing fascination with "natural" philosophy. This is far from the most scientific of his lyrics. The minor work on "The Great Bones Dug Up at Clavarack" and the preceding poem to Meditation 1.8, wherein Taylor envisions the incarnation of Christ (and his own inspiration) as an experiment in alchemy, are more obvious examples.[10] Meditation 1.8 more neatly than these, though, intimates the complete range and extent of Taylor's Ramist epistemology. The occasioning thought of the poem is a stray, but entirely systematic, assumption. When Taylor "kens" divine astronomy, he also initiates a quest whose terms are presumptively scholastic in content and Ramist in execution. A general art (astronomy in this case) reduces to a particular instance (the world). This relation is further imagined as a spatial progression premised on the peripatetic accident of location, and predictably the movement is traced via degrees of cosmological significance. Taylor is moved to "finde the Bread of Life" (6) by passing through the starry sky to the "Worlds bright Battlement" (2) before reaching the "Threshold" (4) of his own life.

What makes this progress specially Ramist, and of a Systematic variety at that, is above all its order. Roland MacIlmaine, in the first English translation of Ramus, put it that any disquisition about a subject should first "intreate of the rules which be generall generallye, and those which be speciall speciallie."[11] When this axiom was combined with the dictate that any art (ars), such as astronomy, should definitively "gather only together that which dothe appartayne to the Arte of which we intreate of,"[12] the effect was a system of knowledge marked by its "technological" drive toward complete analysis of a subject.[13]

---

[10]   For "The Great Bones Dug Up at Clavarack," see *The Unpublished Writings of Edward Taylor*, ed. Thomas M. and Virginia L. Davis. 3 vols. (Boston: G. K. Hall, 1981), 3:211–216; on Taylor's employment of alchemical images, see Cheryl Z. Oreovicz, "Investigating 'the America of nature': Alchemy in Early American Poetry," in *Puritan Poets and Poetics: Seventeenth-Century American Poetry in Theory and Practice*, ed. Peter White (University Park: Pennsylvania State University Press, 1985), 99–110.

[11]   Roland MacIlmaine, *The Logike of the Moste Excellent Philosopher P. Ramus Martyr*, ed. Catherine M. Dunn (Northridge: San Fernando Valley State College Press, 1969), 5.

[12]   Ibid., 4.

[13]   Perry Miller, *The New England Mind: The Seventeenth Century* (1939) (Cambridge: Belknap Press, 1982), 121. I should also note here that Alan Pope proved

The second stanza employs much the same Systematic Ramist technique in the apparently very different context of history. Having somewhat precipitously decided on a meditation about the physical material—the communion loaf—that signifies the act of redemption (a topic that resurfaces in stanza three as a characteristic comprehension of grace as the material cause of election), it might seem that a discourse on history would be unnecessary to Taylor's meditation, but this anomaly looks less unusual when Taylor's acceptance of Aristotelian causation is recalled. The descent into time is shown in this regard to be the necessary efficient cause of the Incarnation and sin itself as a first, formal cause gone awry. The effect is that if by sin, suffering came into the world, by sin, too, salvation entered in. Taylor, then, frankly marvels at how

> When that this Bird of Paradise put in
> This Wicker Cage (my Corps) to tweedle praise
> Had peckt the Fruite forbad: and so did fling
> Away its Food; and lost its golden dayes;
> It fell into Celestiall Famine sore:
> And never could attain a morsel more. (7–12)

Humanity in Taylor's theology had at first been conceived for the same purpose as the angels, who were fashioned only to praise God eternally, but when the original types had spurned the reason for their being, they also discarded their reason and thereby plunged themselves and all their progeny into a temporal desert all but devoid of the divine presence. Nevertheless, even in a postlapsarian world there remains this dim shadow of a lost cosmology: as in the first stanza, where astronomy is anatomized as movement toward greater comprehensiveness, so in the second, history is figuratively located as an effect analyzable into two disjoined types of cause.

This is why Taylor continues by construing grace as the material (and metaphorically physical) cause, leading to an effect of a redemptive human state. "Alas! alas! Poore Bird," Taylor apostrophizes, "what wilt thou doe" (13)?

---

in 1985 that the syllogistic and Aristotelian roots of Ramism showed through the poetry of Michael Wigglesworth. On this matter, see Alan H. Pope, "Petrus Ramus and Michael Wigglesworth: The Logic of Poetic Structure," in White, ed., *Puritan Poets*, 210–226. Taylor's dependence on Ramism, however, is substantially different from that of Wigglesworth's. Whereas Wigglesworth restricts himself in his work to the firmest of scholastic connections within Ramism (Pope, 210), Taylor extends the method along the historical lines that had been laid down in Reformation Europe. This difference marks Taylor as much more relatively radical—if not outright reactionary—than Wigglesworth, since Taylor was writing some twenty years after the Restoration. By the same token, Wigglesworth's writing is not the only example of how Ramist thought exercised an "important and subtle influence" upon American Puritan culture (Pope, 225), even if it is strikingly representative of that development.

> The Creatures field no food for Souls e're gave
> And if thou knock at Angells dores they show
> An Empty Barell: they no soul bread have.
> Alas! Poore Bird, the Worlds White Loaf is done.
> And cannot yield thee here the smallest Crumb. (14–18)

The course of history since Adam's fall is portrayed as an Augustinian search for satisfaction that will never succeed under the circumstances of origination. Because the animals are distinct from humanity by topical definition, they have never been able to give "food for Souls" (14). The angels offer no better hope. In this aspect, they are identical with rather than distinguishable from the scriptural beasts of the field and birds of the air; "they [too] no soul bread have" (16).

Given the scope of such existential vanity, the abrupt reversal of human fortunes in stanza four appears all but unexpected. Certainly, the figural shape taken by that change is one of the most startling and disquieting shifts in English devotional verse. "In this sad state" of sin,

> . . . Gods Tender Bowells run
> Out streams of Grace: And he to end all strife
> The Purest Wheate in Heaven, his deare-dear Son
> Grinds, and kneads up into this Bread of Life.
> Which Bread of Life from heaven down came and stands
> Disht on thy Table up by Angells Hands. (19–24)

In spite of the jarring nature of these images, there is a definite method to Taylor's imagery at this particular place. One way in which he will routinely answer the mystery of mercy is to posit it as a thing of ultimately minor import to God, though almost never so vulgarly as he does here.[14] Indeed, the very next stanza will take up this thread and envisage the visible sign of invisible election as "Heavens Sugar Cake" (30). But Taylor's aim in this crucial stanza is much more daring and disturbing than a simple statement of relation. It makes plain the terrible cost of redemption. Like some grim giant, God grinds up the bones of his own son in order to feed humanity what it had repudiated by an originating act of will: "The purest Wheate in Heaven, his deare-dear Son / Grinds, and kneads up into this Bread of Life" (21–22). Rather than fulfilling human desire for understanding, grace fundamentally interrupts and reverses it. This is the cognitive equivalent of Christ's maxim that in the kingdom of heaven the first shall become last and the last first (Mt 19:30). It is experience made impenetrable, and knowing through a glass, darkly. It is, most of all, a complete inversion of categorical thinking. Of course, whenever the gracious mind of God defies human expectation, it follows that He will, just then, elude the intellectual grasp of His creation.

---

[14]   In Meditation 1.2, Taylor asks to be made a small accoutrement in God's dress. "Yet may I Purse," he prays, "and thou my Mony bee" (29).

The final paradox of the Incarnation is that this horrible sacrifice was the only way whereby right reason could conceivably be restored. The cipher of election solidifies into the communal bread on which Taylor had been contemplating from the start, but with the resurrection of the emblem, he grasps its import in a new way. He wonders again at the priceless gift he has been given entirely without grudge, and perceives afresh the import of the invitation proffered by God to His chosen few:

> Did God mould up this Bread in Heaven, and bake,
> Which from his Table came, and to thine goeth?
> Doth he bespeake thee thus, This Soule Bread take.
> Come Eate thy fill of this thy Gods White Loafe?
> Its food too fine for Angells, yet come, take
> And Eate thy fill. Its Heavens Sugar Cake. (25–30)

If the fall itself was the most tragic event of human existence, it is in the power of the Divine to make it a fortunate occurrence. The provision of Providence surely cannot mean much to God—even if the shape His caretaking assumed was unimaginably costly—but its outcome is infinitely valuable to those whom it benefits.

Put less lyrically, but no less significantly, the wonder of redemption is that the material cause of that signal deed should so far outweigh the formal shape it takes of logical necessity. The broken body of incarnate God is transformed into a dainty desert, as it is elsewhere in the *Meditations*, such as Meditation 1.11, where the communion elements are imaged as the "Choicest Dainties Paradise e're bred" (16). Therefore, in the concluding stanza, it is as a soul reconciled to difficult new meanings that Taylor inquires:

> What Grace is this knead in this Loafe? This thing
> Souls are but petty things it to admire.
> Yee Angells, help: This fill would to the brim
> Heav'ns whelm'd-down Chrystall meele Bowle, yea and
>   higher.
> This Bread of Life dropt in thy mouth, doth Cry.
> Eate, Eate me, Soul, and thou shalt never dy. (31–36)

Poetic language that has been redeemed can imagine what reprobate discourse cannot: asking for help in shaping speech from those who lack apprehension of the subject. In God's redemptive scheme, it is possible to turn to linguistically innocent heavenly messengers for aid in expressing the experience of mercy pressed down and overflowing from heaven, as it is equally possible that the refuse of God should become the means by which ordering sanity is restored to an insanely disordered world.

There is a terrible symmetry here that, if it is not yet Blakean in an American vein, is far from disintegrating into philosophical incoherence. The case is quite the obverse. In his devotion, Taylor never encounters any problem of cognition that some variety of Ramism cannot solve in some (albeit sometimes an unsatisfactory) way. As late as 1718, he was reformulating his experience as one of the elect in terms that are more than a little reminiscent of the Christology of John Flavel and the meditations of Richard Baxter.[15] As completely as Taylor had employed Ramism in a Systematic manner, he put it to use as a vehicle for generating an affective response, especially in the later poems such as Meditation 2.146. Ironically, due to the vast amount of criticism that has tended simplistically to classify Puritans along twentieth-century political lines, this particular verse shows exactly how close Taylor was to the language that would produce the Great Awakening. Taylor is no anachronism preaching an already extinct political vision; he is the herald of its later shape as much as Solomon Stoddard or any other putatively "progressive" Puritan. The language of American evangelical belief derives as fully from the likes of Taylor as anyone else, and his later *Meditations* prefigure the religious culture of periodic revival that would flourish in the environment of colonial America in ways that it did not (and could not) in England.

Meditation 2.146, upon Canticles 6:13, where the male speaker of the Hebrew lyrical cycle cries with the voice of his entire people, "Return, oh Shulamite, return, return, that we may look upon thee," deserves a passing comment, if nothing else, because so many examinations have focused on Taylor's poetic use of the Canticles, though these studies have rarely reached any concord on what to make of Taylor's habitual recurrence to the most intensely erotic work contained in Christian scripture. Grabo, for instance, construes the text as an allegory of mystical union, which is something very like how Taylor himself would have understood the work given the long hermeneutic tradition that views Christ as the male speaker, who woos his bride, the church.[16] Ivy Schweitzer, by contrast, interprets Taylor's insistence on his own (feminized) passivity as a deconstructive sign of his own cultural anxieties.[17]

These and other readings of Taylor's employment of scripture are plainly not without merit but rarely do any of them note the cognitive assumptions actually inherent in his poetic meditations on biblical topics, nor do they typically observe the cultural situation in which Taylor finds himself thereby. Ursula Brumm and Karen Rowe have both analyzed well the typology underwriting the *Meditations*, but they do not remark how Taylor's theories of communication exhibit an identical (and still correspondential) structure that likewise motivates and guides the lyrical practice of his regular devotions.[18] At least as much as it represents his allegorically eroticized love of God, the constant return of Taylor to the

---

15   I am attempting to demonstrate a cultural connection, not a biographical one, between Taylor and Flavel, but it is important to note that if Taylor had read Flavel, he did not own any copies of his works. Taylor did, however, own several texts of Baxter.

16   Grabo, *Taylor*, 46.

17   Schweitzer, *Self-Representation*, 87.

18   Ursula Brumm, *American Thought and Religious Typology*, trans. John Hoaglund (New Brunswick: Rutgers University Press, 1970), 57–85; Karen E. Rowe, *Saint and Singer: Edward Taylor's Typology and the Poetics of Meditation* (Cambridge: Cambridge University Press, 1986), 231–266.

Canticles epitomizes his abiding attraction to coherent forms of order. To comprehend the use of the Canticles in his poetry, then, entails knowing how and to what ends Taylor's own semantic theory operated within the range of his active poetic life.

From this perspective, Meditation 2.146 evinces the final evolution of Taylor's Ramist beliefs. It reflects both the consistency of his thought and its still surprising flexibility. It patently shows how in his later poetry, as in later Puritan colonial culture at large, the youthfully exuberant application of Systematic Ramism underwent a process of distillation, but also indicates that Ramist logic did not necessarily lose any of its original aims as a result. Rhetorical modes of persuasion return to favor in the techniques of Philippo-Ramism, but for Taylor and many early eighteenth-century Congregationalists, this change simply allowed the individuals in devotion to address themselves as a reluctant (and rhetorically pliable) audience. Rather than effecting change in a literal society, as had been the aim of the classical rhetoric against which Ramus had reacted, the goal of Philippo-Ramism when it was applied in Puritanism was to appeal to one's own affections exactly as if (and because) the private self is the social body (in miniature). The individual is condensed or, more accurately, reduced to a synecdoche, an all but representative man in the manner of Emerson. Therefore, what can influence the mob applies to the individual. The results may appear ludicrous in the context of contemporary discourse, but the record of the Great Awakening attests to the efficacy of the practice.

Taylor's frequent recourse to exactly the affective and repetitive rhetorical method of Flavel is the best proof of his proximity to the discourse of revivalism that marked the course of the Great Awakening. If his steadfast refusal to acquiesce to the ecclesiology of Solomon Stoddard ultimately inspired a strong negative reaction in Taylor's own congregation, causing them to embrace the principles of Stoddardeanism shortly before the death of Taylor in 1729, that fact does not mean that his devotional practice was any less characteristic of the future of New English history than it was indicative of its past.[19] Stoddard's polity, in other words, has too long been identified as heralding an American advance into modernity. The similarities among the writings of Flavel and Taylor and Thomas Prince, a major publicist of the Awakening, all suggest that Taylor was as much a viable part of the emergence of a prerevolutionary American discourse as was the most committed evangelist working his or her way through the colonies during the early years of the 1740s.

The first stanza of Meditation 2.146 does unmistakably reverence the past, since the opening lines are a patent evocation of the spirit of the early Puritan Ramist, Alexander Richardson. "My Deare Deare Lord," Taylor prays, "I know not what to say: / Speech is too Course a web for me to cloath / My Love to thee in or it to array" (1–3). The image of speech as cloth that Taylor produces here is one of the primary tropes of Puritan discourse. As John Charles Adams states, Richardson's seventeenth-century "clothing

---

[19]   For a contrary view, see Mark A. Peterson, *The Price of Redemption: The Spiritual Economy of New England* (Stanford: Stanford University Press, 1997), 216.

metaphors" provided one of the first rhetorical instances of how "Ramus's precepts [were applied] to social values and philosophic assumptions drawn from the fields of fashion, psychology, and Puritan theology."[20] Ever since the 1629 publication of *The Logician's School-Master*, Puritans had equated clothing with language. Plainness in dress and speech became in this way a dominant metaphor of Puritan identity throughout the century of Civil War and Restoration. Consequently, whenever Taylor images his failed devotional expression as drab clothing as he does here, he is participating in an established allegorical tradition that correlates fineness of speech with extravagance of dress. In this special cultural sense, his inadequate attempt at language is as foreordinate as his own eternal fate.

Yet the true saving grace of semantic intent is the depressing familiarity of this shortcoming. Just like Augustine at the other outer limit of European culture, Taylor finds meaning between the horns of his will and his ability. So he repeats himself: "Thy Love to mee's too great, for mee to shape / a Vesture for the Same at any rate" (5–6). Hereafter, the poem will find a rich variety of signification in the triune themes of love, sensation, and economy, and Taylor will furnish a near final demonstration of reason's consummate revelation in sentimentalism. Repetitiveness is not, then, a sign of political despair as Miller supposes; it is a focal point of historical change inspired and only inspirable by the instrument of rationality.[21] Method, to recall the Flavelian formulation, was shown in motive.

Among other things, this use of repetition surely signals the poetic debt that Taylor owed to the Psalms as did many Puritan versifiers. Rosemary Fithian has demonstrated with fair conclusiveness that Taylor not only drew on the parallel structure of Hebrew poetry in his own writing, he employed four other techniques acquired from the Psalms: "interrogation, shifting of person addressed, amplification, and antithesis."[22] All of these devices are put to good use in Meditation 2.146, but, again, they need to be understood as ingredients that are added to a Philippo-Ramist mixture of order and affect.

Discernibly, the system in place in stanza two is founded on a sensational psychology, as it is dependent on a natural theology derived from correspondences:

> When as thy Love doth Touch my Heart down tost
> It tremblingly runs, seeking thee its all,
> And as a Child when it his nurse hath lost
> Runs seeking her, and after her doth Call.

20　John Charles Adams, "Linguistic Values and Religious Experience: An Analysis of the Clothing Metaphors in Alexander Richardson's Ramist-Puritan Lectures on Speech, 'Speech is a Garment to Cloath Our Reason,'" *The Quarterly Journal of Speech* 76 (1990): 58–68, 58.

21　Perry Miller, *The New England Mind: From Colony to Province* (1953) (Cambridge: Belknap Press, 1981), 405.

22　Rosemary Fithian, "'Words of My Mouth, Meditations of My Heart': Edward Taylor's Preparatory Meditations and the Book of Psalms," *Early American Literature* 20 (1985): 89–119, 90.

So when thou hidst from me, I seek and sigh.
Thou saist return return Oh Shulamite. (7–12)

In part, this technique is a natural extension of Taylor's play with acrostics during his days as a Harvard student, though in the later lyrics the maneuver is much more subtle and deftly directive. Thus, the heart that "tremblingly runs, seeking" (8) its own essence is transmuted two lines later into the child that more urgently "runs seeking" its nurse "and after her doth Call" (10). Another two lines, and the action shifts its focus without losing its bearing on movement. The poet's desperately searching heart hears the call of Christ, the Israelite King: "Thou saist return return Oh Shulamite" (12). Long before the moment of this poem, Taylor had ceased to be the ingenious wordsmith, who visibly draws attention to his skill. By the time of it, he has become instead the artist confident in his abilities, who guides the reader through a map of his own imaginative landscape on his terms.

The abrupt metaphorical reconfiguration that occurs in the central third and fourth stanzas, therefore, again seems not to be truly haphazard, albeit that the maneuver is as definitely abrupt as it is in any of Taylor's earliest works, such as Meditation 1.8:

Rent out on Use thy Love thy Love I pray.
My Love to thee shall be thy Rent and I
Thee Use on Use, Intrest on intrest pay.
Theres none Extortion in such Usury.[23]

I'le pay thee Use on Use for't and therefore
Thou shalt become the Greatest Usurer.
But yet the principall I'll neer restore.
The Same is thine and mine. We shall not Jar.
And so this blessed Usury shall be
Most profitable both to thee and mee. (13–22)

Few transitions could "Jar" (20) on the modern ear as much as one from love to economy, but an evident preparation was made in the first two stanzas for every move undertaken in these. Taylor, for instance, images the attempt to produce a linguistic mantle of devotion with which the meditation is initiated as a priceless artifact: "Thy Love to mee's too great, for mee to shape / A Vesture for the same at any rate" (5–6). Rate is here a pun on loquacity, but it is also a sure signifier of creditor-debtor relations. Even the repetitive "thy Love thy Love I pray" (13) appears less unexpected when it is compared to the immediately preceding plea of "return return Oh Shulamite" (12).

Moreover, because every public relation (including marriage) in Puritan culture was understood as a covenant, it is no surprise that Taylor

---

[23]   This is almost the only instance of a quatrain in the *Preparatory Meditations*. In virtually every other lyric, Taylor never deviates from the six-line stanza typical in George Herbert's *The Temple*.

should address the object of his faith in legal and economic terms. It is more remarkable, but not finally very startling, that Taylor envisions a utopian society in which John Winthrop's "modell" of Christian charity no longer obtains. Taylor can endlessly exchange and owe a debt of love for Love and word for Word and "yet the principall . . . neer restore" (19), simply because the "Same is thine and mine" (20). Taylor might well be hoping for an age when economic strife would be put to rest, if Peterson is correct in his assertion that the church in Westfield, and Taylor as its minister, both suffered from the hard economic conditions of the Massachusetts frontier.[24] There can, however, be little doubt that this poem distinctly unites opposites, as language redeemed from its categorical fractures always had been rhetorically and logically rejoined in Taylor's verse. As ever, the dream at the end of his life is still of a return to an originally lost, holistic epistemology. At the last, he only refocused his efforts by reducing them to their essentials. Like a frontier Descartes, Taylor wanted to begin with the indubitable. In this case, the endeavor simply takes the shape of a repeated, infinitely longing, call to come back to a dimly remembered home of unified cognition.

As a result, Taylor is able nimbly to convert the image again in the concluding stanza:

> And shouldst thou hide thy shining face most fair
> Away from me. And in a sinking wise
> My trembling beating heart brought nigh t'dispare
> Should cry to thee and in a trembling guise
> Lord quicken it. Drop in its Eares delight
> Saying Return, Return, my Shulamite. (2.146, 23–28)

The refrain of futilely searching speech becomes newly dominant, and takes the place of the symbol of the desired relationship—that of a lover's debt—with one fine difference. The prayer to return is specified this time as it had not been previously. Dialectical generality once more elides into particularity, in this case attended by a note of property rights. The Shulamite is made coextensive with Taylor himself (and, by implication, with all of the same elected "race"). He again identifies his own affective experience with the concord of a larger congregation and thereby revalidates his own demanding ecclesiology using the correspondential methods of Philippo-Ramist logic.

Ultimately, that standard would not suit his congregation and along with many other churches in the Connecticut River valley they would be led to adopt a practice of open communion, but, then, it could well be specially significant that Westfield did not participate very much in the Great Awakening.[25] If Taylor's *Meditations* show anything at all, it is that he far more than his congregation was primed for revival. Despite (or, perhaps, due to) his own fervor, he might have known – as his church might not

---

24   Peterson, *Redemption*, 96.
25   Ibid., 222.

have—that both the "heart" and the people "brought nigh t'dispare" were ripe for religious rededication (2.146, 25). If nothing else, that was the lesson of the Jeremiad. To all appearances, the grandson of his controversial foe, Jonathan Edwards, agreed entirely with Taylor. Edwards's refusal to administer communion to his own congregation in his later years as the pastor at Northampton reflects his acceptance of the same distinctions of motive that inspired Taylor's life-long stringent application of membership requirements in Westfield. Few attitudes could be more Puritanical; few Puritans could better represent the early emergence of a systematically experiential discourse in modern American culture.

These two strands of discourse are not, it must finally be said, fully united in Taylor. By the time of the Great Awakening, however, Systematic and Philippo-Ramist techniques would merge into a seamless expectation of redemptive history. Taylor is no Edwards, nor is he a budding Congregational Methodist, but he does patently anticipate such developments in American Christianity. Perhaps nowhere is this similarity better shown than in one of the earliest texts of the "awakening" in America. The circular distributed by Bostonian Thomas Prince, advertising for accounts to be included in his periodical, Christian History, proves how the affective rhetoric of those like Taylor was later melded to a more distinctly sentimental, but still systematic, version of Christian belief.

Prince's "solicitation," reproduced in Frank Lambert's study, *Inventing the "Great Awakening,"* is richly evocative of much later educated colonial New English thought and fully deserves lengthier consideration than it can be given here.[26] Summarily, though, Prince is pointedly interested in the visible "effects" of revival (he repeats this word twice in the first two paragraphs), as Taylor was not. Seeking "the most Remarkable Instances of the Power and Grace of GOD," Prince implicitly presumes in an entirely commonsensical way that the accuracy of accounts of spiritual experience will be sensed by those who read them.

At the same time, he establishes a catalogue of those affected by the revivals that would have made Bartholomew Keckermann proud. Prince specially asks that his contributors include narratives of the "Power and Grace of God on the ſe four Sorts of People." There follows a numbered list of "Young Perſons," "Immoral Perſons," "The Oppoſers of this Work at firſt," and "Those who have been before in Repute for Morality and Religion." That this breakdown is presented in no discernible order can be very misleading: in actuality, Prince's categorization is so comprehensive that it includes every possible circumstance. The subjects are subdivided into two classes of origin: those who at first were "outside" the church (the young and immoral), and those at first "inside" it (the opponents and hypocrites).[27]

---

[26]   Frank Lambert, *Inventing the "Great Awakening"* (Princeton: Princeton University Press, 1999), 146.

[27]   The "young," as members of the Halfway Covenant, would, of course, have occupied a position of particular significance for New English Puritans seeking signs of revival. As Michael Colacurcio observed in a different context, such a class is presumed in Taylor's *Gods Determinations Touching His Elect.* See

The boundaries of these sets are also plainly intriguing: innocence and experience, duplicity and sincerity. Each displays an interest in psychology yet undeveloped in Taylor. By so much are Taylor and Prince separated, but, by their cognitive structures, they are obviously united.

Michael J. Colacurcio, *Doctrine and Difference: Essays in the Literature of New England* (New York: Routledge Press, 1997), 28–29.

Dualities of the Divine in Pope's *Essay on Man* and the *Dunciad*

Katherine M. Quinsey

The curious parallels between Pope's *Essay on Man* and its unholy relative the *Dunciad* have been observed at intervals over forty years, by scholars as diverse as Aubrey Williams, Maynard Mack, Miriam Leranbaum, Don Nichol, and Laura Brown.[1] The relation between these two poems, however, is more intimate, comprehensive, and dynamic than has hitherto been suggested. Not only do the formal elements of structure, subject, imagery, and generic matrix interpenetrate throughout, but, more tellingly, the two works are closely interwoven in their textual and production history. This complex interaction of Pope's two major "religious" (or irreligious) works creates a dynamic of the unstated, an energetic instability of textual process, that reveals more about Pope's religious thought and imagination than do the assertions of either poem.

Both the *Essay* and the *Dunciad* locate their purpose in relation to Milton's in *Paradise Lost* (1.1–26), a shared allusion generating much of the interplay and the subversiveness. *The Essay on Man* declares itself to be an attempt to "vindicate the ways of God to Man," yet it attempts the vindication without recourse to overt Christianity, relying instead on a great

---

1   Aubrey Williams, *Pope's Dunciad: A Study of Its Meaning* (London: Methuen, 1955), 84; Maynard Mack, *Alexander Pope: A Life* (New York: Norton; New Haven; Yale University Press, 1985) 540, 774; Miriam Leranbaum, *Alexander Pope's "Opus Magnum" 1729–1744* (Oxford: Clarendon Press, 1977), 131, 150–154; Laura Brown, *Alexander Pope* (Oxford: Basil Blackwell, 1985), 150–151; Don Nichol, "Pope's 1747 Ethick Epistles and The Essay on Man Frontispiece: An Abandoned 'Opus Magnum'?" in *Alexander Pope: Essays for the Tercentenary*, ed. Colin Nicholson (Aberdeen: Aberdeen University Press, 1988), 150–151.

cosmo-ethical system embodied in a rationalizing, hortatory, and at times conversational form. The *Essay* is itself the schematized introduction to what was to be a full-scale schematized attempt to make sense of human experience—Pope's projected "system of Ethicks, in the Horatian way,"[2] which existed conceptually from the mid-1720s if not earlier, helped generate both the *Essay*, the *Dunciad*, and the early Horatian satires, slept in the mid-1730s, and was revived under William Warburton's influence in the 1740s. In this scheme, even satirically-noted inconsistencies and vices are drawn up into a larger Providential order, seen for example in the optimism of the *Epistle To Burlington*, the closing climactic poem of what was generally published as "the Second Book of Ethic Epistles": "Yet hence [from Timon's vanities] the Poor are cloath'd, the Hungry fed" (169).[3]

The *Dunciad* precisely inverts both the *Essay's* Miltonic purpose and its discursive strategy. It celebrates the restoration of the reign of Chaos and Night, enacting Satan's vow to undo God's creation.[4] It works by an intuitive process of myth, fantasy, and vision, beyond the framework of rational, rhetorical, and moral justification; and it aims not to elicit a response from the reader in a traditional rhetorical mode but rather to preempt that response in an immersing narrative. There is no peroratio—no distancing coda—even the Popeian signature is problematic. In the *Dunciad* (all versions), the Providential process by which partial evil becomes universal good (*Essay*, 1.292) is not parodied but rather transmogrified; all partial evil disappears in universal darkness, in the complete obliteration of the distinction between good and evil, harmony and discord. (Note that the use of the terms "darkness" and "Unison" replace "evil" and "discord," which imply judgment, a point of reference outside). More significantly, in the *Dunciad* the overt Christian elements erased from the *Essay on Man* come bulging out, swarming with new, grotesque, and distorted life; they appear not only in the poem's allusive substance, but also in its central shaping principle—an incisive, multilayered, and thorough parody of the central mysteries of Christian theology.[5]

---

2   Pope to Swift, November 1729, in *The Correspondence of Alexander Pope*, ed. George Sherburn (Oxford: Clarendon Press, 1956), 3:81.

3   Quotations from Pope's poetry are from John Butt, ed., *The Poems of Alexander Pope: A One-Volume Edition of The Twickenham Pope* (London: Methuen, 1963). Pope comments on the significance of these lines to Spence (May 1–7, 1730): "As to the general design of Providence, the two extremes of a vice serve like two opposite biases to keep up the balance of things." Joseph Spence, *Observations, Anecdotes, and Characters of Books and Men*, ed. James M. Osborn (Oxford: Clarendon Press, 1966), 1:130–131, no. 297.

4   Sanford Budick, *Mythopoeic Displacement in the Verse of Milton, Dryden, Pope, and Johnson* (New Haven: Yale University Press, 1974), 140.

5   The Christian parody in the *Dunciad* has been discussed variously by Williams, *Pope's Dunciad*, 131–158; B. L. Reid, "Ordering Chaos: *The Dunciad*" (1974), rprt. in *Pope: Recent Essays By Several Hands*, ed. Maynard Mack and James Winn (Hamden: Archon Books, 1980), 678–706; Robert Griffin, "Pope, Prophets, and the *Dunciad*," *Studies in English Literature* 23 (1983): 435–446; Thomas Jemiely, "Consummatum Est: Alexander Pope's 1743 *Dunciad* and Mock-Apocalypse," in *"More Solid Learning": New Perspectives on Pope's Dunciad*, ed.

Both these works coexist in process during the entire period 1726–1744; Pope was actively revising both until his death (including numerous revisions to both text and commentary of both poems during reprintings and productions of his works in the 1730s). There is only time to suggest briefly what their textual and editing history reveals of how these two poems were conceived in relation to one another, in both the presentation and orderings of editions of Pope's *Works* in the 1730s and 1740s, and in the shifting outlines of the opus magnum. In arrangements of the *Works* from 1735 to 1739, the *Essay* is consistently presented as (literally) the "First Book of Ethic Epistles," the introduction to Pope's moral poetry (that is later Horatian epistles, satires, epitaphs, such short pieces as "To Mrs M. B. on her Birthday" and the *Universal Prayer*).[6] The *Dunciad*, however, usually appears in an independent volume following this body of work—separated, yet concluding Pope's serious moral works with its anarchic energies and vision of final dissolution, coyly qualified by his alter ego Martinus Scriblerus (indeed, concluding even more anticlimactically with its apparatus, which is increasingly appendicized from the poetic text until 1742, when Warburton takes over as the somewhat ponderous presiding spirit).

It can be argued that *Dunciad* was present from the very conception of the *opus magnum*, hovering constantly behind it, wings outspread; certainly it appears in shifting and embryonic forms in those plans, as Brown (128–129) and Leranbaum (passim) have shown, until 1742 when its role becomes much enlarged. David van der Meulen, in the introduction to his incomparable bibliographical study of the 1728 *Dunciad*, suggests that plans for the fourth book existed even prior to 1728.[7] The metaphysical section and satire on freethinking were added to Book 3 in the *Dunciad Variorum* (1729), anticipating the concerns of the fourth book, but also coinciding with the genesis of early plans for the great moral work. There are hints of a satire on false learning and false use of reason as early as 1722, 1714, or even earlier, in the Scriblerus project;[8] and it is notable that

---

Catherine Ingrassia and Claudia Thomas (Lewisburg: Bucknell University Press, 2000), 166–188, as well as by James King, "Alexander Pope and Roman Catholicism" (diss., Princeton University, 1970), 135–165. Williams and Reid suggest the scope of these religious parallels; King and Griffin something of their precision—but the parody is more complete and more comprehensive than these studies indicate.

[6]   I wish to express my warmest gratitude to the Beinecke Rare Book and Manuscript Library, the Houghton Library, the Bodleian Library, the Huntington Library, and the British Library for the opportunity to examine in detail numerous editions and variant editions of Pope's Works. I would also like in particular to thank the Pierpont Morgan Library and the Houghton Library for the opportunity to examine the original working manuscripts of the *Essay on Man*, discussed below.

[7]   David L. Van der Meulen, *Pope's Dunciad of 1728: A History and Facsimile* (Charlottesville: University of Virginia Press), 59.

[8]   Alexander Pope et al., *Memoirs of the Extraordinary Life, Works, and Discoveries of Martinus Scriblerus, Written in Collaboration by Members of the Scriblerus Club*, ed. Charles Kerby-Miller (New York: Russell & Russell, 1966), 29, 38, 58ff, 57ff.

education, science, and the use/misuse of reason become the theme of the "Second Book of Ethic Epistles" in Pope's revised structure for the moral scheme in 1736[9]—not long after Pope inherits Arbuthnot's Scriblerian materials on the latter's death in 1735 (Kerby-Miller, 63). Under Warburton's encouragement, Pope returns to his "studies" (his own pet term for the opus magnum project) in 1741, and shortly thereafter, again with Warburton's encouragement, he completes and publishes not only the expanded *Dunciad* but also the *Memoirs of Martinus Scriblerus* (1742), the final compilation of Scriblerian materials, whose major focus is a satire on false learning, pedantry, metaphysical speculation, and freethinking.

Indeed, the *Dunciad* seems to take on a far-reaching and multi-faceted significance in relation to Pope's other works in the editions of the 1740s, in particular his other didactic poems. In the editions of 1743, Pope appears to have reconceived both his earliest major didactic work (*Essay on Criticism*) and his last (*Essay on Man* and the four-book *Dunciad*) as commenting on each other; they are printed together in a quarto "Sett" and linked through Warburton's commentary.[10] Pope writes to Warburton late in 1742 that his commentary on the *Dunciad* is to be "a kind of Prelude or Advertisement . . . of your Commentary on the Essays on Man, and on Criticisme" (27 November 1742, *Correspondence*, 4:427–428). The preparation of the so-called "death-bed edition" of his works, Pope's consummative effort to complete his artistic self-presentation—"I must make a perfect edition of my works, and then I shall have nothing to do but die"[11]—is a process closely linked in time with the production of the 1743 *Dunciad*, a fact that lends interesting support to Brown's claim that the *Dunciad* rewrites Pope's works (128–129); we see them as in a funhouse mirror, as the *Dunciad's* holistic, sweeping indictment of the contemporary print culture that plagues the "honest unwriting Subject"[12] is linked inextricably to the production of the "perfect edition" of Pope's works.

The close-knit opposition of the *Essay* and the *Dunciad* is further deepened by their links to three related publications of 1738, the last poems of any completeness written before the *New Dunciad*: the two *Dialogues of Seventeen Hundred and Thirty Eight: Epilogue to the Satires*, and the *Universal Prayer*. These are published almost as a triad, in similar formats,

---

See also James Sutherland, ed. *Alexander Pope: The Dunciad. The Twickenham Edition of the Poems of Alexander Pope*, rev. ed. (London: Methuen, 1963), 5:ix–x.

9   Pope to Swift, 25 March 1736, in Sherburn, *Correspondence*, 4:5.
10   And were apparently advertised as such, as observed by R. H. Griffith: "The two Essays were not infrequently bound with the quarto *Dunciad* of 1743 in a single volume; the note on the verso of the title-leaf of the *Dunciad* reads: 'Speedily will be publish'd,/ [In the same Paper, and Character, to be bound up with this,] / *The Essay on Man*, / The *Essay on Criticism*, / And the rest of the Author's Original Poems, / With the Commentaries and Notes of / W. Warburton, A. M.'" Note to entry no. 590, in R. H. Griffith, *Alexander Pope: A Bibliography* (London: Holland Press, 1962), 2:472–473.
11   January 1744; Spence, *Anecdotes*, 1:258, no. 622.
12   "Martinus Scriblerus, of the Poem," *Dunciad Variorum* (1729), in Butt, *Poems*, 344.

as folio pamphlets.[13] Published within a few weeks of each other, they are all shadowed by the context of Pope's declaration of his intention to publish no more, at the end of the second *Dialogue*, in visionary despairing tones characteristic of his Opposition writing at its height—a curious contrast to the bland and generalized pieties of the *Universal Prayer*. The *Dunciad* is related both historically and thematically to this grouping. Warburton sees the *Dunciad* as continuing this "PROTEST" with which Pope resolved to print no more in the Dialogues of 1738: he writes to William Oliver on 24 July 1742: "I am sure you have been well entertained with our excellent friend's last noble work, the new Dunciad. It may be considered, after his having so long attempted to stem the torrent of vice & folly, as a solemn protest left upon record against the overbearing barbarity & corruption of the age."[14]

As seen by its title (*The Universal Prayer. By the Author of The Essay on Man*), the *Universal Prayer* is presented as a postscript to the *Essay*, expressing similar sentiments in a more religious but still largely Enlightenment rationalist, non-denominational vein.[15] The *Dialogues*, however, seem to culminate a process by which, through the epistles and satires (and editions) of the 1730s, Pope repudiates, if not the *Essay* itself then the optimism on which the *Essay* is founded. The process begins with the problematics of the composition of the *Essay* itself in which the absence of overt Christian theology is the (literally) erased trace that unsettles the logic of the poem's commitment to cosmic optimism.[16] The poem is

---

[13] The three appear in identical formats and fonts, with the same printer's ornament on the title page identifying them as done by John Wright (Griffith, 2:388–389), who was, according to David Foxon, faithful to a fault in carrying out Pope's extremely specific requirements; see David Foxon and James McLaverty, *Pope and the Early Eighteenth-Century Book Trade* (Oxford: Oxford University Press, 1991), 104. *The Dialogue Something Like Horace (Dialogue 1)* was published on 16 May (by T. Cooper), the *Universal Prayer* on 22 June (by Robert Dodsley), and *Dialogue I* on 18 July, also by Dodsley; it was reset and reprinted in August. Also of interest is the fact that Pope's equivocal Horatian Epistle I.i (To Bolingbroke) was published on 7 March of this year, and Bolingbroke arrived for an extended stay in July (*Correspondence*, 4:91). It is tempting to speculate that some of the ambivalence of Epistle I.i is reflected in the striking contrasts and interrelationship of the three poems that follow so closely.

[14] Signed autograph letter pasted into a folio edition of Boswell's *Life of Johnson* (1874), vol. 13, following p. 416, located at the Beinecke.

[15] Although the poem existed as early as 1715, according to Pope, he sent a revised version of it to Ralph Allen in September 1736, claiming that it addressed some of the critiques of the orthodoxy of the *Essay on Man*: "I've sent you the Hymn, a little alterd, & enlargd in one necessary point of doctrine, viz: the third Stanza, which I think reconciles Freedom & Necessity; & is at least a Comment on some Verses in my Essay on Man, which have been mis-construed" (*Correspondence*, 4:31).

[16] The dualities in critical reading of the *Essay* across the Warburton-Crousaz divide persist to this day, suggesting a fundamental instability within the text of the *Essay*. See for example A. D. Nuttall's introduction to *Pope's "Essay on Man"* (London: Allen and Unwin, 1984). This hermeneutic instability is adumbrated in

shadowed throughout by the Creation, Fall, Incarnation, Atonement—by uneasiness surrounding a personal and affective belief in a particular Providence, and by conventional Catholic views of Christian immortality, original sin, the need for atonement, and the significance of suffering, as opposed to the poem's didactic and rhetorical commitment to general Providence and a benignly omniscient but distant Disposer. The *Essay* was conceived as a Christian work by "our divine Pope,"[17] but one that was intended to be palatable to the Enlightenment rationalist project, of which it indeed became, to this day, a notable, and notorious, exemplar; this was the view of both Bolingbroke and George Berkeley, Bishop of Cloyne, philosopher, and author of *Alciphron, or the Minute Philosopher* (1732), his satire on free-thinking. As Pope noted to Spence, Berkeley had advised Pope to omit an address to "Our Saviour," originally planned for the *Essay*.[18] Not only is the poetic text of the *Essay* charged by these powerful ambivalences, but the circumstances of its production show the extent to which the *Essay* was both Christianized and de-Christianized in its conception and realization: through manuscript revisions and erasures (e.g., such literally erased Christian elements as "Thy Will be done," as the gloss on the famous "Whatever Is, Is RIGHT"; elsewhere, "Charity ye greatest of ye three . . ." as an earlier version of 3.308);[19] through the circumstances of its composition, in particular the role of Bolingbroke (as either Horatian adversary or presiding spirit), and the association of the *Essay* with other of Pope's works then in process; through Pope's careful manipulation of the book trade, and timing of publication, to reinforce the *Essay's* Christian contexts and purposes by associating it with overtly Christian and bibliographically related works, id est Arbuthnot's *Know Your Self* (1734), and Walter Harte's *Essay on Reason* (1735), in the production of both of which Pope appears to have been involved;[20] through precise articulation of visual effects, accidentals (for example, italics are continually revised in doctrinally

---

a recent full-length study, Harry M. Solomon, *The Rape of the Text: Reading and Misreading Pope's Essay on Man* (Tuscaloosa: University of Alabama Press, 1993).

17   Bolingbroke and Pope to Swift [20 March 1731], Sherburn, *Correspondence*, 3:183. An alternate reading, found in 1741 and 1742 editions of Pope's correspondence, is "Pope, our Divine" (183n).

18   "In the Moral Poem I had written an address to our Saviour, imitated from Lucretius' compliment to Epicurus, but omitted it by advice of Dean Berkeley." Spence, *Anecdotes*, 1:135, no. 305.

19   See Maynard Mack, *The Last and Greatest Art: Some Unpublished Poetical Manuscripts of Alexander Pope* (Newark: Delaware University Press, 1984), 226, 281; see also autograph MS, Morgan Library, fols. [13] [40].

20   For example, MS quotations from "Dr. a" appear in the margins of the Houghton MS in Pope's hand, later to appear in *Know Your Self* (see Houghton MS, fol. [34]; Mack, *Last and Greatest*, 379), and, as Foxon and McLaverty point out (*Pope and the Early Eighteenth-Century Book Trade*, 64n), this work and the *Essay* are closely linked bibliographically. Pope was extensively involved in the editing (and possibly the composing) of Harte's *Essay on Reason* (see letter to Mallet, May/June 1734, *Correspondence*, 3:408, and to Caryll, 12 May 1735, *Correspondence*, 3:455).

sensitive passages), and engravings (discussed below); through repeated revisions, edition by edition, of both the poetic text and of the modest commentary Pope developed through the 1730s, well predating Warburton's voluminous notations.

Pope's ambivalence towards the optimism of the *Essay* and the opus magnum culminates in the final lines of the Epilogue to the Satires, Dialogue 2, the poem in which he declares his resolution to abandon public poetry, which takes the form of a dialogue between Pope (P.) and a wordly time-serving adversarius (Fr.).[21] The climactic passage in which Pope anoints himself as satirist-prophet, speaking from a transcendent realm of value ("Truth guards the poet, sanctifies the line, / And makes immortal, Verse as mean as mine . . ."), is punctured as if it were a balloon by the Fr's reply, coming from an alternate – and ultimately encompassing—framework of value and perception.

> Yes, the last Pen for Freedom let me draw,
> Where Truth stands trembling on the edge of Law:
> Here, last of Britons! let your Names be read;
> Are none, none living? let me praise the Dead,
> And for that Cause which made your Fathers shine,
>   Fall, by the Votes of their degen'rate Line!
>
> Fr. Alas! Alas! pray end what you began,
> And write next winter more Essays on Man.

Note how the passage implicates the contemporary reader, invoking the Horatian mean, the *nil admirari* response, in another context by its hyperbolic rhetoric (is it hyperbolic? or do we believe? by what value system do we make that judgment?). The *Fr*'s reply is the concluding, framing response, returning us to the world we know—pragmatic, materialistic, (or, in other terms, ordered, rational), where Pope's words sound strident and bombastic. If we try reading the passage without the final couplet, the lines hang in the void, lacking the sense of closure they seem to demand, the epigrammatic twist so common to Pope's endings, but here the required signature is displaced.

Here the *Essay* (and by implication the *opus magnum*) is placed squarely in the world and value system of the *Fr*. It is invoked as a non-mythic, useful (and harmless) work, an empirical study of observable human nature, laying its mysteries open to the equalizing Enlightenment gaze; nice, general, cosmically justified, drawing as its conclusion, not "the strong antipathy of Good to Bad," but "Whatever is, is RIGHT." It is associated with the amoral and corrupt, placed opposite the sacred duty of the satirist (represented as stepping into the void left by the abdication of

---

21 Another version of this reading of *Dialogue 2* appears in my essay, "Ridicule's Two Edges: Myth, Parody, and the Reader in Pope," in *Comedy: Essays in Honour of Peter Dixon*, ed. E. Maslen (London: Westfield and Queen Mary College, 1993), 157–158.

Church and legal authority, a recurring image in Pope going back to the *Essay on Criticism*). When the ethic scheme is picked up again in 1741 at Warburton's encouragement (Pope to Warburton, 12 November 1741, *Corresp.* 4.370; Leranbaum, "*Opus Magnum*," 140ff.), and as part of Pope's urge to make the "perfect" or "true Edition" of his works at the end of his life, it translates itself into Pope's apocalyptic visionary mode of "PROTEST"—characteristic of Opposition literature at this time—but it also casts the affirmation of the *Essay* into that questioning shadow.

The material relationship between the *Essay* and the *Dunciad* is also eloquently apparent in the illustrations of quarto editions of Pope's *Works*, volume II (1735–1739). The quarto of 1735 was more fully revised than the small folio that preceded it, with the *Essay on Man* being newly revised and completely reset (Griffith, *Bibliography*, 2:286, no. 372), and it featured numerous opulent engravings from designs by Pope's friend the famous landscape gardener and artist William Kent, done by Peter Fourdrinier, advertised by Gilliver as such ("This Day is published, in large Quarto, with Copper Plates, design'd by Mr. Kent, The Works of Alexander Pope, Esq" *Grubstreet Journal*, No. 278, Saturday, April 24, 1735, cited in Griffith, *Bibliography*, 2.287). Pope's involvement in and control over ornamentation and visual effects is evident in many ways, from his own artistic efforts, including illustrations to the posthumous quarto of the *Essay* (1745), to his close relationship with painters such as Jonathan Richardson and Charles Jervas, to his extraordinary control over visual effects in the production of his works—white spacing, font ("Letter"), accidentals, and illustrations (not to mention paper quality, format, and binding).[22] He owned the engravings for the Homer editions (Foxon, *Book Trade*, 93); the Kent/Fourdrinier engravings, one of which appears in the Homer as early as 1726,[23] appear in made-up and reissued editions of his *Works* through to 1739. These energetically detailed rococo pieces create an alternate level of discourse ironically interacting with the verbal text, and not infrequently subversive of it. For example, the initial letter B to the opening lines of the *Dunciad*, "Books and the Man I sing," consists of not a man but a scholarly rodent with reading glasses and a tome (see figure 1)—part of a consistent bestiary theme throughout the *Dunciad* illustrations. The engravings also set up a powerful link between the *Essay* and the *Dunciad*; these are the works that are by far the most extensively adorned with headpieces, tailpieces, vignettes, and initial letters, owing to the complexity of their four-part divisions. The illustrations themselves suggest various central thematic

---

22   Based on my own examination of revision and editorial production in both manuscript and successive editions, as well as on the seminal work of Foxon and McLaverty, who argue for Pope's unprecedented engagement in the material production of his works, both physical and economic (*Pope and the Early Eighteenth-Century Book Trade*, 81ff, 93, and passim). Pope clearly saw the editorial and even the marketing process as an extension of the poetic, though not without ambivalence. My work in progress, *Rhyme and Print: Pope, Poetry, and the Material Text*, explores this relationship in detail.

23   W. K. Wimsatt, *The Portraits of Alexander Pope* (New Haven: Yale University Press, 1965), 126n.

connections, subversive parallels, and mutual commentary that further reinforce the interaction between the two poems.

The *Essay's* title-page vignette and tailpiece to Epistle 4 are the same "Know Thyself" engraving (see figure 2), representing a human head in a glory, surrounded by floating papers and books in a cloud, one open book in front with a butterfly on it, cobwebs with butterflies caught in them. These are familiar as symbols of false knowledge in the *Dunciad*, and there is in this a certain family resemblance to both ass and owl frontispieces to the 1728 and 1729 *Dunciads*, not to mention the more direct echo in the Curll headpiece to the *Dunciad* Book 2 (see figure 3.). Also suggestive is the inscription, which recalls Arbuthnot's poem of the same title (in Greek), which is closely linked bibliographically to Pope's *Essay*, as mentioned above, and which takes an overtly Christian approach to human limitations and faith. The headpiece to the *Dunciad*, Book 2, represents presumably Curll in the pillory, surrounded by the bounty of print, based on ll. 3–4, which itself parodies some of Pope's deepest harvest values—the "boundless bounty" of Nature at the ending of the *Essay on Man*, Epistle 4, and the Psalmic triumph of "laughing Ceres" in the *Epistle to Burlington*:[24] "Or that, where on her Curlls the Public pours / All bounteous, fragrant grains, and golden show'rs." The engraving links print culture and physical punishment (rods, tickling cones, eggs, rolls, Weekly Journals) with these deeper enviro-religious values of Pope's, while its overall design is parallel to the human head in a glory surrounded by the emblems of pedantry and false knowledge, in the *Essay* vignette.

The textual reading to follow concentrates first on the invocations of the two poems, suggesting something of the *Dunciad's* multilayered re-creation of the theology erased from the *Essay*, focusing particularly on those submerged elements of Creation and Atonement. The *Dunciad's* travesty extends further yet, to religious values overtly affirmed in the *Essay*, rewriting those parts of the *Essay* that express Pope's deepest-held religious principles, such as cosmic and natural harmony, and that outward-looking charity that links man to God. This leads into a consideration of the respective endings of the two poems. One is a Popeian signature, which restores the conversational framework and diminishes the vindication of the ways of God to a mere topic of gentlemanly debate, easily resolvable in aphoristic terms encapsulating (and containing) the *Essay* itself. The other is an eyewitness account of the swallowing up of the known world and the obliteration of all external positive standards, identifying poetic inspiration with Dulness itself, and blurring the poet's own subjectivity with a curious indeterminacy.

The Miltonic account of the Holy Spirit brooding over the abyss in *Paradise Lost* 1.1–26 is a passage whose absence speaks loudly in the opening lines of the *Essay on Man*, whose claim to vindicate the ways of God to man clearly points to it. When read in conjunction with Milton's

---

24   See Mack: "the conviction . . . ran very deep in Pope . . . that the natural world contains some sort of retributive and resuscitative power." (*Life*, 497).

invocation, Pope's invitation to Bolingbroke seems almost insufferably constrained by reason and its limitations:

> Let us (since life can little more supply
> Than just to look about us and to die)
> Expatiate free. . . .

The meaning of this couplet hovers in the contradictions between the main sentence and the parenthesis. "Expatiate" was a favorite verb of Pope's, used not in its regular sense of "to talk at length," but rather to express the freedom of the mind and soul from the limitations of the body (for example, later in the *Essay*, "The soul, uneasy and confin'd from home, / Rests and expatiates in a life to come"). Here it is placed next to a definition of life so limited as to be absurd (in the existential sense)—and the parenthesis is placed so as to create a long separation between the verb "expatiate" and its subjects, Pope and Bolingbroke. In this conjunction the action and purpose of the poem become open to question—a kind of exercise to stave off ennui and despair. The entire rationalist view of life can be so defined, in this reductive phrase. It thus teeters on the edge of the absurdity that becomes actualized in the *Dunciad*; indeed, absurdity, the absurdity of mortal human existence, becomes its logical conclusion.

As has been noted, in both the Houghton Library MS of the poem and in Pope's note to this passage in later editions, Pope conceived this opening passage itself as a rationalized, schematized introduction to his schematized system of ethics (the *Essay* in microcosm).[25] Here Milton's inner vision is replaced by Lockean observation as Pope deliberately excludes mystery to focus on the "Scene of Man"; the Holy Spirit is replaced by Bolingbroke's companionship; two hunting gentlemen trample casually through the garden of Eden looking for human follies to shoot with words. They might possibly stumble upon the plan of the garden's maze; and either by this discovery or by satirizing human failings they will vindicate God's ways to men—answer the ancient human anguish over evil and absurdity. Pope ends this passage with the direct allusion to Milton, which both calls to mind the larger meaning of the "vindicate" expression and calls his own intent into grave question: "Laugh where we must, be candid where we can; / But vindicate the ways of God to Man." Horatian conversational decorum and compulsive laughter meet the highest epic intent proclaimed in English; and what is the effect of their limited candor on a declaration that aspires to absolute truth? Yet, according to Pope, these are the two lines that "contain

---

[25] Marginal notes keying the lines of the exordium to topics covered in the opus magnum plans appear in rudimentary form in the Morgan MS (fol. [1]) and in more developed form in the Houghton MS (fol. [1]). See Leranbaum 20–22. In addition to the published "Design" of the 1734 quarto edition, which describes the *Essay* as a "general Map of MAN" preparatory to a larger scheme to follow, Pope describes the *Essay* as fulfilling this function to Spence (May 1730; 1733–1734); Spence, *Anecdotes*, 1:129–130, 1:133, no. 274.

the main design that runs through the whole" (November 1730; Spence, *Anecdotes*, 1.131, no. 299).

When the Miltonic image actually surfaces in the opening lines of the *Dunciad* (both versions) [lines 27–28], it comes to us inverted and physicalized and absurd. Dulness becomes a "gross malign fowl" (Reid 687) brooding over the abyss of unmeaning, evidently about to deliver herself of the "one vast Egg" from which the anti-creation will spring. Note that, as in the *Essay*, this image is buried within a tribute to Swift, one that also invites Swift in balanced couplets to share in Horatian observation and rational wit, a community of value. Yet in the syntactical blurring of this opening passage (in both versions), the poem becomes oddly identified with its subject, the products of Dulness:

> The Mighty Mother, and her Son who brings
> The Smithfield Muses to the ear of Kings,
> I sing. Say you, her instruments the Great!
> Call'd to this work by Dulness, Jove, and Fate;
> You by whose care, in vain decry'd and curst,
> Still Dunce the second reigns like Dunce the first;
> Say how the Goddess bade Britannia sleep,
> And pour'd her Spirit o'er the land and deep. (1743, 1.1–8)

Here it seems "the Great" are invoked to do the singing; it is unclear what "this Work" refers to; the Miltonic creation imagery is conflated with prophecies of the coming of Christ's Kingdom in Joel, bringing Genesis and Revelation together in a single image. Furthermore, in Scriblerus's note to the 1743 edition the action of the poem is made coterminous with, even identified with, the "hatching" of Dulness's progeny: "She is said here only to be spreading her wings to hatch this age; which is not produced complete till the fourth book" (note to line 18, 1743).

In one of the books owned by Pope, Cambridge Platonist Ralph Cudworth's *True Intellectual System of the Universe* (1678), a description of Orphic creation myths in which creation springs from an egg of night and chaos occurs in the midst of Cudworth's extensive discussion of the absurdity of such atheistical accounts of Creation as opposed to Platonic accounts of creation directed by Mind and Love (concepts central to the cosmos depicted in the *Essay*).[26] Here in the mighty hen of Dulness we have a creation myth that negates the whole concept of the shaping logos and the

---

[26]   "[Epicurus] . . . fetcht the original of all things in the Universe, even of Soul and Mind . . . from senseless Atoms fortuitously moved. He together with Democritus, hereby making the World to be, in the worst Sence . . . an Egge of the Night, that is, not the off-spring of Mind and Understanding, but of dark senseless Matter, of Tohu and Bohu, of Confused Chaos; and deriving the Original of all the Perfections in the Universe, from the most Imperfect Being and the lowest of all Entities, than which nothing can be more Atheistical," *The True Intellectual System of the Universe: The First Part; wherein, All the Reason and Philosophy of Atheism is Confuted; and Its Impossibility Demonstrated* (London, 1678), 61.

chain of love—mindless, "hatching," self-enclosed, reductive. (Indeed, the image of Dulness about to drop her egg into land and deep anticipates the Dutchman of Book 2 of which more later.) Through this image, Dulness is also linked with another Creator, John Rich, the producer of cheap theatrical spectacle, who is the active Word of Dulness in Book 3, creating heaven and earth in a parody of both Genesis and Revelation; he is described in terms evoking not only the Psalmist's God but also the God of the *Essay on Man*, who "mounts the storm, and walks upon the wind" (2.110)—"And proud his Mistress' orders to perform / Rides in the whirlwind, and directs the storm" (1729, 3.259–260). It is Rich who produces the "vast Egg" from which the "human race" springs—actually a pantomime actor, but Pope makes it sound like a new Genesis ("At last, to give the whole Creation grace. . . ."), interweaving the traditional (and Miltonic) notion of humanity as the pinnacle of creation with his own multivalent term "grace," here suggesting also the sweep of redemption history, with humanity as the avenue through which Christ's atonement brings grace to all creation.

This eschatological metaphor is further elaborated in the Kent/ Fourdrinier headpiece to Book 3 in the 1735 quarto (see figure 4), which portrays Rich's theatre with apocalyptic overtones. The owl of the 1728 frontispiece has been transformed into a monstrous embodiment of Dulness herself, its mighty wings outspread, not hatching but devouring a human figure (notably, head-first). The gaping maw is reminiscent of medieval stage representations of hell mouth, a layer of reference linked to its descendant in the pantomime-stage apocalypse described in 3.231–236 (1729). More deeply, however, the open mouth is itself the cognate image for the Greek term *kaos*.[27] Reid suggests that the "uncreating word" is in fact the vacuum-like yawn of Dulness ("Ordering Chaos" 685; he also sees it as evocative of hell mouth); we can go on to say that it negates all word, all things, sucking all into itself, as the archetypal image of evil in medieval-Renaissance Christian tradition, the ultimate solipsism, the single appetite seeing itself as the final purpose of creation—a portrayal of evil satirized in both Milton's *Comus* (710–714) and the *Essay on Man*, and consummatively envisioned in the *Dunciad*. The picture of the dragon in the lower left corner, apparently excreting another human figure, and thus linked with the owl in one digestive continuum, continues this eschatological theme, as a monstrous pantomime version of the dragon of Revelation, in specific fact a picture of Elkanah Settle in his home-made dragon costume.[28]

---

27 G. F. C. Plowden, *Pope on Classic Ground* (Athens: Ohio University Press, 1983).
28 In fact, this image embodies a nexus of political and eschatological references. Although this image suggests the dragon of Revelation, embodiment of Satan, associated by Reformation polemic with the Roman Catholic Church (an image appropriated by British nationalism in Spenser's *Faerie Queene*, Book I), it in fact portrays Elkanah Settle, the central figure of Book III—former City-poet, Anchises-prophet of Dulness, and architect of pageants and Pope-burnings— donning his home-made dragon costume (3.287–290, 1729). Pope's portrayal of Settle turns Protestant polemic on its head, a link foregrounded by the illustration.

In the power, pervasiveness, and multiplicity of its creation references (add to this hatching and uncreation the false creation of the pantomime stage in Book 3, and the teeming womb of Book 1. 53ff, "the Chaos dark and deep / Where nameless somethings in their causes sleep . . .") the *Dunciad* gives swarming life to ideas resoundingly absent from the *Essay on Man*, which celebrates a cosmos without any cosmogony. Yet there are ways in which the creator/creation relationship in the *Dunciad* resembles that of the *Essay*, a resemblance that serves to highlight submerged or contradictory elements. The *Essay* itself creates a dynamic gap between platonic and dionysian concepts of creation, between "the great directing MIND of ALL" (1.266) and the immanent God who breathes, warms, and refreshes through His creation (1.271–276), a creation that itself teems like the womb of Dulness, "all matter quick, and bursting into birth" (1.234). These contrarieties are the dynamic center of the climactic description of the cosmos at the end of Epistle I, in which the vitalism of "all matter quick, and bursting into birth" gives way to the interlocking rigid hierarchy of the "Vast chain of being" that has been extended by new technologies "from Infinite to thee, / From thee to Nothing!" (1.237–241), and is seemingly held together by a contained balance of force, so much so that the whole would fly off in all directions should one link of the great chain be broken. In an odd conjunction of physical and spiritual, empirical and mythic, Pope combines the Newtonian and Miltonic universes, the traditional hierarchies of the Miltonic cosmos with the Newtonian universe of interstellar space, gravitational pull and planetary orbits with ruling angels—and centers all in original sin of pride, again with imagery from *Paradise Lost*:[29]

> Let Earth unbalanc'd from her orbit fly,
> Planets and Suns run lawless thro' the sky,
> Let ruling Angels from their spheres be hurl'd,
> Being on being wreck'd, and world on world,
> Heav'n's whole foundations to their centre nod,
> And Nature tremble to the throne of God:
> All this dread ORDER break—for whom? for thee?
> Vile worm!—Oh Madness, Pride, Impiety! (1.251–258)

This image is countered, however, by one immediately following, a description that challenges—even obliterates—hierarchy. It is equally traditional in its formulae, drawing on patristic and scholastic formulations of God in the creation and of the soul within the body (see Mack's commentary in *Twickenham* 3.1.48–49), and portraying God as immanent, as fully and equally present in all parts of His creation:

---

[29]   Specifically, Satan's account of the battle in heaven, which according to him "shook [God's] throne" (1.105), and Milton's account of the Fall itself in the moment it happens (9.1000). All citations from Milton are from John Milton, *Complete Poems and Major Prose*, ed. Merritt J. Hughes (New York: Bobbs-Merrill, 1957).

> That, chang'd thro' all, and yet in all the same,
> Great in the earth, as in th'aethereal frame,
> Warms in the sun, refreshes in the breeze,
> Glows in the stars, and blossoms in the trees,
> Lives thro' all life, extends thro' all extent,
> Spreads undivided, operates unspent,
> Breathes in our soul, informs our mortal part,
> As full, as perfect, in a hair as heart,
> As full, as perfect, in vile Man that mourns,
> As the rapt Seraph that adores and burns;
> To him no high, no low, no great, no small;
> He fills, he bounds, connects, and equals all. (1.269–280)

This passage specifically echoes the language and hierarchical oppositions of the previous passage, only to refute them. Note the repetition of the term "vile" applied to man again, but now in a redemptive context, associated not with pride but with humility and repentance.

Dulness's relation to her universe (which, by Book 4, is Pope's universe) is uncannily precise in its similarities to the creator/creation relationship in the *Essay*. The entire action of the poem, of course, traces the process by which her non-mind controls her subjects and, ultimately, all intellectual and spiritual space. She is also immanent, filling creation with her "amplitude" (Reid 687, 690), as God in the *Essay* is full and perfect in every part of His creation; she is not seen except in her effects (Reid 692), and neither is the power of God in the *Essay* (and in orthodox teaching)— "Itself unseen, but in th'effects remains."

These resemblances are all part of an extensive and detailed parody of Christian theology at all levels of the poem, from its story line on inward. The *Dunciad* centers precisely on those elements that are erased or suppressed in the *Essay on Man*: Christian eschatology, Creation to Judgment;[30] Messianic and incarnational theology; Eucharist; Atonement; Trinitarian concepts. The appearance of these elements in the *Dunciad* has the effect of highlighting both the Christian elements and the Christian absences in the *Essay*. The Second Coming of Dulness in Book 4, heralded by the "posterior Trumpet" of Fame with its multiple comic and apocalyptic meanings, begins an extended and detailed parody of both redemption history (see Jemielity, passim) and the Catholic theology of penance and reconciliation, the theology most noisily erased from the *Essay*—that of sin, sacrifice, and atonement. In the final judgment of Dulness, the forgiveness of sins is closely parodied, as her initiates are freed, not from guilt or the burden of sin, but from the sense of sin: "wrap[ped] in her veil, and free[d] from sense of shame" (4.336). The parousia of Dulness in fact obliterates all judgment, all distinction between good and evil, sheep and goats, ultimately eliminating consciousness itself.[31] In the *Essay*, this power of distinction

---

30   Cf. Jemielity, *Consummatum*; independently observed.
31   In fact, the entire process of the summoning, witness, and judgment of the dunces follows closely Catholic sacramental theology, being presided over by Dulness and her Pontiff, who celebrates her "greater Mysteries": baptism,

and judgment is internalized—"This light and darkness in our Chaos join'd / What shall divide? The God within the mind" (2. 203–204) – but inadequate – "And oft so mixt, the diff'rence is too nice / Where ends the Virtue, or begins the Vice" (2. 209–210). The "God within the mind" degenerates shortly thereafter into the "weak queen" reason; the language of lines 203–204 then serves only to remind the reader of the revealed theology that is not supposed to be there, theology that closely connects the power of distinction with the divine act of creation.

Not only submerged Christian elements, but also the positive religious assertions of the *Essay on Man* have distinctive analogues in the *Dunciad*. The *Dunciad's* four-book structure parallels that of the *Essay*, expanding outward in the same concentric circles of reference, investing the local and particular with universalizing meaning, and, equally precisely, inverting the purpose of that vision in the *Essay*. Where the *Essay* commands vision repeatedly (Awake—See!) and with it all the traditional associations of light with knowledge, reason, enlightenment, the *Dunciad* permits vision to witness itself succumbing to blindness (darkness). Where the *Essay* absolves satirically-denounced human limitations and prideful subjectivism in the widening structure that culminates in the "boundless heart" that unites the human individual with God, the *Dunciad* expands the satirized defect itself to encompass all the "mighty Maze" of providential history, human culture, and intellectual existence (as outlined in Epistle 3 of the *Essay*). The process by which in Book 1 (1743) the whole world seems to contract to something inside Cibber's head ("What then remains? Ourself." [217–218]) expands eschatologically to suggest the created and moral universe as a figment of the mind of Dulness, or even of the poet himself. In the consummation, the poet invokes not light, but darkness ("dread Chaos, and eternal Night"), and the Muse itself becomes identified with Dulness, to vindicate the ways of an alternate Providence: "Of darkness visible so much be lent, / As half to shew, half veil the deep Intent" (4.3–4). Where the

---

marriage, Eucharist, ordination, catechism, reconciliation, along with the sevenfold gifts of the Spirit, those of Dulness being Impudence, Stupefaction, Self-conceit, Int'rest, Flattery, Ambition, and Gluttony. All sacraments appear except final unction, for the poem outlives consciousness itself. In a parody of the theology of baptism, an inversion both of the creation of man as a "living soul" by the breath of God in Genesis, and a parody of the regeneration of the soul in Christ, the Grand Tour culminates in the transformation of the soul into mere "Air, the echo of a sound." Similarly, the mock-Eucharist celebrated by Walpole, pontiff of Dulness, erases all sense of community, or the common union of Christians in the Mass; whoever "tastes, forgets his former friends, / Sire, Ancestors, Himself." Indeed, as in the parodic baptism, the soul is sucked out (a Marlovian image of damnation); in an inversion of transubstantiation, the appearance of the body remains but an animal nature, not a divine soul, is the reality. The description of the "specious miracles" of French cookery ("What cannot copious Sacrifice attone?") suggests some of the more technical points of the Anglo-Catholic debates of the 1680s on transubstantiation, debates with which Pope claimed familiarity (letter to Atterbury, 20 November 1717, *Correspondence*, 1:453–454). See also James King's discussion of the eucharistic parody in the cup of the Magus (157–165).

Essay moves from its transcendent humanistic vision to a conventional Horatian tribute, encapsulating itself in a series of aphorisms, the *Dunciad* enacts the loss of external perspective in an encompassing vision that writes itself out of existence. The dream/prophecy of Book 3 in 1729 shifts to its fulfillment in present reality (1742), from a comic fantasy with its presumed framework of judgment, to an eyewitness account from which even the author has disappeared, and the poem, a tattered physical object, "Found in the Year 1741," is all that is left. We lose the satiric distance by which Cibber's pertness may be ironically compared to heroic courage; rather, we are in an epic world of Miltonic proportions, where heroic value has been replaced by a parody of heroic proportions and comparable moral significance. The final couplet—"Thy hand, great Anarch! lets the curtain fall; / And universal Darkness buries All"—completes a movement in the poem by which metaphor and thing signified become one: the whole of creation and history become one of Rich's extravaganzas. In this precisely inverted apocalypse (by which the curtain falls rather than being raised to reveal) the God of Pope's universe becomes a producer of cheap theatrical spectacle.

Even here, however, where the *Essay* and the *Dunciad* seem to be most deeply opposed, curious and non-inverted connections appear. One of the most striking parallels between the two poems (noted independently by Laura Brown and myself) occurs at the end of Book 2 of the *Dunciad*, anticipating Book 4, and at the end of Epistle 4 of the *Essay on Man*, in the rhetorically climactic position. This is, of course, the very passage in Epistle 4 where Pope asserts most compellingly the expanding and redemptive meaning of human charity. This passage is anticipated in 1728 by the bedtime scene at the end of Book 2, where the dunces fall asleep like tired children, and then both are echoed in 1742, in the stupefying Unison of the consummation of Dulness. The connection is more than merely verbal. The *Essay* passage concentrates ideas reiterated throughout Pope's works and personal documents, deeply held beliefs in the divine significance of human social love and the redemptive rhythms of nature; it triumphantly transcends earlier gaps and inconsistencies, bridging the distance not only between man and God but also between Christian theology and mystery and the poem's commitment to secular rationalism, as the unifying force of love recreates man in God's image.

> Self-love but serves the virtuous mind to wake,
> As the small pebble stirs the peaceful lake
> The centre mov'd, a circle strait succeeds,
> Another still, and still another spreads,
> Friend, parent, neighbour, first it will embrace,
> His country next, and next all human race,
> Wide, and more wide, th'o'erflowings of the mind
> Take ev'ry creature in, of ev'ry kind;
> Earth smiles around, with boundless bounty blest,
> And Heav'n beholds its image in his breast. (4.363–372)

In the *Dunciad*, this image has a transmogrified form, in the quintessence of subjectivism and mindlessness:

> As what a Dutchman plumps into the lakes,
> One circle first, and then a second makes,
> What Dulness dropt among her sons imprest
> Like motions from one circle to the rest;
> So from the mid-most the nutation spreads
> Round and more round, o'er all the Sea of heads (2.405–410)

Although, as Brown points out (150), the expanding concentric circles recur throughout Pope, the parallel here is far more precise and far-reaching, especially when read with the end of Book 4, as the vacuum-like effect of the yawn of Dulness spreads "Wide, and more wide," and her un-mind overflows to take in creation. The vivifying and unifying force of love has been replaced by a force equally unifying, but negating. The motive original is not a pebble but a turd—that quintessential Scriblerian image of subjectivity, unrelatedness, art produced by the autonomous nervous system and equatable only with its physical medium (cf. Dryden's *MacFlecknoe*, "Loads of Sh[adwell] block'd the way")—an utter inversion of the boundless heart. In replacing the chain of love with the bond of boredom, and the potent pebble with one of the most subjective products of all, Pope is describing the loss of the living principle of his poetic cosmos— the death of charity.

Yet there are points of contact in these passages that highlight the subjectivism latent in the *Essay*'s own description. Earlier in the *Dunciad* (all versions), as Dulness beholds her own image "exprest" in her sons, she is uncomfortably like Heaven contemplating its image in the charitable breast. Indeed, in the overflowing action of charity, the whole creation is "taken in" by the subject's mind. In the *Essay*, Pope promptly shifts the point of view back over to Heaven, reasserting the objective framework, but, in the *Dunciad*, he goes on to depict one un-mind taking "ev'ry creature . . . of ev'ry kind" into itself, and the framework dissolves as the poet becomes one of them ("take at once the Poet and the Song").[32] He is no longer the charitable subject; Dulness is the only subject (in a double sense), and all other subjectivity becomes hers.

In the ending of the *Essay*, control and distance are further exerted, as the climactic assertion of the redemptive power of charity gives way to a conventional tribute to Bolingbroke, the infinite sweep of vision to the clipped, balanced opposites of Horatian decorum. Pope's MS revisions show

---

[32] The idea of the poet's complicity with Dulness, ironically stressed by the Scriblerian commentary ("this is an invocation of much Piety" in which the poet declares his impatience to be reunited with Dulness), is seen in the frontispiece to a 1749 octavo (Griffith no. 638) produced by the Knaptons, publishers of the Warburton edition of the Works, featuring a hugely fat Dulness, on her throne supported by four guardian virtues, and, in the lower left corner among the Hogarthian crowd surrounding her, an emaciated figure in black strongly resembling Pope, holding up a book as though in offering.

that he had conceived this ending early on, but he had problems placing the passage as the shape of the *Essay* changed; more, the revisions themselves reveal that these lines were conceived as emphasizing Bolingbroke's restraint of the Muse rather than his inspiration. This is clearest in a version of these lines appearing in the last page of the Houghton Library MS, intended for the second book of Ethic Epistles, "Epist. I. of ye Limmits of Reason"—notably, one of the projected forms in which elements of the *Dunciad* would have appeared in the *opus magnum*.

> And now, transported o'er so vast a Plain,
> While the free Courser flies with all ~~her~~ the Rein;
> While heav'nward, now his mounting Wings she feels,
> Now ~~stoops where~~ scatterd Fools fly trembling from his heels;
> Wilt thou, my Laelius, keep ye Course in sight,
> ~~Or urge~~ Confine the ~~my~~ Fury, or ~~restrain~~ assist my^e Flight?
> Laelius, whose Love excus'd my labours past,
> Matures my present, & shall bound my last.[33]

As in the opening, Horatian moderation is not adequate to the subject; this tension and the revisions may also reveal other perspectives on the role of and relationship with Bolingbroke. The rhetorical questions, though conventional, end in a certain lack of resolution anticipating the ambivalences of the *Epistle to Bolingbroke* ("Shall then this verse to future age pretend . . . ?) Indeed, the syntax here (following from the conjunction that ["urg'd by thee . . ."]) would turn all the remaining lines, all the capitalized assertions that aphoristically encapsulate the *Essay*, into an open-ended question (Shall it?). It is tempting to suggest that the answer comes in the fourth book of the *Dunciad*, and it is No.

In Book 3 of the 1729 *Dunciad*, in an odd, gratuitous passage that well predates Warburton's heavy-handed orthodoxy, Settle (of all people) warns the Dunces not to scorn their God (the God of light, ordered creation, knowledge, and clarity). In Book 4, however, just as Milton invokes the Holy Spirit to help him describe the mysteries of heaven and man's redemption in *Paradise Lost* Book 3, so the poet invokes not this God of light and learning but the powers of Night and Chaos themselves to help him describe their own mysteries ("yet, yet a moment . . ."). Unlike the conventional epic invocation, in this one the "song" is not going to outlast and immortalize the epic action, to commemorate the friendship of Pope and Bolingbroke and the charity of the boundless heart, or to vindicate (or justify) the ways of God to men. Here the action itself, the restoration of the empire of Dulness, will outlast the song: it replaces the song, consumes it. This point is stressed in the material nature of the text. The asterisks, or "chasm," immediately following the final desperate command to the Muse turns the poet's song into a sub-verbal absurdity, or even an absence, a portion of the

---

[33]   Mack, *Last and Greatest*, 413; Houghton MS fol. [51].

page ripped away from the tattered and flimsy document that is all that is left of civilization and Arts. Pope was able to speak mockingly of the death of satire in *Epilogue to the Satires, Dialogue I* ("So—Satire is no more—I feel it die"); but now he constructs an eyewitness account (evolved through repeated revisions of this section of the *New Dunciad*, and only complete in the four-book edition of 1743):

> Oh Muse! relate (for you can tell alone,
> Wits have short Memories, and Dunces none)
> Relate, who First, who last resign'd to rest;
> Whose Heads she partly, whose completely blest;
> What Charms could Faction, what Ambition lull,
> The Venal quiet, and entrance the Dull;
> 'Till drown'd was Sense, and Shame, and Right, and Wrong—
> Oh sing, and hush the Nations with thy Song!
>   * * * * * * *
> In vain, in vain,—the all-composing Hour Resistless falls;
> The Muse obeys the Pow'r

Note how even before the Muse obeys the power, distinctions begin to dissolve: the Muse is to hush the nations into reverence (as of Christ's second coming, the power of judgment with which Pope associates her), but the nations are already hushed in moral and spiritual oblivion—it is as if the Last Judgment has come too late and is irrelevant.

In their comment on one another, the *Essay on Man* and the *Dunciad* can be seen as expressing two sides of Pope's religious imagination: one, rationalizing, optimistic, attempting to make sense of suffering through a "ballance of Opposites"; the other, visionary, irrational, and subversive of balance and order. One side invokes a divinity of logos and nous, everlasting, a Word both encompassing and transcendent, the God of light and reason, harmony, full consent of things; the other side is aware of divinity as dionysian, ever-changing, immanent and pervasive, a vital principle within the creation yet containing within itself a darkness and fluid irrationality that can either give life to or destroy the forms of order. Pope engages both sides of the divine nature with a radical and creative ambivalence, and his religious thought can be better traced in the movement between the two *Dunciads* and the *Essay on Man* than it can in any of his overt declarations of faith. It is the contention of this paper that "religion" is more clearly evident in the *Essay's* absences and inconsistencies, and in the *Dunciad's* subversive linking of the spiritual substance of myth with the parodic emptying of religious forms, than it is in the affirmations or negations of either poem.

Figure 1. Pope, *Works* (1717–1735, made-up quarto), vol. 3. Initial letter to Book 1 of the *Dunciad*. By courtesy of the Beinecke Rare Book and Manuscript Library, Yale University.

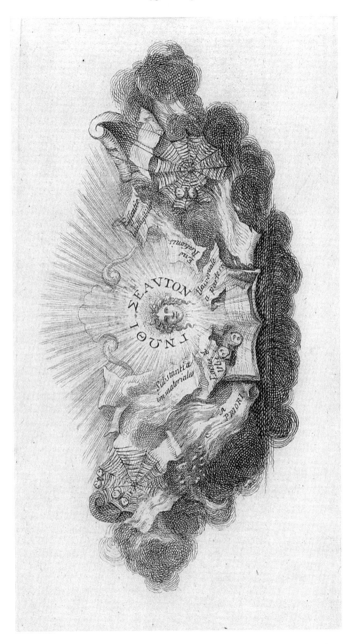

Figure 2. Pope, *Essay on Man* (1734, quarto). Title page vignette. By courtesy of the Beinecke Rare Book and Manuscript Library, Yale University.

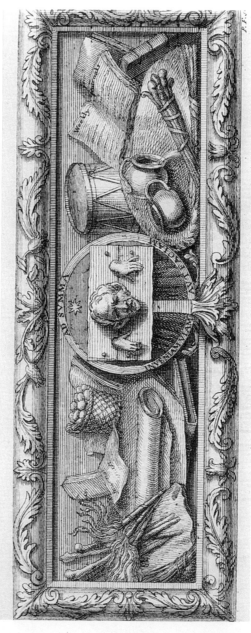

Figure 3. Pope, *Works* (1717–1735, made-up quarto), vol. 3. Headpiece to Book 2 of the *Dunciad*. By courtesy of the Beinecke Rare Book and Manuscript Library, Yale University.

Figure 4. Pope, *Works* (1717–1735, made-up quarto), vol. 3. Headpiece to Book 3 of the *Dunciad*. By courtesy of the Beinecke Rare Book and Manuscript Library, Yale University.

"Dishonest Scars": Holiness, Secrecy, and the Problem of Perpetual Peace

Michael Rotenberg-Schwartz

In *Spectator* no. 523 (12 October 1712), which puffs Thomas Tickell's poem on the treaty of Utrecht, Addison proscribes the use of myth by those who would celebrate the controversial peace. An "edict" against the "Effusion of Nonsense," his essay requires the author "who shall write on this Subject, to remember that he is a Christian, and not to Sacrifice his Catechism to his Poetry."[1] This is a criticism particularly of Pope, who is mentioned in the first paragraph of the essay, and whose draft of *Windsor-Forest* Addison had seen. The poem, especially its conclusion, Johnson writes in his *Life* of Pope, "gave great pain" to Addison "as a poet and a politician."[2] As noted by others, Pope's reaction was to add more of those elements Addison considered anathema.[3] Readers have lately focused more on the poem's imperial, political, and economic contexts, but the degree to which *Windsor-Forest* might be considered a "Christian" work, as compared to Tickell's poem or the writings of others, is worth consideration as well. What does "peace" mean? What is celebrated by writers like Pope and Tickell, when an Addison can claim that writing like a Christian does not entail distancing oneself from war, when dead soldiers may be "accounted for by the Christian System of Powder and Ball?"[4]

---

1   Joseph Addison, *The Spectator*, 6th ed. (London, 1723), 7:190.
2   Samuel Johnson, *The Lives of the Poets*, ed. Roger Lonsdale (Oxford: Oxford University Press, 2006), 4:11.
3   Robert Cummings, "Addison's 'Inexpressible Chagrin' and Pope's Poem on the Peace," *Yearbook of English Studies* 18 (1988): 143–158.
4   Addison, *Spectator*, 7:191.

Of course, one might "Christianize" a work simply by referring to the Bible. Thus a short lyric by William Bush compares the zero-sum nature of war to the experience of plagues in Exodus: "So, *Egypt* Pensive sat in Dismal Night, / While bord'ring *Goshen* saw the cheerful Light."[5] His couplet also serves to represent Britain as a new Israel enjoying a green and prosperous land and France as a new Egypt suffering darkness. Marshall Smith's *On the Peace* uses the same allusion to domestic affect:

> With specious Shews of *Liberty* beguil'd,
> Beneath *Aegyptian Bondage* long we Toyl'd,
> *Brick without Straw* at last compell'd to make,
> And *mortgag'd* (e'er enjoy'd) our latest *Stake*;
> *Factions* who durst their Saucy Notions own,
> Like *Pharaoh's Frogs* sat Croaking round the Throne,
> Audaciously presuming to defy
> The Anger of Affronted *Majesty.*[6]

In this case, the Egyptian taskmasters are Whig war financiers, attacked for making money off taxes that force landowners to take out loans on their last pieces of property, while the Tories are Israelite slaves, who complain of Pharaoh's decree that bricks be made without straw. Here all factions are implicated in the image of the second plague, "Pharaoh's frogs"; at the conclusion of the second book of *The Task*, however, William Cowper describes England as infested and stinking with "the croaking nuisance" of Egyptian (French) culture.[7] This is religious in a rather basic sense.

Less so, but more interesting and more immediately relevant to Pope, is the final couplet of Bush's lyric, which speaks of Queen Anne: "Let there be Peace, the Awful Goddess said; / At the commanding Word all Kings obey'd."[8] The all-creating word of Genesis emanates not from God, but the "Goddess" of Britain, Queen Anne. Pope's famous couplet extends the jurisdiction (literally, the "saying of law") of the queen's illocutionary speech but has the queen embody only human greatness: "At length great *Anna* said 'Let Discord cease!' / She said, the World obey'd, and all was *Peace!*" (lines 327–328).[9] David Morris has noted that the couplet originally read: "Till Anna rose, and bade the Furies cease; / *Let there be Peace*—She said; and all was *Peace*." He suggests Pope made this revision because, whereas

---

5   William Bush, "Wars Humble Some, whilst Other States They Raise," in *Verses on the Peace by the Scholars of Croyden School, Surry. Spoken in Public May 13, 1713* (London, 1713), 4.

6   Marshall Smith, *On the Peace: A Poem. Humbly Inscrib'd to the Most Honourable the Earl of Oxford and Mortimer, Lord High Treasurer of Great Britain, &c.* (London, 1713), 3.

7   William Cowper, *The Task and Selected Other Poems*, ed. James Sambrook (New York: Longman, 1994), line 830.

8   Bush, *Verses*, 4.

9   All quotations of Pope's verse are from *The Twickenham Edition of the Poems of Alexander Pope*, vol. 1, *Pastoral Poetry and an Essay on Criticism*, ed. E. Audra and Aubrey Williams (New Haven: Yale University Press, 1961) and will be cited parenthetically.

the Furies, representations of the underlying causes of war, cannot be stopped (certainly not by mere human decree), actual warfare personified as Discord may be.[10]

Either version obscures a significant point: that, hardly the spontaneous occurrence of a public declamation, the treaty had been long and sometimes quietly in the making.[11] Though plenipotentiaries in Utrecht publicly advocated and even achieved consensus, the treaty they produced (actually, eleven separate bilateral agreements) was in many ways the outcome of private meetings.[12] The hush raised noise both in Parliament and the press. "Secrets" and cognate metaphors became bugbears of Whig propagandists. This was fair since many Tories were themselves feeling uncomfortable about abandoning the Grand Alliance to negotiate a separate peace with an untrustworthy France.[13] (That said, Joseph Trapp's *Peace, A Poem* responded by contrasting Anne's mandate—"At her Command intestine Discords cease, / And all th'inferior Pow'rs lie hushed in Peace"— with the confounding clamor of factionists who "Pronounc'd the World undone, should Fighting cease, / And taught Mankind th'Absurdity of Peace.")[14] These secrets generated their own fictions, often produced for

---

[10]   David Morris, "Virgilian Attitudes in Pope's *Windsor-Forest*," in *Pope: Recent Essays by Several Hands*, ed. Maynard Mack and James A. Winn (New York: Archon Books, 1980), 236–238. Cited in Pat Rogers, *The Symbolic Design of Windsor-Forest* (Newark: University of Delaware Press, 2004), 61.

[11]   Rogers notes: "At the same time that the poem recognized Anne as the titular architect of the peace, it *implicitly* endorsed the part played by Oxford and Bolingbroke, along with lesser instruments of government policy" (emphasis added). Pat Rogers, *Pope and the Destiny of the Stuarts* (Oxford: Oxford University Press, 2005), 207.

[12]   Andreas Osiander, *The States System of Europe, 1640–1990: Peacemaking and the Conditions of International Stability* (Oxford: Oxford University Press, 1994), 90–165. The treaty between Britain and Spain may itself have had three secret clauses; see, Edward Grosek, *The Secret Treaties of History* (Xlibris, 2004), 49.

[13]   Rogers, *Pope*, 209. The author of *Pacata Britannia*, warns the Queen to smile gently, "lest Peace and too much Joy / Above the Terrors of the War destroy; / And *France* at last the fatal Secret find, / Secure while hated, to undo You kind." Thomas Newcombe, *Pacata Britannia. A Panegyrick to the Queen, on the Peace, and the Interest of the British Nation* (London, 1713), 11. See, however, William Law, *A Sermon Preach'd at Hazelingfield, In the County of Cambridge, On Tuesday, July 7, 1713* (Cambridge, 1713) and Edmund Chishull, *The Duty of Good Subjects, in Relation to Publick Peace. Being a Sermon Preach'd at the Assizes at Hertford, on August 11th, 1712* (London, 1712), which tell people not to meddle too deeply in government affairs. Those who do, Law suggests, pose a national threat on the order of the Fall: "When therefore they [who are against the peace] court us out of love to our selves, to quit the mean serenity of Peace for the glorious noise of War, we shall bid them look at Satan raging with despair and anguish at the sight of Man in Paradise, and remember that their care for us, is like that Hellish Kindness which perswaded the happy Innocent to eat in order to be a God" (16).

[14]   Joseph Trapp, *Peace, A Poem: Inscrib'd to the Right Honourable the Lord Viscount Bolingbroke* (Dublin, 1713), 10, 5.

factional purposes.[15] For example, the Whiggish *The History of the Treaty of Utrecht* sums up the differing interpretations of Ormonde's withdrawal of British troops from the field: "Thus were both Sides amusing the World with Fictions: On the one Hand the Duke of *Ormond* was to be affronted by Prince *Eugene*; on the other . . . Prince *Eugene* to be betray'd by the Duke of *Ormond*, both of which were equally True."[16]

Not coincidentally, the year of the peace also saw the publication in French and English of St. Pierre's *Projet de Paix Perpetuelle*, in which the establishment of an international court and league of states is advocated. Knowing how often rulers have justified their untoward actions by alleging either that the terms of an old treaty were ambiguous or that they were forced into accepting them, St. Pierre premises his system on the proscription of secret meetings and separate peaces. For him, a crucial step toward peace involves the increase of transparency and openness in the arbitration of international conflicts. Such openness, he claims, will stabilize civil as well as international society:

> I do not say that in the System of Peace a Sovereign will never have any thing to conceal; but it is certain he would have three times less to conceal, whether from his Neighbours, or from his Subjects. Because with respect to his Neighbours, as all the future Treaties he shall make with them, will be made in the City of Peace, in the Sight, with the Knowledge, and with the Consent of all the other

---

[15] These fictions took a variety of forms. Tories commonly figure Anne as a second Elizabeth with Whigs following the same strategy for the purposes of critique. See Samuel Croxall's *An Original Canto of Spencer* (London, 1714) and the anonymous *Reasons Pro and Con: Being A Debate at the Council-Table, Between the Treasurer and the General, for Making a Peace, or Carrying on the War, in the Reign of Queen Elizabeth; wherein the Force of the General's Arguments Prevailed against the Sophistry of the Treasurer's*. Croxall's Spenserian allegorical romance may be compared with a passage in Trapp, *Peace*, 4–6. Dialogues are also common; see, for example, the anonymous *A Dialogue Between Jack High and Will Low, About the Peace* (London, 1713). For other examples of narrative shaping, see *A Review of the Report of the Secret Committee; Digested into Alphabetical Order, which Distinguishes the Transactions of the Late Ministers One from Another. And Is Also an Useful and Easy Index to the Report* (London, 1715) and *An Index to the Report of the Secret Committee . . . In a Letter to a Friend* (London, 1715). The former condenses the Report of the Secret Committee into an index of biographical entries arranged alphabetically, while the latter provides a summary of the report in epistolary form and proceeds according to date; the former is chronological only within a given biographical sketch.

[16] Anon., *The History of the Treaty of Utrecht* (London, 1712), 368. Throughout, Louis XIV and his government are labeled dissimulators; see, for example, pages 18, 23, 25, 50, 154, 190, 253, 266. The French people, however, are said to be held in "Darkness and Ignorance" by state regulation of the press (267). Also see 280, which recounts Count Zinzendorf's pricking of Marshall de Uxelles by challenging him to publish the king's response to Allied proposals. (French ambassadors had long delayed negotiations by refusing to put anything in writing.)

> Sovereigns, he will have no fear of being deceived, nor any
> Hopes of deceiving. . . . On the contrary, in the System of
> War, the most powerful Sovereign is under a very great
> Constraint, by being obliged to Secrecy. . . .Because in this
> System he has both Neighbours and Subjects to fear . . .
> he is even often as it were forced to conceal his Designs,
> and to deceive both the one and the other, for fear of being
> ruined by them.[17]

By 1713, then, secrecy had come to seem indicative of private interests, a Hobbesian state of war and Christian sin. St. Pierre hoped his plan would effectively create a peaceful civic body out of sovereign states. How to hold rulers accountable for dishonesty remained a problem; a deeper one was the susceptibility of civic bodies to civil war, which the disclosure of truths was often said to foster.[18] Allowing that a ruler might need to conceal information even in a time of peace ("I do not say . . . [he] will never . . ."), St. Pierre invites the behavior he legislates against. His containment of secrecy within what is explicitly considered a Christian body resembles Pope's silencing of the protracted and private deliberations in Utrecht by Anne's creating word.[19] Through exploring other such moments in *Windsor-Forest* and a few contemporaneous panegyrics and comparing them to related passages in sermons devoted to Utrecht, this essay suggests that readers should look for a "Christian" poetic of peace where texts, most threatened by the realities of war, strain hardest but fail to contain violence. Their failures manifest in holy scars.

The contemporary American poet Allen Grossman has suggested that the cultures of poetry and war are the same. Where war (Grossman focuses on nuclear war) represents the power to annihilate the human image (as well as human existence or history), poetry limits absolute violence with "eidetic checks," "lovely, order-conferring, and ultimately world-maintaining countenance[s]" that regulate fundamental visions of perfection by

---

17 Abbé de St. Pierre, *A Project for Settling an Everlasting Peace in Europe* (London, 1713), 82–83.

18 For example, in a charity sermon titled *The Methods of Cultivating the Arts of Peace* (London, 1713), Samuel Hilliard worries about those who "take upon them to canvas and controul the Actions, Counsels and Designs of their Superiours" and dare to "pass their Censures" on current affairs, thereby confounding "the Ranks and Orders of Men . . . the Harmony of the World, and supplants and throws out of its Place the publick Tranquility" (17). Writers often trace the root of this problem to the war in Heaven. More interestingly, James Davies refers to the corruption of the early Church in *A Sermon Preach'd at the Parish-Church of Randilo [sic], in the County of Radnor* (London,1713): "We read that a long Peace and Prosperity having somewhat corrupted the primitive Christians, brought upon them the tenth Persecution," which "as it was the last, so the fiercest" (9).

19 He explains, for example, that European states should "suffer the *Czar* to enter into the Union," because although "the Christianity of his Dominions is very different," nevertheless its practitioners "hope for Salvation through *Jesus Christ*; therefore they are *Christians*" (105).

incorporating, for example, "courteous" violence.[20] Just as the gods protect Hektor's body from mutilation by Achilleus, so the epic contains as well as glorifies war. Defining holiness as the assimilation of all existence into God, Grossman theorizes that image making, or the "creational violence" of religious sacrifice, coincides with the regulation of society by institutions such as poetry, church, and civil government. Though all such institutions apparently limit human experience, they also make the world livable: the "sign of obliteration is the same as the sign of immortality—the sign of poetry." Consequently, though developments like secularization, scientific discovery, and modern eschewals of meter and literary gore seem liberating, they confuse "the violence of the structure of the image" with "the violence that opposes the image altogether," and thereby make the obliteration of humanity a likelier threat.[21] Holy poetry succeeds insofar as its recording of death intends to remind readers that humanity once and still exists.

To put it slightly differently, a poem on peace will be most Christian not when it speaks overtly of doves or the metamorphoses of swords into ploughshares and spears into pruning hooks but when it makes violence a primary theme. In his fast-day sermon of January 16, 1711–1712, Roger Altham reminded members of the House of Commons that to "seek" peace in Greek has "a double Import[;] it signifies both to pursue and persecute, and seems to intimate that the Pursuit of such a Blessing as Peace is, may be sufficient to justify even some kind of Violence for the Accomplishment of it."[22] The phrase "blessings of peace"—used frequently in poems and sermons on the Treaty of Utrecht—conveys bloodshed. Etymologically, to "bless" means to consecrate by marking with the blood of a sacrificial victim.[23] Thus, in the Book of Exodus, the Israelites are commanded to put the blood of paschal lambs on the doorposts and lintels of the entrances to their homes to protect themselves from God's smiting of all first born creatures in Egypt. Though not called a blessing, this act symbolizes a giving over of every aspect of the Israelites' former existence to God, according to Samson Raphael Hirsch, the father of neo-Orthodox Judaism in nineteenth-century Germany. In Grossman's terms, this is one of many "transactions of holiness" in Exodus marking an existential shift in the nation: "The historical moment of the alienation of humankind from

[20] Allen Grossman, "Nuclear Violence, Institutions of Holiness, and the Structures of Poetry," in *The Long Schoolroom: Lessons in the Bitter Logic of the Poetic Principle* (Ann Arbor: University of Michigan Press, 1997), 170. Also see, "Holiness," in the same volume.
[21] Ibid., 177 and 174.
[22] Roger Altham, *A Sermon Preach'd before the Honourable House of Commons, At the Church of St. Margaret Westminster, on Wednesday, Jan. 16, 1711–12, Being the Fast-Day for a General Peace* (London, 1712), 19. William Fleetwood warns that enduring too many insults and injuries from a foreign nation during peacetime, is "neither Christian nor Princely, nor indeed Manly" and hazardous to the nation. Here he uses the image of a polluted, stagnant body of water: "For the Blood of a People does sometimes, like standing Waters, stagnate, putrify, and breed corrupt and dangerous Humours." William Fleetwood, *A Sermon on the Fast-Day, January the Sixteenth, 1711–12* (London, 1712), 12.
[23] This sense is in the *OED* but not in Johnson's *Dictionary*.

unmediated relationship to reality—the Egyptian servitude and consequent multiplication of the people—requires the reconstruction of that relationship within a system of mediation toward a God whose name is being itself."[24] The system of mediation includes words, acts, and signs. For example, God tells Moses their paschal service "shall be to you for a token upon the houses." Hirsch explains it is through the bloody doorposts, which separate the Israelites from the rest of society, and the bloody lintel, which shields them from the natural elements, that they merit providential protection.[25] The token of the blood-spattered doorway brings about a transformation on that day. Through an annual commemoration of the event, it will do so forever; this is indicated in Exodus XII.14, where God commands the Israelites to make of the day "a memorial": "ye shall keep it a feast to the Lord throughout your generations; ye shall keep it a feast by an ordinance forever."[26] A more accurate translation of the Hebrew reads, "for your generations, you shall celebrate it as an eternal statute."[27] History collapses in the token, the actions of the Israelites proleptically accomplishing this law for later generations. But the token also keeps history going, allowing the people to substitute sacrificial for all-consuming holiness.

In this light, William Waller's eulogy of Marlborough in *Peace on Earth. A Congratulatory Poem* looks overtly Whiggish but also subtly religious:

> Stay Muse, be not ingrate, brave *Marlbro*'s Name
> Pass not in Silence, whose Illustrious Fame,
> The World thro'out a glorious Sound will make,
> 'Till the last Trump shall sleeping Mortals wake.
> Nor will prepost'rous Rhymes disgrace thy song,
> Or the great Patriots of Concord wrong,
> If warlike *Marlborough* to them be join'd;
> Peace the Result of War we often find.
> ...
> O gentle Muse, may'st thou for ever be
> From such too strict *Examinations* free:
> Whose nice Remarks thou justly must expect
> Will for one Beauty num'rous Scars detect.
> Howe'er proceed, thou'lt suffer more Disgrace,
> If in thy Work Great *Marlbro'* has no Place.[28]

---

24 Grossman, *Long*, 182–183.
25 *The Pentateuch with a Translation by Samson Raphael Hirsch and Excerpts from the Hirsch Commentary*, ed. Ephraim Oratz (New York: Judaica Press, 1986), 253.
26 All citations of the *King James Bible* are from the online edition hosted by the University of Michigan library. <http://quod.lib.umich.edu/cgi/k/kjv/kjv-idx?type=DIV1&byte=220736> (accessed 8 August 2007).
27 *The Sapirstein Edition Rashi Torah*, vol. 4, *Numbers*, trans. Rabbi Yisrael Isser Zvi Herczeg (Brooklyn: Mesorah Publications, 1997), 116–117.
28 William Waller, *Peace on Earth. A Congratulatory Poem* (London, 1713), 5–6.

Waller "places" Marlborough with Tory "patriots" such as Ormonde and Oxford (Bolingbroke is notably absent) and defends him from Tory propagandists like Swift, to whose *Examiner* he alludes, because otherwise the poet's muse would suffer "disgrace."[29] Though meant in a secular way, "disgrace" possesses religious meaning; it is also of clear import in the passage, being used twice. The poem successfully channels heavenly grace because it refers to Marlborough's battles as instruments of peace ("Peace the Result of War"). Moreover, the great general's name, a "glorious" sound, will last until a trumpet blast signals the end of days, precisely when humanity will be subsumed fully into the holy and the need for poetry will end. Where Pope concludes *Windsor-Forest* by casting out personifications of discord, Waller finishes by dismissing the unholy: "Hence ye Profane, hence then, away be gone."[30] This is unsurprising, given that Waller—unlike most of his contemporaries—begins his poem by praising God, to whom thanks are "in the first Place due": "the Mighty Work does plainly shew; / Not the best Industry of Human Kind, / Unaided by the All-directing Mind, / Cou'd Pow'rs cement so horribly disjoyn'd."[31] Structurally speaking, from first to last, the poem hangs (suspended until Judgment Day) on the idea that holiness is manifested in the interplay of war and peace. Critics of Marlborough may detect "num'rous scars" for any one beauty, but the poem itself symbolizes a holy scar, a blessing, and a reminder of the difference between God and man.

In his *Dictionary*, Johnson defines "scar" as a "mark made by a hurt or fire; a cicatrix."[32] Two of his illustrations connect these marks to holiness or, more accurately, the loss thereof. The first comes from Book II of *Paradise Lost*, when Beelzebub suggests the fallen angels' indirect attack on God through man may allow them to reenter Heaven or occupy some mild zone where: "The soft delicious air, / To heal the scars of these corrosive fires, / Shall breathe her balm." The scars of the fallen angels are from the war in Heaven and the fires of Hell, a consequence and reminder of their rebellion. The second prooftext is from Thomas Burnet's *The Sacred Theory of the Earth*, from the well-known chapter in which he explains that the Biblical flood (again, a punishment for sin) caused the Earth to lose its uniform smoothness. When still in a state of perfection, "this earth had the beauty of youth and blooming nature, and not a wrinkle, *scar*, or fracture on all its body." In both texts, then, bodily and geological scars mark the inevitable separation of sacred and profane, a perfect deity and His flawed faithful, the start of a new historical or spiritual era and catastrophic destruction. Scars reveal that nothing in time is easily healed or restored.

---

29   The author of *Some Thoughts Concerning the Peace and the Thanks-Giving* records that the Tory attack on Marlborough for misappropriating funds "gained thus much by it, that the Duke was *disgraced* and turned out of his Command" (7, my emphasis).

30   Ibid., 8.

31   Ibid., 1.

32   All references to the dictionary are from Samuel Johnson, *A Dictionary of the English Language*, 1st and 4th eds., ed. Anne McDermott (CD-ROM) (Cambridge: Cambridge University Press, 1996).

Preparing for a Miltonic comparison of the fallen angels in Hell and the political factions in Britain, the anonymous author of *Anna Triumphans* expresses interest in the causes of human rage. For example, he asks his "Celestial Muse," who has surveyed all "Nature's Secret Laws, / . . . / E'er since the Earth's stupendous Origin," to "declare the Cause" and:

> Paint the black Offspring of immortal Rage,
> Which groaning Lands in Tragic Wars engage,
> Who form'd to Slay, and furious to Oppress,
> Wish the whole World a barb'rous Wilderness,
> Direct Reverse to Peaceful Heav'n and You,
> Just Heav'n Ordains ev'n these to have their Due.[33]

From one who knows "secrets," the poet would learn what made a war-ravaged world the "Direct Reverse" of "Peaceful Heav'n." Significantly, an answer is possible because God gives Rage's "black Offspring" their "Due." Earlier, an active battlefield renders the poet speechless: "Amazing Actions quite ov'rwhelm'd the Sense, / Silence in Wonder was our Eloquence."[34] In hell, however, the angels make "one Universal Roar" as they upbraid each other. They are immediately drowned out when the "Infernal Vault" itself rings with the "dire Clamour" of righteous kings acting righteously. The poem thus begins to perform its holy work, conceiving peace not by silencing but drowning out war. Yet the fires of Hell spill out as the poem continues in the eruptions of Aetna and Vesuvius (geological cicatrices of sorts). From their noxious eruptions humans learned "T'involve themselves in Military Sin":

> Curs'd Cain himself, a Demi-World, defil'd
> One wretched Part, when t'other Part he spoil'd,
> And current Times in endless Wars embroil'd.
> Mysterious Weapon! Iron, Wood, or Stone;
> But Happier Secret was Thy killing Art unknown!
> If Clanks of Arms, cleaving Funeral Cries,
> At Might Numbers Slain; if Mother's Sighs,
> Intestine Scuffle, Storms of Party-Strife,
> (The sad Lugubrious Scenes of Human Life)
> If fatal He, who gave such Mischiefs Birth,
> Himself had prov'd Abortive to the Earth![35]

The world may have been better had Cain been stillborn, but his existence must be acknowledged. What should have remained secret, the "killing Art," inspires a cacophony ("clanks," "cries," "sighs") as noisy as the clamor of rebel angels. As with Pope, the emphasis here is both on foreign and domestic ("Intestine" fights and "Party-Strife") unease. Shifting to an account of Britain's great victories in the War of Spanish Succession, the

---

33   Anon., *Anna Triumphans. A Congratulatory Poem on the Peace* (London, 1713), 4.
34   Ibid., 3.
35   Ibid., 5.

poet compares the summoning of "Sanguine Youth" to "Foreign Fields" to the assignment of Cherubim to the gates of Eden after Adam and Eve's fall:

> For measuring Justice with that Flaming Sword,
> Which executes th'Almighty Sov'raign's Word,
> (Such as preserv'd fair *Eden*'s Sacred Mound,
> When Guardian Cherubs did that Place surround).[36]

If the soldiers' swords are like the Cherubim's, then the places they protect may also share some attribute. Still sacred and preserved as the site of man's first sin, Eden is also slightly diminished; it would not otherwise need to bar the violence of a sinful world by violent means.[37] The border between sacred and profane, Eden and the world, is the same as that separating war and peace.

Addison excuses pagan authors from "interweaving the Actions of Deities with their Atchievements" but judges the Christian writer who would do the same to be childish. Despite acknowledging its "sweetness," Johnson too calls this writing practice a "ready and puerile expedient."[38] Yet as the poems discussed so far have shown, these actions are not as different as either critic thinks; the sign of their intersection resides in the godlike, indestructible, and sometimes inscrutable "Word." Even Tickell engages with this conception of holiness. Immediately following the opening invocation in his dedicatory poem, "To the Lord Privy-Seal," for example, he describes John Robinson, the Bishop of Bristol (a representative at Utrecht), as formed "to heal the Christian wounds," to "give each kingdom bounds," "the face of ravag'd nature to repair," and finally to "gain by love, where rage and slaughter fail, / And make the crosier o'er the sword prevail." Next, the Bishop's crosier is compared to the rod of Aaron:

> So when great Moses, with Jehovah's wand,
> Had scatter'd plagues o'er stubborn Pharaoh's land,
> Now spread an horde of locusts round the shore,
> Now turn'd Nile's fatt'ning stream to putrid gore;

---

36 Ibid., 6.
37 R. Franks, *Truth and Righteousness: Or, the Peace of God. A Sermon Occasion'd by the Great Discourse and Expectation of Peace* (London, 1713), describes the fall as a declaration of war against God: "a War begins, Man becomes an Enemy to God, and therefore, God most justly becomes an Enemy to Man . . . thunders against Man, drives him from his Presence, and puts a *flaming Sword* into the Hands of Justice" (11). The casting out of Adam and Eve is described as a merciful act, a deferral of judgment until the crucifixion. The factionalized debate over a peace without Spain was also described by Hooper, before both houses of Parliament, as a threatened attack on God: "to persist longer in [the war] than is necessary, is to change the Side; to begin to War against the Gospel; and by a bold Appeal to provoke the Almighty to judge for himself." George Hooper, *A Sermon Preach'd before Both Houses of Parliament, in the Cathedral Church of St. Paul, On Tuesday, July 7, 1713* (London, 1713), 6.
38 Johnson, *Lives*, 67.

Plenty and gladness mark'd the priest of God,
And sudden almonds shot from Aaron's rod.[39]

Remarkably, the poem portrays the "sudden" almonds of plenty as coexistent with the plagues, which are set in the immediate present ("now" and "now"). In the Book of Exodus, Aaron's rod is used to administer the first three plagues.[40] And only his rod, not Moses's, exhibits miraculous powers on its own: once, when Moses and Aaron first approach Pharaoh, the second time, after Korah's rebellion.

The latter is crucial here, having been started because of dissatisfaction with the choice of Aaron as High Priest. After being twice punished, the rebels are finally silenced by God through the demonstration of a miracle. Commanding twelve candidates (one from each tribe) to leave their staffs overnight in the Tent of Meeting, God says his favor will manifest on the staff of the rightful priest. The favorite, of course, is Aaron, whose staff blooms with almonds: "and, behold, the rod of Aaron for the house of Levi was budded, and brought forth buds, and bloomed blossoms, and yielded almonds." As with the paschal sacrifice, God then commands that this staff be saved as an eternal safeguard, reminding the people not to rebel: "And the LORD said unto Moses, Bring Aaron's rod again before the testimony, to be kept for a token against the rebels; and thou shalt quite take away their murmurings from me, that they die not."[41] The great rabbinic exegete of eleventh-century Troyes, Shlomo Yitzhaqi (Rashi), comments that, as the quickest-growing fruit, almonds represent the haste with which God punishes rebels. He adds that the Hebrew word for complaint in Old French is "murmurdiz," related to the Old French "murmure," from which English derives the verb "to murmur"—which Johnson translates as "to grumble; to utter secret and sullen discontent."[42] The rebel angels murmur, for example, in Milton's *Paradise Lost*. Aaron's rod ends civil war but also signifies it. According to rabbinic tradition, it bore sweet almonds on one side and bitter on the other. When the Israelites conformed with Godly behavior, the sweet almonds became ripe and edible; when they did not, the bitter almonds flourished. Additionally, some commentators explain that the staff sprouted in the tent but blossomed only when held by Moses.[43] Like the flaming swords, the brothers' two staffs mark the permeable bound between war and peace. According to a different midrash, Aaron's rod, passed down from every Israelite king but hidden by God after the destruction of the Temple in Jerusalem, is "destined to be held

---

[39]   This and the previous quotation are from Thomas Tickell, *A Poem, To His Excellency The Lord Privy-Seal, on the Prospect of Peace* (London, 1713), ii.

[40]   According to rabbinic tradition, Moses, having as a baby been protected by the Nile and as an adult by Egyptian soil that covered the body of the man he murdered, could not cause them harm.

[41]   *KJB*, Nm 17:8, 10.

[42]   *Sapirstein*, 4:211–212.

[43]   *Etz Hayim: Torah and Commentary*, ed. David L. Lieber (New York: Rabbinical Assembly, 2001), 869.

in the hand of the King Messiah."[44] Christianizing the midrash, Origen writes that the staff was used as the transverse beam of Jesus's crucifix. Thus, it also symbolizes the eventual victory of Judeo-Christian holiness over the earth. In his thanksgiving sermon, James Davies blames the war in part on domestic schisms and the masking of private agendas with public faith: "the wide Passage, that lies between the Faith, and lives of those who pretend to be Christians."[45] Representing the tenuous hold of peace in the world, Aaron's rod demonstrates that the difference is not so wide as Davies would have. The same holds for Bristol's crosier and his peacemaking activities in Utrecht.

While concern about faction and civil war is expressed in many thanksgiving sermons (including George Hooper's, preached before both houses of Parliament), Tickell's *A Poem on the Prospect of Peace* shows that, under conditions of peace, even the international scene can in a certain sense be thought of as domestic:

> Brave minds, howe'er at war, are secret friends,
> Their gen'rous discord with the battle ends;
> In peace they wonder whence dissension rose,
> And ask how souls so like could e'er be foes.[46]

The difference between enemies and friends is slight but not as inclusive as it seems. "Secret" may allude to the backdoor negotiations between Britain and France, but it may also refer to their shared religious beliefs.[47] This much becomes clear in a second apostrophe to the Bishop of Bristol, where the poet asks for Bellona to be sent "where Tartar-clans and grisly Cossacs reign; / Let the steel'd Turk be deaf to matrons' cries."[48] Association with the "th' untam'd barbarian" is fine, because "'tis a godlike work to civilize."[49] Unless they convert, however, the uncivilized, ungodly, and grisly non-

---

44   *Midrash Rabbah*, vol. 2, *Numbers*, trans. Judah J. Slotki (London: Soncino Press, 1983), 744.

45   Davies, *A Sermon*, 8.

46   Tickell, *A Poem*, 2.

47   Before the Queen's representatives in Utrecht, William Ayerst called it a good and blessed work "for Men to endeavour to reconcile those that are *Brethren*, not only as Men, all sprung from the same Common Stock, but as Christians, Redeem'd by the same Blood of Christ." Like the almonds, members of all sects are brothers "sprung" from the same stock. William Ayerst, *The Duty and Motives of Praying for Peace. A Sermon Preach'd before their Excellencies The Lord Privy Seal, and the Right Honourable Thomas, Earl of Strafford, Her Majesty'd Plenipotentiaries at the Congress of Utrecht* (London, 1712), 22. Hooper, by contrast, condemns political faction by making reference to the "Venemous Weed" of Matthew 13:25, which did not grow suddenly but was sown by enemies at night (15). The author of the anti-Papist *Some Thoughts Concerning the Peace and the Thanks-Giving* expresses concern for Protestants at home and in Europe (8, 15–17).

48   Tickell, *A Poem*, 7.

49   Ibid., 8.

Europeans will remain outsiders in Tickell's world. By comparison, as John Richardson and Pat Rogers have shown, Pope's vision is more inclusive.[50]

Among the insiders are fond wives who, tearing over every wound, listen to the experiences of their recently returned husbands, who draw their spouses in by depicting the battlefield as a set dining-room table:

> Near the full bowl he draws the fancied line,
> And mark's the feign'd trenches in the flowing wine,
> Then sets th'invested fort before her eyes,
> And mines that whirl'd battalions to the skies.[51]

Unlike Pope's *Rape of the Lock*, the domestication of war here is not intended to mock but sentimentalize epic virtues. Indeed, the husband's "little list'ning progeny," turned pale, begs to hear the tale repeated. Unlike his mother, the child seems moved by its romance, the genre of which Tickell next briefly speaks. Weaned on stories of "palfrey'd dames, bold knights, and magic spells," like-minded children become eager youths who travel abroad to "visit fields their valiant fathers won; / From Flandria's shore their country's fame they trace, / 'Till far Germania shews her blasted face."[52] Like his father at the table, a mournful guide takes the young Briton through Blenheim and Hocstet, the view of the latter being compared to a painting by Raphael or Kneller. Though he next desires to "see the horrors of the field / By plough-shares levell'd, or in flow'rs conceal'd," when he describes a visit to Blenheim Palace, Tickell once again juxtaposes a child's experience with a painting:

> If Churchill's race perhaps some lovely boy
> Shall mark the burnish'd steel that hangs on high;
> Shall gaze transported on its glitt'ring charms,
> And reach it struggling with unequal arms;
> . . .
> So, in the painter's animated frame,
> Where Mars embraces the soft Paphian dame,
> The little loves in sport the faulchion wield,
> Or join their strength to heave his pond'rous shield;
> One strokes the plume in Tityon's gore embru'd;
> Another's infant brows the helm sustain,
> He nods his crest, and frights the shrieking train.[53]

---

[50] John Richardson, "Alexander Pope's *Windsor Forest*: Its Context and Attitudes toward Slavery," *Eighteenth-Century Studies* 35 (2001): 1–17. Rogers, *Pope*, 226–239.

[51] Tickell, 3.

[52] Ibid., 4.

[53] Ibid., 13. In Nicholas Brady's *A Sermon Preach'd at Richmond in Surrey, Upon July the 7th, 1713. Being the Day of Thanksgiving Appointed by her Majesty for a General Peace* (London, 1713), looking back in time at the miserable "scene" of war serves, like "Shades in Painting, to set off the Lustre of our present Happiness" (5). War and peace share the scene.

In an earlier passage, Tickell imagines newly gained ore being melted into commemorative coins on which, among other things, "Churchill's sword hang[s] o'er the prostrate foe."[54] Now the sword hangs above a descendant of Marlborough, who hopes one day to stand, like Marlborough, in an ascendant position. The child reaches for it like the figures in the unnamed painting, which at the very least recalls Botticelli's *Mars and Venus*. The putti are playing in the background, but such sports, as Johan Huizinga shows, forebode good as well as ill.[55] Between a loving mother and a veteran father, the child at home and abroad—above and beneath the sword—contains within him the possibilities of friendship and enmity.

Addison excuses Tickell's mythological allusions by calling them mere "fable," as though fables were not essential to the Gospels.[56] In *The Genesis of Secrecy*, Frank Kermode discusses the power of fables to construct outsiders and insiders—the insiders ostensibly being those who do not need the spiritual truth of stories explained. And yet, like all readers, Jesus's disciples often prove incapable interpreters. As Kermode shows, their failures, plus the complications of variant manuscripts, give the lie to fabulous simplicity.[57] Neither perfectly accessible nor free from interpretive ambiguity, holy secrets (like scars) are as readily transmitted through mythological as Christian fable. This may be illustrated by a passage in *An Hymn on Peace*, where Samuel Wesley (the father of John and Charles of Methodist fame), mourns Anne's lack of an heir:

> *Retire* we then to the wise *Pollio*'s Seat,
> That Scene of all *Agreeable* and *Great*;
> Where, in the *Town*, thick *Rural Shades* he sees,
> And views the World in *Emblematic Trees*:
> . . .
> Tho' long his weighty *Thoughts* intent remain
> A *Pleasing Interruption* breaks their Chain:
> See thro' the Grove a *Shining Form* appear,
> The parting Shades Confess a Vertue near:
> She, o'er th' *Illumin'd Herb* Majestic treads,
> And in her Hand a *Little-Love* she leads:
> . . .

---

54   Ibid., 10. On numismatics and Pope's use thereof in *Windsor-Forest*, see Rogers, *Symbolic*, 64–69 and *Pope*, 89–90, 142–144.

55   "The idea of warfare only enters when a special condition of general hostility solemnly proclaimed is recognized as distinct from individual quarrels and family feuds . . . It is elevated to the level of holy causes, becomes a general matching of forces and a revelation of destiny . . . Even if it were no more than a fiction, these fancies of war as a noble game of honour and virtue have still played an important part in developing civilization, for it is from them that the idea of chivalry sprang and hence, ultimately, of international law." Johan Huizinga, *Homo Ludens* (Boston: Beacon Press, 1950), 95–96.

56   Addison, *Spectator*, 189.

57   Frank Kermode, *The Genesis of Secrecy: On the Interpretation of Narrative* (Cambridge: Harvard University Press, 1979); see especially, 23–47.

With Lips untaught, *less-than-Half-Words* he tries,
But more the *Charmer* prattles with his *Eyes*:
He rais'd the *Infant Honours* of his Head,
Young *blooming Joys* around profusely shed,
And if he could have Spoke, he *Peace* had said.[58]

This imitates Virgil's fourth *Eclogue*, a celebration of the treaty of
Brundisium and Antony's consul, Gaius Asinius Pollio. In his invocation to
the "Sicilian Muses," Virgil asks them to "Let woods, if woods we sing be
worthy of a consul."[59] These are Wesley's "*Emblematic Trees*." Throughout
the poem, Wesley makes nature a reflection of politics; Adam and Eve's fall
thus generates "th' ill-scented *Weed*, and *Warriour-Thistle*."[60] Like fables,
the trees are readable but also subject to misinterpretation. How does the
child relate to them and the world? His entrance interrupts (albeit
pleasantly) the poet's retirement, breaking the direct transmission of meaning from nature. Lacking the power of speech, however, he cannot yet make
"peace." While Virgil makes the child a savior, Wesley renders his "*Little-
Love*" a mere figure.[61] Crucially, this is in keeping with the tradition of the
Church fathers. As Guy Lee notes, Lactantius and Augustine accepted
Virgil's poem as a fabulous prefiguration of the birth of Christ. So too,
Wesley's child prefigures the Messiah; after this passage, the poem
concludes by thinking of Jesus, "*Father* of *Peace*, a Friend to Human Race:
/ Serene in Wounds; Impenetrably *Calm;* / Whose *Hands* are Healing, and
whose *Words* are Balm," and hoping for his return.[62] Here, the end of time
("*Eternal Peace*") is like the beginning, when "all was *Mind*" and "Th'Almighty
Word the Heav'n of Heav'ns sustain'd."[63] For as God heals "the *Scars* of
Heav'n" after the rebellion, so Jesus bears the earthly wounds of ambition,
pride, and sin with his healing hands and holy words.[64] Rather than
dismiss fable, then, Wesley appropriates it, like Augustine before him, for
Christian purposes.

And like Tickell, Wesley would have the secret nature of Gospel truth
spread worldwide. Speaking of the Thames, he prays the river will:

Th' inestimable *Pearl* of *Truth-divine*
His *Floating Castles* waft beyond the *Line;*

---

58   Samuel Wesley, *An Hymn on Peace. To the Prince of Peace* (London, 1713), 11–12.
59   Virgil, *The Eclogues*, trans. Guy Lee (New York: Penguin Books, 1984), p. 57, line 3.
60   Wesley, *An Hymn*, 5.
61   Even for Virgil's readers, the newborn child was ambiguous, referring to the
     child of Octavian, Antony, or Pollio. As a peacemaker, Pollio is a good candidate,
     but Octavian's Julian lineage and Antony's marriage to Octavia make them
     naturally fitter to sire a godlike child. See M. Owen Lee, *Death and Rebirth in
     Virgil's Arcadia* (Albany: State University of New York Press, 1989), 44.
62   Wesley, *An Hymn*, 12.
63   Ibid., 3.
64   Ibid., 3.

And safe *return'd*, to his *Augusta* bear,
The Wealth of *Peace*, not Spoils or *Scars* of *War*.[65]

Dreams of mass conversion are fairly common. In the forebodingly titled thanksgiving sermon, *Peace the Gift of God, But the Terrour of the Wicked*, Luke Milbourne labels those who are unhappy with the treaty a "*Discontented, Hypocritical, Atheistical Crew*" who will never enjoy the benefits of concord: "such unhappy Persons shall reap no Benefit from the best, the most honourable, and the most advantageous Peace that ever was made among contending Nations. God calls not such wicked Men into his Counsels."[66] Likewise, the author of *Peace, or, No Peace* wishes "everlasting War, and all its Woes," upon all those who Satanically oppose the peace— namely, "Whigs and Atheists" who "curse the fruitful Ground, / And, in Revenge, the Gifts of Heav'n confound."[67] Joseph Trapp's fast-day sermon expresses more shame and self-implication:

> It is indeed a Disgrace to Christianity, that there should be at *all* any such Thing as *War*, among it's [sic] Professors; were it's [sic] Precepts duly obey'd, there would be nothing like it in these Parts of the World . . . But that Christians should not only have Wars *like* other Nations, but *more than* other Nations; more Sharp, Cruel, and Bloody Wars, than any other People upon the Face of the Earth, directly contrary to the Genius and Tendency of the Religion they profess; is a most deplorable Scandal.[68]

Often enough, though, self-critique is premised on Christian solidarity against non-Christians. Though he mostly concentrates on disunity and schism, after allowing that war may at times be justified, James Davies adds an interesting historical reminder:

> May we not forget how that profess'd Enemy of our Saviour, the Scourge of Christians, the Rod of God's Indignation, hath not only overthrown those glorious Countries, those Churches modeliz'd by the blessed Apostles and their Successors; but also cover'd them with Tartarian Darkness, *Mahomet's* Doctrine, the Alchoran Religion, and all this, (to our Shame be it spoken) through our Pride and Contention.[69]

65   Ibid., 10.
66   Luke Milbourne, *Peace the Gift of God, But the Terrour of the Wicked; In a Sermon Preach'd on the Thanksgiving for the Peace, July the 7th, 1713. At the Parish-Church of St. Ethelburga* (London, 1713), 3 and 17.
67   Anon., *Grandsire Hambden's Ghost. And Peace, or, No Peace. Two Poems.* (London, 1712), 42–43.
68   Joseph Trapp, *A Sermon Preach'd at the Parish-Church of St. Martin in the Fields; January the 16th, 1711* (London, 1712), 9.
69   Davies, *A Sermon*, 10.

Read generously, the passage merely warns Britons that ceaseless in-fighting will endanger their very existence—possibly from anyone, probably from Muslims. It hardly takes a giant leap, however, to imagine this as encouraging not so much the laying down as the redirection of weapons. Other treatments are less belligerent but essentially bigoted. Like Trapp, William Ayerst feels scandalized over Christian bellicosity when: "Even the *Mahometans* themselves, whose very Religion was founded upon the Sword, seem of late Years more humanely inclined, and keep themselves freer from Dissensions among themselves, and Quarrels with their Neighbors, than those that pretend to be Followers of the Gospel of Peace."[70] Construing Muslims oppositely from Davies, Ayerst's contrastive "even" indicates surprise at their more peaceful behavior. In both, Muslim unity highlights Christian disunity and the susceptibility of all nations to war. While Augustus proved Virgil's prophecy wrong, Wesley's advocacy of missionizing makes his nominal celebration of peace, if not suspect, at least worthy of scrutiny.

Clearly, then, the troping of violence in *Windsor-Forest* engages with language both ubiquitous and religious in Pope's day. Less focused on international war or missionary work than some others, Pope worries about Britain's history of civil strife, the chronology of which he superimposes onto the forest. In a discussion of Pope's reluctant patriotism, Dustin Griffin notes that "the recurrent figure of blood and gore [throughout the poem] suggests an awareness that the patriotic story of British triumph is a dark story of the spilling of blood."[71] To this can be added the image of scars. In the two couplets preceding Anne's fiat, the figure of Albion tearfully watches her nation punished for the murder of Charles I:

> . . . her sons with purple deaths expire,
> Her sacred domes involv'd in rolling fire,
> A dreadful series of intestine wars,
> Inglorious triumphs, and dishonest scars. (323–326)

The Twickenham editors suggest that these lines refer to the outbreak of the bubonic plague in 1665, the Great Fire of London in 1666, and the Glorious Revolution. Of greater interest presently are the "dishonest scars." The editors also note that, in his *Iliad*, Pope frequently uses "dishonest," meaning shameful, to describe wounds received in the back. Only generally can one know from where such wounds come. And in any event, even with the cessation of discord, traces of them remain.

Though these haunt Pope's poem, signaling the potential of violence to break out suddenly and mysteriously, they are nearly erased in the passage concluding the Lodona episode. Breaking from her community only to pray for Diana's protection when chased by Pan, Lodona is metamorphosed into a tributary of the Thames. This may seem a rescue, but in fact Lodona is doomed to an eternity of tears: "The silver Stream her Virgin Coldness

---

70 Ayerst, *The Duty*, 4.
71 Dustin Griffin, *Patriotism and Poetry in Eighteenth-Century Britain* (Cambridge: Cambridge University Press, 2002), 58.

keeps, / For ever murmurs, and for ever weeps." Perhaps because of this disturbance, Pope added six verses to the conclusion of the episode:

> Oft in her Glass the musing Shepherd spies
> The headlong Mountains and the downward Skies,
> The watry Landskip of the pendant Woods,
> And absent Trees that tremble in the Floods;
> In the clear azure Gleam the Flocks are seen,
> And floating Forests paint the Waves with Green. (211–216)

The famous quatrain on the Thames in Denham's *Cooper's-Hill* emphasizes, among other things, the river's clarity: "Though deep, yet clear; though gentle, yet not dull."[72] Here, however, Lodona-as-river reflects the world, hiding what lies beneath its surface. Like a fable, the river closes the world off from the untoward actions of creatures like Pan.

   Hardly ideal or peaceful, in so doing it also shakes and turns the world upside down ("headlong," "downward," "pendant," "trembling"). Terming his use of Virgilian motifs "eco-political," Rogers writes that Pope uses landscape as "an index of the vulnerability of the state and of all human contrivances."[73] Similarly, Susanne Wofford argues that epic is "a genre that mystifies rather than reveals origins, and that demonstrates the reasons *not* to expose the cause."[74] Whereas the epic impulse renders opposition inert and forgettable, especially in Ovid, from which Pope's Lodona borrows, metamorphosis often generates a "mournful landscape that continually points to the crime and grief that it hides."[75] Wofford's reading applies equally well to the inverted world of Lodona's reflection. The phrase "for ever" also gives the reader pause. It is used just four times in the poem: twice here, once in the aforementioned passage on Charles I ("Make sacred

---

[72]   I quote from Brendan O Hehir, *Expans'd Hieroglyphicks: A Critical Edition of Sir John Denham's Cooper's Hill* (Berkeley: University of California Press, 1969), line 190. In 1642, the famous quatrain of which this is a verse, read: "O could my verse freely and smoothly flow / As thy pure flood, heaven should no longer know / Her old Eridanus; thy purer streame / Should bathe the gods, and be the poet's theame" (76). A mythological river in Hades, in Book II of Ovid's *Metamorphosis*, it is the site of Phaeton's death. There the Heliades mournful tears create amber. Through the power of Denham's verse, the Thames replaces Eridanus twice: in these lines and in their excision. Though early in the poem Pope dismisses "the weeping amber" (30), by the conclusion, he similarly appropriates it for Britain with father Thames triumphantly declaring: "For me the balm shall bleed, and amber flow" (390). Through literary allusion, the episode is scarred once more.

[73]   Rogers, *Pope*, 243–244.

[74]   Susanne L. Wofford, "Epics and the Politics of the Origin Tale: Virgil, Ovid, Spenser, and Native American Aetiology," in *Epic Traditions in the Contemporary World: The Poetics of Community*, ed. Margaret Beissinger, Jane Tylus, and Susanne Wofford (Berkeley: University of California Press, 1999), 257. Wofford is countering David Quint's interpretation of epic as a teleologically closed narration of national origin that projects imperial power as inevitable and irreversible.

[75]   Ibid., 249. On the use of Ovidian myth in this episode, see David R. Hauser, "Pope's Lodona and the Uses of Mythology," *SEL* 6 (1966): 465–482.

Charles's Tomb for ever known, / (Obscure the Place, and uninscrib'd the Stone"), and finally in lines that suggest that should Granville (a minor poet, and a secretary of war from 1710–1712) sing of Edward's acts and Crecy's field, the French will "bleed for ever under *Britain*'s Spear" (lines 319–320, 308). Buried with Henry VIII, Charles's hidden body resembles Lodona as river. As Lodona's eternal tears expose Pan's desire, so Pope's cry for Charles's tomb to be "for ever known" may extend to a recuperation (or at least a sympathetic memorial) of the Stuart cause. These passages are in turn exposed by the image of eternally flowing French blood. Effectively, the recurrence of "for ever" indicates an endless cycle of counter-narratives (the world and its upside-down image) in which the victim of one story becomes the violent perpetrator of another.

Embedding the history of peace in a landscape, Pope also admits the superficiality of the gesture. Functioning as a transition from the local forest to the wide world, the Lodona episode also resembles a scarred border.[76] Beyond any of the poem's other religious references, this structural concession/confession (Lodona's reflection is at the exact center of the poem) makes *Windsor-Forest* deeply Christian. Pope's *Messiah*, published anonymously in *Spectator* no. 378 (14 May 1712) with a subtitle announcing it as "Written in Imitation of Virgil's Pollio," highlights why. For one, upon the birth of the Son, both "Peace o'er the World her Olive-Wand extend, / And white-roab'd Innocence from Heav'n descend" (19–20). In an alchemical reading, Rogers identifies Lodona as a figure of innocence.[77] Moreover, Peace is a harbinger of the world to come (imagined at the poem's conclusion), where the holiness of Heaven eradicates all mater:

> See Heav'n its sparkling Portals wide display,
> And break upon thee in a Flood of Day!
> No more the rising *Sun* shall gild the Morn,
> Nor Evening *Cynthia* fill her silver Horn,
> But lost, dissolv'd in thy superior Rays;
> One Tyde of Glory, one unclouded Blaze,
> O'erflow thy Courts: The Light Himself shall shine
> Reveal'd; and God's eternal Day be thine!
> The Seas shall waste; the Skies in Smoke decay;
> Rocks fall to Dust, and Mountains melt away;
> But fix'd *His* Word, *His* saving Pow'r remains:
> Thy *Realm* for ever lasts! thy own *Messiah* reigns! (97–108)

Diana rules in the Lodona episode, but here her moonlight is dissolved in God's rays. When the poet earlier rouses the natural world to acknowledge the Son, he commands its topography to smoothen, like the world before

---

[76]   For sunnier readings of the poem's mediation of aggression, see Vincent Carretta, "Anne and Elizabeth: The Poet as Historian in *Windsor-Forest*," *SEL* 21 (1981): 425–437, which considers Lodona's a "fortunate fall"; and Howard Weinbrot's chapter on *Windsor-Forest* in *Britannia's Issue: The Rise of British Literature from Dryden to Ossian* (Cambridge: Cambridge University Press, 1993).

[77]   Rogers, *Pope*, 258–260.

the flood: "Sink down ye Mountains, and ye Vallies rise: / . . . / Be smooth ye Rocks, ye rapid Floods give way!" (36–37). The end of days having arrived, now the perfected world melts away. Likewise, earlier the Son silences all before him with new music: "No Sigh, no Murmur the wide World shall hear, / From ev'ry Face he wipes off ev'ry Tear" (45–46). Lodona weeps forever, but Jesus "wipes off ev'ry Tear." In the end, however, all that is left is "*His* Word," power and realm—all of which will survive "for ever." Pope's *Messiah* embraces the holiness described by Thomas Cooke in his fast-day sermon: "the most glorious Perfections of the Divine Nature, and the blessed Emanations from it; *Is the Peace of God which passeth all understanding.*" Human experience and knowledge are nullified under God's absolute word.[78] Attracted to what Cooke calls a more "restrain'd" notion of peace, *Windsor-Forest* evades this extreme.[79]

In recent years, scholars have suggested that a primary element of Augustan literature is its refusal of stable expressions of belief. In this view, Pope's is a deeply satirical age.[80] Prior to this recent scholarship, Earl Wasserman essentially argued the opposite, that the couplets of *Windsor-Forest* hold contraries in balance and thereby embody cosmic order.[81] Eric Auerbach's famous chapter on Odysseus's scar also categorizes two types of realism: one being multilayered and various, and the other, logical and detailed. The scar proving an apt detail for identifying Odysseus, Auerbach sees it as exemplary of the latter.[82] What I hope to have shown is that, in scars, tokens, secrets, and fables, one will find these extremes simultaneously tending toward and away from each other. The violence tearing through peaceful landscapes also instantiates holiness in it. The same holds for fables, which promise to create in-groups by coding meaning

78 Temporal peace is providentially ordained, achieved by God's ministers, the rulers of nations: "When Princes proclaim Peace in their respective Dominions, they are only so many deputed *Heralds* of the *Prince of Peace*, acting under him *Ministerially*, in whom is inherent, *Originally*, the Indisputable Right, as well as Uncontroulable Power of Uniting the World." Benjamin Loveling, *Peace the Gift of God: Rest, Safety, and Opportunities of Piety, the Fruits of Peace. A Sermon Preach'd at Banbury, in Oxford-shire, on Tuesday the Seventh of July, 1713. It being the Day of Thanksgiving, Appointed by Her Majesty, For a General Peace* (Oxford, 1713), 4.
79 Thomas Cooke, *The Way to Peace, and Lamentation for the Fall of the Righteous. Two Sermons on Two Fast Days; January 16. The Fast for Peace. And January 30. Being the Martyrdom of King Charles I. Preach'd at Kingston in Surry* (London, 1711–1712), 5.
80 See, for example, Blanford Parker, *The Triumph of Augustan Poetics: English Literary Culture from Butler to Johnson* (Cambridge: Cambridge University Press, 1998); and Christian Thorne, "Thumbing Our Nose at the Public Sphere: Satire, the Market, and the Invention of Literature," *PMLA* 116 (2001): 531–544.
81 See the chapter on *Windsor-Forest* in Earl Wasserman, *The Subtler Language: Critical Readings of Neo-Classical and Romantic Poems* (Baltimore: Johns Hopkins University Press, 1968) and also Isabel Rivers, *The Poetry of Conservatism, 1600–1745: A Study of Poets and Public Affairs from Jonson to Pope* (Cambridge: Rivers Press, 1973), 179.
82 Erich Auerbach, *Mimesis: The Representation of Reality in Western Literature* (Garden City, NY: Doubleday, 1957), 1–20.

and restricting access to the key. This is not "Christian" in a doctrinal sense but as a way of thought or practice of writing. And it pervades texts that readers might not otherwise associate with religious contexts. Propagandizing the Tory agenda, for example, Defoe's definition of a "good peace" nonetheless speaks to the ambiguity of holy scars:

> Two Men quarelling together in this Town, One a *West* Countryman, the other a *North* Countryman; among some Scurrility that part between them, says *West* to his Antagonist, I am no *Yorkshireman*; why, says *North*, *What have you to say to* Yorkshire? Are there not a great many Honest Men in *Yorkshire?* I would have you know, *There are as Honest Men in* Yorkshire, *as in any Part of* England; Ay, ay, says *West*, that may be true for ought I know; *but that is called Honesty in* Yorkshire, *which is not Honesty in other Places.*[83]

This story teaches readers that concepts such as honesty are relative and depend especially on point of origin. Yet, premising everything on the treaty of the Grand Alliance, Defoe goes on to argue unashamedly that a peace without Spain is acceptable and good. His story of ambivalent meaning thus leaves a structural hole in the text, an access point for any who might advocate the continuation of the war. Kant indicates the darker side of this ambivalence when he describes the sign of a Dutch inn on which a cemetery and the phrase "eternal peace" comment upon each other.[84] The paths of peace lead but to the grave, the sign seems to say. As Tobin Siebers has shown, throughout his meditation on perpetual peace, Kant struggles to reconcile individual reason and the public processes necessary for peace.[85] His suggestion that peace may be deferred until the end of life would not be out of place in a sermon or Pope's poem.

---

[83] Daniel Defoe, *An Essay at a Plain Exposition of that Difficult Phrase A Good Peace* (London, 1711), 11.
[84] Immanuel Kant, "Eternal Peace," in *Essays and Treatises on Moral, Political, and Various Philosophical Subjects* (London, 1798), 243–244.
[85] Tobin Siebers, "Politics and Peace," *Contagion* 3 (1996): 85–100.

Jonathan Edwards on Nature as a Language of God: Symbolic Typology as Rhetorical Presence

Brian Fehler

In recent years, scholars have paid increasing attention to the rhetoric of the Puritans. One rhetor, in particular, has received notice: Jonathan Edwards, that giant of late Puritan thought. Edwards's rhetoric, after all, whipped up the embers of a dying Puritan discourse into the flame that became the Great Awakening. Edwards's Awakening, though, was not only—or even especially—maintained by his famous fire-and-brimstone sermons, such as the justifiably famous "Sinners in the Hands of An Angry God." Indeed, not all of Edwards's rhetoric was preached from pulpits; he produced a large body of writings never delivered as sermons. In two of these works, *Images or Shadows of Divine Things* and *Dissertation Concerning the End for Which God Created the World*, Edwards investigates the topic of natural, or general, revelation, that is, God's presence in the things of nature, in creation. [1]

Natural revelation was the source of Puritan typology, ways of thinking that saw in every action, every movement, "shadows" of divine purpose and will. Traditionally, typology concerns the Biblical Old Testament as prefiguring the New Testament. Thus, Christ, for example, is seen as fulfilling the prophecies of the Hebrew prophets such as Isaiah. The

---

[1] All quotations from Edwards's *Dissertation Concerning the End for Which God Created the World and Images or Shadows of Divine Things* are taken from *Jonathan Edwards, Puritan Sage: The Writings of Jonathan Edwards*, ed. Vergilus Ferm (New York: Library Press, 1953).

Puritans extended this notion to their own era and considered New England to be a New Israel. Richard Slotkin writes that "the Puritans saw the New World as a desert wilderness, like that through which Bunyan's pilgrim travels."2 Primary revelation, then, God's own sacred scripture ordained the notions of typological thinking; for example, the Puritans' confrontations with the Native peoples they faced could be read as mirroring early conflicts between Israel and its enemies. But Puritan views of the symbolism of nature—expressed by Edwards—served another purpose as well. Especially in the days of declining faith, the age of the Great Awakening, Edwards's emphasis of natural symbolism demonstrated the power of rhetorical presence, that is, the use of concrete symbols to lend authority to an oration or text. For Edwards, the words of Scripture, the words of any written language, are symbolic of spoken language, and nature is certainly no less symbolic. By viewing nature as imbued with divine presence, Edwards helped concretize his Calvinistic theology. This emphasis on the visual, on the everyday occurrence, helps us to view the Great Awakening as an era of epideictic rhetoric, when, for a time, the faith of traditional Puritanism was strengthened.

Typology and Rhetorical Presence

The notion of rhetorical presence, upon which Edwards relied so well, is described by Chaim Perelman and L. Olbrechts-Tyteca in *The New Rhetoric: A Treatise on Argumentation*. Perelman and Olbrechts-Tyteca write that by "selecting certain elements and presenting them to the audience, their importance and pertinence to the discussion are implied. Indeed, such a choice endows these elements with a presence."3 The Puritan thinkers realized the importance of presence for an argument, and they never avoided considering their theology as an argument. Perelman and Olbrechts-Tyteca further explain their notion of presence: "when two things are set side by side [. . .] the thing on which the eye dwells, that which is best or most often seen, is, by that very circumstance, overestimated. The thing that is present to the consciousness assumes thus an importance that the theory and practice of argumentation must take into consideration."4

Presence need not, of course, depend on the actual, physical presence of concrete objects. Indeed, a speaker can demonstrate his or her skill in producing "by verbal magic alone, what is actually absent." Such a purely verbal display, moreover, has the benefit of keeping an audience's attention fully focused on the speaker, while physical evidence may "distract the viewer's attention." Nevertheless, physical presence, Perelman and Olbrechts-Tyteca insist, should be utilized when possible, for things like

2   Richard Slotkin, *Regeneration through Violence: The Mythology of the American Frontier, 1600–1860* (Middletown: Wesleyan University Press, 1973), 59.
3   Chaim Perelman and Lucie Olbrechts-Tyteca, *The New Rhetoric: A Treatise on Argumentation*, trans. John Wilkinson and Purcell Weaver (Notre Dame: University of Notre Dame Press, 1969), 116.
4   Ibid., 116–117.

Anthony's use of "Caesar's bloody tunic" can produce "quick results."[5] An examination of Edwards's use of symbolic typology, though, shows that presence can produce more than quick results. For Edwards, a skilled orator with verbal magic of his own, managed to balance his oratory and Calvinist theology with an appreciation of things of Creation. This appreciation and recognition of the divine in all things resulted in an inescapable rhetorical presence—one could never hide from God, when God was everywhere and in everything.

Edwards receives attention from many disciplines—literature, history, theology, American studies—and these diverse fields reflect the far ranging nature of his own thought. Jonathan Edwards lived in an age when scientific explanations were beginning to take precedence over purely theological reflections, when to believe in a literal creation story meant being labeled a "medieval" rather than an enlightened thinker. But Edwards, though he was interested in Newtonian science, considered himself first and foremost a theologian, one who clung to the Calvinist rather than Deist tradition. Michael McClymond suggests that Edwards's position rendered him "a Christian apologist in an increasingly secular world."[6] The title of Edwards's principle work on the theology of nature, *Dissertation Concerning the End for Which God Created the World*, published posthumously in 1765, reveals that he believed in a God who purposefully created the world and who remains active in its concerns. Why did Edwards feel compelled to cling to the idea of a literal creation? In answering this question, one must examine Edwards's theology of nature, his theology of God, and the intellectual milieu into which his ideas were introduced. Ultimately, Edwards hoped to establish humanity's relationship with God in the wordless realm of nature. Edwards would never endorse abandoning Scriptural revelation, but he believed that God could be experienced through nature as well. It was this important theology of nature that successfully imbued Edwards's message with a powerful rhetorical presence.

In many works, Edwards utilized religious symbolism in nature, though his reliance on images of nature involved far more than reflections on nature for nature's sake. Nature always and only possessed a status as a creation of God. Interestingly, intellectual historian R. C. DeProspo finds fault with Edwards on this very point. DeProspo writes that Edwards "studies the natural world only to the degree that he thinks it manifests the design of its Creator."[7] This statement of DeProspo's, of course, represents exactly what Edwards hoped to do, that is, to defend his theology of a divinely created world, a world in which God still took an active role, against the growing skepticism of an age that Leslie Stephens describes as "intellectually deist."[8]

---

5   Ibid., 117.

6   Michael McClymond, *Encounters with God: An Approach to the Theology of Jonathan Edwards* (Oxford: Oxford University Press, 1998), 48.

7   R. C. DeProspo, *Theism in the Discourse of Jonathan Edwards* (Newark: University of Delaware Press, 1985), 58.

8   Leslie Stephens, "Jonathan Edwards," in *Critical Essays on Jonathan Edwards*, ed. William Scheick (Boston: G. K. Hall, 1980), 73.

Without much difficulty, one can accept DeProspo's charge that Edwards was no scientist. Truly, Edwards did not share the cool empiricism of Newton or Locke, but detached empiricism was not his aim.

Indeed, Edwards was not convinced, as were some of his more scientifically-minded contemporaries, that wisdom could be presented through the intellect alone. In the intellectual tradition that has come down to us from Ramus, Descartes, and Newton, formal reason and demonstration are the only legitimate sources of knowledge. But Edwards was a holdout of an earlier age, something of an "anachronism," as Vernon Parrington suggests.[9] Edwards repeatedly demonstrated the power, the everyday relevance, of a reason dependent on feeling, not merely on logical demonstration. Perelman's "new rhetoric" project is largely concerned with recognizing these forms of dialectical, practical reasoning. In this way, Edwards can be seen as similar to Pascal, whom Perelman often cites. For both these men of the Church, Pascal and Edwards, do "not hesitate to declare that the truths that are the most significant [. . .] that is, the truths of faith—have to be received by the heart before they can be accepted by reason."[10] Edwards, like Pascal, did not reject arguments that were not purely demonstrative, for Edwards recognized the importance of other means of persuasion, especially rhetorical presence of non-verbal "rhetoric."

Edwards, as a master of oratory in an age of "heavy oral residue,"[11] understood the power of the spoken word. His oratorical performances are justifiably famous; he could reportedly send men and women into states of trembling. Patricia Roberts-Miller writes that Edwards "compared a minister with a sermon to a surgeon with a scalpel."[12] What is not as commonly known is that Edwards produced these effects while often reading from a page, speaking in a monosyllabic tone, or by staring over the heads of his congregation, rarely engaging eye contact. Edwards's sermons, then, were often highly literate; he almost always prepared them beforehand. Yet Edwards realized that the rhetorical presence of his own person was a powerful tool (as a cipher for God's word, of course, not important through his own merits). What effect would his messages produce in the absence of his own person? Edwards succeeded in introducing into his purely literate texts, such as *Dissertation Concerning the End for Which God Created the World* and *Images or Shadows of Divine Things*, typological presence. If, during his sermons, Edwards himself was God's representative, in his writings Edwards pointed to God's representative in nature. No wonder,

9   Vernon Parrington, *Main Currents in American Thought*, vol. 1, *The Colonial Mind, 1620–1800* (New York: Harcourt, 1954), 151.
10   Chaim Perelman, *The New Rhetoric and the Humanities: Essays on Rhetoric and Its Applications*, trans. William Kluback (Dordrecht, Holland: D. Reidel, 1979), 28.
11   The phrase "heavy oral residue" is borrowed from Walter J. Ong, *Orality and Literacy: The Technologizing of the Word* (New York: Routledge, 1982), 11. In his book, Ong suggests that societies that have recently moved from an oral stage to a literate one continue to exhibit a heavy oral residue. Thus, I refer to Puritan New England as a society with considerable oral residue.
12   Patricia Roberts-Miller, *Voices in the Wilderness: Public Discourse and the Paradox of Puritan Rhetoric* (Tuscaloosa: University of Alabama Press, 1999), 105.

then, that the topic of nature appears so frequently in Edwards's thought. Langdon Gilkey rightly suggests that in order "to discover Jonathan Edwards' theology of nature, it is necessary to consult a dozen sermons and essays, as well as many private notebook entries."[13] Nature was everywhere and inescapable: what better subject for rhetorical presence?

Rhetorical Presence in the *Dissertation*

Some critics assert that Edwards, in the opening pages of *Dissertation*, cannot decide if he is being guided by revelation or reason. Perhaps this perceived confusion is a result of the battle between logic and rhetoric, formal and practical reasoning, that existed at the time of Edwards's writings. In fact, Edwards does seem to begin logically with a discussion of motives and actions and the implication that reason may examine behavior in order to discover the disposition of the "will." Edwards divides motives or ends according to importance. The least important is the "subordinate end," which is pursued "not at all upon its own account." Instead, this end is followed in pursuit of an ultimate end. Any number of ultimate ends may be pursued, but even these ends are subject finally to the "chief end," which is "most valued and most sought after." Edwards provides an example to illustrate how these ends contribute to motivation. In the example, a man goes "on a journey to obtain a medicine to restore his health."[14] The man's desire to obtain the medicine is "subordinate" to the end of curing himself, which is the "ultimate" end. This ultimate end, however, is "supreme" only if health is the most sought after end in the man's life.

In a Puritanic typology, life becomes itself an allegory of God's greater purpose. If Edwards rejected a view of knowledge based on reason alone, he did not reject reason altogether, so long as reason remained balanced by emotion and revelation. Reason, despite its limitations, may indeed allow one to arrive at plausible truths regarding the always symbolic cosmos. For reason to be useful in Edwards's system of thought, it had to surpass the realm of "common sense," by which Edwards meant—as did Descartes— knowledge available through the senses. Common sense, Edwards felt, often led people to protest any claim that could not be verified by sensual experience. One of Edwards's favorite quotations, which he reproduced in his *Images*, appeared in Andrew Ramsay's *Philosophical Principles of Revealed and Natural Religion*: "Though seeing clearly be a sufficient reason for affirming, yet, not seeing at all, can never be a reason for denying."[15] Though Edwards's proofs are not Cartesian proofs—and, indeed, proofs found normally in rhetoric—he hoped to develop a worldview or maintain a worldview in which "unseen" proofs—the divine hand at work beyond the typology—could be regarded as normal to any rational audience. Edwards would certainly protest against the idea that Descartes and Locke had

---

13 Langdon Gilkey, *Nature, Reality, and the Sacred: The Nexus of Science and Religion* (Minneapolis: Fortress, 1993), 23.
14 Ibid., 595, 596, 597.
15 Quoted in Jonathan Edwards, *Images or Shadows of Divine Things, Puritan Sage*, ed. Vergilus Fern, 460.

discovered the only legitimate notion of reasonableness. To prove his point—
that the idea of a literal creation and an ever-present Creator could be
intellectually respectable in an age of science—Edwards found himself
relying not merely on fire-and-brimstone, but on a symbology of nature.

While we may apply Perelman's notion of *presence* to Puritanic
typology, Edwards had no specifically rhetorical model to follow. The power
of presence in Edwards's message had to result from a strong conviction
that God was everywhere observable through Creation itself. Edwards
hoped to show, then, that without the controlling agency of God, the whole
of creation would be only so many disconnected moments. Paul Lewis writes
that, in Edwards's theology, "[t]he world not only exists because of God, it
continues to exist. The very rotation and movement of the universe depend
upon God's eternal control."[16] Edwards himself writes: "It is certain with me
that the world exists anew every moment, that the existence of things every
moment ceases and is every moment renewed."[17] According to Edwards,
God's relation to the world is "an inevitable one, and one of spirit."[18]

In order to construct a system of persuasion based on typology,
Edwards needed to demonstrate that the "spiritual" relation between
Creator and Creation was also manifested in the concrete, through acts of
divine communication. Edwards insisted, then, that the infinite mind of God
is the foundation for all of creation and that God is a "communicating
being" who uses the creation as a divine language. In *Images*, Edwards
writes: "The works of God are but a kind of voice or language of God to
instruct intelligent beings in things pertaining to himself."[19] Interestingly,
Edwards limits this communication to "intelligent" hearers; these hearers
have something in common, perhaps, with Perelman's universal audience,
for they are a reasonable group of people who will be persuaded to
Edwards's side upon hearing/witnessing his rhetorical proofs. In any event,
Edwards declares that God communicates through a creation-language
neither out of some inner compulsion, nor because something outside of
God's self requires it. Instead, God communicates in the language of
creation in order to "be glorified."[20] Both Scripture and Creation—specific
and general revelation—are the manifestations of God's glory.

In the *Dissertation*, Edwards develops his notion of creation-as-
language-of-God, suggesting that God's relationship to this language is one
of "emanation" and "remanation." Despite the fiery image Edwards presents
in "Sinners in the Hands of An Angry God" and elsewhere, Edwards believed
his God to be a loving one, and communication through Creation provided
evidence of that love. Paula Cooey writes that "as divine communication,
divine self-love expresses itself through the act of creation and includes love

16 Paul Lewis, "The Springs of Motion: Jonathan Edwards on Agency," *Journal of Religious Ethics* 22 (1994): 275–297, 280.
17 Edwards, *Images*, 469.
18 Ibid., 470.
19 Ibid., 453, 596.
20 Edwards, *Dissertation*, 600.

for the resulting created order."[21] The world is itself an emanation of God's loving fullness, but the creation speaks a language back to God as well: it speaks back as a remanation of God's glory. Edwards writes that "[t]he whole is of God, and in God, and to God, and God is the beginning, middle, and end in the affair."[22] As is often the case, though, Edwards finds it necessary to qualify, to explain, an absolutist comment with more temperate, persuasive language. Thus, in order to clarify this relationship between God and the language of nature, Edwards utilizes metaphors, which, as Perelman and Olbrechts-Tyteca suggest, helps create a shared view of reality. The "wheels of a machine" are used to symbolize the parts of the cosmos working for God's ends; the wheels may benefit a person's work, but that benefit ultimately pleases and glorifies God.[23]

In order to imbue creation with a sense of sacred presence, Edwards had to make explicit the idea that God was revealed in nature; that nature, indeed, was proof enough of God's existence and love. Edwards, therefore, turns quickly enough from metaphors of machinery to metaphors— examples of typology—from the natural world. Perhaps unsurprisingly, given his interest in "emanation," Edwards primary symbol of the divine presence is light. In Edwards's judgment, it is no accident that Scripture so often compares God's glory to the reflection of light. Edwards writes, "light is the eternal expression, exhibition, and manifestation of the excellency of God." He further states that the image of light best captures the manner in which the things of nature are beautiful solely by virtue of the Creator. Moreover, the image of light best signifies the creation's reflection of God's glory back to its originator. Edwards writes that "the beams of glory come from God, or are something of God, and are refunded again back to their original."[24] Light, in short, is imbued with divine meaning, and illuminates the rest of typological creation as well, bringing to the eyes of the faithful the presence of God.

Light, therefore, gives humans visual access to a creation that provides symbolic evidence of God's presence; this point is especially important, for in Edwards's thought, humanity's knowledge of God is imaginative or symbolic in that humans have no access to the interior being of God. Humanity knows God through the images of the world and words of Scripture. In the *Dissertation*, Edwards writes: "Jesus Christ is admitted to know God intimately, but the knowledge of all others in heaven and earth is by means or by manifestations of signs held forth."[25] These "signs held forth" are the symbolic markings upon a page of the Bible or the symbolic signature of God upon natural creation.

When Edwards describes the language of God that he reads in natural creation, he is careful to avoid any notions of pantheism. The role played by rhetorical presence in Edwards's theology did not require putting God's

---

21   Paula Cooey, *Jonathan Edwards on Nature and Destiny: A Systematic Analysis* (Queenston, ON: Mellen, 1985), 48.
22   Edwards, *Dissertation*, 628.
23   Ibid., 601.
24   Ibid., 612.
25   Ibid., 612.

being on display, but symbolic evidence of God's love. In Perelman and Olbrechts-Tyteca's description of presence, it is helpful to recall, they did not suggest that Anthony display the dead body of Caesar; symbolically, Caesar's bloody tunic worked as well. In the same way that the bloody tunic *was not* Caesar, but represented him, God's natural creation *is not* God, but it does symbolize God's existence. Edwards, in short, believes that the natural creation gives symbolic evidence of God, but is not itself God. As we might expect, Edwards draws a rather clear distinction between God's being and God's glory. To Edwards, it is God's glory that is the "end" of creation. He writes: "God does not make his existence or being the end of creation . . . . His being and existence cannot be conceived of but as prior to any of God's acts or designs."[26] Edwards further rejects the idea of pantheism by suggesting that God requires nothing from nature. Following Edwards's beloved light metaphors, one could compare his idea to the sun casting out its rays and receiving nothing in return. According to Edwards, God is, quite apart from creation, complete in being and glory. Edwards writes that the notion of "God's creating the world in order to receive anything from the creation is not only contrary to the nature of God, but inconsistent with the notion of creation."[27] Nature is indeed sacred because it is a creation of God, not because it contains God.

Critics have tried to explain Edwards's attraction to nature—an attraction, as we are seeing, that is best explained by allowing Edwards to draw upon the rhetorical power of presence. Conrad Cherry suggests that it was the "eventfulness of nature" that most attracted Edwards, providing material for thought to an active mind.[28] But Edwards saw beyond nature's activities to the inherent essence of all creation, an essence dependent upon God. In *Images or Shadows of Divine Things*, Edwards suggests that the "temperate air of the visible heavens awakens images of the saints in glory," and the "green fields and trees and colors of the rainbow" symbolize the "grace and love of God."[29] But, as Cherry suggests, Edwards is indeed fascinated by the movement of nature, and his imagery often draws upon nature's functions, particularly in relation to human livelihood. Indeed, we often read in Edwards of the acts of creation, though these acts do not merely interest Edwards; they point to a deeper relationship with God. For example, in Edwards, spiders sucking flies and serpents "charming" birds are "lively representations of the Devil's catching our souls by his temptations," thus proving that in the grand allegory of nature, "all temporal sweets are mixt with bitter."[30] These types of passages have led critics to conclude that Edwards's eyes were those of an "anachronistic Puritan," trained to recognize the events of nature as the "remarkable providences of God."[31] This anachronistic Puritan, though, was also able to

---

26   Ibid., 623.
27   Ibid., 600.
28   Conrad Cherry, *Nature and Religious Imagination: From Edwards to Bushnell* (Philadelphia: Fortress, 1980), 116.
29   Edwards, *Images*, 457.
30   Ibid., 445.
31   Parrington, *Colonial Mind*, 151.

demonstrate the powerfully rhetorical presence of a God who was everywhere.

Rhetorical Presence in *Images or Shadows of Divine Things*

In *Images or Shadows of Divine Things*, Edwards deals more specifically and concretely with symbolism than in the *Dissertation*. Critics have recognized that Edwards often makes "the same feature of nature stand for widely different spiritual truths."[32] The often used image of the sun stands both for God's glory as well as human suffering. The color green, when it emerges from the grays of winter, represents God's grace; when green leaves give way to autumn, the color represents humanity's finitude. Certainly, these varying representations may be due to the nature of *Images*, for it is by no means a systematic book. Rather, Edwards makes no effort to correlate what was essentially a rough notebook. However, in view of our project, we may recognize another reason for Edwards's copious symbolisms. Edwards, as we have seen, believed that when nature was observed in its functions, it necessarily must take on many meanings. Nature, according to Edwards, never exists in a "static state."[33] Stephen Yarbrough has recognized the multiplicity of meanings within Edwards's metaphors, and makes a distinction between typology and allegory. In "Jonathan Edwards on Rhetorical Authority," Yarbrough writes: "typology is led by the fact to the symbolic meaning, rather than establishing ahead of time a fixed equivalent between image and thing imaged."[34] Yarbrough recognizes in Edwards's metaphors a useful fluidity. This fluidity allows Edwards to see nature as presenting eternal truths about God but also commenting on the ongoing human struggle.

As already noted, Edwards made extensive use of the image of light in his *Dissertation*. This symbol is the dominant one in *Images* as well. The sun and its rays most frequently represent the Trinity, God's glory, and the resurrection. As in the *Dissertation*, light serves as rhetorical presence by presenting an unavoidable encounter with God. In *Images*, the variety of color that exists within a ray of light leads Edwards to examine the rainbow as an emblem of God's spirit, one that, while unified, possesses a variety of operations and attributes. Edwards cannot but admire the penetration of light, and he writes: "[t]he beams of the sun cannot be scattered, nor the constant stream of their light interrupted by the most violent winds." In Edwards, of course, "light" faces a more fierce challenger than the wind: "the heavenly light communicated from Christ, the sun of righteousness, to the soul, uninterrupted by the Devil." Symbolically, the light of the sun reminds believers of the presence of God, even during times of trial. Like most educated people of his day, Edwards was aware of contemporary science, and this science generally suited Edwards's light metaphors. Edwards admits having read Isaac Newton's *Optics*, and he understood the

---

[32] Cooey, *Jonathan Edwards*, 243.
[33] Edwards, *Images*, 452.
[34] Stephen R. Yarbrough, "Jonathan Edwards on Rhetorical Authority," *Scottish Journal of Theology* 50 (1997): 39–60, 40.

Newtonian principles. He writes: "That mixture we call light is a proportionate mixture, that is harmonious to each particular sample colour [. . .] and each plays a distinct tune to the soul, those lovely mixtures found in nature."[35] Science, in the study of light at least, did not challenge Edwards's typology but only revealed knowledge of the wonders of God, a God always present in the Creation.

In addition to light, water is also a symbol of presence in the *Images*. In the notebook, one reads about the running waters of rivers, which symbolize the "infinite flow of God's goodness," while the oceans represent God's "enormity and power."[36] Alternatively, Edwards does not associate deep, still waters with peaceful reflection, as did the psalmist; rather, "depth of water" in Edwards often symbolizes human shortcomings, as do "valleys and caverns."[37] Edwards, while utilizing the beauty of nature as evidence of God's presence, also sees negative connotations in nature. Often these types of negative symbols are contrasted with the good, providing Edwards the opportunity not only to demonstrate God's presence, but also to encourage moral behavior. Yarbrough suggests that Edwards relied upon a "rhetoric of contrasts, which he perfected in his sermons."[38] Though he perhaps "perfected" this rhetoric in his sermons, Edwards uses contrasts throughout his *Images*. In *Images*, for example, the clear sky is contrasted with dark caverns and thunderclouds with a calm afternoon. For Edwards, such distinctions represent the sharp contrast between good and evil. Nature was proof of God's loving presence, surely, but also provided proof enough of judgment should any congregant wander astray.

Edwards's notions of general revelation (nature) and special revelation (the Bible) are not mutually exclusive ideas. The natural world gives us insights into the nature of God, but these insights add to scriptural revelation; they never contradict it. In *Images*, Edwards writes: "Wherever we are, we may see divine things excellently represented and held forth. And it will abundantly tend to confirm Scripture."[39] Edwards felt that Scripture set the tone for how to read nature, and the Bible directed his notions of typology. As Janice Knight points out, Edwards believed that Scripture and "the book of nature" are linked by a "perfect and natural harmony."[40] Edwards, as any good rhetorician would do, attempts to utilize all the available means of persuasion, and the natural world, by sheer power of rhetorical presence, "is also recognized as a language of God."[41] Edwards is occasionally quite explicit about his project; in the *Images*, he writes:

> There is a wonderful resemblance in the effects which God
> produces, and consent in his manner of working in one

---

[35] Edwards, *Images*, 455, 457, 536.
[36] Ibid., 477, 479.
[37] Edwards, *Images*, 557, 582.
[38] Yarbrough, "Rhetorical Authority," 48.
[39] Edwards, *Images*, 469–470.
[40] Janice Knight, "Learning the Language of God: Jonathan Edwards and the Typology of Nature," *William and Mary Quarterly* 48 (1991): 531–551, 535.
[41] Knight, "Learning the Language," 540.

thing and another throughout all nature. It is very observable in the visible world; therefore, it is allowed that God does purposefully make and order one thing to be in agreeableness with another. And if so, why should we suppose that He makes the inferior in imitation of the superior, the material of the spiritual, on purpose to have a resemblance and shadow of them.[42]

Here Edwards defends the idea that nature itself is an "image" of divine things, an essential point in establishing a typology of rhetorical presence.

Edwards and Epideictic, the Puritans and Presence

Edwards's use of rhetorical presence, as Perelman and Olbrechts-Tyteca describe the concept, served to make a theological, omnipresent (and, thus, never *actually* present, in a human, concrete sense) God more easily observable through the things of natural creation. The Puritans' typology served as a powerful rhetorical tool. By Edwards's own era, though, thousands of new settlers were coming to the colonies every year. The old, closely guarded theocracy in New England began to lose influence in the face of many newcomers, newcomers who did not necessarily share Mayflower surnames or Calvinist doctrines. The revival movement, then, that Edwards helped to ignite became known as "the Great Awakening," a time in which new believers joined "old believers," whose faith, or orthodoxy, at least, had been rekindled. The rhetoric of Edwards's Great Awakening may thus surely be seen as an epideictic rhetoric, serving, as it did, to intensify devotion to Puritan Reformism. Perelman and Olbrechts-Tyteca suggest that in the Aristotelian tradition, the epideictic "is concerned with praise and blame [. . .] with what is beautiful or ugly."[43] Of course, in the popular image of Edwards, drawn from "Sinners in the Hands of An Angry God," it would be difficult to determine which characteristic of God, the beautiful or the ugly, is being discussed. But even Edwards's seemingly "ugly" references—the divine tyrant suspending believers over the fires of hell by the merest spider's web—reflect awe and thus the sublimely beautiful.

Of Perelman's many contributions to rhetoric, his thoughts on epideictic are among the most valuable. Perelman judges epideictic as an important form of persuasion, a form of persuasion that helps us to understand the importance of concepts such as rhetorical presence. Perelman and Olbrechts-Tyteca write that "[o]ur own view is that epidictic oratory forms a central part of the art of persuasion," an art that is "designed to secure a proper degree of adherence of an audience to the arguments presented to it."[44] Edwards was as concerned as any Puritan minister in securing his congregation's adherence to the principles of the Puritan theocracy. History records many details of the "Great Awakening,"

---

[42] Edwards, *Images*, 464.
[43] Perelman and Olbrechts-Tyteca, *New Rhetoric*, 48.
[44] Ibid., 49.

but less recognized is what Yarbrough and Adams term the "little awakening." This little awakening began in the winter of 1735–1736, when Edwards was already preaching at Northampton. In his account of those early days, *A Faithful Narrative*, Edwards records that "there was a gradual decline of the general, engaged, lively spirit in religion, which had been before."[45] This little awakening apparently burnt out quickly but was reignited because of a purely temporal matter: the old church meetinghouse at Northampton fell down during a worship service in March of 1737. Yarbrough and Adams report that this event "was taken, of course, by Edwards and his flock as a sign to repent their sins." Yarbrough and Adams may be imprudently suggesting that the event was "of course" taken as a sign. Undoubtedly, Edwards's rhetorical mind—and the typological tenor of the times—strongly interpreted this event as divinely meaningful. In any event, by the time the new, larger church was constructed, it was "swollen with the newly converted."[46] Edwards's typological interpretation set the scene for the "Great" Awakening, and this time from a roomier but still troubled meetinghouse.

The description of these early events in Northampton would seem to have little to do with our topic of "natural" rhetorical presence, but it helps modern people to understand how almost any event in a typological culture could be seen as an opportunity to practice epideictic rhetoric. In their discussion on epideictic rhetoric, Perelman and Olbrechts-Tyteca write: "argumentation in epideictic discourse sets out to increase the intensity of adherence to certain values, which might not be contested when considered on their own but may nevertheless not prevail against other values that might come into conflict with them.[47] Certainly Edwards's rhetoric, by its very example, attempted to increase intensity. Edwards's Great Awakening, for such it must surely have seemed at the time, can better be seen, with the benefit of hindsight, as a temporary resurgence in Puritan ideals. Parrington metaphorically describes the situation well: "the old [Puritan theocracy] was too deeply entrenched to be routed, and stricken with palsy it lingered out a morose old age." The Puritan theocracy, as with any closed society, had to be constantly on guard against any innovative ideas, and it also had to find new ways to maintain the dedication of those already in the fold. Parrington writes that "rationalism was in the air [. . .] and it spread its subtle infection through the mass of the people."[48] Edwards did his part to invigorate the faith, to make typology seem, if not rational, then at least natural. But new settlers and new ideas crowded into the colonies, making Puritanism only one religious option among several.

Many critics have suggested that Edwards in his use of natural metaphor and typology was very much accepting his Puritan heritage, was acting, as Parrington puts it, as an "anachronistic Puritan." And indeed he

---

45 Quoted in Stephen R. Yarbrough and John C. Adams, *Delightful Conviction: Jonathan Edwards and the Rhetoric of Conversion* (Westport, CT: Greenwood, 1993), 41.
46 Ibid., 41.
47 Perelman and Olbrechts-Tyteca, *New Rhetoric*, 51.
48 Parrington, *Colonial Mind*, 151, 152.

was. McClymond suggests that the "puritan was convinced that his natural typologies were rendered possible by one grand and historical fact, the appearance of Christ." For Edwards, certainly, Christ represented the "antitype" unifying all other symbols and their shadows. What inspired the Puritans in general, and Edwards in particular, to search for the spiritual meanings within the parts and functions of nature was the appearance of God incarnate. Puritan typology and symbology rested on the secure foundation that "the invisible had assumed the visible."[49] Edwards's unshakable belief in this "grand and historical fact" lent his message a passionate example of the power of rhetorical presence.

Edwards never disowned his Puritan heritage, and he owes to this heritage his appreciation of natural symbolism. Cooey suggests that "[t]he symbolic consciousness of the Puritans was Jonathan Edwards' deepest heritage."[50] Elisa New lyrically writes that "[t]he Puritans' keen eyes for detail were legacies for Jonathan in the swamp, young Edwards in the pasture, and Rev. Edwards in the pulpit."[51] Edwards was always eager to extend his theories of typology to nature and to advocate the Christocentrism of that process. Edwards, above all, seems to have shared a theological viewpoint that unified the essence of nature. Edwards insists that "God is holy originally, the creatures are so by derivation."[52] Even as a derivation, or an image, nature is closely connected to the divine, a divine presence never far from the Puritans' persuasive appeals.

Edwards was a product of interesting times, and Calvinistic theology and Newtonian science helped shape his identity. Edwards observed God in nature not to find an alternative to Scripture, but to find epiphanies complementary to Scripture. Edwards was careful about this distinction, and his use of rhetorical presence was by no means limited by his seeing nature as an "image" of divinity. Edwards did not need to rely on a Pantheistic philosophy, for his intent was to point to the meaning behind nature. Roland Delattre suggests that nature, in this view, bears a heavy responsibility, "symbolizing the mystery and grandeur of God, yet also the struggles of the human spirit."[53] If Edwards could convince his parishioners, as he sincerely believed, that the struggles they recognized in nature provided proof of God's sustaining presence, nature would be viewed, as he hoped it would, as a language of God. If he could convince an increasingly diverse audience of this view, his epideictic would succeed.

We have been viewing Puritan typology as an effective means of rhetorical presence, for, as Perelman and Olbrechts-Tyteca suggest, "illustration seeks to increase presence by making an abstract rule concrete

49   McClymond, *Encounters*, 45, 49.
50   Cooey, *Jonathan Edwards*, 243.
51   Elisa New, "Beyond the Romance Theory of American Vision: Beauty and the Qualified Will in Edwards," *America Literary History* 7 (1995): 381–414, 383.
52   Edwards, *Images*, 452.
53   Roland Andre Delattre, "Beauty and Theology: A Reappraisal of Jonathan Edwards," *Critical Essays on Jonathan Edwards*, ed. William Scheick (Boston: G. K. Hall, 1980), 140.

by means of a particular case."[54] By the very nature of metaphysics, theology must present abstract cases, and Edwards's theology proved no exception. Successful theologies understand rhetorical practice, if not particular terms and traditions, at least the principles. Edwards theology of natural presence succeeded in organizing a complete system of thought, one in which nature powerfully represented God's presence in the world.

---

[54]   Perelman and Olbrechts-Tyteca, *New Rhetoric*, 360.

Method or Madness: Methodist Devotion and the Anti-Methodist Response

Brett C. McInelly

Near the end of *The Life and Adventures of Sir Launcelot Greaves* (1760–1761), Tobias Smollet's title character finds himself confined to a madhouse. Among the inane ramblings of his fellow inmates, Greaves listens to the following monologue, presumably delivered by a Methodist-gone-mad: "Assuredly . . . he that thinks to be saved by works is in a state of utter reprobation—I myself was a prophane weaver, and trusted to the rottenness of works . . . but now I have got a glimpse of the new light—I feel the operations of grace—I am of the new birth—I abhor good works—I detest all workings but the workings of the spirit."[1] The monologue cuts to the heart of Smollett's apprehensions regarding the Methodists' insistence on salvation through faith[2] and points to his concern that Methodism encourages enthusiasm at the expense of reason. Methodism, according to Smollett, is a sure path to Bedlam.

---

[1] Tobias Smollett, *The Life and Adventures of Sir Lancelot Greaves*, ed. Peter Wagner (London: Penguin, 1988), 228–229.

[2] Smollett detested any teachings that did not promote a charitable disposition in their adherents, and he was leery of religious doctrines that downplayed work's righteousness, which helps to account for his hostility toward Methodism. While my focus in this essay is on the anti-Methodist critique of Methodist enthusiasm, I address Smollett's concerns regarding the belief that people are saved solely by faith in another essay (see Brett C. McInelly, "Redeeming Religion: Wesleyan and Calvinistic Methodism in *Humphry Clinker*," *Bulletin of the John Rylands University Library of Manchester* 85, nos. 2 and 3 (2003), 285–296.)

Smollett's attack resonates with a host of other anti-Methodist writings that associate Methodist devotion with madness. While Smollett and these other writers certainly take Methodism to absurd extremes, we should not be surprised that participation in the Methodist revival culminates in confinement to a madhouse in anti-Methodist literature. Methodism did encourage a kind of religious experience that defied Enlightenment rationalism. As Foucault argues in *Madness and Civilization,* the eighteenth century set out to silence the discourse of unreason by associating such expressions with madness. While later historians have challenged Foucault's claim that madness was subjected to a rigorous physical confinement during the period,[3] forms of behavior that ran counter to nature and reason were effectively relegated, if not to an insane asylum, at least to the periphery of eighteenth-century society. "We can have no excuse," Clement Hawes argues, "in the wake of Foucault's work, for failing to reckon the extent to which a label of individual madness may have participated in a repressive history of segregating, confining, and silencing the 'mad,' along with vagrants, beggars, debtors, and other stigmatized social nuisances."[4] Although early Methodists may not have been confined in the same ways or to the same degree as vagrants and beggars, the anti-Methodists were vigilant in making sure the Methodists were at least symbolically confined in print.

Writers like Smollett certainly viewed Methodism as a "social nuisance" for authorizing the activities of lay ministers, encouraging female participation, and insisting on a kind of religious experience that evades rational explanation. Methodism itself pushed at the boundaries of reason and, in so doing, indicated that religious faith may have more in common with unreason than some contemporaries were willing to acknowledge. Perhaps the most threatening aspect of Methodism for rational observers like Smollett was the recognition that religious faith is always questioning reason and its authority and, consequently, is always flirting on the edges of madness, at least when madness is associated with non-rational ways of knowing as it was during the eighteenth century. As Allan Ingram argues, "The eighteenth century's obsession with madness was not, in fact, simply the desire to silence the alternative discourses of unreason. Behind the impulse to restrain was a very real fear of the terrifying proximity of insanity."[5] The anti-Methodist writers' fixation on Methodist enthusiasm may very well reveal a truth that these writers preferred not to acknowledge directly: that engagement with the spiritual may necessitate the surrender of one's rational faculties and the possibility of a direct encounter with unreason and, by extension, insanity.

---

3   See Clement Hawes, *Mania and Literary Style: The Rhetoric of Enthusiasm from the Ranters to Christopher Smart* (Cambridge: Cambridge University Press, 1996), 6–7, and Roy Porter, *Madmen: A Social History of Madhouses, Mad-Doctors and Lunatics* (Stroud: Tempus, 2004), 19–20.
4   Hawes, 6.
5   Allan Ingram, *The Madhouse of Language: Writing and Reading Madness in the Eighteenth Century* (London: Routledge, 1991), 12.

This essay explores the extent to which the anti-Methodists' efforts to stymie the Methodist revival via claims of enthusiasm were informed by such an unsettling proposition. While critics worried that the Methodist movement threatened the social order and consequently needed to be confined—both literally and symbolically—to the madhouse, they were equally unsettled by Methodism's implicit critique of Enlightenment rationalism. This essay also examines the ways John Wesley, generally regarded as the founder of Methodism,[6] responded to charges of enthusiasm, both to answer his critics and to pacify his own anxieties regarding his followers' susceptibility to enthusiastic flights. Perhaps even more than the anti-Methodists, Wesley recognized that religious experience could easily devolve into enthusiasm and, in extreme cases, madness (though, as I point out, Wesley's understanding of mental illness differed widely from many, if not most, of his contemporaries). Curiously, he tried to rationalize faith at the same time he acknowledged faith's incompatibility with an epistemology based solely on reason. Wesley's efforts and the theology he promulgated ensured that Methodism in the eighteenth century straddled the line between real conviction and the madhouse. This is not to suggest that Methodism did, in fact, encourage mental illness; rather, since madness was largely a cultural construction and Methodism's claims of supernatural influence had more in common with unreason than reason, the argument about Methodist enthusiasm unavoidably teetered between what was for the believer spiritual realities and what was for the skeptic manifestations of madness.

Enthusiasm was, of course, a volatile term in the eighteenth century. It brought to mind the calamities of civil war from the previous century and was generally associated with emotional forms of religious expression and false conviction in supernatural experience. Johnson defines enthusiasm as "A vain belief of private revelation."[7] Bishop George Lavington pushes the definition to its furthest extreme in *The Enthusiasm of Methodists and Papists Compar'd* (1749): "*Enthusiasm . . . is Religion run mad.*"[8] Portrayals of Methodist enthusiasm[9] fluctuate between "vain belief" and outright madness. Less virulent and primarily comic portrayals include Smollett's Tabitha from *Humphry Clinker* (1771) and Samuel Foote's procuress, Mrs.

---

6   Methodism was an internal movement within the Anglican church. Wesley was an ordained Anglican minister and remained committed to the established church throughout his life. His primary goal in establishing the Methodist societies was to revive primitive Christianity, something the Anglican church, in his view, had strayed from. It was not until after his death that the Methodist leadership decided to break with the Church of England and become a distinct sect.

7   Samuel Johnson, *A Dictionary of the English Language*, vol. 1 (London: J. Knapton, 1756).

8   George Lavington, *The Enthusiasm of Methodist and Papists Compar'd* (London: J. and P. Knapton, 1749), 81.

9   Enthusiasm was the most common charge leveled against the Methodists. See Albert M. Lyles, *Methodism Mocked: The Satiric Reaction to Methodism in the Eighteenth Century* (London: Epworth Press, 1960), 32.

Cole,[10] women who rely on religious whim to justify their own immorality. The narrator of *The Story of the Methodist-Lady: or, The Injur'd Husband's Revenge* (1770)—purportedly a "True History"—recounts more serious consequences of Methodism's supposed influence: "Miss *Dolly F----h* has hang'd herself out of Despair of being happy" and "There is *Roger* the young Miller of *Heathfield*, drown'd himself but about a Month ago."[11]

These accounts suggest that the Methodist societies attracted women and members of the lower social ranks, a cause for concern among many social and political observers. Writing in 1741, William Fleetwood claimed that the majority of John Wesley's followers were merely "silly *Women*,"[12] and the ex-Methodist James Lackington similarly observed, "I believe that by far the greatest part of [Wesley's] people are females."[13] In his account of the Methodist revival in *The History of England* (1766), Smollett reports, "Many thousands of the lower ranks of life were infected with this species of enthusiasm."[14] Because women were thought to be less emotionally stable than men and members of the lower ranks were seen as weak minded, both groups were thought to be particularly susceptible to enthusiastic flights, and their participation in the Methodist societies—as class leaders and even preachers[15]—was seen as a threat to the social order. Smollett in particular advocated a stratified social order and was leery of social climbers. Lay ministry flew in the face of his ideas regarding social decorum and proper religious practice, and those who claimed divine influence or a special witness or calling were, in his view, merely pretentious and inflated by their own self-importance. In addition, social disturbances in some communities were regularly blamed on the Methodists. The Wednesbury Riots (1743), for example, were reportedly caused by a woman who had abandoned her husband and children and was found at a Methodist meeting. Such riots indicated that domestic strife could incite social and political discord. As Roy Porter states, "Methodistical madness struck real fear into the polite and propertied, alarmed lest a popular religion of the heart should foment civil disorders, as in the bad old times of the Civil War."[16]

Charges of enthusiasm in the anti-Methodist literature intersect with and are informed by a larger discourse that makes possible the kinds of claims they make. Including discussions of religious enthusiasm generally

---

10   See Samuel Foote, *The Minor* (Dublin: G. Faulkner, 1760).
11   *The Story of the Methodist-Lady: or the Injur'd Husband's Revenge* (London: John Doughty, 1770), 8–9.
12   William Fleetwood, *The Perfectionists Examin'd; Or, Inherent Perfection in this Life, no Scripture Doctrine* (London: J. Roberts, 1741), 2.
13   James Lackington, *Memoirs of the Forty-Five First Years of James Lackington* (London: J. Lackington, 1794), 72.
14   Tobias Smollett, *The History of England* (Oxford: Talboys, 1827), 5:280.
15   Wesley's societies were subdivided into classes of about twelve people with an assigned leader. These groups met regularly, and the leader was responsible for the spiritual welfare of the class members. The need for lay preachers naturally increased as Methodism spread, and Wesley employed both men and women in his efforts to regularly minister to his followers.
16   Porter, 86.

as well as Methodist enthusiasm specifically, the larger discourse invests the charges leveled by even overtly fictional accounts with meaning and influence in spite of the questionable veracity of their claims. The charge of enthusiasm gains much of its significance from its associations with the Puritan Interregnum as well as from the intellectual heft of Johnson's dictionary and the religious authority conveyed by Bishop Lavington's critique in *The Enthusiasm of Methodists and Papists Compar'd*.[17]

In addition, all of the discussions of Methodist enthusiasm converge with a substantial body of medical writing on madness that further validate the idea that Methodism sits on the threshold of a myriad of pathological disorders. The medical records most often deal with religious enthusiasm generally, but they frequently make specific reference to Methodism as the cause of such disorders as melancholy, mania, and delusion. Thomas Arnold's *Observations on the Nature, Kinds, Causes, and Prevention of Insanity, Lunacy, or Madness* (1782) classifies enthusiasm as one of the causes of "Pathetic Insanity," a *"Species of Insanity* [in which] One Passion *is in full, and complete possession of the mind."* "Enthusiasm," he writes, "not only originates, for the most part, from religious *distress*; but is often interrupted by *intervals of depression*, is at best ardent and *restless*; and not infrequently *tumultuous*, and *turbulent*."[18] In *Select Cases in the Different Species of Insanity, Lunacy, or Madness* (1787), William Perfect partly attributes a perceived increase in "instances of insanity" to enthusiasm: "so humiliating a degradation of our reasoning faculties owes much to its accession to the absurd tenets and ill-founded notions of an epidemic enthusiasm, whose type is absurd and gloomy notions of God and religion derived from vulgar prejudices, which excites the attention of weak understandings to points of religion, which they contemplate without comprehending, to the entire subversion of their rational faculties." In one case study, Perfect attributes the condition of one mentally deranged patient to "the noisy and dangerous harangues of a Methodist preacher."[19]

---

[17]   In talking of a discourse of enthusiasm, I do not mean to suggest that such a discourse is unique to the eighteenth century. Charges of enthusiasm, albeit via a different vocabulary, likely are as old as religion itself. For all intents and purposes, Christ was branded an enthusiast by the Jewish leadership that insisted on his crucifixion, and many living in the Western world today might construe the activities of Muslim extremists as bordering on madness. My concern is with the ways the discourse of enthusiasm is deployed during the eighteenth century in relation to the Methodist revival and its particular resonance in the Age of Reason. Primarily because Methodism encouraged a kind of religious experience that could easily be construed as enthusiastic and so diametrically opposed to the reigning epistemology of the period, discussions of Methodist enthusiasm became a prominent feature of the cultural landscape and the anti-Methodist literature.

[18]   Thomas Arnold, *Observations on the Nature, Kinds, Causes, and Prevention of Insanity, Lunacy, or Madness* (Leicester: G. Ireland, 1782), 235 and 236–237.

[19]   William Perfect, *Select Cases in the Different Species of Insanity, Lunacy, or Madness, with the Modes of Practice as Adopted in the Treatment of Each* (Rochester: W. Gillman, 1787), 118–119 and 211.

No treatise singles the Methodists out more pointedly than William Pargeter's *Observations on Maniacal Disorders* (1792).[20] After stating that *"Fanaticism* is a very common cause of Madness" and that many of the cases he has observed "proceeded from religious *enthusiasm,"* Pargeter gets much more specific: "The *doctrines* of the Methodists have a greater tendency than those of any other sect, to produce the most deplorable effects on the human understanding. The brain is perplexed in the mazes of mystery, and the imagination overpowered by the tremendous description of future torments." Pargeter includes among his case studies several accounts that attribute the onset of madness to an individual's participation in the Methodist revival. One man who was "under great distress concerning his future state" eventually "attached himself to the *Methodists."* "I could not learn on strict enquiry," Pargeter records, "that previously to this circumstance, he had exhibited any symptoms of mental derangement." In another study, Pargeter again attributes a fit of madness to a woman's involvement with Methodism: "I was told by her husband, that there was not the least predisposition to Insanity before this attack, and it appeared that a *Methodist preacher,* who had much infested the parish, was frequently in her company, and they were perpetually conversing on religious topics."[21]

At the beginning of the nineteenth century, William Black, a London physician, reported among the "Causes of Insanity" of those patients admitted to Bethlem hospital "Religion and Methodism." In Black's list of suspected causes, "Religion and Methodism" account for approximately 10 percent of admitted cases. Of the sixteen causes listed, only "Misfortunes, Troubles, Disappointments, [and] Grief"(24 percent), "Family and Heredity" (13 percent), and "Fevers" (13 percent) rank higher. Methodism is the only specific religion Black mentions.[22] Although it is difficult to determine if Methodism did, in fact, lead to mental illness to the degree suggested by Black's data and indicated in the medical record, the Methodist revival clearly invited the gaze of satirists and physicians alike.

Certain Methodist activities undoubtedly drew the attention of critics and the medical establishment. As already indicated in the medical accounts, Methodist preaching in particular was viewed with suspicion.

---

20 Pargeter, much more than the other medical writers included here, seems to have had a personal axe to grind in singling out the Methodists. He lapses into what seems personal bias much more often than these other writers. He refers to Methodists as a "deluded people" and characterizes the penetration of an itinerant preacher into a local community as an infestation. Pargeter did eventually take religious orders and served as a chaplain in the Royal Navy, so it is quite possible that his fixation on Methodism was theological as well as medical. Nonetheless, his study, like the others quoted here, forges a link between religious activity, particularly of the Methodist variety, and the mental state of the devotee.

21 William Pargeter, *Observations on Maniacal Disorders,* in *Patterns of Madness in the Eighteenth Century: A Reader,* ed. Allan Ingram (Liverpool: Liverpool University Press, 1998), 180–181.

22 Quoted in Richard Hunter and Ida Macalpine, *Three Hundred Years of Psychiatry, 1535–1860* (London: Oxford University Press, 1963), 646.

Wesley's friend and colleague, George Whitefield,[23] was especially well known for his flamboyant preaching style. Lackington reports that "of all the preachers that ever I attended, never did I meet with one that had such a perfect command of the passions of his audience. In every sermon that I heard him preach, he would sometimes make them ready to burst with laughter, and the next moment drown them in tears; indeed it was scarce possible for the most guarded to escape the effect."[24] Whitefield, according to one anti-Methodist tract, had a talent for "Preaching his Hearers from their senses."[25] Even Wesley's less florid preaching style attracted its share of negative attention, and the anti-Methodists repeatedly insisted that enthusiastic fits and bouts with madness were commonplace reactions to Methodist preaching. Given that some Methodists exhibited their faith in energetic and emotional ways, outside observers could easily draw such conclusions. The location of both Wesley's and Whitefield's London chapels in Moorfields, a stone's throw from Bethlem hospital, merely proved a convenient coincidence for critics wanting to make the associations with madness particularly poignant.

Another feature of the revival that attracted its share of negative attention was the frequent band and class meetings. Such meetings brought small groups of Methodists together to read scripture, to sing hymns, and to strengthen the participants' faith through exhortation and mutual soul searching. Part of Wesley's intent in organizing such meetings was to regulate the religious experiences of his follower. As I discuss later in this essay, Wesley understood that even the devout can be deceived in spiritual matters and that the search for a personal spiritual witness can easily slide into enthusiasm. Hence, the meetings became a place to temper religious zeal. Outside observers, however, viewed these meetings with skepticism. Instead of regulating religious experience, the meetings were thought to give way to collective religious frenzy and looked more like a scene at Bethlem than a church.[26]

Of course, those who suggested that Methodist meeting houses were merely extensions of an insane asylum were probably more interested in lambasting Methodism than with the truthfulness of their claims. But the

---

23   Although Wesley and Whitefield remained friends until Whitefield's death in 1770, their relationship was tested by their competing theological views. Specifically, Wesley placed more emphasis on work's righteousness and free will than Whitefield, who held to a more staunchly Calvinist view. The rift between the two men fractured the movement and led to the formation of Wesleyan and Calvinist societies. Wesley was also skeptical of Whitefield's more flamboyant and, from Wesley's point of view, enthusiastic preaching style. I discuss the tension between Wesley and Whitefield in more detail in the essay referenced in footnote 2.

24   Lackington, 104.

25   Evan Lloyd, *The Methodist* (London: E. Lloyd, 1766), 26.

26   We might recall, for example, William Hogarth's "Credulity, Superstition, and Fanaticism" (1762). The satiric print depicts a Methodist meeting in which many in the congregation are experiencing violent fits while listening to a Methodist preacher. The whole scene looks more like a madhouse than a house of worship.

degree to which early Methodists actually experienced mental illness[27] is in some ways less relevant than what the fascination with Methodism and madness suggests about how madness was thought about in the eighteenth century. Madness as a category remained relatively fluid throughout the period; it was associated with what was perceived as unrestrained and extreme forms of behavior. "In common parlance," Porter observes, "people were typically called 'mad' when impassioned beyond moderation and 'reason.'" Of course, what counts as "moderate" and "reasonable" was as culturally determined and arbitrary as what was perceived as "madness" or "lunacy," and one wonders the extent to which popular attitudes influenced medical opinion. As Porter goes on to argue, ideas about madness "were constructed out of grassroots experiences and community tensions rather than being essentially medical codifications serving the interests of a 'psy profession' or a 'therapeutic state.'"[28] Medical interpretations of Methodist religious experience were undoubtedly informed by the larger culture at the same time those interpretations bolstered cultural commonplaces.

The negative reaction to Methodism owes much to the fact that Methodism encouraged what was thought of in the eighteenth century as extreme forms of religious observance. Wesley and his followers accepted what previous generations of Christians accepted as fundamental tenets of Christianity—for example, that the devotee may have to forsake all her worldly possessions, perhaps even family relationships, in pursuing salvation. Indeed, Christianity, defined in the strictest biblical terms, is anything but a "moderate" religion. Methodism in the eighteenth century similarly required much from its people, both in its demands for a personal spiritual witness and in its outward observances. Early Methodists were encouraged to rise early for personal scripture study and prayer; they were required to attend several society meetings each week; and they were discouraged from participating in such diversions as card playing and attending the theater. Wesley even encouraged celibacy in *Thoughts on Marriage and a Single Life* (1743). Merely living what Wesley and others taught could land the pious devotee in a madhouse. Whitefield records in his journal the circumstances under which one man was committed: "I . . . went and talked with his sister, who gave me the three following Symptoms of his being mad. *First*, That he fasted for near a Fortnight. *Secondly*, That he prayed so as to be heard four Story high. *Thirdly*, That he had sold his Cloaths, and given them to the Poor." Whitefield goes on to explain that the man sold his clothes after reading in the Bible that Christ had instructed a

---

[27]   I do not want to suggest here that all claims of enthusiasm were unfounded, nor do I want to imply that the degree to which early Methodists actually experienced mental illness is unimportant to our understanding of Methodist religious experience in the eighteenth century. Such issues are merely beyond the scope of this study.

[28]   Porter, 35 and 43.

man to do likewise.[29] "To Georgian churchmen this was crazy," Porter explains, "once it would have been holy."[30]

Medical interpretations of seemingly extreme forms of religious behavior could certainly reinforce, if only indirectly, the anti-Methodist position. As Hawes asserts, "The label of madness, retroactively buttressed by medical authority, then served to naturalize and universalize [the] persecution [of so-called enthusiasts], concealing its basis in historical conflict."[31] The editors of The Anatomy of Madness similarly argue that "the recognition and interpretation of mental illness, indeed its whole meaning, are culture-bound, and change profoundly from epoch to epoch, in ways inexplicable unless viewed within wider contexts of shifting power relations, social pressures, and ideological interests."[32] Foucault's influence is clearly evident in such claims, and it is difficult, if not impossible, in light of Foucault's work not to see the history of madness as an assertion of social and political power.[33] When surveying the reaction to Methodism, it becomes clear that what previous generations accepted as commonplace—Julian of Norwich's visions, for example—the eighteenth century refigured as madness as a way to counteract the supposed threat of religious enthusiasm.

Although Smollett and others were likely more concerned with preserving the status quo than with the actual mental state of those whom they criticized, the fixation on Methodist enthusiasm betrays an obsession with madness and religious experience that indicates a more complex response to the Methodist revival. At the core of this fixation is an anxiety regarding the viability of assessing religious experience from the vantage point of Enlightenment rationalism. In an age that set out to rationalize everything, including the spiritual, Methodism threatened to undermine the primacy of reason by situating religious experience outside the Enlightenment paradigm at the same time the anti-Methodist writers did all they could to wrestle it back.

From the point of view of those outside the movement, Methodism appeared to attack the rational grounds on which Enlightenment epistemology based its authority. This notion materializes in the mock epic,

29 George Whitefield, A Continuation of the Reverend Mr. Whitefield's Journal, from his Arrival at London, to his Departure from Thence to Georgia (London: James Hutton, 1739), 98.
30 Porter, 28.
31 Hawes, 5.
32 W. F. Bynum, Roy Porter, and Michael Shepherd, eds., The Anatomy of Madness: Essays in the History of Psychiatry (London: Travistock, 1985), 1:4.
33 According to Foucault, confinement in the name of madness was initially a "police matter" more than a medical one, a way of preserving bourgeois hegemony when faced with the possibility of social unrest. (See Madness and Civilization: A History of Insanity in the Age of Reason, trans. Richard Howard [New York: Vintage, 1965], 46.) While threats to the social order undoubtedly fueled much of the anti-Methodist attack, the point I make throughout this essay is that critics were equally threatened by the extent to which Methodism questioned reason, its authority, and the category of madness as it was constructed in the eighteenth century.

Methodism Triumphant (1767). After invoking the twin muses of "Mania" and "Phantasia," the poet recounts in ironic strains how, in the name of Methodism, the "godlike" Wesley wages war on "reason": Methodism's "shock drive[s] Reason from her seat; / It saves the Soul; which Reason would destroy."[34] Set up as the antithesis of reason, Methodism and the kind of experience it promoted ostensibly fall within the same register of experience as lunacy. "From Reason free," writes the author of *The Fanatic Saints*, "they give their *Frenzies* wing, / *Groan, weep, rave, rant, confess, exhort,* and *sing*."[35]

Such accounts indicate that the revival cut to the core of deep-seated attitudes about religion and, perhaps more importantly, about how we know and experience the world. In setting out to restore "primitive Christianity," Wesley and the early Methodists mounted a significant challenge to those who would have religion answer the demands of reason. By the time the revival began to pick up steam in the late 1730s, the Deists and Freethinkers had dismissed as mere fable the unexplainable and miraculous features of the Bible; some questioned the probability of the devil and his existence. Even mainstream Anglicans doubted the likelihood of what previous generations of Christians had accepted as commonplace, including miracles, divine and demonic possession, and the idea of a personal spiritual witness. In reclaiming the supernatural for Christianity, Methodism put faith in the unexplainable at the heart of Christian religious experience, which partly accounts for the success of the Methodist revival: "What got Wesleyan Methodism off the ground in the 1740s was the Wesleys' encounter with and response to the demands of primary religion, a passionate hunger for access to invisible powers, and so for ways of changing the life and prosperity of the adherent."[36] Methodism made religion more a matter of the heart than the intellect and reemphasized the spiritual dimension of human experience at a time when at least some in English society wanted to feel the divine in their everyday lives. But in so doing, Methodism indicated that religious experience may, in fact, have more in common with unreason than some contemporaries were willing to acknowledge.

This is the point Whitefield unabashedly makes in his response to what was one of the more widely known anti-Methodist tracts during the period, Joseph Trapp's *The Nature, Folly, Sin, and Danger of Being Righteous Over-Much* (1739). In charging the Methodists with enthusiasm, Trapp insists that they cannot provide "*Evidence*" or "*Proof*" for their claims of a spiritual witness, the baseline qualification for the "new birth" and what could be regarded as the essential attribute of Methodist religious experience. "What *Proof* have they of such Motions or Impulses?" Trapp

---

34   Nathanial Lancaster, *Methodism Triumphant, or, the Decisive Battle Between the Old Serpent and the Modern Saint* (London: J. Wilkie, 1767), 34.
35   *The Fanatic Saints: or, Bedlamites Inspired* (London, 1778), 9.
36   John Kent, *Wesley and the Wesleyans: Religion in Eighteenth-Century Britain* (Cambridge: Cambridge University Press, 2002), 8.

asks.[37] Whitefield countered by asking, "*What Proof do they give?* Says the Writer [Trapp]: What Sign would they have?" Whitefield goes on to argue, "This Writer . . . tells us, it is against *Common-Sense to talk of the Feeling of the Spirit of God*: Common-Sense . . . was never allow'd to be a Judge yet; it is above its Comprehension, neither are, nor can the Ways of God be known by Common-Sense."[38] In short, Whitefield insists that reason ("Common-Sense") is an inadequate conduit for accessing and understanding God and spiritual phenomena, and he elevates a heart-felt experience over the intellect.

Even Wesley, who tended to take a more rational view of religious matters than Whitefield, insisted on the supernatural nature of religious experience, and his discussion of the "new birth" implies a need for what might be termed extra-sensory perception. As Wesley writes, "While a man is in a mere natural state, before he is born of God, he has, in a spiritual sense, eyes and sees not. . . . He has ears, but hears not." Being born again requires an inner awareness of God's grace: the devotee "feels, is inwardly sensible of, the graces which the Spirit of God works in his heart. He feels, he is conscious of, a 'peace which passeth all understanding.'"[39] Of course, Wesley did not coin such teachings. As an ordained Anglican minister, Wesley was generally orthodox in his beliefs, though he chose to emphasize those doctrines he felt the established church had come to neglect. In addition to the new birth, Wesley placed renewed interest in the doctrines of justification by faith and of assurance—the beliefs that people are saved by faith and that an individual could be assured that God had forgiven her sins, respectively. But how does one know for sure if he has been born again or justified? Wesley recognized that even the most sincere Christian could deceive herself, and he submitted his lay ministers to rigorous examination before authorizing their activities. Rationalizing spiritual experience to the satisfaction of the skeptic was thus only part of the problem; understanding the nature of one's own religious experience was a more pressing concern for Wesley since the search for a personal spiritual witness, as numerous personal accounts attest, could elicit complex mental and emotional responses in the devotee.

Sarah Colston's story is typical of the kind of mental and emotional fluctuations early Methodists experienced in their quest to be born again. Following an initial awakening in which she explains, "I felt such a change in my soul which was unspeakable," Colston goes on to say that "the enemie came, reasioning with me, telling me it was only delusion, that I only thought my sins were forgiven." Following weeks of spiritual affliction, during which time "the devil told me I should never hold out to the end," Colston experienced the new birth while in the company of Wesley and other Methodist leaders: "I felt in a moment such a witness in my heart that

37   Joseph Trapp, *The Nature, Folly, Sin, and Danger of Being Righteous Over-much* (London: S. Austen, 1739), 41.
38   George Whitefield, *The Folly and Danger of Being Not Righteous Enough* (London: C. Whitefield, 1739), 9–10.
39   John Wesley, "The New Birth," in *John Wesley's Sermons*, ed. Albert C. Outler and Richard P. Heitzenrater (Nashville: Abingdon Press, 1991), 339, 340.

I was a child of god that I never had any douts or fears from that hour to this."[40] Colston's narrative uses the same language of feeling found in Wesley's sermon on the new birth and Whitefield's response to Trapp and encapsulates the point both men make regarding the nature of religious experience—that it is something that the devotee feels rather than comprehends through rational means.

Paradoxically, Colston initially fails to understand the "unspeakable" nature of her experience precisely because she views it in purely rational terms. "I gave way to reasoning,"[41] she explains as she tries and fails to make sense of her feelings. She eventually surrenders to the idea that the reasoning faculties, at least when applied to religious experience, are a tool of the devil[42]—"the enemie came, *reasoning* with me, telling me it was only delusion" [emphasis added]. Before fully accepting her experience as authentic, Colston thus takes the same view of her experience as did the anti-Methodist writers: she assumes she suffers from delusion. Viewed from a rational viewpoint, Colston's experience does not even make sense to her.

While critical and circumspect when assessing her experience, Coltson acknowledges that subjecting spiritual promptings to rational inquiry was a futile project. At a certain point, the kind of conviction at which she arrives is the product of her faith in an internal experience. Methodist conviction, as Wesley taught in *Advice to the People Called Methodists* (1745), was founded on "supernatural Evidence of Things not seen; of an inward Witness." Thus, Wesley goes on to say, "To Men of *Reason* you will give Offense, by talking of Inspiration and receiving the Holy Ghost."[43] In a 1755 sermon entitled "The Nature of Enthusiasm," Wesley writes, "If a Man is indeed alive to God, and dead to all Things here below; if he continually sees him that is invisible, and accordingly walks by Faith and not by Sight: then they account it a clear Case; beyond all Dispute, *much Religion hath made him mad*."[44] Wesley seems to concede that the Methodists would likely never escape charges of enthusiasm in an age that placed such a premium on empirical knowledge.

But Wesley's more pressing concern involved regulating the religious zeal of his followers. "Carefully avoid *Enthusiasm*," he counsels. "Impute not the Dreams of Men to the all-wise God."[45] Wesley acknowledges that people

---

[40] Sarah Colston, "Manuscript Account of Sarah Colston," in *Her Own Story: Autobiographical Portraits of Early Methodist Women*, ed. Paul Wesley Chilcotte (Nashville: Kingswood Books, 2001), 44–45.

[41] Ibid., 44.

[42] Interestingly, Colston's view here contrasts sharply with the idea that reason is a gift from God, a commonly accepted idea during the eighteenth century. Colston, of course, probably does not intend to disparage reason, at least in a general sense; she only suggests that it may be among the tools the devil uses to lead people astray. It is clear that, in her mind, the type of experience she has had does not make sense when subjected to the dictates of reason.

[43] John Wesley, *Advice to the People Called Methodists* (Newcastle upon Tyne, 1745), 5, 7.

[44] John Wesley, "The Nature of Enthusiasm" (London: T. Try, 1755), 6–7.

[45] Wesley, *Advice to the People Called Methodists*, 9.

are easily deceived, especially the devout: enthusiasm "easily besets those who fear or love God." The central issue for Wesley and his followers was establishing the authenticity of spiritual experience for themselves, and Wesley's 1755 sermon does not provide any clear-cut answers on this matter. He allows for "Visions or Dreams," "strong Impressions or sudden Impulses on the Mind," if only in "very rare Instances," but then asks the obvious question: "But how frequently do Men mistake herein? How are they misled by Pride and a warm Imagination to ascribe such Impulses or Impressions, Dreams or Visions to God?"[46]

So how does the earnest Christian distinguish between real conviction and mere enthusiasm? Wesley answers this question by essentially invoking reason at the same time he has insinuated that private religious experience does not stand up to rational analysis. One deciphers the will of God "Not by waiting for supernatural Dreams. Not by expecting God to reveal it in Visions. Not by looking for any *particular Impressions*, or sudden Impulses on his Mind. No: But by consulting the Oracles of God. *To the Law and to the Testimony*. This is the general Method of knowing what is *the holy and acceptable Will of God*." He later states that "a Flood of *Enthusiasm* must needs break in, on those who endeavour to know *the Will of God*, by unscriptural, irrational Ways."[47]

Curiously, Wesley discusses enthusiasm in ways reminiscent of the anti-Methodists, and he would contend that he was as much an enemy of enthusiasm as Smollett or Bishop Lavington, and not unlike the mad doctors of his day, Wesley classifies enthusiasm as a "Disorder of the Mind" that "greatly hinders the Exercise of Reason." Enthusiasm, he claims, is "a religious Madness arising from some falsely imagined Influence or Inspiration of God."[48] Wesley would likewise argue that he was a champion of reason. His faith made perfect sense to him, and he undoubtedly saw reason as one means to help bring people to Christ. Maldwyn Edwards states that Wesley's "special strength lay in his logical power of reasoning" and that "the strength of his preaching lay in his refusal to despise reason."[49] What distinguishes Wesley's discussion of enthusiasm from other accounts is that he allows for and even expects the supernatural. The soundest and most logical arguments one can muster in support of faith cannot compensate for a personal spiritual witness. While Wesley would readily agree that some individuals may act on false conviction, he would just as easily accept as evidence of divine influence what skeptics would write off as mere enthusiasm. Wesley's position may appear contradictory, and it was certainly difficult to successfully argue, which may explain why he never fully reconciles, at least in his writings on enthusiasm, his conventional attitude toward enthusiasm with his belief in supernatural

---

46   Wesley, "The Nature of Enthusiasm," 34, 22.
47   Ibid., 23, 26.
48   Ibid., 12, 13.
49   Maldwyn Edwards, "John Wesley," in *A History of the Methodist Church in Great Britain*, ed. Rupert E. Davies and Gordon Rupp (London: Epworth Press, 1965), 1:42.

kinds of experience. Ultimately, the contradictory nature of his outlook was
a paradox he readily accepted.

Wesley's discussion of enthusiasm also indicates that Wesley himself
believed that madness is, in fact, a hair's breadth away from spiritual
conviction. Wesley viewed madness as one of many human ailments, of
which he considered himself a bit of an expert. He dabbled in medicine,
dispensing homemade medications as well as medical advice from his
London chapel and during his extensive travels; he even wrote a book of folk
remedies for a host of ailments (*Primitive Physick* [1747]), including hysteria,
hypochondria, and lunacy. One of his favorite cures for madness and other
diseases involved what we would call shock therapy, and he even designed
and built an electrical machine for such purposes. Though satirists were
fond of suggesting that Wesley was a quack in spiritual as well as medical
matters, Wesley possessed more than a passing interest in the medical arts,
and his reading in the field was significant.

Nonetheless, Wesley's medical opinions were strongly influenced by
his religious views. Most notably, he traced all human ailments to the Fall,
a common view in previous eras and still popular among some eighteenth-
century medical practitioners, including George Cheyne. As a consequence
of the Fall, Wesley writes, "The Seeds of Weakness and Pain, of Sickness
and Death, are now lodged in our inmost Substance: Whence a thousand
Disorders continually spring."[50] In addition, some ailments, particularly
mental illness, could be traced to spiritual and other worldly sources.
Wesley accepted that the struggle for salvation may be accompanied by
emotional fits and agitations. Such agitations could be induced by the
recognition of one's sinful state, or they may derive from even demonic
influences. For Wesley, then, madness could be as much a spiritual affliction as a psychological or physical one, and he became, as Porter puts it,
"the most energetic apostle of divine madness." "He was alert all his life,"
Porter states, "to interpreting all manner of mystery illnesses as symptoms
of diabolical possession."[51] When treating a person "tormented by an evil
spirit," Wesley argued that only a spiritual cure would suffice: "Yea, try all
your drugs over and over; But at length it will plainly appear, that *this kind
goeth not out, but by prayer and fasting.*"[52] Such an opinion a century
earlier would have been accepted as a cultural norm; in the mid-eighteenth
century, it undoubtedly appeared antiquated and superstitious.

Ironically, the same scenes of religious ecstasy that typify accounts of
Methodist meetings, particularly during the first decade of the revival,
confirmed for Wesley his ideas regarding spiritual madness at the same
time those scenes fueled the anti-Methodist argument. In Wesley's and the
anti-Methodists' view, these scenes illustrated that religious practice can, in
fact, flirt with madness. The difference for Wesley was that the devotee was

50   John Wesley, *Primitive Physick: or, an Easy and Natural Method of Curing Most
     Diseases* (London: Thomas Trye, 1747), iv.
51   Porter, 77.
52   John Wesley, *An Extract of the Reverend John Wesley's Journal, from September
     3, 1741, to October 27, 1743* (Bristol: Felix Farley, 1749), 33.

driven to the brink of madness, and even beyond, by supernatural forces, whereas the skeptic only saw evidence of delusion. Wesley's own journal provides several examples of spiritual madness that became fodder for claims of enthusiasm. In one passage, Wesley records walking in on the following scene after being woken at two or three in the morning by a "confused Noise": "One whom I particularly observed to be roaring aloud for pain was one J--- W---, who had always 'till then been very sure, that 'none cried out but Hypocrites': So had Mrs. S---ms also. But she too now cried to God with a loud and bitter Cry. It was not long, before God heard from his Holy Place. He spake, and all our Souls were comforted."[53]

Such passages appear with regularity in the Methodist archive; conversion stories in particular are characterized by devotees collapsing to the floor, crying aloud, and convulsing uncontrollably. Thomas Rankin, one of Wesley's traveling preachers, described one meeting this way: "Numbers were calling out loud for mercy, and many were mightily praising God their Saviour; while others were in agony for full redemption in the blood of Jesus."[54] In light of such accounts, it is no wonder that accusations of enthusiasm became the hallmark of the anti-Methodist literature. But where the anti-Methodists argued the Methodists needed to be committed and treated by medical experts, Wesley insisted they only needed God: "The plain Truth is, they wanted God, they wanted Christ, they wanted Faith. And God convinced them of their Want, in a Way their Physicians no more understood than themselves."[55] Wesley's rebuttal to the anti-Methodists as well as the medical establishment is that they had misunderstood and, consequently, misdiagnosed the problem. Ironically, Wesley agreed with his critics that Methodism could lead to madness; he just disagreed emphatically with the cause and cure advocated by the skeptic and the medical community. The impulses that gave rise to fits and agitations derived, in Wesley's mind, from real and not imagined places.

For Wesley, arriving at conviction and not the madhouse involved following a logical method of religious observance. Paradoxically, what for Wesley was a reasonable means produced what even he acknowledges as not wholly reasonable ends. Visions and impulses of the mind are, indeed, possible, but for these impulses to be attributed to God, the devotee must follow a systematic and methodical study of the Bible while adhering to the teachings of the Christian gospel. Curiously, the name that fixed itself to Wesley and his movement—originally given to a small group of Oxford students, of which Wesley became a part, for their regimented religious practices—was generally applied with derision. Wesley, however, accepted the label and defined it to his advantage. "A Methodist," according to his own dictionary, is "one that lives according to the method laid down in the

---

53   John Wesley, *An Extract of the Reverend John Wesley's Journal, from November 1, 1739, to September 3, 1741* (Bristol: Felix Farley, 1749), 52.

54   Quoted in Kent, 13.

55   John Wesley, *An Extract of the Reverend John Wesley's Journal, from August 12, 1738, to November 1, 1739* (Bristol: Felix Farley, 1742), 66.

bible."[56] But as Wesleyan theology makes clear, a Methodist is also someone who readily accepts what the world writes off as enthusiasm—that is, the authenticity and irrefutability of supernatural phenomena. Henry Rack, who wrote the definitive biography on Wesley, refers to the Methodist leader as a "reasonable enthusiast."[57] Indeed, the label captures the paradoxical nature of Wesley's faith and the religious life he led and encouraged in his followers. Wesley toed the line between two competing epistemologies, trying to answer the demands of rationalism while privileging a deeply personal and not always logical kind of religious experience.

But in his efforts to extricate Methodism from charges of enthusiasm, Wesley reinvokes that same discourse that set out to confine the Methodists and Methodism to the madhouse. Wesley's highly conventional discussion of enthusiasm as well as his attempts to rationalize spiritual experience must eventually surrender to the unstated conclusion that underlies those efforts: some types of experience cannot be rationally explained. The inane ramblings confronted by Greaves at the end of Smollett's novel are thus partly made possible by Wesley himself, not because his theology necessarily contributed to pathological disorders, but because he asserted a system of belief that, despite his own best intentions to the contrary, insisted on the unreasonableness of religious faith. If by confining Methodism to the madhouse the anti-Methodists set out to silence the rival, it was from that same space that Methodism pressed back, asserting both method and meaning to its perceived madness. What is finally evident in the debates over enthusiasm is that the supposed madness of Methodism is contingent on the cultural and historical context in which the debate took place. In addition, the debate illustrates that there was a certain inevitability in its trajectory, both within the anti-Methodist literature and within Methodism itself.

---

[56]   John Wesley, *The Complete English Dictionary, Explaining Most of those Hard Words, Which Are Found in the Best English Writers* (London: W. Strahan, 1753).

[57]   Henry D. Rack, *Reasonable Enthusiast: John Wesley and the Rise of Methodism*, 3rd ed. (London: Epworth Press, 2002).

The Changing Legacy and Reception of John Foxe's "Book of Martyrs" in the "Long Eighteenth Century": Varieties of Anglican, Protestant, and Catholic Response, c. 1760–c. 1830

Peter Nockles

One of the key elements highlighted by recent historians of Britain in the so-called "Long Eighteenth Century," notably Linda Colley in her ground-breaking *Britons: Forging the Nation* (1992) and Colin Haydon in his *Anti-Catholicism in Eighteenth-Century Britain* (1995), has been that of the potent power and influence of Protestantism and of an attendant virulent anti-Catholicism (Catholicism being demonized as an unacceptable "Other" to an evolving British national identity and self-understanding).[1] Haydon has delineated the ingredients of an eighteenth-century anti-Catholicism that was ingrained in the national and popular religious consciousness and fed by such potent symbols of supposedly popish cruelty and persecution as the fires of Smithfield, the St. Bartholomew's Day Massacre, the Spanish Armada, and the Gunpowder Plot. He has emphasized the important part played in keeping alive a popular and elite anti-Catholic historical memory

---

[1]   Linda Colley, *Britons: Forging the Nation 1707–1837* (New Haven: Yale University Press, 1992), esp. 11–54.

and English "Protestant" self-image by the seminal influence of the gruesome accounts, visual as well as textual, given in John Foxe's *Acts and Monuments*, commonly known as his "Book of Martyrs." Foxe helped link Catholicism in the minds of English people with religious persecution, foreign interference, arbitrary government, and despotism. Haydon has argued that a previous reluctance by historians to recognize the force of eighteenth-century English anti-Catholicism as symbolized by a continued popularity and propagation of Foxe's martyrology can be ascribed to a historiography of post-Revolution toleration, growing secularism, and latitudinarian or somnolent Anglicanism.[2]

Much evidence can be brought to bear to support Colley's and Haydon's emphasis on the binding power of anti-Catholicism in helping shape and cement a shared sense of Protestant nationalism in eighteenth-century England. Colley has argued that Foxe's "ageing classic went through a new and much wider period of fame and was interpreted in a far more aggressively patriotic fashion in the eighteenth century and after."[3] Colley cites Foxe as an example of the Protestant literature that became more accessible in geographical terms and in terms of price as a consequence of the loosening of press censorship in 1695, enabling it to reach a plebeian audience.[4] Various other scholars such as J. F. Mozley and William Haller,[5] and more recently, John Miller, Edward Hodnett, and Tessa Watt, have argued for the seminal status of Foxe's *Acts and Monuments*, especially through its illustrations and woodcuts, in perpetuating English perceptions of popery in the eighteenth century.[6] Particular emphasis has been made on the impact or potential impact of its woodcuts on the unlettered. It has also been assumed that there was a narrowing of the book's original purpose from that of a work of wider ecclesiastical history to one designed merely to kindle anti-Catholic propaganda, a tool to club Catholics. Many of the popular reprints and new

[2]   Colin Haydon, *Anti-Catholicism in Eighteenth-Century England* (Manchester: Manchester University Press, 1993), esp. 131–161; G. Newman, *The Rise of English Nationalism: A Cultural History* (New York: St. Martin's Press, 1987). See also Edwin Jones, *The English Nation: The Great Myth* (Stroud: Alan Sutton, 1998).

[3]   Colley, 25.

[4]   Ibid., 42.

[5]   J. F. Mozley, *John Foxe and His Book* (London: Macmillan, 1940); William Haller, *Foxe's Book of Martyrs and the Elect Nation* (London: Jonathan Cape, 1963). For a questioning of the application of the protestant national identity model (derived from Foxe) to the "long" eighteenth century by Colley and others, however, see Tony Claydon and Ian McBride, "The Trials of the Chosen People: Recent Interpretations of Protestantism and National identity in Britain and Ireland," in *Protestantism and National Identity, Britain and Ireland, c. 1650–c. 1850*, ed. Tony Claydon and Ian McBride (Cambridge: Cambridge University Press, 1998), 3–29.

[6]   John Miller, *Popery and Politics in England 1660–1688* (Cambridge: Cambridge University, 1973), 72–75; Edward Hodnett, *Image and Text: Studies in the Illustration of English Literature* (London: Scolar Press, 1982), 30; Tessa Watt, *Cheap Print and Popular Piety 1550–1640* (Cambridge: Cambridge University Press, 1991), 158.

editions were timed with periods of national crisis associated with an imagined threat from "Popery," such as the expulsion of the Salzburger Protestants in 1731 and the Jacobite uprisings of 1715 and 1745, the latter prompting publication of an anonymous *Select History of the Lives and Sufferings of the Principle English Protestant Martyrs* (1746), the editor of which made clear that it was designed "to confirm my countrymen in the principles of the pure doctrine of the Church of England," at a time, *"when the enemies of our happy constitution, and established religion, have made such a bold and daring attempt, to ruin the one, and abolish the other."* The preface to the work even includes a panegyric on the military valor and exertions of the Duke of Cumberland in putting down the '45.[7] It would seem, as Kendra Packham has argued in a forthcoming study, that the "Foxe tradition" retained its cultural currency in the years between the Restoration of the monarchy in 1660 and collapse of the Jacobite rising in 1745.[8]

In her article, "Eighteenth-Century Foxe: Evidence for the Impact of the Acts and Monuments in the 'Long' Eighteenth Century," Eirwen Nicholson has questioned assumptions about the influence of Foxe's martyrology as not securely based on the evidence of print runs and publication history.[9] The fact that, prior to the nineteenth century, the last major new edition of Foxe's *Acts and Monuments*, produced with reasonable fidelity to the original, was in 1684, is certainly in itself significant. The eighteenth century witnessed new editions of the *Acts and Monuments* such as that of the Methodist Martin Madan in 1761, but they were abbreviated or formed parts of larger collections of Protestant martyrologies. For example, in 1751 John Wesley published an abbreviated version of Foxe's work in his *Christian Library*.[10] The lack of a complete edition of the *Acts and Monuments* is perhaps not surprising given that the text was so voluminous and would have been a daunting project for any publisher.

There were certainly concerted attempts to produce cheap editions that might reach a wider and more popular audience. Martin Madan had the explicit aim of publishing weekly installments of his edition by subscription, so "that the common people might be also enabled, by degrees, to procure it."[11] Nicholson, however, has challenged the assumption of scholars such as

---

7   Preface to *A Select History of the Lives and Sufferings of the Principal English Protestant Martyrs: Chiefly of Those Executed in the Bloody Reign of Queen Mary. Carefully Extracted from Foxe, and Other Writers, Being Designed as a Cheap and Useful Book for Protestant Families of All Denominations* (London, 1746).

8   K. Packham, "Representations of Catholicism and English Literary and Polemical Culture, c. 1660–1750" (PhD diss., University of Oxford, 2008), ch. 3.

9   E. Nicholson, "Eighteenth Century Foxe: Evidence for the Impact of the *Acts and Monuments* in the 'Long' Eighteenth Century," in *John Foxe and the English Reformation*, ed. David Loades (Aldershot: Scolar Press, 1997), 143–177.

10 John Wesley devoted four and a half books of the fifty in his *Christian Library* to Foxe's *Acts and Monuments* and to a supplement of Foxe's martyrology published in 1751.

11 Preface to *The Book of Martyrs: Containing an Account of the Sufferings and Death of the Protestants in the Reign of Queen Mary the First . . . Originally Written by Mr. John Fox, and Now Revised and Corrected with a Recommendatory Preface by the Rev. Mr. Madan* (London, 1761).

Haller and Miller that even what she calls popular "video nasty" versions of
Foxe's "Book of Martyrs" in pirated or "bastard" editions reached a wider
audience in any great numbers, concluding that there was a real "gap in the
bookshelf" during the "long eighteenth century."[12] She also finds a paucity of
versions of Foxe in represented or iconographic form in the genre of post-
1660 prints that she has examined. She concludes by questioning the extent
to which Foxe shaped the national Protestant mythology and the extent to
which the seminal status of his book was itself part of that mythology.

Devorah Greenberg has confirmed Nicholson's evidence of a "gap in
eighteenth century examples" of Foxe, noting that her own bibliography of
just over fifty printings of the "Book of Martyrs," "hardly begins to reach the
increasingly literate populace of eighteenth-century England."[13] She also
notes that some eighteenth-century editions such as *The Book of Martyrs*
(1732) justified republication of the text on the specific ground that it had
grown so "scarce as to be rarely found but in the closets of the learned or
curious."[14] Later eighteenth-century editions, such as Paul Wright's *New and
Complete Book of Martyrs* (1784), also were produced with at least the
intention of attracting a wide readership, the preface to Wright's work stating
that it was being presented, "to the public in eighty numbers, that, by this
means, the middling class, and indeed all ranks of people, may be enabled, by
the weekly mode of publication to purchase it."[15] However, what matters is
that the belief that Catholics persecuted Protestants under Mary and would
do so again if they attained power in England was widely circulated among
people who had never set eyes on a copy of Foxe, even though they might
have used Foxe's "name" to prove these assertions. Greenberg also nuances
Colley's and Haydon's simple equation of Foxe with anti-Catholicism by
suggesting a variety of other and more subtle uses to which Foxe's
supposedly "bastardised" text was put during the "long eighteenth century":
universal histories of martyrdom and persecution, martyrologies that
primarily promoted tolerance of Protestant Dissenters and mutual Protestant
accord, and Foxe's martyrology presented, notably by John Wesley in the
third volume of his 50-volume *Christian Library* (1751) as a means of didactic
instruction in godliness and support of a learned ministry.[16] Although, as in
his defense of Lord George Gordon's Protestant Association in 1780, Wesley
was capable of exhibiting a robust anti-Catholicism, his edition of Foxe was
far from being colored by anti-Catholic rhetoric. On the contrary, as he
explained: "I set upon cleansing Augeus' stable, upon purging that huge
work, Mr Foxe's *Acts and Monuments*, from all the trash which that honest,

12 Ibid., 168–171.
13 D. Greenberg, "Eighteenth-Century 'Foxe': History, Historiography, and
   Historical Consciousness," in John Foxe's *Book of Martyrs* Online Variorum
   Edition—Introductory Essays <http://www.hrionline.ac. uk/johnfoxe/apparatus/
   greenbessay.html>.
14 "An Impartial Hand," *The Book of the Martyrs* (London, 1732), i.
15 P. Wright, *New and Complete Book of Martyrs, or, an Universal History of
   Martyrdom: Being Fox's Book of Martyrs, Revised, Corrected, with Additions and
   Great Improvements* (London, 1784), iii.
16 Greenberg, "Eighteenth Century 'Foxe.'"

injudicious writer has heaped together and mingled with those most venerable records which are worthy to be had in everlasting remembrance."[17] Wesley's editorial priority of exhibiting 'the power of God . . . so eminently shown forth both in the lives and deaths of these his saints', involved his excision from Foxe of not only doctrinal disputes and, "all the secular history; but likewise those accounts, writings, and examinations of the Martyrs, which constituted nothing particularly affecting or instructive."[18]

A similarly broad-based didactic message of godly example was evident in the Anglican Evangelical Hannah More's Cheap Repository Tract series edition of a *Book of Martyrs. An Account of Holy Men who Died for the Christian Religion* (1795).[19] Moreover, the model of Foxe's martyrology was even used as a basis for political satire against Lord North and on behalf of Charles James Fox in 1784, symbolizing at least an assumption of familiarity with its text in contemporary political discourse. Thus, *An Entire New Work. Fox's Martyrs, or a New Book of the Sufferings of the Faithful* (1784) with "lists of martyrs and places of martyrdom" and "a complete system of the political martyrology of the present day" was, in the words of the anonymous author, complied "for our edification and encouragement" and to show that "the constitution" was "in as much danger from Prerogative and Secret Influence, as it was" in earlier times from Popery.[20]

In many of the later eighteenth-century editions such as Henry Southwell's two-volume *The New Book of Martyrs or Complete Christian Martyrology or Complete Christian Martyrology* (1764–1765), and Matthew Taylor's *England's Bloody Tribunal* (1769), the classic Foxean account of the Protestant martyrs who suffered in Mary's reign occupied a modest part of a text that was supplemented by later accretions necessarily not to be found in Foxe: accounts of the Gunpowder Plot, persecutions of Irish Protestants in 1641, and the supposed assassination by "five Popish officers" of a Justice involved in uncovering persons involved in the so-called "Popish Plot" in 1678.[21] Typical of the more broad-based and irenical genre of Foxean literature identified by Greenburg are Thomas Mason's two-volume *Book of Martyrs, or, the History of the Church* (1747–1748) and Paul Wright's *New and Complete Book of Martyrs, or, an Universal History of Martyrdom* (1782). Although, like Mason's work, edited by a member of the Church of England

---

17   J. Wesley, ed., *A Christian Library, Consisting of Extracts and Abridgements of the Choicest Pieces of Practical Divinity Which Have Been Published in the English Tongue, in Thirty Volumes First Published in 1750* (London, 1819), 2:iii. For links between Wesley and the "Puritan" tradition and reliance on Foxe's early biographer, Samuel Clarke, see R. C. Monk, *John Wesley: His Puritan Heritage* (Nashville: Abingdon Press, 1966), 49–59. 41.

18   Ibid., 3.

19   *The Book of Martyrs. An Account of Holy Men Who Died for the Christian Religion* (London, 1795).

20   *An Entire New Work. Fox's Martyrs, or a New Book of the Sufferings of the Faithful* (London, 2nd ed., 1784), 1.

21   H. Southwell, *The New Book of Martyrs or Complete Christian Martyrology* (London, 1765), 377. Southwell also included (365–406) long accounts of persecutions against Presbyterians in Scotland.

and intended to appeal to "members of our national establishment,"[22] Wright addressed his work to "Protestant Readers of Every Denomination." He went out of his way to conciliate Protestant Dissenters, acknowledging that "you also have suffered from the violent spirit of persecution."[23] The link between Protestant Dissent and what can be termed low church Anglicanism in the Hanoverian era has been well recognized in the work of James Bradley,[24] and one area of convergence between the two traditions was in a mutual Protestant celebration of the iconic status of Foxe's "Book of Martyrs" against what both regarded as the evils of "Popery."

As Greenberg acknowledges, however, many of the eighteenth-century Foxean texts that appeared to promote tolerance came from the Protestant Dissenting stable and were actually directed against what was regarded as the intolerant principles of Anglican high churchmen, if not relics of popish ritual within the Church of England itself.[25] Their intrinsic anti-Catholicism was more evident than Greenberg perhaps allows, though anti-Catholicism was readily transposed into anti-high churchmanship as a form of popery. As Andrew Thompson and Grayson Ditchfield have demonstrated, for many eighteenth-century Protestant Dissenters, "Popery" was often viewed as residing in the Church of England itself, the term symbolizing not merely papal tyranny but any rigorous imposition of clerical or episcopal authority in religious matters that could be perceived as curtailing the right of private judgment.[26] It was an attitude shared by some latitudinarian Anglicans, notably Benjamin Hoadly and his allies and later by Francis Blackburne,[27] and had a long lineage. Many Protestants, firstly Puritans within the Elizabethan church establishment, then Dissenters or separatists outside it, argued that the Church of England retained "rags of popery," was not sufficiently Protestant and needed further "reformation." Those within this tradition, such as the eighteenth-century Dissenting historian Daniel Neal, Samuel Chandler, and Caleb Fleming looked to Foxe for inspiration and used his martyrology to their own advantage; claiming Foxe's sanction for their sectarian views and citing Foxe's own siding with a "Genevan" party among the Marian exiles in Frankfort in the 1550s. Chandler's *History of Persecution* (1736), though professedly inspired by Foxe, gave no space to the Marian martyrs and, instead, focused on persecutions of Puritans under the Elizabethan as well as Laudian regime, with Elizabethan bishops such as Parker, Aylmer, and Whitgift, charged with having "entered their sees with

---

22 Wright, preface to *New Complete Book of Martyrs*.
23 Ibid., iv.
24 James Bradley, *Religion, Revolution, and English Radicalism: Non-Comformity in Eighteenth-Century Politics and Society* (Cambridge: Cambridge University Press, 1990).
25 Greenberg, "Eighteenth Century 'Foxe.'"
26 A. Thompson, "Popery, Politics, and Private Judgment in Early Hanoverian Britain," *Historical Journal* 45 (2002): 333–356, esp. 343–344.
27 B. W. Young, *Religion and Enlightenment in Eighteenth-Century England: Theological Debate from Locke to Burke* (Oxford: Oxford University Press, 1998), 48–51; Andrew Starkie, *The Church of England and the Bangorian Controversy, 1716–1721* (Woodbridge: Boydell Press, 2007), 107–108.

persecuting principles."[28] It thus reflected an anti-Anglican as much as an anti-Catholic agenda.

Moreover, Foxe's well-attested apocalypticism especially appealed to late-seventeenth- and early-eighteenth-century Protestant Dissenters of the Salter's Hall school. Packham cites numerous Salter's Hall sermons in the period that drew upon Foxe in this way to highlight "Romish persecution and cruelty."[29] Furthermore, as is well known, many early Nonconformists, including Presbyterians, Congregationalists, and Quakers, had from the seventeenth century onwards compiled their own martyrologies and Books of Sufferings, with a conscious harking back to Foxe's *Acts and Monuments* as a model.[30] It was a tradition, as evidenced by Edmund Calamy, that continued into the eighteenth century. Foxe's legacy was already becoming problematic and contested. However, the paucity of references to Foxe in the pamphlet literature of the ultra-latitudinarian Bishop Hoadly (1676–1761) and his supporters in the Bangorian controversy of 1716–1721[31] is perhaps indicative of the way in which the Hodleian rhetoric of private judgment and concept of "sincerity" as touchstones of religious belief were not in tune with the apocalyptical "enthusiasm" and dogmatism of the Foxean tradition. The eschatological basis of Foxe's anti-Catholicism and any concern for tracing a doctrinal "true church" succession back to Wycliffe, Lollards, or Hussites was just as much *terra incognita* for Hoadly as was the traditional high church ecclesiological concern for establishing valid episcopal succession. This *lacuna* in the Bangorian controversial literature further supports Nicholson's argument for a Foxean "gap in the bookshelf" in the period.

When faced with a renewed round of what they regarded as Anglican "persecution" in the run up to Lord Sidmouth's bill restricting itinerancy in 1813, Protestant Dissenters and also Methodists looked to Foxe's martyrology for inspiration. As the Methodist Philip Oliver noted in the preface to his *Short Account of the Reformers and Martyrs of the Church of England . . . Compiled from Foxe and Other Writers* (1812): "I confess, I found the imputation of being a Methodist once the greatest misfortune; I now rejoice in it . . . One means of strengthening me was the lives of the martyrs."[32] Again, the emphasis is on a wider history and geographical spectrum of "persecution" than that contemplated by Foxe himself. The context of Sidmouth's bill probably also

---

28 S. Chandler, *The History of Persecution in Four Parts* (London, 1736), 344.

29 Packham, "Representations of Catholicism," ch. 3.

30 B. W. Griggs, "Remembering the Puritan Past: John Walker and Anglican Memories of the English Civil War," in *Protestant Identities: Religion, Society, and Self-Fashioning in Post-Reformation England*, ed. Muriel McClendon, Joseph Ward, and Michael MacDonald (Stanford: Stanford University Press, 1999), 160.

31 The religious controversy provoked by a sermon in 1716 denying the visibility of the church by Benjamin Hoadly, Bishop of Bangor, drew a celebrated response from the nonjuring divine William Law. For a detailed study of the whole controversy and its significance, see Starkie, *The Church of England and the Bangorian Controversy.*

32 P. Oliver, *A Short Account of the Reformers and Martyrs of the Church of England, and of the Various Cruelties, and Persecutions in Germany, France, and Ireland. Compiled from Fox and Other Writers* (Bala, 1812), iv.

explains the timing in 1813 of a new edition of Samuel Chandler's *History of Persecution* by the Methodist Charles Atmore.[33] The Protestant Dissenting exclusivist appropriation of Foxe's martyrology with an anti-Anglican animus, increasingly tapped into by Methodists, encouraged a reaction on the other side of the Protestant divide. Whereas, many "long eighteenth century" Anglican writers such as Paul Wright had sought to accommodate or enlist such Dissenters on behalf of Foxe in a pan-Protestant united front against Catholicism, from the 1830s onwards Anglican apologists for Foxe sought to downplay or explain away his "nonconformity," recasting his image in more exclusive terms as an ideological bulwark of the Protestant church establishment as enshrined in the Elizabethan settlement.

Although anti-Catholicism remained undiminished at a popular level, as evidenced by the Gordon riots in 1780, it had been on the wane in elite circles in the later part of the eighteenth century.[34] However, the rise of anti-Catholicism within the Church of England after 1801, fuelled by events in Ireland, the debates over Catholic Emancipation and the perceived threat to the Protestant constitution represented by a resurgent Catholicism, and the growth of a narrower brand of evangelicalism in the second quarter of the nineteenth century helped to breathe new life and interest in Foxe and his martyrology. Several of the new editions or adaptations of Foxe's text in this period, such as the Methodist Henry More's *History of the Persecutions of the Church of Rome, and Complete Protestant Martyrology* (1810) and J. Milner's *Universal History of Christian Martyrdom* (1817), were designed to bolster the anti-Emancipation case by countering the perception that Popery had changed and was no longer a threat to civil or religious liberty. In the renewed Protestant-Catholic controversy from the 1800s onwards, the reliability and integrity of Foxe's historical evidence was put more closely under the spotlight than had been the case for several generations.

There was a long English Catholic tradition of direct controversial responses to Foxe, beginning with Nicholas Harpsfield (died 1575) and subsequently continued by Robert Parsons in his *Three Conversions of England from Paganism to Christian Religion* (St. Omer, 1603–1604). Richard Challoner's two-volume *Memoirs of Missionary Priests* (1741–1742) also served as a kind of Catholic reply to Foxe. John Lingard's widely acclaimed *History of England* (1819–1830), which impressed most readers by its impartiality, and Bishop John Milner's more combative *End of Religious Controversy* (1822), like his earlier more irenical *Letters to a Prebendary* (1802), sought to overcome the latent fear and hostility of British Protestants towards Roman Catholics. This could be achieved by showing that such fear and hostility rested on the insecure foundations of the "black propaganda" of the erroneous and "lying" testimony of Foxe's martyrology. In his *Letters to a Prebendary,* Milner had sought to embarrass Protestants by highlighting Cranmer's part in the executions of John Lambert, Ann Askew, and John

---

[33] C. Atmore, ed., *The History of Persecution, from the Patriarchal Age, to the Reign of George II* (Hull, 1813).

[34] See James J. Sack, *From Jacobite to Conservative: Reaction and Orthodoxy in Britain c. 1760–1832* (Cambridge: Cambridge University Press, 1993), ch. 9.

Frith, under Henry VIII, criticizing Foxe for overlooking "the share which Cranmer had in these executions."[35] He also sought to embarrass Anglican high churchmen by highlighting the "non-conformity" and "Puritanism" of some of the martyrs, notably John Rogers and John Hooper, and by implication Foxe himself. Certainly, Anglican high churchmen would have felt discomfited by Milner's raking up of Laudian charges such as that of Peter Heylyn against Hooper and others for their "sacrilegious robberies" of the church.[36] In the same work, Milner had made a similar point at the expense of his adversary, prebend and Chancellor of Winchester Cathedral, the Reverend John Sturges, a latitudinarian disciple of that *bete noir* of both high church and Evangelical churchmen, Benjamin Hoadly (1675–1761): *"if Cranmer and Ridley were now alive and sitting in judgment on some of your publications . . . they would infallibly sentence you to the same cruel fate which they themselves suffered."*[37] In short, Foxe's brand of Reformation Protestant orthodoxy was presented as just as antithetical to the principles and temper of eighteenth-century Protestant latitudinarianism, with its Socinian overtones, as it was to traditional Roman Catholicism. Indeed as Andrew Starkie has argued, an eighteenth-century Anglican high churchman by making a concern for purity of doctrine the cornerstone of his anti-Catholic rhetoric, was actually much closer to the "Puritan" or Foxean basis of anti-popery than was an eighteenth-century latitudinarian of the Hodleian type, with his overarching concern for religious liberty and distaste for doctrinal rigor of any variety.[38]

The whole thrust of the non-Catholic radical pamphleteer William Cobbett's *History of the Protestant Reformation* (1824–1827), which drew heavily on Catholic apologetic on the subject, aimed at undermining Foxe's reputation among a popular audience. The *Acts and Monuments* was described as "lying Foxe's lying book of Protestant Martyrs!"[39] Although intended to be a popular work that came out in cheap monthly installments and sold over 700,000 copies, it sent shock waves through the higher echelons of the established church and caused consternation in Anglican high church as well as Anglican Evangelical circles.[40]

The nineteenth-century champions of Foxe's martyrology noted a Laudian tradition of lack of sympathy for Foxean historiography within a

---

35 J. Milner, *A Letter to a Prebendary: Being an Answer to Reflections on Popery, by the Rev. J. Sturges, LL.D . . . with Remarks on the Opposition of Hoadlyism to the Doctrines of the Church of England* (London, 2nd ed., 1801), 206.

36 Ibid., 194.

37 Ibid., 212–213.

38 Starkie, *Church of England and the Bangorian Controversy*, 111.

39 W. Cobbett, *A History of the Protestant Reformation in England and Ireland* (London, 1st ed., 1824), Letter VIII.

40 Cobbett almost went beyond Catholic critiques of Foxe, asserting: "The real truth about these 'Martyrs', is, that they were, generally, a set of most wicked wretches, who sought to destroy the Queen and her government, and under the pretence of superior piety, to obtain the means of again preying upon the people." W. Cobbett, *A History of the Protestant Reformation in England and Ireland.* 2 vols. (London, 1829), 1:249.

section of the Church of England. In his introduction to the first of the four complete Victorian editions of the *Acts and Monuments*, published (1837–1841) by Seeley & Burnside, the Reverend George Townsend complained that "to despise Foxe, and to believe the rulers and senate of their own Church to have erred in approving him, has been made the proof and pledge of high churchmanship."[41] In fact, a public repudiation of Foxe by high churchmen only ensued in the later 1830s. Pre-Tractarian orthodox or high churchmen such as George Pretyman-Tomline (1750–1827) and Archdeacon Daubeny (1745–1827) had engaged theological dispute with Anglican Evangelicals over the doctrines of grace, free-will, and the nature of Justification, but both sides trumpeted the merits of the English Reformers and Reformation. Their differences focused on whether or not Calvinism or Arminianism could be read into the teaching of the Reformers and Reformation formularies and as to which side could thereby lay claim to being the true spiritual heirs of the sixteenth century.[42] In this dispute, the evidence or witness of Foxe's martyrology was not widely utilized. Foxe continued to be a unifying force among groups within the Church of England against the external threat posed by Roman Catholicism.

Anglican Evangelicals such as Leigh Richmond were prominent early in the nineteenth century in trying to rescue Foxe from relative neglect. Richmond's eight-volume *The Fathers of the English Church; or a Selection from the Writings of the Reformers and Early Protestant Divines of the Church of England* (1807–1812) drew heavily on Foxe. However, mindful of conflicting interpretations of the Church's doctrinal Articles, he professed a non-partisan approach. Richmond also explained the timing of his republication of accounts (largely from Foxe) of the life and writings of the Reformers by the contemporary need, in the context of opposing Catholic political claims, of informing or reminding Protestants "as to the ground of their forefathers' separation from the Church of Rome."[43]

Contemporary high churchmen were at one with Anglican Evangelicals in promoting this aim. They were just as forward in utilizing Foxe's *Acts and Monuments* as a weapon in the Protestant polemical armory against the perceived Catholic challenge of the 1810s and 1820s. Thus, in his six-volume *Ecclesiastical Biography* (1810), the prominent high churchman Christopher Wordsworth (1774–1846), Master of Trinity College, Cambridge, made extensive, if abbreviated, use of Foxe's martyrology. The memoir of Archbishop Thomas Cranmer, which comprised the third volume, was entirely transcribed by Wordsworth from Foxe's *Acts and Monuments*.

---

41 *The Acts and Monuments of John Foxe. With a Life of the Martyrologist, and Vindication of the Work, by the Rev. George Townsend, M.A.* (London, 1843), 1:164.

42 On this, see P. B. Nockles, "A Disputed Legacy: Anglican Historiographies of the Reformation from the Era of the Caroline Divines to That of the Oxford Movement," *Bulletin of the John Rylands University Library of Manchester* 83 (2001): 121–167, esp. 124–128.

43 [L. Richmond, ed.,] *The Fathers of the English Church; or, a Selection from the Writings of the Reformers and Early Protestant Divines, of the Church of England* (London, 1809), 4:vi.

Wordsworth maintained that "the most valuable parts of his volumes" were taken from the *Acts and Monuments*. In his introduction to the first volume, Wordsworth explained the contemporary anti-Catholic controversial context to his publication. Wordsworth was responding to the attacks by Bishop Milner in his *Letters to a Prebendary* (1802) on "the frequent publications of John Foxe's lying Book of Martyrs," and to "what has been said by Dr J. Milner's predecessors in the same argument, by Harpsfield, Parsons, and others."[44] Robert Southey, in his *Book of the Church* (1824), Henry Soames, in his *History of the Reformation of the Church of England* (1826), also relied heavily on Foxe, "the venerable martyrologist" who has "presented us with a series of valuable documents and important statements."[45] In a significant comment on its then priorities, Lingard privately dismissed Southey's *Book of the Church* as having "plainly been written for a purpose to please the high-church party."[46] According to Sheridan Gilley, Southey's *Book of the Church* (to which Butler's *Book of the Roman Catholic Church* was a response) "signified a new heat in the relations between the churches, and the reversal of the latitudinarian tendencies of eighteenth-century Christianity."[47]

Lingard was privately scathing about the uncritical reliance of Protestant churchmen such as Wordsworth, Southey, and Soames on Foxe, complaining in 1824 of Southey's *Book of the Church*, that in, "his reigns of Henry, Edward and Mary he has done little more than make a compendium of Foxe, and has related without the least semblance of a doubt as to their accuracy the hearsay stories collected by that writer."[48] It would seem that Milner and later, his still more outspoken Catholic coreligionist, William Eusebius Andrews in his *Critical and Historical Review of Fox's Book of Martyrs* (1824), touched on a particularly sensitive nerve as far as high or orthodox churchmen such as Wordsworth and Soames were concerned. One of the familiar tropes of English Catholic controversial literature was an appeal, albeit selective, to other Protestant historical authorities in order to discredit standard laudatory accounts of the Reformation and its English martyred Reformers in general and the evidence of Foxe in particular.[49] Protestant annalists of a "high church" character, such as the Laudian Peter Heylin (1600–1662) and Nonjuror Jeremy Collier (1650–1726), who were highly critical of the sacrilege and spoliation of church property that

---

44   C. Wordsworth, ed., *Ecclesiastical Biography; or Lives of Eminent Men Connected with the History of Religion in England, from the Commencement of the Reformation to the Revolution, Selected and Illustrated with Notes.* 6 vols. (London, 1818), 1:xxi.

45   H. Soames, *History of the Reformation.* 4 vols. (London, 1826–1828), 4:722.

46   J. Lingard to J. Mawman, 14 February 1824, [M.] Haile and [E.] Bonney, eds. *Life and Letters of John Lingard* (London, 1911), 204.

47   S. Gilley, "Nationality and Liberty, Protestant and Catholic: Robert Southey's 'Book of the Church,'" *Religion and National Identity.* (*Studies in Church History* 18: 1982), 431.

48   J. Lingard to J. Mawman, 14 February 1824, Haile and Bonney, 204.

49   See my "'The Difficulties of Protestantism': Bishop John Milner, John Fletcher and Catholic Apologetic against the Church of England in the Era from the First Relief Act to Emancipation, 1778–1830," *Recusant History* 24 (1998): 193–236, esp. 209–210.

accompanied some phases of the Reformation, were particular favorites in this respect. Thus, Andrews drew on evidence from Heylin's *History of the Presbyterians* in order to highlight the supposedly tumultuous violence inspired by Protestant preachers in the Netherlands in the 1590s and to use this as a weapon to discredit those whom Foxe sought to canonize. Heylin, a favorite author of nineteenth-century high churchmen when they sought to distance the Church of England from associations with Calvinist Predestination or with the excesses of Puritans and Protestant sectaries, was hailed by Andrews as a "Protestant historian and divine, who wrote when the circumstances he recorded were fresh upon the minds of every intelligent person, to show the irreligious and blasphemous pretensions of those religion-menders."[50]

Andrews's *Critical and Historical Review of Fox* came out in installments between 1823 and 1826. Andrews claimed that the work met with a greater sale than any Catholic controversial work ever before published in this country. The third volume, entitled *An Examination of Fox's Calendar of Protestant Saints, Martyrs, etc. Contrasted with a Biographical Sketch of Catholic Missionary Priests and Others Executed under the Protestant Penal Laws from the Years 1535 to 1684* (1826–1829), was a response to the publication of a cheap edition of Foxe's "book of martyrs" in 1823.

The attempt in the later 1820s to publish a more complete edition emanated from more reputable Anglican sources than the Southwark "bigots" who had provoked Andrews and involved the patronage of prominent figures in the high church party within the Church of England. In 1827, plans were made for a new edition of Foxe's "book of martyrs" when Thomas F. Dibdin, sometime rector of St. Mary's, Bryanston Square, London, persuaded the high churchman William Howley, then Bishop of London, "to accept the dedication to himself."[51] Dibdin also received encouragement from other prominent orthodox and anti-Evangelical churchmen such as Thomas Rennell (1763–1840), Dean of Winchester, praised for his anti-Catholic exertions by various Evangelicals, and Henry John Todd, Archdeacon of Cleveland and Canon of Durham, author of a new edition in 1825 of Cranmer's *Defence of the True and Catholic Doctrine of the Sacrament, and Life of Archbishop Cranmer* (1831) which relied heavily on Foxe. The proposals for a new edition of Foxe's work could not have been more timely for Protestant high churchmen fighting a rearguard action against the threat of Catholic Emancipation. Rennell assured Dibdin that it was "impossible to conceive an undertaking of more importance to the best interests of our protestant cause."[52] However, Dibdin's

---

50   W. E. Andrews, *A Critical and Historical Review of Fox's Book of Martyrs, Showing the Inaccuracies, Falsehoods, and Misrepresentations in That Work of Deception* (London, 1824, 1826), 380.

51   G. Townsend, "Preliminary Dissertation," in *Acts and Monuments of John Foxe: A New and Complete Edition,* ed. S. R. Cattley (London, 1837–1841), i., pt. ii, sect. i, 284.

52   T. Rennell to Dibdin, 23 February 1827, quoted in Townsend, "Life of Foxe: and Vindication of the Work," *The Acts and Monuments of John Foxe* (London, 184349), I, pt ii, sect. ii, 235 Hereafter A & M (1843–1849). While my conclusions are my own, I am indebted to and partly draw upon in this section, Andrew

project was not carried through, and the impetus for a new edition now passed to members of the Evangelical party in the Church of England.

Foxe had been reclaimed for the establishment in the eighteenth century, but he was shared property between Anglicans and Protestant Dissenters. However, in the new theological climate of the 1830s and 1840s, the championing of Foxe within the Church of England increasingly became a mark or symbol of party spirit and formed an aspect of the Protestant (albeit not exclusively Evangelical) reaction against the Oxford Movement (the great movement of high church revival within the Church of England from 1833). Anglican Evangelicals from the 1830s onwards increasingly took up Foxe, but this was only very partially because Foxe's virulent anti-Catholicism had become a useful polemical weapon to employ against the forces of a revived English Roman Catholicism. The real "enemy" would now become the supposed "crypto-papists" within the Church of England itself.

Foxe's status had survived Protestant Nonconformist readings and republications of Foxe that often carried an inherent anti-Anglican animus, even though some Anglican reworkings of Foxe had aimed at conciliation of Protestant Dissenters. However, from the 1830s onwards, Protestant consensus broke down. Thereafter, the reception of Foxe's martyrology came to involve far more than a mere denominational dog fight between Protestant and Roman Catholic controversialists, with each side striving either to vindicate or discredit Foxe's credibility as a historian. During the later part of the "long eighteenth century" under consideration, the polemical use of Foxe's martyrology and assumptions of his reliability had united Anglican high churchmen and Anglican Evangelicals against the challenge posed by a resurgent English Catholicism, notably in the lead up to Emancipation. A revived sense of the importance of dogma and even eschatology shared by both sides in reaction against Hodleian "indifferentism" on these questions aided this process. Significantly, in his *Book of the Church*, Robert Southey had been able happily to combine his protestant martyrology from Foxe's *Acts and Monuments* with a high church historiography from divines like the Laudian Peter Heylin.

The rise of the Oxford Movement in the 1830s, however, coincided with a growing Anglican Evangelical agenda of appropriating Foxe's "book of martyrs" not only as a stick with which to beat Roman Catholicism but in order to discredit the loyalty of Tractarian churchmen and to support the Anglican Evangelical claim to be the true mouthpiece of the theology of the English Reformers. By promoting Foxe's martyrology, some Anglican Evangelicals also hoped to gain support and credence for their own eschatological views concerning the prophetical interpretation of Scripture. In short, debates over the merits or otherwise of the martyrologist were not only

Penny, "John Foxe: An Historical Perspective. Evangelicalism and the Oxford Movement," in *John Foxe: An Historical Perspective*, ed. D. Loades (Aldershot: Ashgate, 1999), 182–221, and more fully in Andrew Penny, *John Foxe, Evangelicalism and the Oxford Movement: Dialogue across the Centuries* (Lampeter: Edwin Mellen, 2002), ch. 4. See also Andrew Penny, "John Foxe's Victorian Reception," *Historical Journal* 40 (1997): 111–142.

a microcosm of wider debates over the increasingly contested nature of the English Reformation but became bound up with an internal struggle for the identity of the contemporary Church of England itself. Anglican Evangelicals were keen to promote Foxe as an icon of not only anti-Catholicism but as a symbol of their own claim for the Protestant identity of the Church of England. This identity had appeared threatened by a resurgent Anglican high churchmanship, which Anglican Evangelicals chose to characterize as "Tractarian," but which represented a far wider constituency. Of course, English Catholics were quick to exploit this Anglican identity crisis in the era of the Oxford Movement. However, this in itself was nothing new. As Packham has demonstrated, there was a long and earlier tradition of English Catholics exploiting tensions within the Protestant tradition in combating Foxe.[53] What was new now was that the tensions and conflict over Foxe's status emanated as much from within the Church of England itself as from promptings from outside.

The Oxford Movement and the response it elicited from Anglican Evangelicals, as well as from Protestant high churchmen, helped reopen old divisions within the Church of England that had lain dormant for much of the "long eighteenth century" (or at least since the end of the divisive "Bangorian controversy" in the early 1720s). In this process of polarization, arguments concerning Foxe and his "Book of Martyrs" played a significant part. However, the nineteenth-century response to Foxe from within the established church shows something much more than this; it reveals the extent to which nineteenth-century "Anglicanism" represented a narrowing of the earlier broader Protestant vision of the 1540s, 1550s, and 1560s, a vision which many "long eighteenth-century" editors of Foxe (such as Martin Madan and Paul Wright) may have wished to revive. Foxe's *Acts and Monuments* in its time can be viewed as part of a wider pan-European, Protestant internationalist agenda, for as Peter Lake has observed, Foxe upheld a "broad bottomed Protestant internationalism" rather than the concept of a Protestant "elect nation" as argued by William Haller.

Foxe's nineteenth-century Anglican defenders, followed those of the seventeenth century rather than eighteenth century, in viewing the "Book of Martyrs" primarily as a founding text of England's national church, as a buttress of the contemporary Protestant establishment and even of the union of church and state. They were embarrassed by the eighteenth-century Protestant Nonconformist championship of Foxe and its legacy in their own age. By their forcing Foxe, in effect, to "wear" an anachronistic "Anglican dress" and by downplaying the sectarian or "nonconformist" aspects of his career and excluding Protestant Dissenters from the Foxean inheritance to which they had laid claim in the previous century, later Anglican Foxe apologists contributed as much to this narrowing process as did Foxe's growing number of Anglican critics. Such critics were suspicious of "foreign" Calvinist influence on the course of the English Reformation and even more decisively turned their back on Foxe's original Protestant internationalist

---

53   Packham, "Representations of Catholicism."

perspective and sought to redefine the catholicity of the English church in older ecclesial terms of external visibility and episcopal descent and succession. It was precisely because Foxean historiography pointed so decisively away from the basic principles underpinning this high church redefinition that not only his nineteenth-century critics but even his erstwhile Anglican apologists, including Anglican Evangelicals anxious to prove their establishment credentials, felt uncomfortable with those radical aspects of his legacy that eighteenth-century Protestant Nonconformists had made their own.

Index